"Julie Carr, in her panoramic exhumation and exposé of the ties—the roots—that bind, precariously and profoundly, the present to the past, is, as it turns out, the ghost jumping on her great-grandfather's bed, rustling his blankets, keeping his life—and history, for the future—unquiet, unable to rest. *Mud, Blood, and Ghosts*—transdisciplinary biography as reappropriation—is not only the title of this book but precisely what it is made of."
—BRANDON SHIMODA, author of *The Grave on the Wall*

"Julie Carr brings alive the disquieting and kaleidoscope history of her great-grandfather, a radical populist who homesteaded in the U.S. West at the turn of the century. She unflinchingly shows how his struggle for survival was characterized by an unruly combination of hardscrabble determination, spiritual longings, eugenic beliefs, and white supremacy. As she poignantly reconstructs an intensely personal past, Carr grapples with the ghosts of violence, silence, and memory in the politically volatile present."
—ALEXANDRA MINNA STERN, author of *Eugenic Nation: Faults and Frontiers of Better Breeding in Modern America*

"Why should readers care about Omer Kem? Because he stands in for a kind of everyman—his hopes, fears, and prejudices represent the legacies that white Americans carry into the present. *Mud, Blood, and Ghosts* powerfully captures what it means to be an American in the twenty-first century, sticky with the residue of history. It is beautiful, evocative, and difficult. This is the right book at the right time."
—KATRINE BARBER, author of *In Defense of Wyam: Native-White Alliances and the Struggle for Celilo Village*

"Written with the prowess of a scholar and full of the insightfulness and precision of a poet, *Mud, Blood, and Ghosts* takes us simultaneously back to the nineteenth-century family origins of this story and into our turbulent present, where the urgent beating of land taken reverberates aloud, reminding us of the structural inequality of this country. *Mud, Blood, and Ghosts* is a masterful multilayered take on the modern history of the United States, an outstanding, genre-bending family memoir that does not let us forget for a minute the fundamental force of land in our lives, a wise and compelling coming-to-terms with racial privilege, and a forceful journey into the heart of the here and now. Based on sweeping research and the reading of the family archive, Carr visits with ghosts and delivers their truth: the past is never the past. The future, if there is one, is up to us. Frankly: a must-read."

—CRISTINA RIVERA GARZA, distinguished professor of Hispanic studies and creative writing at the University of Houston

MUD, BLOOD, AND GHOSTS

MUD BLOOD AND GHOSTS

Populism, Eugenics, and Spiritualism in the American West

JULIE CARR

University of Nebraska Press Lincoln

© 2023 by Julie Carr

All rights reserved

The University of Nebraska Press is part of a land-grant institution with campuses and programs on the past, present, and future homelands of the Pawnee, Ponca, Otoe-Missouria, Omaha, Dakota, Lakota, Kaw, Cheyenne, and Arapaho Peoples, as well as those of the relocated Ho-Chunk, Sac and Fox, and Iowa Peoples.

Library of Congress Cataloging-in-Publication Data
Names: Carr, Julie, 1966– author.
Title: Mud, blood, and ghosts: populism, eugenics, and spiritualism in the American West / Julie Carr.
Description: Lincoln: University of Nebraska Press, [2023] | Includes bibliographical references and index.
Identifiers: LCCN 2022026301
ISBN 9781496228024 (hardback)
ISBN 9781496235060 (paperback)
ISBN 9781496235527 (epub)
ISBN 9781496235534 (pdf)
Subjects: LCSH: Kem, Omer M. (Omer Madison), 1855–1942. | Carr, Julie, 1966– —Family. | Politicians—United States—Biography. | Populist Party (U.S.: 1892–1908) | Populism—United States—History. | Eugenics—United States—History. | West (U.S.)—History—1860–1890. | West (U.S.)—History—1890–1945. | United States—Race relations—History. | United States—Politics and government—1865–1933. | BISAC: BIOGRAPHY & AUTOBIOGRAPHY / Historical | POLITICAL SCIENCE / History & Theory
Classification: LCC E664.K28 C37 2023 | DDC 320.56/620973 [B]—dc23/eng/20221220
LC record available at https://lccn.loc.gov/2022026301

Designed and set in New Baskerville ITC Pro by L. Auten.

For Stephen Carr

From the sixteenth century onward race and gender divided humans into three categories: owning property, becoming propertyless, and being property.
—AILEEN MORETON-ROBINSON

Our present can be reckoned with, and a different future emerge, but the way forward for the left, in my world, is through the past.
—ELIZABETH CATTE

You know, anytime the story is simple, it's probably wrong.
—RHIANNON GIDDENS

Contents

	List of Illustrations	xi
	Acknowledgments	xiii
	Introduction: Ownership and Thievery	1
1.	Mud	13
2.	Sod	34
3.	Law and Order	50
4.	Ghosts	76
5.	Water in Relation	97
	Interlude: "A Real Everyday Feeling," Portland, February 2020	125
6.	Daughters	133
7.	Blood	159
8.	Power	187
	Notes	215
	Bibliography	281
	Index	313

Illustrations

PHOTOGRAPHS

1. Kem family, Montrose, Colorado, ca. 1905	2
2. Mary Kem in costume, 1925	12
3. Hagerstown shop, 2018	17
4. Burned clay, ca. 2012	26
5. Kem family, Broken Bow, Nebraska, 1885	35
6. Nebraska farm, 2019	43
7. Susette La Flesche, ca. 1900	92
8. Norma-Marie Kem, 1895–98	100
9. Jack Nicholson in *Chinatown*, 1974	118
10. Belinda Palmer in *Chinatown*, 1974	119
11. *The Ute Massacre*, 1959	119
12. Kem family house after the fire, Montrose, Colorado	124
13. Mary Kem in *The Kem Story, Part* 2, 1925	127
14. Jenny Kathleen Kem, ca. 1919	130
15. Iris Kem letter of September 29, 1931	138
16. Iris Kem, ca. 1907	139
17. Front page of the *Woman Rebel*, March 1914	147
18. James D. Ream, ca. 1925	177

19. Jazz on the Green,
    Omaha, Nebraska, 2017   185
20. Brown sawmill and Cottage Grove
    Electric and Light   191
21. Alice Kem, Lottie Mellett, Thelma Kem,
    Louise Mellett, Sophronia Mellett,
    Omer Kem, ca. 1916   192
22. & 23. Victor's enlistment papers   195
24. Carolyn Carr, Cambridge,
    Massachusetts, 1967   205
25. Victor Kem, 1917   207
26. "Added Adendun," March 1934   208

MAPS

1. Indiana's Underground Railroad   28

Acknowledgments

Every book creates its own community. This book has especially relied on the help of many people who have offered me necessary companionship, guidance, support, and generous feedback along the way. It has been my deepest pleasure to be in conversation with all of them.

A heartfelt thanks to Tish Fobben, Sara Springsteen, Rosemary Sekora, and especially Clark Whitehorn at the University of Nebraska Press for believing in this book and bringing it into the world. Thank you to Richard Feit for meticulous and thoughtful copyediting. Thank you to Judy Staigmiller for creating the excellent index. I am enormously grateful also to the two anonymous readers who offered their professional discernment. Thank you!

My colleagues at the University of Colorado have taught me what a true intellectual community looks like. Thank you to Thomas Andrews for being the first historian to encourage me in this project and for tolerating my uninformed ramblings while patiently guiding the beginnings of my research. Thank you to Paul Sutter, Tom Zeller, and Penny Kelsey for assisting my research on water, grass, war, and Indigenous history. Thank you to Sue Zemka for encouraging me and standing by me, always. Thank you to Ruth Ellen Kocher for sharing your stories with me, for listening to mine, and for sustained friendship. May we write our collaboration one day. Thank you to Joe Bryan, Emmanuel David, Emily Harrington, Cheryl Higashida, Janice Ho, Jennifer Ho, and Ramesh Mallipeddi for conversations, help, and solidarity during the years of writing this book and for your own engaged scholarship and care. Thank you to CU Boulder's Center for the Humanities and Arts fellows of 2022. Thank you to CU Boulder's College of Arts and Science for a 2022 College Scholar

Award. Thank you to Donna Axel for all your passion, your brilliant editing, and your faith in this project and in me. Thank you to all my students for helping me to think harder about archives, history, gender, race, and writing and for always giving me joy and hope. Thank you especially to Beatriz Lacombe for traveling and dancing with me and to Jenna Gersie for pedagogic collaboration and for building this book's website. Enormous thanks to Micaela Cruce, the greatest research assistant anyone could ever wish for. Your sharp eye and quicksilver mind made every page of this book better. You are astounding. Thank you in memoriam to David Shneer for bounding across cafés to greet me. Your energy, determination, and warmth move me still.

I owe endless thanks to the many scholars and specialists who responded to random emails from a stranger, giving of their time and expertise with astonishing generosity. Thank you especially to Steve Anderson, Katrine Barber, Steven Beda, Brett Chapman, C. Joseph Genetin-Pilawa, Robert D. Johnston, Annie McClanahan, Sean O'Brien, Richard Peltier, Sarah Rovang, Daniel O. Sayers, and Alexandra Minna Stern. In your debt.

Thank you to the librarians and archivists at Camp Etna; the Cottage Grove Historical Society; Creighton University; the Denver Public Library; Earlham College; the Indiana Historical Society; the Oregon Historical Society; the University of Colorado, Boulder; and the South Bend History Museum.

Thank you to the editors of *Territory* for publishing an early draft of the introduction and to Emma Gomis and Jenny Cookson, editors of *Manifold*, for publishing an early version of "Ghosts," and for friendship.

Thank you forever to my beloved friends and collaborators Gillian Conoley, Cristina Rivera Garza, K. J. Holmes, Laird Hunt, Chad Kautzer, Lisa Olstein, Jennifer Pap, Jeffrey Pethybridge, Beth Robertson, Jeffrey Robinson, Nicholas Sammond, Selah Saterstrom, Brandon Shimoda, Yasmeen Siddiqui, Eleni Sikelianos, Sasha Steensen, Catherine Taylor, Rodrigo Toscano, and Jenny Weyel for reading sections of this book, offering astute feedback, or engaging with me in deep and crucial discussions about its themes.

Enormous gratitude especially to Margaret Ronda for reading nearly every word in manuscript form, helping me see what I needed to do, and pushing me to do it. You are the rarest of things: a truly passionate and discerning reader. Your nonstop intelligence and love have made me a better writer and, more importantly, a better person. Special thanks also to John-Michael Rivera for nearing two decades of rich and complex conversation about race, power, history, gender, family, and work, for always being on my side, for laughing with me, and for being an inspiration.

Thank you, most of all, to my family. To Chris Christensen, whose enthusiasm for this archive rivals mine; thank you for generously sharing so much with me. Thank you to Valerie Christensen for telling me about your dreams, showing me your archive of photos, and welcoming me into your home. Thank you to my loving siblings and parents: James, Kim, Anna, Claire, Sasha, Louise, John, Anne, and Linda, and in memoriam, Carolyn Grace, Raymonde Roberts, and Kathleen Carr. Thank you especially to my father, Stephen Carr, for accompanying me to the archive, for preparing the photos, and most of all for being a beacon of love, courage, generosity, and lifelong dedication to justice and equity.

Thank you to Benjamin, Alice, and Lucy for being the center of my life, the reason to write, and for bringing joy to every one of my days. And finally, to Tim Roberts, thank you for listening to far too many hundred-year-old stories and for always keeping my world and heart wide open. Never forget that anything is possible. I love you.

MUD, BLOOD, AND GHOSTS

Introduction   *Ownership and Thievery*

I-90 runs right along the top of Indiana, truck-heavy with glare. Just a little to the north lies Lake Michigan. A little to the south, ancestral ghosts. So bland and so bad, America's highways, where it feels like nothing good could ever begin.

Fifteen and determined, Alice drives her body through her namesake's birth state. A farmhouse, a silo, a cluster of cows: Days Inn, Ramada, Motel 6. Under all that road lie the swamps that are no longer there, wetlands fed by glacial melt, slashes where ample trees once rose straight out from water. There is no history that's not in the day.

Just over the Illinois border we check into a Best Western built into the parking lot of a Target. Alice sleeps. I lie on my side, staring at the past as it slips in and out of focus on my phone.

It was September of 2016 when the faces arrived in my inbox. I studied them, there on the screen. My grandmother Kathleen, in the bottom-left corner, her little hand cupping the air by her jaw, outlived every one of her siblings, even the one not yet born. Beside and a bit behind her, Maude, her older sister, inclines her head as if it had become too heavy to hold. With hands hidden behind their backs, the standing women gaze out from under low, straight brows. The dog in front would, I felt sure, be named somewhere in the pages of the eleven-volume autobiography that the one man in this picture had left behind.

Omer Madison Kem (1855–1942), father of all those girls, two older boys, and the one boy shown, named Victor, was my great-grandfather, a radical Populist homesteader and congressional representative

1. Kem family, Montrose, Colorado, ca. 1905. Chris Christensen personal archive.

from Nebraska. Each volume of his extensive autobiography sits in its own box carefully stored in Omaha; Omaha—where the wide streets seem deserted as if it's Sunday on a Tuesday, or as if it's early morning on a Sunday on a Tuesday midday.

On the day this photo showed up in my email, I had not yet read a word of what was stored in those boxes. A month earlier, I had been barred from doing so by a Creighton University librarian concerned, as we would soon learn, about a legal issue having to do with these same obscure volumes. Dave Crawford took seriously his responsibility to protect the rare books room of Creighton's Reinert Alumni Memorial Library, and although he was more than willing to describe the contents of these boxed books for me, he firmly but politely refused my request to look inside.

In that quiet room with its long empty tables, my husband and I stood talking with Dave, while behind us our son, Benjamin, faced a glassed-in bookshelf that guarded other old volumes, gathered from the decrepit home of Stephen Blumberg, the Book Bandit, in 1990. At the time of his arrest, Blumberg had stolen almost twenty-four thousand volumes from 327 university libraries across the nation. Blumberg's methods ranged from impersonating a professor whose library card he had filched to "squirm[ing] through ventilation ducts and the eight-inch gap between the top of a caged enclosure and the ceiling."[1] In some old libraries he had shimmied up book dumbwaiter cables to access the hidden crevices of a bibliomane's dreams.

Why these stolen books were here in Omaha keeping company with my great-grandfather's autobiography was explained to us by an elderly second librarian whose name I did not catch. After Blumberg's arrest, she told us, she had taken on the job of locating the home libraries of many of the volumes, a project that involved considerable detective work—tracking fonts, bindings, and other identifiable characteristics. Her labor had been rewarded by the gift of all those books whose homes could never be found.

These stolen and homeless books in their glass case had attracted Benjamin's interest only because he had noticed that one of the authors was named Humboldt, the name of the street in Denver on which we lived. He'd been mostly quiet on that trip, gazing into his phone or out at prairie grass, farms, or just highway whirring by. He was eighteen and we were taking him to college, using the occasion of that long, nervous drive to pursue this bit of family research. He'd been quiet, too, in the rare books room, until he caught that word—*Humboldt*—and said it out loud, as if his home was calling him back just as he was now leaving it.

But this leave-taking was not the only event that charged that drive with a kind of somber intensity. It was the summer of 2016. Trump was about to be elected, which is to say, America was about to experience a "psychic break."[2] And though we didn't quite know that yet, we felt it coming. In Cleveland, where we'd gone to protest the GOP's convention in July, excited people in MAGA hats flooded the streets, but protestors were few and far between. Herds of police in impeccable formation kept those of us who were there far apart, kettling us with their bikes, motorcycles, horses, and cars. Just outside the convention hall they had formed an unbreachable barrier, a kind of enclosure, around a Black man on his knees who was openly weeping for Tamir Rice. Inside the hall, Trump warned Americans about the "illegals" "roaming free" and announced the turn to "Americanism, not globalism" as his "credo." Cruz and Giuliani blew their dog whistles with both gravity and shrill fury and mocked the "politically correct" with their "safe spaces." The people cheered; they still cheer now. These, we were told, were the populists.[3]

So what had happened to U.S. Populism between 1891, when my great-grandfather ran for office under that banner, and 2016, when Trump did? Or more to the point, what forms of racist exclusion functioned in the earlier agrarian Populist (or People's) Party, formed by poor farmers in the South and West in protest against the vast abuses and inequalities of the Gilded Age? What had gone wrong, and what was left of their radical critiques of industrial capitalism and fervent expressions of equality? These questions were political, historical, and deeply personal. I had gone to the library because I needed to trace the inexhaustible threads of invitation and rejection, belonging and barrier weaving through the ghosts in my family, weaving through our lives now.

After the older librarian had completed her tale of robbery and retrieval, she went back to her work, and Dave went back to his refusal. Omer Kem's autobiography, though it sat in its boxes before us, would not be opened. We could not read it, because there was an issue with Legal. Legal would have to be consulted, and this would take some time. We were intrigued, a little amused; we pressed him to explain.

Another relative, said Dave, an older man in Portland, Oregon, had shown interest in the autobiography and had even claimed to be in possession of a missing volume, one entirely about Kem's long-held beliefs in ghosts and spirit guides.[4]

Having tracked down the location of the rest of the archive, my unnamed relative in Portland wrote to Dave, seeking access. At first he and Dave had been enthusiastically emailing about Kem's homesteading, Populism, and spiritualism. But then the conversation suddenly turned sour. The relative had grown hostile, accusing Dave of keeping things from him, of mishandling the archive, of withholding documents he had no right to withhold. This relative wasn't shy about these accusations either. He had cc'd the dean of libraries and even the president of the university in his accusatory emails. It occurred to me then, in a hazy way, that the Book Bandit and my possibly litigious relative had something in common, something that could be described as a passion, a deep desire, a feeling of unlawful ownership over things written long, long ago. Or perhaps their shared passion could more accurately be called a rejection of ownership, of the particular kind of ownership that university libraries enforce, which might be an especially aggressive form of ownership because of how it purports to be no ownership at all.

For Blumberg's thieving was certainly an act of resistance to the seemingly well-meaning barring and withholding performed in the quiet halls of the security state, for which academia was just a proxy. As his Wikipedia page explains, "Blumberg believed that the government was plotting to keep the ordinary person from having access to rare books and unique materials, and so sought to liberate and release them in an attempt to thwart the government plot." This is presented as evidence of his delusional mind. But Blumberg has a point. While Duke University's librarian, John L. Sharpell, is quoted on Blumberg's Wiki as saying, "I think he betrayed everything that we try to represent in making information available as freely and as uninhibitedly as possible," it currently costs $81,488 per year to attend Duke University.[5] Creighton's annual costs hover around $47,184. In 2022 fewer than a third of American families have an annual income above $100,000, and only 8 percent have an income above $150,000. The cost of one year at Duke is twice the yearly income of about half of America's families.[6] And even beyond and before the obscene cost of higher ed (higher ed as citadel), it is also true—and obviously so—that the United States has historically barred certain people from acquiring formal educations and has, in fact, often been in the business of enforcing ignorance. Banning enslaved people from literacy or prohibiting Native children from knowing their own languages are just two quite blatant historical examples of such enforcement. In the present, one could also point to the many states that have decimated their public-education budgets in recent decades, as have Georgia, Alabama, Mississippi, North Carolina, North Dakota, Kentucky, and Colorado, where I live.[7] As I write, forty-two state legislatures have proposed bans or restrictions on the teaching of (especially but not only) critical race theory, that field of study through which we might begin to understand how our institutions—law, education, medicine, politics—have functioned to maintain racial hierarchies.[8] What political desires are met, whose interests are served, by ignorance?

This story of stolen books, of protest against the sequestration of knowledge, this urge to break into the library, is a populist story. The principle of inclusion, the critique of protections and barriers, is central to the populist dream that was, I knew, running through the pages in the unopened boxes before me.

But what is it to approach the archive, to unlock the cabinet, lift the top off the box, to begin to read? It is to invite a haunting, which nevertheless begins long before we open any books. And to invite the ghosts into the open, one must be ready to hear what they teach. No doubt I did not know then what ghosts I was about to reckon with.

In short: Omer Madison Kem began his adult life at the age of sixteen as a hand-to-mouth tenant farmer in the swamps of Indiana. In 1881, married with three children and facing all-out destitution, he took advantage of the Homestead Act (1862) and moved his family to Custer County, Nebraska. Like thousands of others, Kem was granted 320 acres to farm (160 from the Homestead Act and 160 from the 1873 Timber Culture Act)—a nearly impossible task, given railroad rates, falling crop values, drought, and a powerful lending industry preying on vulnerable farmers. He sold half this claim within the first year. Further poverty and debt pushed Kem toward politics, as he became a founding member of the Populist Party. Elected to the Fifty-Second to Fifty-Fourth Congresses (1891–97), Kem, like progressives and populists today, was an outspoken critic of capitalist greed and income inequality. He also became an avid spiritualist, visited by the ghosts of his mother, sister, and son and receiving guidance from the (dead) Radical Republicans, including Abraham Lincoln himself.

In 1898 Kem moved his family to Colorado, where he raised cattle and fruit, participated in a massive irrigation project, and developed a decades-long relationship with an invented Indian spirit he named Fleet Wind. In a remarkable instance of racial projection and appropriation, Kem believed that Fleet Wind visited him regularly throughout the rest of his life to massage and heal his ailing body and those of his loved ones. In his later years, Kem owned a power company in Oregon and became a passionate advocate for eugenics, including the forced sterilization of people he considered unfit to breed. In the 1910s, '20s, and '30s, he eagerly trafficked in the scientific racism that has long influenced U.S. immigration and criminal justice policies and both European and American fascism to this day.

To study this narrative requires of me a kind of transdisciplinary will, or willingness. At once a biography and a narrative history of Populist and Progressive Era politics in the West from the late nineteenth century to the Depression, this book is also a meditation on the present, a sort of memoir. For as I move through this archive and try to address the complex entanglements of violence, power, and resistance running through and around it—stories of enslavement and *marronage*, of Indigenous dispossession and resilience, of interracial alliance and betrayal, of life-long hauntings and mental illness, of home, homelessness, and transit—I don't leave myself out. In fact it would be impossible to do so, impossible to act as if my kin were not running through my body and my home, as if their remains were not in plain sight.

Right after the 2016 election, mortified Democrats and progressives tended to divide into two camps: those who accepted the dominant narrative that said Trump was elected by working-class and poor whites who had been "left behind" by globalism and the liberal elite, and those who believed that the entire phenomenon of Trumpism was a function purely of racism, a white-supremacist response to a shifting demographic, to #BlackLivesMatter, and especially to the presidency of Barak Obama. I had this fight with my father, Omer's grandson, each of us passionately sticking to our side. We were both wrong, of course. What ails this country was and is both racism and unsustainable capitalism as entwined forces, not two distinct harms.

Because of our history, racial and class formation are "bound to penetrate each other at every turn," as David Roediger has written.[9] There is an ongoing history of how white people, fighting just to survive this particularly brutal form of capitalism—under the name of populism or not—have been hobbled in that struggle by a violent attachment to whiteness. That story was in Kem's autobiography as much as it was anywhere.

Almost a year after that first visit to Creighton's rare books room, I returned for a second time, now not with my son and husband but with my father. At this point the older librarian's job had, for reasons of budget, been cut, and Dave was alone. The issue with Legal had been cleared up (and my Portland cousin revealed to be Chris Christensen, neither elderly nor litigious), and so my father and I spent three days reading almost at random from Kem's seemingly endless writing—page after page of political rants, ghost stories, letters to editors, and long poems in rhyming quatrains (ballad meter, often written in midwestern farm-boy slang).

A muted light. The one window looks out over the general reading room where undergraduates sprawl in chairs, asleep with their mouths open or with their heads cradled in their arms. I read through the poems, stories, and transcribed letters, looking for something like trauma or the willingness to inflict it, trying to understand origins and arrivals. My father, perhaps more simply and perhaps not, is looking for his mother.

The stories are many. The attempts at humor, the Populist's serious, if sardonic, railing against injustice, the legislative fight for the common man, the atheist's disgust at religious hypocrisy, the deaths of pets, babies, children, and women—all of this was adding up to a complex history of bad and good luck, of power struggles, and of property. And then, as I skimmed through all this flux, I snagged on a transcribed letter from 1925 addressed to Omer and his wife, Alice, from their now-grown son Huxley, describing a birthday party for Huxley's seven-year-old daughter, Mary, to which another little girl was not invited.

The little girl who was not invited to the seventh birthday party of Huxley's daughter and Omer's granddaughter simply could not *be* invited, for reasons perfectly obvious to everyone involved. And yet despite this inevitable and obvious situation, the story must be told, must take two paragraphs of this grown man's letter to his father. The decision must be defended, even though inevitable, as nothing but common sense. She cannot be invited, though she likes the celebrated seven-year-old so much that she gives her not one but four presents at school, and though all the other girls in the class *are* invited, and she does not know why. She does not know why, so the other seven-year-old tells her why. It is because unlike all the other little girls who have been invited, she is not white. As the white seven-year-old's father explains, the uninvited girl's mother is white, but her father, in the language of the time, is an "octoroon," which means that of his eight great-grandparents, one had been Black, and most likely enslaved, and most likely a woman who had been raped. The matrilineal line of racial formation that was at once a form of capitalist reproduction is the root of and route to practices of exclusion that are both structural and, as in this case, precisely personal.

The girl looks, as Huxley tells his father, "entirely white," but Huxley and his wife, Happie, have looked into it; they've asked around, and they've learned the truth.[10] And so despite the little girl's tender age and despite her professed love for Mary, the family follows the spirit of the law, as had been affirmed by *Plessy* thirty years before, and she is not invited.[11] A tiny insult, a small thing, and yet it would have been felt keenly, was felt keenly, by the child who was seven.[12]

Kem's response is to articulate, as I would discover he had done many, many times in letters, speeches, and editorials, the concept of race purity, which was expressed in those years with the formula "a single drop of blood spoils the whole" and which would play itself out in barriers against non-white people's participation in all sorts of private and public spaces, structures, and events, including, as we see here, rituals in which white people celebrate their births. This very ordinary, absolutely common, and minor event in my family's history (and what could be more minor than a child's birthday party?) was only one expression of their committed racism. And it's a mild act of bigotry when compared to how Omer and his feminist daughter Iris pushed for the forced sterilization of eventually all disabled people, the poor, and anyone who could be deemed "morally degenerate," anyone, in the end, who was criminalized by the white-supremacist state. Vehemently against "blood-mixing," Omer considered the "Great White Race" to be vulnerable, in need of vigilant protections.[13]

Why whiteness must be guarded has everything to do with property (with ownership and with thievery) in a country where whiteness and property have always been deeply entwined. To protect whiteness against invasion or infiltration, to keep whiteness safe, is synonymous with protecting the private property white people hold, believe themselves entitled to, or jealously desire. At the time of the correspondence about the birthday, Kem is nearing seventy. He has owned 320 acres of grasslands in Nebraska, a ranch and apple orchard in southern Colorado, a house in the wet woods of Cottage Grove, Oregon, and a family home in Indiana that he had inherited from his older sister. None of this land had come without cost to someone.

Whether in 1925, 1825, or 2025, property ownership in America cannot break free of the colonial war that stole the land and nearly cleared it of its original people or from the stolen lives forced to farm it. "Property's a measure of elimination," writes the poet C. S. Giscombe in his *Prairie Style*.[14] And it only gets more invidious in the particulars, as property ownership by white families so often follows quickly on the heels of the dispossession, removal, or exclusion of Black people, Native people, and non-white immigrants, as these pages will reveal.

An archive survives to be revived. The archive as a limit, a thing in a box, is always also an opening. It opens on losses sustained, harms inflicted, the tenacity of survival, and on the persistence of lineages both proud and shameful. The archive, like Paul Celan said of the poem, is lonely. This loneliness compels it, like a ghost, toward another, toward its reader: "It is lonely and *en route*. . . . It intends another, needs this other."[15] To answer this intention by beginning to read, however haltingly and imperfectly, however quietly and slowly, is also to be en route, preparing for a present time worth waiting for, even if we do not live to see it.

In the end and at the beginning, this is a book about fathers: the father as law, as lawmaker, as authoritative imposition; the father as white American patriarchy that demands and holds power, both in our origins and at our present moment; the father as slaver, as settler, as border police, as power broker. And this is also a book about *my* fathers, both the persons and the patrilineal side, and as such, it is a book about love. For though I did not know Omer Kem to love him, I know his grandson, my father, who has worked throughout his life to create more equitable public spaces, who inherited his grandfather's righteous rage against injustice and whose love for me, and mine for him, infuses everything I do.[16] For these reasons, and not only because the book demands a complex kind of study, this is a book that is hard to write. I am not and do not want to be an apologist for power, white-masculine-settler-capitalist or any other kind. And yet in placing my lens on these very forces in my family, I also do not intend to only accuse and blame (as if doing so would exalt myself). We are all living in the fallout of the settler-capitalist model. The fires and floods, the mass incarceration, the police killings of Black and brown people, the ballooning housing costs and corresponding rise in homelessness—these are only some of the most glaring signs of the violence that has been visited upon the land and so many of the people in the name of progress. What pieces of that history of violence do I carry? And what forms of resistance do I also inherit? And how can I learn from both? These are the questions I begin with.

This, then, is not one story but many stories of protest and participation, of fighting back and giving in. The people I will focus on here are just one family. Their stories tell only a tiny portion of the many histories I touch on in these pages. But each of us is a node in an infinite network that moves horizontally in all directions, as well as backward and forward at once. I begin where I am and tell what I can in the time that I have.

Early on, as I was reading these histories, finding so many things that pained me, I asked a wise friend, "How can I love these people"? "Love them through their loves," she instructed. So inasmuch as love

2. Film capture of Mary Kem (in costume), approximately seven years old. *The Kem Story, Part 2*, by Huxley Darwin Kem, 1925. Chris Christensen personal archive.

is lawlessness, is an energy that opens, that refuses boundary and border, that asks to be entered over and over, I have tried to orient my writing toward that call.

Let me return, then, to what was stolen in 1990, to the thievery of language and knowledge. Blumberg the Book Bandit was not interested only in books. Rather, he was obsessed with all things nineteenth century, wearing (says one researcher) Victorian underwear and carrying a nineteenth-century revolver.[17] His special literary interest was, in fact, American history, and he met that history repudiating what could be called its primary force. Blumberg's intention was not possession but dispossession, not ownership but release. Almost ten years after he had completed his four and a half years of jail time, Blumberg was arrested again for theft. This time the object of his thievery was not books but carefully removed doorknobs—as if his true aim was to leave all doors open.

1 Mud

> A dismal swamp, on which the half-built houses rot away: cleared here and there for the space of a few yards; and teeming, then, with rank unwholesome vegetation, in whose baleful shade the wretched wanderers who are tempted hither, droop, and die, and lay their bones.
> —Charles Dickens, *American Notes*, 1842

Birth

In November of the year 1855, in Hagerstown, Indiana, a town near the eastern border of that still fresh state, Malinda Kem gave birth to her eighth and final child, a boy named Omer. Malinda, the first daughter of Martha and Uriah Bulla, had been raised mostly in her uncle Thomas's house, for when she was eight years old, her father, a great fiddler and dancer, abandoned the family, and shortly after that, her mother died.

Malinda's uncles and father were the sons of William Bulla, who had migrated to Indiana from the North Carolina farm on which he was raised. Quakers, the family opposed slavery, and by the 1820s, William Bulla had become an active participant in the Underground Railroad.[1] With his father-in-law, Andrew Hoover, he took part in an 1822 "rescue" of a man named George (or Peter) Sheldon (or Stellow), who, having escaped enslavement in Kentucky, was then fleeing recapture.[2] Bulla and Hoover reportedly helped Sheldon escape through the window of the courthouse by grabbing an agent "by the back of his neck and throwing him across the room." The "Sheldon rescue" was one of the earliest recorded of such incidents in Indiana, written about in the papers at that time and after.[3]

William's son (and Malinda's uncle) Thomas followed in his father's footsteps, becoming known as an Underground Railroad "stationmaster." Not only did he provide shelter to the orphaned Malinda, but also, according to *his* son, "he was ever the friend of the escaping colored man who might be on his way to Canada and freedom, rendering such assistance as was in his power to do, whether in affording assistance to an escaping fugitive, or refusing to play the part of blood-hound in aiding in his capture."[4]

Bet, Amy, and Mourning. These are the names of the three enslaved people once the legal property of William Bulla's father and Thomas's grandfather and namesake, referred to as Thomas Jr. Bet, Amy, and Mourning were sold at Thomas Jr.'s death (in 1809) to a man named Alexander Gray for $840, about $20,000 now.[5] The money from this sale was divided among the three surviving Bulla sons, including William. That is to say that even this family of sometimes active abolitionists received wealth from the sale of enslaved people, wealth that by 1820 clearly had been converted into property in Indiana and thus was contributing to a habit of ownership that the family carries to this day.

I do not know what happened to Bet, Amy, or Mourning once they became the property of Alexander Gray; one aspect of being owned rather than owning is that one's history is unlikely to have been written down or saved.

Madison Kem—Malinda's husband and Omer's father—was born in West Virginia to a fifteen-year-old mother who would birth twelve subsequent children. The Kems, like the Bullas, were motivated in their journey north and west (say their descendants) by their similar, if less active, opposition to slavery. Both families were mobilized (says history) by their government's desire to populate the continent with whites.

In the Supreme Court's 1823 decision in *Johnson v. M'Intosh*, Chief Justice John Marshall ruled that the United States had the "exclusive right to extinguish . . . by purchase or by conquest" Indian ownership of land. In this prime example of the law adjusting itself to meet the aspirations of the powerful, Marshall based his decision on the principle of "discovery," which gave "absolute title" to the colonizer.[6] Indians, he explained, could not own full title to land, because they had not settled it, only "wandered over" it, and moreover were no longer "an independent people" capable of national sovereignty.[7] The immediate effect of the ruling, and indeed its purpose, was to privilege the many purchases of Indigenous land that settlers had negotiated with the federal government over any that had been negotiated with the tribes themselves, thus destroying tribal land sovereignty in a single blow. Following this ruling, Andrew Jackson signed the contentious Indian Removal Act of 1830, which led to the forced removal of the Cherokees in Georgia—the Trail of Tears—and to many other forced dispossessions.[8] Two years after that, the "Act to Enable the President to Extinguish Indian Land Title within the States of Indiana, Illinois, and Territory of Michigan" provided legal cover for the removal of almost all remaining Miamis and Potawatomi in Indiana (the Winnebago, Shawnee, Delaware, and Kickapoo tribes had by that time already been mostly devastated or removed).[9]

The Kems' and the Bullas' migrations to Indiana, however motivated by their opposition to slavery, were concurrent with this series of legal genocidal actions that thoroughly dismantled Indigenous land rights in the area as elsewhere. The two events—white arrival and Native decimation or forced removal—are, from the point of view of history and law, one. As historian Thomas Campion succinctly puts it, "Land became more accessible during the great flood of sales in the 1830s, as Indian removal reached its climax. Indian policy and land policy worked together."[10]

By the time of Omer's passage through his mother's body, Malinda had already lost most of her teeth, and despite his own father's large and successful farm, Madison had not done well.

Madison was at times a farmer, at other moments a laborer, and always also a carpenter, paid sometimes in firewood and, when not paid, shivering with his family of ten in whatever rented or borrowed home they then shared. In the tales Omer tells of his childhood, the family is frequently on the move, looking around the state and sometimes across its borders for something that could be profitable, or at least livable.

In one journey, before Omer's birth, the Kems headed northwest toward the banks of the Eel River, where they hoped to farm. Along the way they came upon a settlement forming around a canal-digging project, and they took a gamble. Madison purchased a bit of land, expecting to sell it quickly, make a profit, and move on. The canal project failed, the area went bust, and the family came down with dysentery, which killed Mary Esther, just eight years old. The others survived, though not without tooth rot. Calomel, a laxative, also known as mercury chloride, was given to treat digestive ailments and could cause both hair and teeth to fall out. In the case of Mary Esther, it also ate a hole right through her cheek.

Land was cheap for whites in the new West then, especially in swampy Indiana, and so despite this disastrous trip, Madison still owned the swath of farmable earth off in the woods, though he could not, being broke, get to it, nor would he have had the means to build a house and clear a farm if he were to arrive.[11] Against the dark premonitions of his daughter Sophronia (who, having just lost her little sister, might well have been raving), Madison traded that "farm in the wilderness" for a sawmill. In a state with ample and variable lumber, this could have been a decent trade had the sawmill not burned to the ground just three months later, leaving the family without land, cash, or second daughter. And so they stayed put in the boomtown gone bust called Hagerstown, which to this day is one block long and wet and poor. There Madison labored for just about $5 a month, renting and hoping to own.

Just after the war—which no one in the immediate family fought in, though they took the side of the Union—another journey was attempted, this time with Omer, about twelve, and this time across two borders into Missouri. "This being at the close of the war everything in the country was in a state of chaos, with negroes predominating to a large extent," writes Omer by way of explaining that having hauled his family some three hundred miles (which by wagon would have taken at least a month), Madison turned them back around without so much as unpacking a bundle.[12] Crossing borders

3. Hagerstown shop, 2018. Author's collection.

is frightening—especially, it seems, as the border crossed was as much racial as geographic. The family's return to Indiana, where since 1851 Blacks had been constitutionally barred from settling, might have provided a certain kind of comfort, the comfort of the familiar but still not profitable, for from this point forward, Madison and Malinda became more or less dependent on their married daughters' families for support.[13]

The eight-year-old girl who died of dysentery (also known as bloody flux), who shat blood and vomited emptiness while mercury rotted her face off its bones in the misery of an illness for which there was no cure while her mother, father, and siblings were also unrelentingly releasing fluids in great pain, was buried in the mud somewhere near the eventually successful Whitewater Canal.

Her little sister, Ellen, seven at the time, would survive long enough to marry a doctor and birth a baby girl given the Dakota name Minnie Ha-Ha but would die at twenty-seven of a different bacterial infection, equally as common, which, though not inducing the shitting of blood, does result in the coughing of it. And while the short lives of women were in those years generally unremarkable or at least unremarked upon, their deaths were quite often cataclysmic, not just because they might have been loved but also because those whom they cared for, the little children, would be immediately in need of a replacement.

And in fact, Minnie Ha-Ha's need of care was the reason Madison and Malinda Kem finally had a place to settle—in the home of their bereaved, though not particularly beloved, son-in-law, Dr. Ross. Ellen's death was therefore also the reason that at sixteen, Omer, who refused to go along with his parents, was left parentless, in a sense twice motherless, for it was Ellen and not Malinda who had rocked him to sleep when he was small, singing his favorite song, "The Old Bachelor," whose precise lyrics I cannot find anywhere on YouTube, Spotify, or even at the Kodály Center's American Folk Song Collection website. "My favorite song was one in which the trials and tribulations of a bachelor's life was set forth in rather tragic terms, and that part that appealed to me in particular, went something like this, 'He threw himself across the bed and tore all the hair out of his head.' This was so thrilling to me I remember it as clearly as the day of its utterance and it's the only part of the song that I do remember."[14]

Twenty years later, Ellen would visit him—a comforting spirit, a ball of light, or just a hand reaching through the folds of a curtain—in the parlors of Washington DC's spiritualist radicals.

This departure of Omer's parents, which he strongly protested, was in the end the reason he left school and went to work, plowing a field in Sulphur Springs, a field populated by midsized boulders left behind long ago by glacial melt, boulders they called "n——heads," just thirty-seven miles west of Westfield, that "hotbed of abolitionism" where Indiana's Underground Railroad had established its most active network, as remembered by Julia Conklin in 1910: "For it was said by slave-hunters that when a runaway . . . got to Westfield it was not worthwhile to look for him."[15] But even more to the point, Omer plowed into such "heads" only a decade after his uncles, aunts, and cousins were, as I said, active members of the UGRR of Indiana, their houses referred to as "stations" along the way.

> Hi, ho, hum! I guess I bin dreamin
> But I must say hit wuz shore nuff seamin,
> Jist like hit did when I wiz young,
> En full uf life el also uv fun.
> I've shore made asnaak on old dad time
> En went back tu my youth while th' goin wuz fine,
> En whatever betides in th' years to cum,
> I've had th' time o' my life en a barrel uv fun.

This is the final stanza of a fourteen-stanza poem about childhood, written by the boy with his plow a half century later, looking back.

Nan Benson, Omer's first wife, was born in the year preceding Omer's birth in a place unnamed though not far from where Omer's plow met those "heads" and broke. Nan and Omer's initial contact would have been in a hayride or at an apple-picking party, as Omer describes (he's so often kitschy—or America is). The specifics of this meeting, however, are not detailed in the pages of Omer's autobiography, for despite the fact that she birthed his five oldest children (only three of whom survived to adulthood), she is peripheral to the narrative's drive, which Omer understandably sends through himself. When he does speak of her, their early love, her death at twenty-seven, he drops his often flamboyant language into generalized praise. One detail he offers: when they first marry, Nan and Omer have a black dog they name Nig.

"Drain the Swamp": The Swamp Lands Act and the Fugitive Slave Act of 1850

> Laws, of course, are not to be taken at face value; they are not an indication of what transpires in any given society.
> —Sylviane A. Diouf, *Slavery's Exiles*

> Law, the preserve of terror, the fief of punishment.
> —Rosario Castellanos, "Limit"

One can begin a history anywhere, in any year, at any moment. Let me fall back now into a year in which to start again, a year selected for its laws. These laws, taken together, have everything to do with the Indiana that Omer Kem was born to labor in, have everything to do with why he, like other poor whites, eventually had to leave.

In 1850 the Thirty-First Congress of the United States passed two bills into law, one well known, one not so. The well-known one was the (second) Fugitive Slave Act. Although the slave owner's right to retrieve his or her human property from even a free state was written into the U.S. Constitution, as the eighteenth century drew to a close, people of the northern states found themselves less and less inclined to aid owners and hunters in their efforts. The first Fugitive Slave Act of 1793 responded to this reluctance and the corresponding pressure from slave states by defining the retrieval of fugitive slaves as a national project. Now the federal government became "virtually an agent of the slaveholding interest within free-state jurisdictions."[16] The 1793 bill (signed into law by George Washington) was not, however, strong enough when by the 1840s, enslaved people were both more valuable and more successful at taking flight.[17] Moreover, many northern states had countered the law's demand by writing and passing "personal liberty laws" of their own, designed to protect free Blacks and fugitives within their borders and (perhaps even more) to unburden their white local governments from incurring the costs of recapture. The conflict between the Fugitive Slave Act of 1793 and these state laws came to a head in the 1842 Supreme Court case *Prigg v. Pennsylvania.*

Edward Prigg was a slave catcher sent by the Ashmores of Maryland, specifically by one Ashmore heir named Margaret, to capture another Margaret, this one a Morgan. Margaret Morgan was living in Pennsylvania with her husband, Jerry, and their children. At no point in her life had she been deemed the property of the Ashmores' now deceased patriarch, John, nor of anyone else. Her parents *had* been considered John's property until he released them from his "service."

Prigg and his colleagues, Forwood, Lewis, and Bemis (who was white Margaret's husband), traveled into Pennsylvania on a sleety winter night and "with force and violence" compelled Margaret Morgan and her children into an uncovered wagon to be delivered as property to Margaret Ashmore in Maryland. Under Pennsylvania law, Prigg was arrested and indicted for kidnapping. Under the U.S. Constitution (Article IV, Section 2, Clause 2), argued Prigg's lawyer, Margaret Morgan and her children, who lacked deeds affirming the free status of Margaret's parents, were the inherited property of white Margaret, and Prigg and his colleagues were simply their legal retrievers.[18] The condition of slaver or slave, of person or property, according to Prigg's lawyer, was an immutable fixture of a bloodline.

Lawyer Thomas Hambly took the side of the State of Pennsylvania all the way to the Supreme Court. The court, under Chief Justice Roger B. Taney, who would later author the *Dred Scott* opinion of 1857, acknowledged that policing, which includes the arrest of kidnappers, lies within the purview of each individual state. And yet, continues the ruling written by Justice Joseph Story, "such regulations can *never be permitted to interfere with or obstruct the just rights of the owner to reclaim his slave*" (my emphasis). Thus, in matters pertaining to the retrieval of human property—which includes, it turns out, any descendants of such property—the Constitution overrides state's rights; the Constitution defers to the rights of property owners (or their descendants). "We have not the slightest hesitation," Story continues, "in holding, that under . . . the constitution, the owner of a slave is clothed with *entire authority*, in every state in the Union, to seize and recapture his slave, whenever he can do it, without any breach of the peace or any illegal violence" (my emphasis again).[19] Edward Prigg, despite having been found guilty of kidnapping in the state of Pennsylvania, was thus acquitted by the Supreme Court of the United States.[20] "The act of the Legislature of Pennsylvania upon which the indictment against Edward Prigg is founded is unconstitutional and void," wrote Story. "It purports to punish as a public offense against the State the very act of seizing and removing a slave by his master which the Constitution of the United States was designed to justify and uphold."[21]

Let me pause in this clarification of the Constitution's *design* to acknowledge the death by drowning of Jerry Morgan, who just a couple of days after the capture of his family was accused of stealing a white man's jacket, a situation so dangerous that he would attempt escape from his accusers, who had tied him up and threatened him, by purportedly leaping from a ferry into the Susquehanna River, where he drowned. Perhaps he leaped. Perhaps he was pushed. We cannot and do not know.[22] And lost also is the fate of Margaret Morgan and her children, for no records have been found of their eventual sale, though sold they most certainly were.

However, even as the ruling in favor of Prigg voided Pennsylvania's "personal liberty laws" (and with them, all such laws in northern states), it also confusingly reaffirmed the independence of states' policing efforts. The ruling in no way *required* states to assist in the recapture of fugitives. "The only part of Story's opinion that was not completely pro-slavery was his acknowledgement that state officials *might refuse* to enforce the Fugitive Slave Act [of 1793]."[23] Thus, the ruling left slavers in an increasingly complicated situation; recapturing slaves without the support of local law enforcement was difficult and expensive.[24] And so the court did what courts often do: sharpened the ambiguities within the law, more or less begging for its revision.

Congress followed suit. In 1850, as the Senate was negotiating the acquisition of lands resulting from the Mexican-American War, Senator Henry Clay of Kentucky rewrote and strengthened the Fugitive Slave Act as a portion of his Great Compromise. Clay's plan appeased southern lawmakers, who had wanted the western territories to be admitted as slave states, by promising them greater protections for their human property. The law clarified that the harboring or helping of fugitives from slavery was a crime, punishable by six-months imprisonment and a steep fine ($30,000 today).[25] It rewarded law officers who successfully captured fugitives and barred all persons suspected of being fugitives from offering testimony on their own behalf. The only testimony that mattered was that of the person claiming to own the other; the only viable word was white.[26]

The Compromise of 1850 is credited with delaying the Civil War by a decade, a decade during which the North grew richer and stronger, more prepared for success in the eventual violence, benefiting, along the way, from cheap southern plantation cotton for its mills.[27] The 1850 U.S. census recorded 1,011 enslaved people escaping to the North that year (one out of every 3,165 slaves), while during the entire decade of 1850–59, fewer than 330 fugitives were returned.[28] A law, then, of dubious success. And a law, nonetheless, that destroyed lives, defined a decade, and motivated the resistance.

Ten days after passing the Great Compromise and the Fugitive Slave Act, the same body of lawmakers passed the much less well-known Swamp Lands Act. This law granted all wetlands to their respective states, directing states to then sell the lands (cheap) to those willing to drain the swamps and farm them. Prior to the Swamp Lands Act, nearly all northwest Ohio and much of Indiana, including a large portion of Indianapolis, lay under water and was not privately owned. Now this public land, held in common, would be rapidly privatized.

The Swamp Lands Act had many social, economic, and ecological consequences. It facilitated the development of the Corn Belt and in this way fed the industrial revolution in the United States and beyond. But draining wetlands not only destroys habitats and increases water pollution; it also heightens the threat of extreme flooding, such as was seen across the Midwest in 2019, because as swamps are given over to raising corn or are paved for highways and housing, there is nowhere for excess water to go. Moreover, and perhaps most devastatingly now, the loss of wetlands massively reduces the land's potential for carbon sequestration.[29]

Although the draining of Indiana's swamplands was a decades-long project, the act nonetheless immediately impacted what environmental historian Donald Pisani refers to as "a vast commons."[30] For impoverished un-propertied families, whether white, Black, or

Native, swamplands had provided bounty, "where property boundaries were nonexistent and formal ownership moot."[31] As one settler in the Grand Marsh of the Kankakee River recalls, "It was one of the greatest wild life habitats in the world. . . . Cranes, geese, ducks, plover, rabbits and other smaller wildlife. When they put a ditch through it, why that ruined the marsh. In order to make a few thousand acres of farm ground they ruined the greatest hunting preserve that there ever was."[32] Draining the swamps, as was necessary for large-scale farming and continued settlement, would eventually destroy this "haven for the powerless and the dispossessed."[33]

The Swamp Lands Act followed earlier legislation aimed at draining off the Everglades in Florida and the wetlands of Louisiana. And while the new law applied to all states with "overflowed lands," the swampiest states were still in the South; Louisiana, Arkansas, Alabama, and Florida held 57 percent of the sixty-four million acres of wetlands granted.[34] In a sense, then, the Swamp Lands Act can be read as an addendum of the Compromise of 1850, since the law would boost the slave economy by expanding the areas available for plantation farming. Indeed, throughout the nineteenth century, it was the congressmen from slave states, themselves almost certainly slavers, who had repeatedly attempted to wrest control of the wetlands.[35]

The Swamp Lands Act could benefit these slavers in another way as well: to drain the swamp was to expose and destroy crucial sites of refuge, not only for poor whites but also for fugitives from slavery, or "maroons." Land deemed worthless to some had often meant survival for others.

Maroons, whether in the United States, the Caribbean, or South Africa, were self-liberators, people who escaped from captivity and managed, under duress and threat of dismemberment, death, or both, to live independently, whether for a few days or for months, years, or generations. American *marronage* was, as archeologist Daniel Sayers puts it, "by no means rare," with maroon communities practicing a "great diversity and range of cultural systems."[36] In her necessary book, *Slavery's Exiles: The Story of the American Maroons,* Sylviane A. Diouf describes how communities of "hinterland" maroons from the very beginnings of the slave trade until the end of the Civil War managed to survive in "woods, bayous, marshes [and] swamps" just beyond or miles from the plantation's Big House, fields, and cabins. As she describes, maroons who settled in the high areas of wetlands fished and hunted, and many in long-term communities grew crops as well.[37]

Sayers stretches the definition of U.S. *marronage* to include self-emancipated people living even in "free" states, such as Indiana, especially after 1850, when the threat of recapture became even more intense. U.S. maroons, he argues, have been woefully underrepresented by historians, since scholarship has relied so heavily on documentary sources with their "gaping lacunae." In 2002 Sayers initiated an archeological study of *marronage* in the Great Dismal Swamp of Virginia, where potentially thousands of maroons had lived for over ten generations (1680–1863). "A nameless site," he calls it. "I don't want to put a false name on it. . . . I'm hoping to find out what the people who lived here called this place."[38] Sayers finds record of centuries of astonishing survival not only in documents and oral histories but also in the physical remains discovered in the mud.

The objects themselves—fragile, nearly nothing, bits of rock, metal, or clay that hold the ghostly shape of a thing—are almost but are not yet dust.

By the early 1800s it seems that the wetlands in central Indiana—the Bacon and Fletcher Swamps and perhaps the Black Swamp and Grand Kankakee to the north—had become sites of *marronage* (the Grand Kankakee marsh was also a known hideout for horse thieves).[39] As journalist Stephen Taylor puts it, "In the 1830s Fletcher's Swamp became one of the slushier stops on the Underground Railroad. . . . Wetlands, usually hard to penetrate, were an ideal hideout, since the bloodhounds that bounty-hunters used to track fugitives lost their scent here."[40] A writer for the *Indianapolis Journal* in 1889 relays the following memory of the Fletcher Swamp: "Near the center of the swamp, about on a line with Twelfth street [in Indianapolis], was an acre, more or less, of high land, at least it was lifted above the surrounding morass. On this spot were, even at a quite recent date, remains of rude huts and beds of charcoal." The writer goes on to

4. Burned clay, no more than two centimeters long, from cabin walls and chimneys, ca. 2012. Dan Sayers/Great Dismal Swamp Landscape Study.

describe how Calvin Fletcher, the swamp's abolitionist owner, would often ride his horse to the swamp's edge in the early morning. There he would meet a "muscular negro, with shirt and breeches of coffee-sacking" to whom he would hand off supplies.[41]

But these scant tales—fragments written not by the maroons themselves but by white reporters piecing together long-ago stories from lore—grant only a glimpse of the history of *marronage* still hiding in the ex-swamps of Indiana. How might one ever narrate such histories when much of their remnants now lie firmly buried under the paved parking lots and housing developments that stand where these swamps once were? "To find . . . subjugated knowledge, even mere fragments of it, requires a different kind of invention," writes Avery Gordon, "one that carries the traces of the history that dismissed it in the first place forward towards something else."[42] And yet invention, from my standpoint, would only feel obscene, unless "to invent" is returned to its humbler origins: *invenire*—"to come upon."

I went to Indiana to feel what I could of the wetlands that remained. In the Loblolly Marsh, where in the early spring one can lie down in the tall grasses and not get wet, I recorded the sound of the wind and the peepers in the ponds, and I watched some blue shirts billow on a clothesline across the property line. How the law got some bodies moving and other bodies killed, how the law made property for some out of land that had once protected those who *were* property or had none, and how the map I carried in my phone marked the paths of capital's flow but not the pathways used for flight—these things did and did not sound through the recordings that I made.

The federal decision to drain and sell the swamps was motivated not only by capitalistic speculation, whether for land or retrievable bodies. The swamps were also seen as dangerous places, replete with disease-causing miasma. "Few American landscapes have historically been more feared, reviled, and stigmatized than wetlands," writes historian Anthony Carlson.[43] Malaria, for example, was thought to be caused directly by the wet atmosphere rather than by the disease-carrying mosquitoes that these atmospheres bred.[44] George Waring's 1867 handbook on the topic, *Draining for Profit, Draining for Health*, puts it poetically:

> Land which requires draining hangs out a sign of its condition, more or less clear, according to its circumstances, but always unmistakable to the practiced eye. Sometimes it is the broad banner of standing water, or dark, wet streaks in plowed land, when all should be dry and of even color; sometimes only a fluttering rag of distress in curling corn, or wide-cracking clay, or feeble, spindling, shivering grain, which has survived a precarious winter, on the ice-stilts that have stretched its crown above a wet soil; sometimes the quarantine flag of rank growth and dank miasmatic fogs. To recognize these indications is the first office of the drainer; the second, to remove the causes from which they arise.[45]

"Dark, wet streaks," "rag of distress," "feeble, spindling shivering grain," "rank growth"; if the swamp were a woman, she'd be poor, she'd be ill, she'd be threatening, and she would not be white. For the two motivations—capitalist development on the one hand and purification on the other (profit and health)—were never really distinct from one another.[46]

ROUTES THROUGH INDIANA AND MICHIGAN
IN 1848.

Map 1. Indiana's Underground Railroad. From Wilbur H. Siebert, *The Underground Railroad from Slavery to Freedom*, 1898.

For even before and beside the potential exposure and destruction of Black maroon communities, this gentrifying/purification impulse had racial goals.[47] As Carlson explains, in nineteenth-century America, the swamps were considered "unwholesome," not only because of their association with "disease and death" but also because like other undeveloped lands, they were associated with Indians: "The only problem with North America's atmosphere, the narrative insisted, was that Indians, and not industrious and enlightened Europeans, had inhabited the continent during the past few centuries. . . . According to this critique, the refusal of Indians to heed the Christian injunction to 'subdue the earth,' . . . made them unworthy of possessing the land."[48]

But if the swamp draining was an aspect of anti-Black and anti-Indian violence throughout the South and Midwest, it also led to the further impoverishment of poor whites, at least in Indiana, where the sale of swamp lands was phenomenally corrupt.

"Laborious Dirty Work"
After 1850 each state did something a little different with its wetlands, writing its own laws around their occupation, sale, and drainage. While prior to the Swamp Lands Act, Indiana's approximately six million acres of swamp were, according to one government surveyor from the time, "rather uninviting to the capitalist and land speculator," the state's handling of the law proved quite lucrative to just those people.[49] Once it became clear that the state did not have the revenue to administer the drainage work itself, it began to offer scrips to developers who would agree to take on the egregious job. This scrip program made it quite easy for the much reviled East Coast speculators to speedily and cheaply buy up tracts in the tens of thousands of acres, renting out swampy plots to those who, like Kem, were desperate enough to dig the ditches, at first by hand—"laborious, dirty work"—and later by steam-powered trenchers.[50]

Indiana's process of sale and drainage included "numerous examples of ineptness and criminality."[51] As a few prominent speculators got wind of the cheap land for sale, they effectively manipulated state officials into selling it quickly and adding perfectly dry land to the deal. And whenever a commissioner refused to participate in such corruption, wealthy investors seemed quite able to facilitate his removal.[52] Counties cut illegal deals, selling to certain developers at prices far below the official price, as cheap as ten cents an acre. In a situation echoed in today's housing crises, profits were thereby maximized while equitable land distribution was deplorably curtailed; what might have been sold to many was sold only to a few.[53] "Draining the swamp," in contrast to its current colloquial usage, produced a swamp of its own—the swamp of corruption, exploitation, and exclusion.

But to be clear, in a pattern we see again and again, the exclusion experienced by poor whites unable to participate in the buying and selling of wetlands (though certainly invited to drain them) was nothing in comparison to the exclusion experienced by people of color. While some historians will no doubt find it a stretch to refer to the Swamp Lands Act as a partner in the plan for fugitive recapture (I found no mid-century lawmakers describing it as such), in Indiana 1850 brings a third pivotal legal adjustment to the state, one that makes its mid-century goals apparent.

At Indiana's 1850 Constitutional Convention, delegates passed Article 13, which, following similar laws in Ohio, Illinois, and Oregon, banned all future migration of free Black and mixed-race people to the state while fining any whites who employed the Black people already there. The law went further still, encouraging the departure of its free Black citizens with a petty bribe of $50 for each male who agreed to leave. Ambitiously hoping to "colonize" Black families by exporting them to Africa, the Indiana legislature also appropriated $5,000 to that end.[54] "Colonization" was, in fact, a favored idea for abolitionists, including, ironically or not, Calvin Fletcher. When Article 13 passed, this avid abolitionist wrote in his diary, "I think I can see the finger of God in this." (There's more to Calvin Fletcher than his abolitionism, his benevolent handouts, and even his faith in colonization. When he was young, a pregnant Black woman named Cresy accused him of being the father of her child. At first, he ignored the accusation, then he stridently denied it. And finally, fearing for his reputation, he decided to "make an experiment by fright to elicit the truth from her," hunting her down in the home of a friend and beating her almost unconscious until she named another man as her rapist.)[55]

Schuyler Colfax, future Radical Republican and vice president under Grant, was one of the sole delegates to reject Indiana's 13th Article, providing the minority viewpoint:

> The slave States drive the free negroes from their borders, and the free States declare they shall not come within their limits. Where shall the negro go? . . . The lust and avarice of the white man stole them from their homes, herded them in the slave factories, doomed them to the horrors of the 'middle passage,' and landed them on our shores to live the bondman's life of unrequited toil. He was dragged from his home, and now by the accidents of life a portion of the race find themselves free but ordered off the earth by constitutional provisions, like the one now before this Convention. Where shall the negro go? Into the Ohio river! . . . Let us not adopt such measures as we shall hate to look back upon, from the future; such provisions as we shall burn with shame to see inscribed on the first page of our organic law.[56]

Colfax was in the minority not just of delegates present. All eligible white men in the state were invited to vote on this special provision. It passed—113,828 to 21,873.

In the decades that followed that critical year, poor white farmers in Indiana would find less cheap land left to buy, while their labor would be put to use serving racial capitalism's goals: draining the state of its non-white populations while converting refuge and shared land into profit for the few.[57] An 1889 *Indianapolis Journal* story title says it all: "The Swamp with a History: The Station in Marion County Where Fugitive Slaves Found a Safe Refuge: It Afterward Became a Rendezvous for Bounty Jumpers, but the Wet Lands Were Reclaimed and Given to the Industrious."[58]

From age seventeen to twenty-six, Omer Kem unsuccessfully attempted farming on approximately six different swampy sites, first going solo and then with Nan, who after their youthful marriage promptly began giving birth. Their first baby died at eight months; their second lived long enough to need something to eat other than what Nan's body produced on its own. Draining, farming, and moving on, often before the crops came in, buying a cow or buying a horse and then selling the animal to pay the rent, doctor, or funeral bills, Nan and Omer spiraled toward desperation as children continued to be born—five babies in just under six years.

Owning even mud was impossible for them. But so was staying anywhere for much more than a year. Under the crop-lien system, a tenant would borrow the rent from the landlord against the promise of future crops, sometimes owing for food and supplies as well. If the crops failed to grow because (for example) the land was under water, then the tenants' only option was to move on, taking nothing with them. "I had to take off my shoes, roll up my pants, and plow through water half knee deep in the low places in order to keep the weeds down on the high points where I hoped to get a few nubbins," Kem writes.[59] Nubbins were so few, in fact, that this particular crop left Kem without food for the family or money for the rent, even after he'd sold what livestock he had left. With no means, no land, and three living children (two had died), he was, as he puts it, "drowning."

In 1881, at age twenty-six, Kem boarded a train headed to Nebraska. There he received, as remedy for his poverty, 320 acres of grasslands that he would again fail to farm. Just as the history of wetlands remains as residue in Indiana's current social, economic, and ecological life, the residue of mud—a commons, a shelter, and finally a site of impossible and exploited labor—clung to Kem's life even as he tried to leave it behind. For while the Homestead Act—like the Swamp Lands Act and the Indian Removal Act before that—encouraged people considered white to become property owners on land previously held in common by people who were not, and thereby lifted up some of the nation's poor laborers, it nonetheless left many of its recipients no better off than they'd been.

And yet ten years after Kem arrives in Nebraska, he will find himself a member of the U.S. House of Representatives, where he will attempt to alter the laws he had been oppressed by. The free mobility of whiteness is a product of and producer of the law.

Mud—as transporter of illness, as trans-material, as temporary home for those in motion, as indicator of all that is not yet, has not yet arrived (as capital), not yet been made to produce—could only present a threat to those who sought to stabilize white ownership of land. The swamp was a borderland, haunted by imaginary creatures and real-life exiles. Mistrusted but desired, it presented a potential site of both illness and sustenance, of future wealth and also of death.

These associations ran deep in the Euro-American imagination. In Europe alone there are at least forty different names for creatures who live half-hidden in a semi-fluid world: nixie, knucker, neker, kelpie, brook horse, melusine, siren, water sprite (recognizable in human form by the wet hem of her skirt), Rhine maiden, Lorelei, naiad. Half in, half out, these beings—often part animal (slit ears, fish tails, horse's hair) and almost always female—want to pull you, too, into the undefined and unknowable space they control. And in the still "new" American continent, a woman half in and half out of the water was likely to have been Native, impoverished, or enslaved.

When Omer Kem left Indiana in 1881, most of the lands bought up for draining were not yet dry. But within fifty years, the state had drained 97 percent of its pre-settlement swamps.[60] Now, where the Fletcher Swamp once was, a poor neighborhood is being rapidly gentrified. On one peeling garage door, someone has painted a cluster of hot air balloons, drifting away.

2   Sod

Everything in US history is about the land.
—Roxanne Dunbar-Ortiz, *An Indigenous People's History of the United States*

What it means to be in transit, then, is to be in motion, to exist liminally in the ungrievable spaces of suspicion and unintelligibility. To be in transit is to be made to move.
—Jodi Byrd, *The Transit of Empire*

Coming and Going: Homesteading on the Plains and the Ponca Trail of Tears

A father and his father, a wife and three children (by the first, now dead, wife) with huge slices of watermelon in their hands—a symbol of their productivity and the land's yield. They sit or stand in front of a house formed of the earth they eat from. It is too dark inside for the camera, so we'll never know just how they arranged their beds, or what, if anything, they had for toys. Those girls in their dresses—Maude and Linda—with their eyes cast down against the sun. I know things they do not know about what their lives will offer. Maude (standing) will live long, marry a Nebraska boy, and raise four children in the Oregon woods. Linda (seated) will die young from tuberculosis after struggles with mental illness, her "troubles." As they pose for the photographer, Solomon D. Butcher, who took just about all the photos of settlers in sod houses that we have and none of the photos of the Native people they replaced or lived near, these girls do not know what I know, but they know other things I can't. They know what it is to be a girl living under dirt with a woman not much

5. Kem family in front of their sod house, Broken Bow, Nebraska, 1885. Photograph by Solomon D. Butcher. Library of Congress, Solomon D. Butcher Collection, G2608.PH:000000-000200.

older than you, now positioned as your mother, your first mother in the ground. They know what drought feels like when you've got nothing to eat but what you can grow or kill, which is not much. And they know what it's like to almost die of the disease that took your mother, to sense that incurable affliction always ready to return.

In 1883, just a year after she followed Omer to the claim outside the town of Broken Bow, Nebraska, Nan came down with typhoid fever. Omer had failed to get the doctor in time, and within three days of taking to her bed, Nan died. Omer had no time to grieve the partner of his youth, however; all the energy he had was dedicated to keeping Linda, Maude, and baby Claude alive. He nursed all three in a one-room soddy (not the one shown here—a much smaller and more rudimentary version) as they suffered through the disease that had also taken Omer's sister and his fourth child, a baby named Earl, in Indiana. Linda lay in bed for over three weeks, during which time she ate absolutely nothing and also, according to Omer, did not shit. Maude's illness was less severe, and Claude, still

Sod 35

in diapers, healed quickly. By spring everyone was well, though Kem was now both broke and unable to start the crops because he had no wife. Without a wife, he was also forced into kinds of labor he had no practice in: "By the time Maude had recovered, I had soaked up a lot of experience [and] had learned some things, among others how to nurse typhoid fever and how to cook common food pretty well, but I never did succeed with cookies."[1] Even children whose mother has just died, it seems, want cookies.

They are two, five, and eight. They cannot be left alone. Omer sells half his land and rents out the rest, and this way they get through the spring and summer. But when fall comes around, it's clear he can no longer care for his children without starving them. In what he describes later as "being enveloped in the darkest cloud of my existence," he sends the children to live with his brother-in-law (just three miles away) and hires himself out to his neighbor James Ream, a sheep herder with a flock of four thousand: "I do not know just how cold it got that winter because I had no instrument with which to measure the temperature, but it was the coldest winter I ever experienced before or since. . . . There was one period of 30 days when the snow did not give a particle on the southern sides of buildings even tho the sun was shining brightly. It takes exceedingly cold weather for this sort of stunt and I never, saw it happen in any other winter."[2]

"I promise you," he continues, "that the care of 4,000 sheep in one blizzard by two men is quite enough, not only for one winter, but for a lifetime."[3] This is because when the wind begins to blow, the sheep huddle together, creating a living barrier for the snow. If not helped, the sheep will suffocate in the snowbank that forms around them. Kem and Ream punch and kick the sheep until they move apart, but as soon as they get one group to scatter, they have to attack another, and on and on until the blizzard ends.

After this difficult winter of separation and struggle, the children are reunited with their father, and shortly after this, when out hocking household goods for cash, Kem meets my great-grandmother, Alice Lockhart, and wins the children a new mother. Alice (whose name both I and my daughter carry) was just eight years older than Maude. Now as they stand, this remade family, with their early fall crop in their hands, they know how the melon juice feels on their fingers, and they know the wind that slightly lifts the hem of Alice's skirt. But they don't yet know of the pain that will course through Omer's body nor of the fantasized Indian healer named Fleet Wind who will visit him nightly, massaging his aching legs. And they also don't know more immediate futures—that this will be the last harvest they'll manage to draw from that claim, that Alice's first baby, a boy named Omer Albert, will die while she's nursing her second.

"I was one proud boy," Omer exclaims, remembering how it felt in 1881 to be the recipient of so much free land. Pages and pages of his assertive, confident, rarely reverent, never apologetic, but often playful narratives wrap themselves around other truths I'm trying to hear, just as the house made of sod in the middle of that flat land holds in its walls the living wildness of what sod was—grasses, insects, and rodents—while seeming to say, "Settle."

In the first comprehensive history of the Great Plains, published in 1931, historian Walter Prescott Webb describes a landscape of great mystery, openness, and—until the arrival of white settlers—emptiness: "We cannot solve the mystery of the influence of the plains. . . . But the evidence indicates that the plains give man new and novel sensations of elation, of vastness, of romance, of awe, and often of nauseating loneliness."[4]

As in so many books, movies, and songs about the region, this "nauseating loneliness" supplies cover to another noxious scene, not of loneliness and romance, of course, but of treachery and tragedy. Historian David Wishart estimates that in 1800 there were at least 14,000 Native people in what is now eastern Nebraska: the Omahas, Pawnees, Poncas, and Otoe-Missourias, primarily. By 1900, reports Wishart, there were only 1,203.[5] This condensed history of Indian genocide and removal in the territory begins right around the time of Omer Kem's birth in Hagerstown, Indiana.

In 1851, following the Department of Interior's cleanly stated goal of destroying "any claim the Indians may have to such portions of the soil as are desirable for the location of white settlers," Congress passes the (first) Indian Appropriations Act, which initiates the reservation system.[6] Three years later, the Kansas-Nebraska Act prepares the way to statehood for both territories, opening the area to floods of white migrants, mostly poor farmers from the Midwest like the Kems. While Native populations in the southern plains had been rapidly shrinking before these dates due to devastating epidemics of smallpox (from encounters with Europeans), inter-tribal conflict, and the decimation of the buffalo, by the time Omer Kem arrived in Nebraska territory, most Native people were living on a few small reservations.[7] In any story of the plains from that time, death, grieving, and exile would have to be central, as they are in the story I am about to tell. But also central is the resistance to exile and the refusal of the criminalization and dehumanization of Native people that undergirds it.

A two-year-long war between the United States and the Lakotas, Cheyennes, and Arapahos—known as Red Cloud's War—came to an end in 1868 (really a pause in ongoing struggle). The resulting Fort Laramie Treaty, a triumph for Chief Red Cloud and the Lakotas, marked the "peace" and created the Great Sioux Reservation. However, a portion of that land had already been reserved for the much smaller Ponca nation in 1865 (following a series of earlier broken treaties).[8] Now, what had historically been Ponca land was, "by the stipulations of the Fort Laramie Treaty, no longer theirs."[9] This situation, whether a function of incompetence or treachery on the part of the government, does not go well, as the Lakotas and Poncas had long been in conflict.

In the treaties between the United States and the Poncas, the government had promised protections against incursions by whites or other Indians. But that's not what they offered in the end. Terrible weather conditions and ongoing conflicts with the Lakota Brulé band meant that the government's requirement that the Ponca farm rather than hunt was not only useless; it was murderous.[10] By 1873 the Poncas were starving. (Government annuities amounted to $11.50 per capita per year, when $5.00 a month was poverty wages.)[11] In what Wishart refers to as "one of the most shameful" events in U.S.-Indian relations, Congress responds to the Poncas' crisis by allocating funds to forcibly remove them from the small hold on ancestral lands they had left, eventually relocating all seven hundred people to Indian Territory.[12]

Sometimes referred to as the Ponca Trail of Tears, this six-hundred-mile forced march through tornados and across flooded rivers in the spring of 1877 was enforced by forty armed soldiers. The phrase *trail of tears* doesn't quite capture the extreme violence of this event or others like it. Indian agent E. C. Kemble had threatened the Poncas with death by gunshot if they did not comply.[13] Nonetheless, nine people died on the march, two elderly women and seven children, including a daughter of Chief Standing Bear.[14]

When they arrived in Indian Territory, the Poncas met even worse conditions than they had left behind—unfarmable rocky land, bad weather, and no sanitation. In addition, their arrival in the territory was not without conflict; their first location was Quapaw land, and the government had done nothing to assure the Poncas' welcome. After about a year they were moved again, this time over one hundred miles west during the brutal heat of July. At least an additional 158 people died within the very first year in the new territory. Within two years, one-third of the Poncas were dead.[15]

When another of Standing Bear's children, a sixteen-year-old son named Bear Shield, was on his deathbed in 1879, he begged to be buried in his homeland. As Standing Bear said later: "At last I had only one son left; then he sickened. When he was dying, he asked me to promise him one thing. He begged me to take him, when he was dead, back to our old burying ground by the Swift running Waters, the Niobrara. I promised. When he died, I, and those with me, put his body into a box and then in a wagon, and we started North."[16]

Standing Bear and a group of other tribal members began their journey in the dead of winter, 1879. While most versions of the story emphasize Standing Bear's paternal grief—his wish to bury his son at home—the journey was also clearly an act of defiance. They had already tried other means; in March of 1877, Standing Bear and seven other Ponca chiefs, including White Eagle and Big Snake, had sent a telegram of distress (drafted by Susette La Flesche, who will return in this story) to President Hayes, declaring themselves "tired . . . and sad at heart." In November of that year ten chiefs, including Standing Bear, had traveled by train to Washington to petition Hayes and Interior Secretary Carl Schurz directly, asking to return to their land, but to no avail.[17]

And so, as they set out for South Dakota, the travelers were well aware that they were unauthorized to leave their assigned location. As historian Kay Graber mentions, they avoided areas where white settlers might detect them. They had reason to fear. Sixty days into their journey, they reached a place of rest on the Omaha Reservation in Nebraska where some family members lived.[18] Brigadier General George Crook, apprised of the Poncas' presence, sent a guard to arrest the group for unlawful travel. For various reasons, including the illness of some of the Poncas, Crook did not demand immediate movement. Instead, they were imprisoned at Fort Omaha.[19]

Thus, a grieving father in forced exile is apprehended by the law. Not long after, another father, Omer Madison Kem, becomes a proud landowner on that very same prairie. Both men experienced transit across roughly the same soil, both were motivated in their movement by a longing for a stable home, both men grieved for lost sons, and both impacted U.S. law to this day. And yet one was Native and the other white, and so the former was exiled and treated as a criminal, while the latter was eventually granted great social and legal power.

Fragmenting

> It is impossible to separate the geologic development of the Great Plains from the development of the earth as a whole.
> —Stubbendieck, Hatch, and Dunn, *Grasses of the Great Plains*

The roots were deep, eight to fourteen feet deep. A house could be built of sod because the dirt is held tight in the weave of these roots. A sod roof was, however, a risk. Sod absorbs rain and melting snow, which will increase the weight of the roof by several hundred pounds. Roofs could and often did collapse, sometimes burying settlers alive.

Prairies once covered 170 million acres of our continent, with forty to sixty species of grass and over three hundred of forb and flower. It's estimated that the North American prairies have been around for ten thousand years, but 1880 was year ten in the beginning of their end. In the 140 years from then to now, the prairies have been reduced to 1 percent of their 1870 magnitude. The North American prairie is now one of the most threatened ecosystems on the planet.

The secret to the prairie's long-term survival, prior to the arrival of settlers, was that 75–80 percent of its biomass lay safely underground. "The visible plants seen on the landscape are merely the photosynthetic leaves gathering sunlight for a much larger community underground. Just beneath the surface lies the main stems or rhizomes, running horizontally. Here they lie protected from drying, grazing, trampling, fire, and frost."[20] One could say, then, that Omer Kem built his house—sixteen by twenty-four feet—out of the commons of the grass. Cutting deep, he made a home of its demise.[21] Environmental scientists' term for the farming of this grasslands is, fittingly, *fragmentation*.

Kem's flat land with its box made of sod was precisely 338 miles northeast of my house in Denver and was not the first property this white family had owned; some members had purchased various houses and farms in Indiana and before that in North Carolina, where at least one patriarch also thought he owned three people. But it was the first property in the West and the only sizable piece that was freely acquired from a government whose clear and often stated goal was precisely to populate the land with white people.[22]

It wasn't just the grass roots that were fragmented when the homesteaders arrived; it was the visible landscape too. While ranchers and Indians probably didn't share much, they did share a sense of what Kem called the "free range," which he and the other settlers sought to destroy.[23] Farmers had come to own, and fences (like walls), especially fences weaponized by barbed wire, defined the land as someone's.[24] "The settlement of the country by the tiller of the soil meant the destruction of the *free range* and they [the ranchers] would be compelled to acquire land for grazing purposes as other people acquired it, or go out of business," Omer writes.[25] This disagreement between ranchers and farmers was not peaceable. The ranchers "discouraged such settlers in every way possible even to burning his hay, cutting his fences so the cattle would destroy his crops and shooting him from ambush."[26] So Kem went to war for farmers' "rights"—which is to say, property rights—with his pen.

For despite having survived the winter of 1884–85, and despite having found someone to bake cookies for his children, crop failures were the norm in the late 1880s, and Kem needed other work. His annoyance about the ranchers and their desire for a fenceless range led him to take a job as a reporter for the Custer County paper, the *Republican*. Kem's beat was to report on the threatening activities of the cowboys: "I could see no reason or justice in a half dozen men using hundreds of square miles of the public domain for grazing purposes, free of charge, when it deprived thousands of other men of the right to comply with the law and use these lands in making homes and . . . civilizing the country, and I mumbled not a bit when I said so," he explains.[27] Thus Kem, who had been forced out of Indiana at least in part because of the privatization of public swamplands and been granted free land that had once been owned in common, now found himself a vocal defender of the rules of acquisition and exclusivity, rules he nonetheless hadn't had to play by.

As it turned out, the battle between the settlers and the ranchers was decided by nature. The brutally hot summer of 1886 was followed by an equally brutal winter; in some areas, 75 percent of the cattle froze to death.[28] "When spring came at last only a few pitiful remnants of the great herds remained," writes John Hicks. "'Cattle barons' and 'bovine kings' ceased to exist."[29] However, even nature might have been forced to respond to the settlers, as some evidence suggests that widespread farming had contributed to this ruthless weather pattern.[30] And even if climactic changes are hard to pin on farmers, it was certainly true that fragmenting had left the land stripped of its defenses and terribly vulnerable to the drought that came, which eventually punished all who lived there, though not equally.

Personhood: The Trial of Standing Bear

Almost immediately after Standing Bear and the other Ponca travelers were apprehended by Crook's guard, they received a visit from a man named Thomas Henry Tibbles. Tibbles, an editor for the *Omaha Herald*, had been an active abolitionist as a teenager. In the 1850s he fought under John Brown and James Lane's Free-State militias defending Kansas from pro-slavery factions. In his later years he would

6. Nebraska farm, 2019. Courtesy Chris Kondrich.

become a prominent Populist, nominated to run for vice president on the party ticket in 1904. As a Nebraska journalist in the 1870s, he was similarly principled.[31] Convinced by the righteousness of the Ponca group, Tibbles interviewed Standing Bear at Fort Omaha, published articles about the situation in the daily and weekly *Herald*, and telegraphed the story to papers in Chicago and New York. Tibbles is also credited with encouraging Standing Bear to fight his imprisonment by suing for a writ of habeas corpus in court.[32]

The trial of Standing Bear was scheduled for the first of May 1879.[33] The legal basis for Standing Bear's right to free movement would hinge on the language of habeas corpus, which does not apply specifically to citizens but to "persons" (few Indians were citizens then).

Sod   43

Thus, "there was really but one question, and one question only, before the court: Was Standing Bear a person?"[34] By the time Standing Bear's lawyer, John Lee Webster, launched his three-hour argument, the case was fully in the public eye, having made it to the front page of the *New York Times*.

"Are they wild animals, deer to be chased by every hound?" Webster asked rhetorically as he set out to prove the Poncas' personhood.[35] How could this question be answered? Well, did Standing Bear wear western clothes? Did he practice the sabbath? Did he send his children to school? Did he farm? Did he strive toward independence and self-sufficiency? These were the qualities that would determine his status. If it was shown that he behaved like a settler, then the white people present could feel not only empathy but affinity with his being.[36]

In his discussion of forced assimilation in the Indian boarding schools, Ojibwe author David Treuer puts it this way: "To be a person was to be a certain *kind* of person: an American . . . who owned property and was culturally white."[37] Interestingly, though, as Webster developed his assimilationist argument, he quoted Frederick Douglass's own claims to autonomous selfhood: "A man belongs to himself. His hands are his own, his feet are his own, his body is his own, and they will remain his until you storm the citadel of heaven and wrest from the bosom of God man's title deed to himself."[38] While Webster is leaning on Douglass to argue that race is not the measure of the human, his choice of language here is telling. The language of deed, this description of the body itself as property, underscores the settler logic at play: ownership was everything, the ground of both individual freedom and political power.

Standing Bear himself, who was an avowed Christian, reportedly corroborated the value of white personhood: "I want to work, and become like a white man," he is said to have claimed.[39] Perhaps so. But another interpretation was offered to me by Standing Bear's descendent, the lawyer Brett Chapman, who spoke with me over the phone. Standing Bear was a strategic rhetorician, skilled at dissimulation, said Chapman. Maybe he just knew what would work.[40]

Regardless, at the very end of his testimony, Standing Bear put aspirational whiteness to the side. Facing the by now crowded courtroom, Standing Bear held up his hand. "That hand is not the color of yours, but if I pierce it, I shall feel pain. . . . The blood that will flow from mine will be of the same color as yours," he pronounced.[41] Here, in this literalization of the term *habeas corpus*, Standing Bear grounds his humanity not in race, not in cultural behaviors or beliefs, but in the body and its vulnerability.

And vulnerability, perhaps more than any other universal fact of embodiment, was key. After holding up his hand, Standing Bear switched tactics, describing himself as "weak and faint and sick," surrounded by a rising flood, in need of Judge Dundy's help if he is not to drown.[42] Reinforcing the doctrine of "dependence," which harkened back to *Johnson v. M'Intosh*, left white dominance intact. This account of Indians' fundamental reliance on whites, this assurance of exhaustion and frailty, was effective; reportedly everyone was crying by the end of his testimony, including General Crook.[43]

From the point of view of the lawyers and perhaps much of the audience, Standing Bear was a person because he had assimilated into white settler ways, he was a person because he *owned* a body and had aspirations, too, of privately owning land, and he was a person because, having proven himself to be weak and therefore unthreatening to his white audience, this audience could now safely empathize with his grief. But through his performative act—holding up his hand as evidence—Standing Bear had asserted something far more radical and fundamental: personhood was none of these things; personhood was a fact of corporality, hinging on nothing but a body that breathed.

After a three-day deliberation, Judge Dundy granted the writ of habeas corpus, and Standing Bear and the thirty other apprehended members of the Ponca nation were set free. It was the first time a Native person had asserted their civil rights in a court of law and won.[44]

This is not the end of the story, however. Directly after the trial, Tibbles, Standing Bear, and Omaha siblings Francis and Susette La Flesche went on a speaking tour to gather sympathy for their cause.[45] The tour is arguably even more important to history than the trial, as they had hoped it would be.[46] While speaking to large and sympathetic audiences throughout the Northeast, the group helped generate the creation of the Boston Indian Citizenship Committee and won the admiration and support of Massachusetts senator Henry L. Dawes.

Senator Dawes, moved by the plight of the "homeless" Poncas, would go on to author the notorious Dawes Act, which transformed tribal lands into "allotments" of 160 acres each. Standing Bear, Susette La Flesche, and Thomas Tibbles all participated in the development of the bill, first introduced by Dawes in 1880 though not ratified until 1887.[47] While allotments had been available to various Indians in various states for many years, the Dawes Act made allotment a federal policy. (Incidentally, the first Indian lands to be allotted were in Nebraska; the first homesteaders were there, too.)[48]

This major act of Indian law reform, modeled on the Homestead Act, was believed by many to be the answer to the problem of ever shrinking and encroached upon Indian land. If Native people owned their own plots like settlers did, it was argued, then they would no longer be victims of land theft, and their lands would no longer be vulnerable to the whims of the federal government. However, in practice, the Dawes Act led to a decrease of Native-owned lands by almost two-thirds, from 138 million acres in 1887 to 48 million in 1934.[49] Allotments were "granted" to heads of households, but any land beyond that was considered "surplus" and was immediately made available for sale to whites (usually to wealthy investors). Many allotments, often useless as farms, were sold off to settlers or fragmented even further when divided among heirs. Historians Valerie Sherer Mathes and Richard Lowitt refer to the Dawes Act as "the most devastating piece of legislation affecting Indians in the history of the American republic," and many others, especially Indigenous scholars, echo this dismay.[50]

The Dawes Act had consequences for the Standing Bear Poncas in particular. Though they had returned to their homeland along the Niobrara River, in 1891 their land was allotted. Seventy thousand surplus acres were sold to speculators, who then resold them to whites at a profit. In 1881 these Northern Poncas had returned to a reservation of over ninety thousand acres. By 1939 they had barely a thousand.[51]

The trial of Standing Bear was in many senses a victory for Native people, and yet the moment was quickly subsumed under the settler-colonial nation's continued aggressions, now in the form of what

Patrick Wolfe calls "a paper-trail of tears."[52] By defining Indians as legal persons, the trial and its aftermath helped pave a new, and newly problematic, approach to the "Indian problem" in the United States. Indians were now potential familiars; as such, the role of the state was no longer to murder, remove, or contain them as "savages." Instead, the state would labor to assimilate Indians into itself, which is to say, into whiteness.[53] Because the case was fought and won under the banner of personal rights and not national sovereignty, it did not protect Native lands from further losses and in fact contributed to these losses in the long run.[54] Under the Dawes Act, the fragmented plains were fragmented yet again, and the beneficiaries of this fragmentation were by and large the white capitalists who successfully monetized the soil.[55]

The Right to Survive: Beyond the Boundaries of Private Property

> never again to
> lie in the dirt on my stomach never
> again to call this a game in America
> —Layli Long Soldier, *Whereas*

Two months into the writing of this chapter, I fell asleep to a voice whispering in my ear. She said, "This ain't dead." Then, almost primly, she corrected herself. "This *isn't* dead." Who was she? I can tell you she was a young woman, white, slight, practically still a teen; I could "see" her. She herself was dead, but also not, speaking to me from the past to encourage me in my dealings with things one might think no longer operative, no longer alive.

I had a second dream that week. Like Alice Kem in Nebraska, I had given birth to two babies, one that would survive and one that would not. The one that would not had been born with my placenta *as* her throat and mouth (just as bloody as that sounds). This part of me that was supposed to feed her only when she was inside me had migrated to her mouth, barring her ability to communicate and to feed herself. In a way of seeing this, I had failed to allow her to separate from me, and for this reason, she would die.[56]

I lived with this strange dream for a while. At first it seemed only an obvious metaphor, associating mothering with smothering. But then this obscene image of nurturing-gone-wrong began to open to broader confusions: the confusion between care and violence, between intimacy and power, between sympathetic love and control.

That winter, during Denver's 2019 municipal election, a group of advocates for the rights of the unhoused, Denver's Homeless Outloud, put forth Ballot Initiative 300, "The Right to Survive." The initiative proposed revising Denver's municipal code so that resting, sheltering oneself, occupying one's own parked vehicle, and eating or exchanging food in public would be legally protected activities. As it was, sheltering oneself on public land (even with just a blanket) was banned in Denver; homeless people reported that police forced them to move throughout the night, often multiple times. Unable to sleep, people would become increasingly vulnerable to health crises and less able to work or go to school.[57] One would think that the basic human right of sleep would be easily granted to all. However, in almost every neighborhood in Denver and along all the major avenues, red yard signs proclaimed "NO on 300" with the slogan below: "We can do better." Yet no "better" plan for Denver's six thousand unhoused people was ever proposed. Initiative 300 failed miserably, and the illegality of sleeping in public, the "urban camping ban," was maintained.

Was this because people who were housed simply felt no sympathy for people who were not? Not exactly. As one woman I spoke to said, "I feel bad for homeless people, I really do, but no one should be allowed to sleep in the street." Her sympathy extended only to those unhoused people who were willing (or able) to sleep in the temporary, inadequate, and sometimes dangerous space of the shelter.[58] In the end, this form of "care," a form of what Saidiya Hartman terms "violent identification," threatened the very survival of the people the woman felt bad for.[59]

What this has to do with the trial of Standing Bear is, I think, obvious. In America there is no room for people who live, whether by choice or necessity, outside the boundaries of private property.[60] Care, in this case, becomes a form of control, a way to contain, enclose, and silence those who proclaim their right to simply survive.[61] Within these contexts, then, I take my dream image as a warning.

When on Thanksgiving Day of 1881 Omer Kem left Indiana, his plan was to drop foot on the eastern edge of Nebraska.[62] He'd been unable to move beyond a hand-to-mouth existence, and so, "like a drowning man grabbing at a straw," he had set out for the former Otoe-Missouria Reservation, which just that year, as he'd been told, had been "thrown open for settlement."[63] Along the way, another traveler told him that the rumor was wrong; the former reservation was not available to homesteaders, because the land along the Big Blue River was too valuable to give away. It would be sold instead to the highest bidders. Omer was broke—he almost turned back—but instead pushed on, hoping to find a homestead farther west.

What I'm saying is this: Omer Kem did not go to Nebraska in ignorance of the Native people whose land it was. He went in full awareness of the process of removal he was participating in and benefiting from through his arrival. He and thousands of others knew full well that their new homes, homes they desperately needed, were predicated on other people's homelessness. He knew that but didn't often say it. Indeed, except for his brief mention of the Indians he had hoped to supplant, nowhere else in the first volume of Omer Kem's two-thousand-page autobiography does he mention either the presence or absence of Native people in Nebraska. Instead, he said this: "I was in full possession of 320 acres of its virgin soil with not a thing on it, but grass, gophers and prairie chickens."[64]

When Omer and Alice's first son died at "one year, eight months, and seventeen days," they buried him beside Nan in the Custer County Cemetery. The location for this boy's bones was not in dispute. His belonging to and in the soil that formed the walls that had briefly housed him was, for the town of Broken Bow, the County of Custer, the state of Nebraska, and the United States of America, a given.

Standing Bear's son, having been exiled from his ancestral land, became a homeless corpse, carried in a box, unburied. To resolve the plight of the body it had refused, the U.S. government could imagine only one thing: the land itself, the living earth, was a thing to be bought and to be sold.

3   Law and Order

> It is through law that persons, variously figured, gain or lose definition, become victims of prejudice or inheritors of privilege.
> —Colin Dayan, *The Law Is a White Dog*

"Death Calls Us Home": The Fifty-Second Congress
They mourn one another. For pages and pages, for hours and hours, they mourn. As they mourn the dead, they praise them—for their patriotism, their evenness of temper, their commitment to the whole. Industry, perseverance, honesty. Frank, rugged, resolute. In praising one another, they praise themselves: "We have been brought here as types of people unrivaled on the earth"; "In our American civilization no bar is raised against any man."[1] It is March of 1892. It will be nearly thirty years before any woman of any race is deemed, by this body, to be worthy of the vote. *Plessy v. Ferguson*, which will lock segregation into the law, is just four years away. That very week, when not mourning, these congressmen debate not so much *whether* to take Indian children from their parents but how far away and for how long such children should be removed. "We lose ourselves, Mr. Speaker, in the byways of our lives. Death calls us home."

"The way to glory is the humble way of service," they say. "Service" in this case refers to the work performed by the late Mr. Gamble, dead at forty-three. Representative Gamble, cousin of Andrew Jackson, helped to establish the three-year-old state of South Dakota. His role in the decision to divide the Dakota Territory is mentioned again and again. This is the "bitter controversy," "the war" he took part in. The Wounded Knee Massacre of December 1890, during which up to three hundred Lakota men, women, and children were murdered and which followed immediately after the establishment of statehood, is not mentioned in the telling and retelling of the story of Gamble's life.² The week following Gamble's three-hour eulogy, Kansas senator Preston B. Plumb is likewise mourned, with at least as many words and minutes.

These hours of public mourning, stretching through the Fifty-Second Congress's first legislative session, make sense when we consider that the members' task, perhaps their *primary* task, is to define the body they belong to and represent.³ Public mourning reorders the profound disorder caused by untimely death, but it creates order in another way as well: it clarifies which lives are considered "grievable" and which will be cast aside. Congressmen then and congresspeople now are charged with the awesome task of deciding who will be supported, sustained, and honored and who will not—in short (to use Judith Butler's words), "whose lives count as lives."⁴ For as they soothe one another with praise, read aloud eulogizing poems, hold each other in this circle of mourning, there are other untimely deaths they don't mention at all, lives whose value is nowhere in this archive recorded. The boundary between the honored and the discarded is thus articulated not only by congressmen's words but also by their silence, a silence made ever more palpable by how surrounded by sound it is.

When I was beginning this research, I traveled to Indiana to search for scraps of Omer Kem's mother's childhood, having learned that she was raised in an Underground Railroad "station." As I entered small town libraries in the middle of the state, I was directed to drawers and folders stuffed with documents that held my family names: Bulla, Helms, Kem. These family archive rooms were quietly busy with others also involved in research, and these others were—when I was there, anyway—exclusively white. They, too, were searching for their families with a kind of passionate discipline. In the delicate remains of newspaper articles celebrating girls' basketball teams or announcing weddings and births, in obituaries and maps of plats, in mortgages and in leases, I found what Patricia Limerick calls "the ongoing competition for legitimacy."⁵ There we established our names, secured our home. Even in quiet rooms, the archive of whiteness is loud.

Law and Order   51

On March 9, 1892, at 2:30 in the morning, in what is now a famous lynching, seventy-five never-identified white men murdered Thomas Moss, Calvin McDowell, and Will Stewart, who were Black. "Butchered," "dismembered," "left to rot," as the papers luridly described. Thomas Moss had been the owner of People's Grocery in Memphis, a successful store that catered to white and Black customers alike. William Barrett, a white grocer, ran a less popular store across the street. When, after a dispute involving neighborhood children, Barrett led a group of white men, including police, to attack the store, Moss and others shot at the armed men in self-defense. Three officers were wounded that night, and dozens of Black men, most of whom were not present, were arrested. Six days later, while awaiting trial for the wounding, Moss, McDowell, and Stewart were abducted from the county jail by the mob, taken out to the railroad tracks, and shot dead. Though many reported having seen or heard the events that night, "no witness could state the name of any individual in the mob," and no one was ever charged.[6]

I found no online records of the House meeting that day, but the Senate met on March 9 and 10, and both bodies met on the 11th. There is no mention of this murder, nor any other lynching, on those days. Searching the entire record for 1892 using the words *lynch*, *lynching*, *murder*, and related terms produced just one result: on May 12, Congress debated whether they had the authority to investigate the use of murderous Pinkerton agents (employed to repress striking workers), a proposal put forth by Georgia Populist Tom Watson. Those who opposed the resolution did so on the grounds of state's rights: "It is not the business of Congress to interfere with the police powers of the Several States of the Union," said Senator Taylor of Ohio. The same was true, he said, of lynching.[7] Lynching was, of course, already illegal, as was any mob violence that could be considered insurrectional after the passage of the 1870 Ku Klux Klan Act. But since the 1876 Supreme Court ruling in *United States v. Cruikshank*, which followed on the heels of the Colfax Massacre, it was clear that enforcement would be a matter for each state's police force.[8] State's rights trumped civil rights when it came to the protection of Black lives. But "state's rights," you will remember, did not stop this same governing body from passing the Fugitive Slave Law of 1850. In that case, property ownership (of human property) overrode a state's independent policing powers.

The resolution to investigate the Pinkertons passed. But no such resolution was introduced about lynching. Though in 1892 more Black people were lynched than in any other year before or since—161 according to the Tuskegee Institute report, a Black person reported murdered almost every other day—Congress remained powerless to interfere. No anti-lynching bills were introduced, and no petitions regarding the killings were read that year.[9] Nor were the widows and children of lynched men attended to, though nearly every day, pensions were granted to the widows of Confederate and Union soldiers alike.

Nevertheless, everyone present knew what was happening, for this "horrendous wave of lynching . . . [with] white people lynching black people ritualistically, one after another" was reported widely in the papers.[10] Historian Jacqueline Goldsby calls these newspaper accounts "staggering" for how voluminous and frequent they were, in both Black and white papers (for different reasons).[11] Moreover, the now infamous lynching postcards, a form of gore porn, circulated freely like baseball cards. The white silence of law and lawmaker is clearly complicit in the terror.[12] Mary Church Terrell, the anti-lynching activist and founder of the National Association of Colored Women, put the matter sardonically: "Only martyrs are brave and bold enough to defy the public will, and the manufacture of martyrs in the negro's behalf is not very brisk just now."[13]

But while the Populists in Congress, like all other representatives and senators, remained silent on the issue of anti-Black terror, other Populists did not.[14] Black Populists, like their white counterparts, were poor farmers and agrarian workers in the South and on the plains who recognized the need for political action as a response to Gilded Age injustice and corruption. As Black Kansas Populist Benjamin F. Foster wrote, the Populists "are in favor of the masses and against monopolies. It is the party of the poor man . . . and would give him a chance to live and heal his present misery."[15] However, while Black Populism, "the largest movement of African Americans in the United States until the modern civil rights movement," according to historian Omar Ali, did share certain demands with white Populism, it had its own demands, too, including criminal justice reform, federal oversight of state and local elections, and an end to lynching (all deeply relevant still).[16] "If a poor Negro is suspected of a capital crime, he is immediately lynched," stated one Black Populist, Lutie A. Lytle of Topeka, Kansas. "If a white man is convicted of a capital offense, he is given a slight jail sentence." (Lytle was the first Black woman to practice law in both Tennessee and Kansas. In the late 1890s, when she was admitted to the bar in both states, she was the only Black woman practicing law in the nation. After her time as a Populist, she became an active member of Marcus Garvey's Universal Negro Improvement Association.)[17]

While no Black Populists were present in the House or Senate, Black Populists were present and took leadership roles at the People's Party conventions in Cincinnati in 1891 and St. Louis in 1892 and at parallel meetings of their own.[18] At the Omaha convention, Black and white Populists stood together onstage, jointly holding the American flag in a show of solidarity, and worked together to develop the party platform.[19] This platform, while founded on the hatred of all forms of "tyranny and oppression," says nothing specific about lynching or other forms of anti-Black terror, despite the fact that in their activism, Black Populists took great personal risks and exhibited courage not at all demanded of their white counterparts.

However, during the same year that the platform was written, Terrell and Frederick Douglass took the issue of anti-Black violence straight to the White House. There they implored President Harrison to condemn the lynching of Moss, McDowell, and Stewart and all lynching, in his annual address to Congress that year. Harrison, like the legislators, like my great-grandfather sitting for the first time on Capitol Hill, remained silent.[20] It seems that all three branches of the federal government were in agreement: there would be no federal actions to protect Black lives.

Later that year, Ida B. Wells-Barnett published a pamphlet titled *Southern Horrors: Lynch Law in All Its Phases*, which she described as "a contribution to the truth, an array of facts." Responding to the murders of Moss, McDowell, and Stewart (who were her friends), she caustically calls out the "injustice, barbarity and crime done to a people because of race and color" and repudiates the dominant justification for lynching Black men—the common claim that they rape white women.[21] Instead, she reminds her readers, it is white men who for generations have customarily raped Black women and girls, crimes for which they have almost never been punished, crimes for which they were instead long rewarded (in increased human property), crimes from which their descendants might benefit still.

Wells-Barnett is absolute in her condemnation of the very men who poetically mourn one another in Congress. These "men who stand high in the esteem of the public . . . for devotion to the principles of equal and exact justice for all," she writes, "stand as cowards who fear to open their mouths before this great outrage. They do not see that by their tacit encouragement, their silent acquiescence, the black shadow of lawlessness in the form of lynch law is spreading its wings over the whole country."[22] Wells-Barnett doesn't only call out silence; she also highlights noise, quoting from papers in which lynching is defended as necessary for the public good. These articles are almost unreadable for their naked and shameless cruelty, with us still and still denied.[23]

Silence and noise. How these two poles plague us. On the one hand, a recursive overabundance of brutal narratives (and images and video) works to maintain a pervasive association of Blackness with violent death.[24] On the other hand, the white silence of lawmakers and others rides under that noise like a current of air, keeping it afloat. But where now is the line between being witness to the viciousness of the murders and being a voyeur in what Saidiya Hartman terms the "spectacular nature of black suffering"?[25] How might repeating the facts of a lynching perpetuate, rather than protest, anti-Black violence as a norm? How might retelling these stories inadvertently reaffirm the paradigm that "fixes power in whiteness and pathology in Blackness"?[26] For these questions I do not have hard answers—or I have only hard answers. Insofar as I find the silence to have been productive—of a certain vision of Omer Kem as a good man, an exemplary man, a fair man, a vision that I inherited in stories and attitudes passed down—I am compelled to mark that silence for what it is and thereby to break it.

When not mourning their dead or handing out pensions to the widows of soldiers, the Fifty-Second Congress debates tariffs, taxes, the rights of workers, and the treatment of Indians and immigrants. On these matters, Omer Kem, the new Populist congressman from Nebraska's Third, had virulent and sometimes radical opinions. During the first session, Kem called for the forfeiture of railroad land grants, voted for an eight-hour work law, and called for the nationalization of transportation and finance.[27] After Pinkerton agents killed approximately seven people during the Homestead Strike of July 1892, he supported Watson's resolution to investigate the use of hired thugs.[28] He advocated for direct election of U.S. senators (rather than election by state legislatures), he demanded safeguards against land speculation in the West so that "men of very meager means" could have the "privilege of making for [him]self and [his] family a home," and in 1894, while the country faced a devastating depression, Kem argued passionately for a graduated income tax so that the rich would be forced to support the needs of the poor and vulnerable.[29]

Kem complained about being marginalized in his Populist corner, but he had voice and influence nonetheless. I wanted to know how he'd gotten there. How did he travel from the blizzard and the freezing sheep, the loss of wife and near loss of children, the mortgaging of the land, the cart full of junk he tried to sell, to arrive on the House floor with all its ordinary and brutal discussions? It is necessary to say, even if perfectly obvious, that both whiteness and maleness carried him there. His poverty was a barrier to power but not an uncrossable one. The order of the day was white male supremacy, and even as a poor man, Omer Kem belonged to that order. But before he could get in line, before he could receive the credit that was due, he first had to get on his knees.

White Debt

> Everyone is a "debtor," accountable to and guilty before capital.
> —Maurizio Lazzarato, *The Making of the Indebted Man*

It wasn't the terrible fall of 1883, when Nan died of typhoid, leaving Kem to care for their three young children, that drew Kem from farming into politics. And it wasn't the following winter of 1884–85, when his poverty was so acute that he sent the children away, bartered off and then rented out what was left of his claim, and took a job tending another man's sheep through days, nights, and blizzards.[30] It wasn't even the unforgiving weather five years later, during which "the dry dust of drought" blew across central Nebraska, "withering crops" in its "waterless wake," as a graduate student named Delloyd Guth, Kem's only biographer, alliteratively put it in 1962.[31] It wasn't any of these things, though these things were hard, that made Omer Kem a politician. It was debt.[32]

In the fall of 1885, nineteen-year-old Alice Lockhart agreed to become Kem's second wife. The next summer's crop entirely failed due to a hailstorm that "beat the corn all off the top side of the cob," slammed bullet-sized holes into the watermelon, and left the Kems with nothing to live on that year.[33] The following year was a little bit better, but though it brought a viable crop, there was also now another mouth to feed: a boy named Omer Albert. In need of a house larger than the one-room soddy in which Nan had died, in need of horses and equipment if he were to reap any profit from the land he had been granted, in 1886 Kem mortgaged his land for $600 and borrowed an additional $1,000. In less than a year, he would up his mortgage by another $1,500—all told, about $90,000 of debt today.

Alice birthed a second boy in the scorched summer of 1888. They named him Huxley Darwin. Then, while she was still recovering, Omer Albert, who would have been walking and stringing words together by then, died. (The significance of both these facts—the death of the first son and the naming of the second—will surface later on.) The ensuing four years of struggling and failing to pay their debt were sharpened by increasing bitterness: "I have been working hard for 15 years, many days 16 hours, have produced much wealth in farm products of various kinds, for which I have received but little money, I am nearing middle life still a poor man. I don't own even a home for there is a mortgage covering it for $1,500 and I cannot feel that it is mine till this mortgage is satisfied and, if the present low prices, which have prevailed for many years, shall continue, I don't feel that I can ever satisfy it."[34]

Kem was not alone in having accrued such debt or in being unable to pay it back. All settlers needed farm equipment, grain, and cattle, but having arrived broke, they often mortgaged their homesteads to buy these things. In the 1880s and '90s, Kansas, Nebraska, and the northern plains states "ranked well toward the top of the list of states in the amount of per capita mortgage debt," writes John Hicks.[35] In Kansas alone, "mortgage debts tripled between 1880 and 1887."[36] Even once they got their farms going, weather-dependent farmers were caught in a bind. During good weather years, crops were bountiful and crop prices correspondingly fell.[37] When weather was bad, a cropless farmer's plight was worse. "Either way, however hard he worked, the farmer could not keep himself from falling more and more uncontrollably into debt."[38]

A ten-year drought hit the plains in the spring of 1889, when "the south winds, warm and dry, came long before their time, and . . . robbed the earth of its snow-given moisture."[39] After that, no rain fell for weeks and weeks. Seed blew away in hot wind, was sown again, and again blew away. By the fall of that year, the cattle were starving, and no one could sell a horse. Nebraska's farmers became idlers, dependent for their survival, if they stayed, on handouts from elsewhere. As Kem writes, "Thousands abandoned their homesteads and returned east and these who remained were only able to do so by reason of the food, clothing and money sent from other parts of the country to prevent starvation and freezing."[40] Those years, many if not most settlers in Kansas and Nebraska failed to fulfill the meager requirements of ownership laid out by the Homestead Act—$1.25 per acre after six months, or land for free after five years of residence. (According to Fred Shannon's often-cited data, two-thirds of all Homestead claims failed in this decade.[41] Though recent research disputes this, even conservative estimates suggest that no more than 55 percent of homesteaders succeeded.)[42]

But despite these difficult conditions, farm debt did not arise naturally out of the plains like so much corn. Rather, it was the precise function of opportunistic lenders, fueled by willing and wealthy investors in the East meeting unprepared individual farmers in an inhospitable climate.[43] Debt was, and still is (far more so), good money for some; well over a hundred mortgage companies sprang up in Kansas and Nebraska during the late 1880s and '90s alone.[44] With eager eastern bankers willing to offer low interest rates on the one side and desperate farmers willing to pay high ones on the other, the mortgage broker would lucratively pocket the difference. In 1881 a broker named Jabez Watkins recorded earning $34,000 (about $840,000 today) in a single year. Within a decade, his business had supervised loans totaling over $18 million, all loans parceled out to the desperately poor.[45] By 1890 in Nebraska (before the worst of the drought), there was one mortgage for every three persons—thus, more than one per family—and most of the farms were mortgaged "literally for all they were worth."[46]

The reasons for the equivocal success of the Homestead Act in Kem's period are thus many—crop prices (influenced also by European markets), weather, predatory lenders. Land speculators presented a fourth problem. Loopholes in the law, especially the 1891 "commutation clause," made it too easy for speculators to buy up multiple claims at once, sit on them until boom times, and then sell for a profit.[47] These speculators, reviled as greedy and opportunistic, were often accused of being merely "figureheads" for the "banks and moneyed interests" form eastern cities, or even England.[48]

Kem, like so many others, had been unable to survive Indiana because vast portions of that swampy land had been gobbled up by landlords from Boston or New York; he never could get out from under that rent. And now, having traveled hundreds of miles on the promise of independence, having lost his wife to disease and almost lost his children as well, he had arrived only beholden, seemingly without end, to the precise same group of elites. You could understand why people like him might have begun to feel as if they'd been had.

But one cannot speak of debt, nor of lenders, without mentioning Shylock, who was himself mentioned in many Populist screeds against lenders, such as when Populist editor and orator Sarah E. V. Emery accused Shylock, "with his hoarded millions," of resting "on a bed of down."⁴⁹ Most scholars of Populism consider such complaints about "Shylock" to be *not necessarily* antisemitic, since "Shylock was not a symbol or collective title for Jews but rather for Wall Street or English moneylenders" (who sometimes happened to be Jewish).⁵⁰ It seems that for some scholars, the term *shylock* to refer to a moneylender in the 1890s was merely conventional. But one could as easily remark that antisemitism itself was conventional in nineteenth-century America:

> Our house stood about three blocks from the main business street of the town and in going up to town we passed by the residence of a German Jew named of Pretzel, who had a daughter, Sophia. Pretzel was a little queer, wizened sort of man with a mind as out of proportion as his body. His house was built close to the street so that the porch came even with the sidewalk. One evening mother sent me to the store on an errand and I started off eating a piece of bread and butter, when I drew near the Pretzel house I saw Sophia standing on the porch and by the time I reached it I had finished my lunch except for a piece of crust, which, boy-like, I tossed at her as I passed. Probably, it struck her in the eye, as she began to scream and cry at a great rate. I knew instantly that I had struck a mine of trouble and that I had better go while the going was good, so I quickened my pace to a run. I looked a block away and saw the old man coming full tilt, shaking his head, with what I thot was a knife in his hand.⁵¹

I wonder if young Kem would have as casually thrown his trash at a Christian girl. Or if he had, I wonder if adult Kem would have found the story memorable or funny enough to retell. The Jew gets a crust in the eye because, whether a girl on her porch, a little queer, or British hoarder, the Jew is a (predatory) outsider. The Indiana farm boy, like the Populist on the plains, *belonged*—even if he had to throw things to prove it.

Well, now would be a good time to say that my mother was Jewish, which means I am, which means Kem's bread toss, you could say, lands right in her eye and in mine. She'll come back, this Jewish girl, my mother, that matrilineal line, me, as will the vexing question of antisemitism. For now, I'll ask a different though related question: whether the "mortgage crisis" of the 1890s, by driving so many homesteaders off the land and making others insecurely attached to it, might supply one of the deep roots for the resentments often assigned to today's "populists." For despite endless differences, both periods—the late nineteenth century and the early twenty-first—share one thing for sure: the dream of self-sufficiency is threatened, if not completely obliterated, by humiliating debt.

"Bound and Prostrate"

There's nothing more powerful than a humiliated man.
—Christopher Wylie, NPR, 2019

But why should debt be so humiliating? Why so much more humiliating than poverty itself, which Kem seemed almost proud of? "We then set up housekeeping with very little of this world's goods in tangible form," he writes of his first year of marriage with Nan in Indiana. "The house we began our domestic operations in was the historical 'log cabin in the clearing' of the most primitive type.... The walls were of round lynn or bass wood, with the bark on and cracks between, large enough to throw a cat through."[52] Poverty is so often presented as a noble condition (and funny), especially for those (white men) who, despite humble beginnings, succeeded in achieving positions of power.

Debt, though; that is something else altogether.[53] "What makes debt different," writes the late anthropologist David Graeber (whose *Debt: The First 5,000 Years* is often referred to as the bible of the Occupy movement), "is that it is premised on an assumption of equality."[54] That is, unlike other social orders—"hierarchy" and "communism"—the debtor-creditor dynamic presumes that a relationship between equals is only temporarily off balance. Rebalancing is, of course, the responsibility of the debtor, no matter how beaten down they might be. "This is what makes situations of effectively unpayable debt so difficult and so painful. Since creditor and debtor are ultimately equals, if the debtor cannot do what it takes to restore herself to equality, there is obviously something wrong with her; it must be her fault."⁵⁵ Debt in this way feels personal, maybe even psychological, rather than structural.

In contrast, what Graeber calls "everyday communism" presumes no such equality of means or abilities. I can help my child with her homework and not demand that she help me with mine. You can bring some food to the shelter and not expect the unhoused teen to cook for you next week. Everyday communism is *perpetually* off-balance, requiring and inspiring a vow of sharing that does not need to be, that cannot be, made even. Debt, on the other hand, carries not only the penalty of interest but also a grave sense of social failure. Of course, this is logical, for when one is in debt, one is always in debt to *someone*. The debtor is demeaned by the creditor's power.⁵⁶

White Populists, like the suffragists and the Knights of Labor from that era, often favored metaphors of slavery to describe their plight.⁵⁷ "I don't own even a home for there is a mortgage covering it," complained Kem. "One who has worked as I have . . . ought to be able to own a home free from incumbrance."⁵⁸ In the next breath, Kem labels this problem "industrial slavery"; the indebted farmer is a slave to the lending and railroad industries, just as the factory worker is slave to the bosses, I suppose. In a speech to Congress in the summer of 1892, Kem decries the "slavery of the masses," and in another the next year he denounces the railroads as "the masters of the people as completely as ever the slave driver was master of the black man."⁵⁹ Populist Mary Elizabeth Lease makes the comparison more visceral: "The great common people of this country are slaves, and monopoly is the master. The West and South are bound and prostrate before the manufacturing East."⁶⁰ And Populist senator William Peffer of Kansas (elected in the same year as Kem) is historically explicit: "To give the employer all the profits is to make slaves of the men, and we have about got through with slavery in this country."⁶¹

The proximity that these white Populists felt to enslavement, a proximity that seemed to increase with each acre mortgaged, provides another window into why indebtedness is such a great and motivating shame. To be thrust back toward landlessness was to draw dangerously close to the degradation of the not-quite human, the slave, or perhaps more generally, the Black—the person who, being property, could never own any. Perhaps now that the category "slave" was no longer assigned, had become a free-floating metaphor that could be applied to any number of oppressed groups—women, workers, farmers, miners, ranchers—the threat of resemblance grew that much more severe. At any rate, in 1890 the worst, most humiliating thing you could be was not poor but unfree, beholden. Everyone, it seemed, was haunted by the commodification of human life.[62]

To be clear, as the recipients of one of the largest handouts that the federal government has ever administered, homesteaders were already among the most indebted white people on the American landscape, even before a lender came knocking on their door. For at least the first five years of residency, homesteaders were living on credit. But while this debt might have threatened homesteaders with homelessness, it pales in comparison to the debt that propertyless Black people held, many of whom were trapped in the debasing and barely survivable debt-peonage or crop-lien system in the South at this time.[63] Moreover, this particular process of American expansion—private property for some, removal for others—meant that settlers' unsteady freedom was quite literally grounded in the displacement, ghettoization, or death of Native people.[64] Property was supposed to be the bulwark against these precarities, but perhaps those whose homes displace the homes of others are more alert to their own vulnerability. As Nick Estes (Kul Wicasa) writes, "The perpetual threat of Indigenous nations is that they are a reminder of the settler's own precarious claims to land and belonging."[65] It might seem, in fact, that Populist outrage about their mortgages masked an even more pernicious feeling: not only were you not independent to begin with; you never *would* be secure in the power you craved.

The internal contradiction—between a desired and assumed independence and an actual, though decried, dependence—can be readily seen in the (familiar to us) phrase Kem used to describe his feelings upon first acquiring his homestead: "I had passed my 26th birthday somewhere on the way, acquired 320 acres of fine land and you may rest assured that I was one *proud boy*."[66] This tension—between the manly pride of self-sufficiency and the childlike shame of dependency—could be said to be a defining characteristic of and motivation for Populism then and now.

This proud but indebted boy began his political career as a member of the Noble and Holy Order of the Knights of Labor. (By the time Kem joined, the Order bragged over seven hundred thousand members, with about a tenth of its members Black and another tenth women.)[67] His first attempt at office was to run for regent on the Labor ticket (he lost). By the mid-1880s he was also a leading member of Nebraska's Farmers Alliance.[68]

Educationally oriented, the alliance offered opportunities for sharing knowledge and for collective study—not only of agriculture but sometimes also of revolutionary texts such as Bellamy's *Looking Backward* and Weaver's *A Call to Action*.[69] By the early 1890s, writes historian Sean Cashman, there were over one thousand alliance newspapers in circulation.[70] It was, as Kem understood, a "recruiting ground" for dissatisfied farmers preparing for "the onslaught."

At alliance meetings where Populism was brewing, Kem began to air his view that "our only hope for real relief was through political action."[71] Only Washington could regulate crop prices and mortgage rates. Only Washington could increase circulating currency, legislate a graduated income tax, and regulate railroads.[72] Kem set to work convincing farmers—men who came from poor families and were themselves barely surviving—to run for public office.

In the fall election of 1889—the same season in which the two-year-old Omer Albert died—the Nebraskans began what Kem would refer to as "a revolution" from the bottom up. In Kem's county, the wins for what was then called the Independent Party were absolute. Treasurer, sheriff, clerk, county judge, recorder, and superintendent of public instruction—all seats won by "honest-to-goodness dirt farmers." The old politicians were "dumfounded," and success proved addictive.

The following summer, the Farmer's Alliance of Nebraska and five other states determined to go next level.[73] As crops failed, the Populists held picnics and parades, wrote songs and slogans: "We farmers raise no crops, so we'll just raise hell!" On July 15, 1890, as Kem tells it, eight hundred delegates from sixty-nine Nebraska counties gathered to nominate national congressional candidates to run against the state's dominating Republicans. Kem was stumping for a man named Knox. However, he was clearly not aware of his own magnetism, for as he reports, minutes before the nominating vote, someone shouted out his name instead. He was, he writes, shocked: "I at once arose in an effort to protest, but the convention arose with me to almost a man, and proceeded to howl me down, whooping and yelling, throwing their hats in the air and swinging their arms like lunatics, then someone moved to make the nomination unanimous and it was done."[74]

Reluctance over with, Kem immediately began a vigorous campaign. While Alice was at home on a failing farm with a new baby, Iris, Huxley (now a toddler), and three older children, Omer drove his wagon all over the district, speechifying from its bed to a crowd who called him Brother Kem. As he railed against income inequality, monopolies, and railroad rates, he waved a prop in the air—not a pitchfork or a hoe but a particular piece of paper: his mortgage.[75]

In 1891, as Populists took over both chambers of the Nebraska state assembly, Omer Kem and ten other Populists from Nebraska, Kansas, South Dakota, Minnesota, and Georgia went to Washington to fight for "Equal Rights for All!" Alice stayed behind, to care for their now five children on her own.

Men, Women, and Children

In September of Kem's first year in Congress, four Menominee boys from the Shawano Reservation in Wisconsin were taken from their families and placed in the Carlisle Indian Industrial School in Pennsylvania, established in 1879 by Civil War veteran Richard Henry Pratt of "kill the Indian save the man" fame. There, like thousands of other Indian children, they would have had their hair cut, their language and religion banned.[76] Their education would consist of learning to read and write in English, "converting" to Christianity, learning farming and domestic skills, and performing physical labor.[77] It took less than one month for these four boys to decide to run home. The journey, which they took on foot, was 825 miles long. When they were within only 4 miles of the reservation's border, one of these boys, a child of twelve, gave up.

Reportedly, he sat down and would walk no more. Reportedly, he chose for his seat of rest a railroad track. And reportedly, the other three who had traveled with him for 821 miles were unable to convince him to rise and walk the remaining 4, unable to convince him not to sit on the track. And so, reportedly, they left him there. When the train came, it killed him. The boy's remains were later discovered and returned to his parents. Representative Lynch of Wisconsin, who relates this tragedy to his colleagues in the Fifty-Second Congress, assures them "that the feeling amongst the members of that tribe on that occasion was intense."[78]

But this story as told is incomplete. Perhaps the boy died of dehydration or starvation. Perhaps his death was a suicide. Perhaps—and this is in any case true—his horrendous death is the fault of the U.S. government itself since his kidnapping was its cause. As a child in the boarding school system, the boy's death was not unusual. As David Treuer reports, "Indian children were six times as likely to die in childhood while at boarding schools than the rest of the children in America."[79] (In 2021 mass unmarked graves holding the remains of hundreds of First Nations children were discovered at the sites of boarding schools in Canada.)[80] Nonetheless, no one listening in that chamber questions Lynch about the event. It is not, we must conclude, all that important to them why the boy died.

The purpose of the story, as Lynch explains, is to demonstrate that boarding schools should be built close to reservations—not to save the lives of children, as one might think, but because parents who are not grieving would be more pliable, more likely to accept the state's assimilationist goals. The story doesn't settle the issue, though. Instead, Mr. Brosius (R-PA), no doubt committed to the success of the Carlisle school in his state, presents the opposing view: "The farther you keep the Indian children from the reservation and from their tribal relations the more rapidly we can hope to civilize them." Brosius goes so far as to argue that Indian children should be kept *permanently* from their parents, lest they revert to tribal customs. Allowing them to reunite with the people he calls "their former relations" is like "milking a bucket of milk and then allowing the cow that gave it to kick it over."[81]

MR. STOCKDALE: Will the gentleman permit a question?
MR. BROSIUS: Yes, sir.
MR. STOCKDALE: Do you think this Government has the right to rob parents of their children and keep them away from them?[82]

The question, for this body of men, has no clear answer.

Mr. Mansur (D-MO) is in agreement with Brosius about the desirability of permanent family separation. He illustrates his position with the following tale. Mansur and a group of other men are touring the Arapaho Cheyenne Reservation (in present-day Oklahoma). A merchant directs them to interview an Indian woman called Mary, who had been at Carlisle. "We hunted up Mary," says the congressmen, and "found her to be a small tidy little woman." This description generates laughter from Mansur's colleagues—one can feel them leaning in. He goes on: "Farmer Funston knows that many of these women are big, flabby, and fleshy, as he or I, and a thundering sight dirtier, and when I said that she was tidy, I meant thereby to say she had not totally forgotten what she had learned at Carlisle." Again laughter. The congressmen seem distracted from their debate, entertained as they are by Mary's body.[83]

Mansur describes at some length the men's efforts to get Mary to talk, but in the presence of her people, she remains silent. Finally, they "pull her aside" and draw from her a confession. Yes, she can speak English, but she will not do so in front of other Indians, for whenever she does, "they cut her in every way and reproach her for being no longer an Indian." This has made her life so intolerable "that she even thought of killing herself."[84]

MR. MANSUR: You could see by looking at her that there was something refined about her in comparison with the other Indians. You could see that she was subdued and sorry stricken. She was evidently a person carrying a burden of sorrow.
MR. LEWIS: And acquainted with grief.
MR. MANSUR: And acquainted with grief, as suggested by my friend.

Law and Order 67

But as these friends acknowledge Mary's grief, they seem confused about its cause. Not loneliness, not isolation—it's that living among other Indians, she cannot exercise her boarding school education. The problem, explains Mansur, is that she has nothing to read.[85] Suicidal misery, he concludes, would be alleviated by a complete and total removal from the tribe, a return to the white world, to its language, and to its books.

Omer Kem's contribution to this debate arrives in his very first extended speech to Congress. In this passionate outpouring, Omer comes out against all boarding schools. He flatly calls them "wrong," believing that Indian children should be educated "on their own territory." For Kem, any discussion of "the Indian question" requires a square look at the centuries of domination that have led to this point. Referencing the recent Wounded Knee Massacre (which had been ignored during Senator Gamble's eulogy a month before), he places blame for the massacre firmly on the shoulders of the U.S. Army. Moreover, he insists that in *all* cases of violence between white people and Indians, the white people have been the aggressors.

> Reviewing the history of this Indian question as we know it in our own country, the fact can be established that every time we have had an Indian war or an Indian depredation, the white man has been the aggressor—has been responsible for the loss of blood and treasure that has ensued. We have taken possession of the land of the Indian; we have dispossessed him of his home, of that which by nature rightfully belonged to him, without making just compensation.
>
> If the white people had treated the Indian justly, if they had done by him as they ought to have done as a matter of common justice between man and man, this country would not have witnessed the disgraceful proceedings that took place in Dakota last winter, when defenseless men, women, and children were butchered like so many animals.[86]

Just after this astonishing admission, Kem shifts gears to a topic closer to his heart: taxes. Since all Indian schools require taxes to support them, Kem uses this opportunity to make a larger point.

All poor people, he says, whether white, Black, or Indian, are in "a deplorably helpless and destitute situation"; all suffer under an unfair system of taxation and exploitation in which the rich never pay their share.

> Now, Mr. Chairman . . . I want to say to you—to recapitulate, as it were—that if we had the amount of money that has been appropriated for Indian purposes, that has been unlawfully and illegally appropriated to the private use of Indian agents throughout this country; if we had the money that has been taken from us through this unjust system of taxation, the money that has been taken from the people, the masses of the people, by the corporations and the trusts of the country in excessive freight rates, by the national-banking corporations, and all of the other institutions by robbery—I say to you if we had that money today in the Treasury, if it had been allowed to remain where it belongs . . . the appropriation for the Indian would not be a burden, and the whites, as well as the blacks, would be able to take care of themselves.[87]

Words and Deeds

I hadn't yet learned how to read the Congressional Record online, didn't even know you could, so in 2017, when I was visiting my sister in DC, I went to the Congressional Library, hoping to find Omer's voice or votes. After extensive security proceedings (stripped of coat and bag, photographed, identified), I sat in a nearly empty room as silent librarians wearing masks against dust delivered the volumes to my desk. I thought I should feel a reverence for these materials. Mostly, I just felt their weight—so much language, so much of it so boring, or if not, then pompously cruel. But when I read Omer's speech about Indian boarding schools, I felt a surge of excitement, even pride. I took photos and sent them to my sister down the street at her job. It seemed a valiant moment; he was indicting the very system of genocidal removal that he himself had benefited from, the very system, you could say, that had delivered him to the floor on which he stood. And here too was an example of Populist solidarity:

the rich get richer while all poor people of all races are made to suffer. But righteous speeches are one thing, and actions, so much harder, are another.

In the 1880s the Choctaw and Cherokee nations began drilling for oil in Indian Territory. As the market for "black gold" grew, so too did settler desire for that oil-rich land.[88] After the passage of the Dawes Act in 1887, two million acres of "surplus" or "unassigned" land had been opened to settlers. The first Oklahoma land rush in 1889 drew fifty thousand people on a single day.[89]

Just as Kem was pronouncing his outrage about Indian dispossession—"We have taken possession of the land of the Indian; we have dispossessed him of his home"—as a member of the Committee on Indian Affairs, he was preparing a bill designed to administer this next wave of displacement.[90] When he discusses this bill in his autobiography, Kem shows no further support for Native sovereignty. Instead, he voices a different concern: he wants the land divvied up among whites through a lottery system rather than a barbaric rush. Settlers must acquire this land, he says, "in accordance with justice, honesty and civilization."[91]

Well, one should say that the land in Oklahoma had already been taken from the Indians before Kem even arrived in Congress; he was merely processing a done deal. But then that same year, Kem submitted another report for the committee. This report recommends the passage of H.R. 67, a bill that would ratify an 1888 agreement with the Southern Ute tribes, removing them from their reservation in Colorado to a new one in Utah. Kem's report makes clear how this removal would benefit whites—those in the nearby city of Durango and those who want the Ute land "for agricultural purposes."[92]

The report asserts that the Utes themselves, under leadership of Chief Ignacio, are in favor of this relocation. This was true, in a sense. In 1883 Coloradan cowboys, incensed by Utes who were not staying on their reservations and who had on occasion stolen horses from whites, attacked a Weeminuche Ute family, murdering at least seven people, including women and children. Ignacio had responded to this outrage by demanding a larger reservation, away from marauding whites.[93] Kem's report doesn't mention this, but it does refer to another reason the Utes had agreed to removal. Ute children were being taken from their families and placed in off-reservation boarding schools. The hope for the Utes, the report reveals, is that if they move to Utah Territory, their children will be returned.[94] Again, the issue was not only separation but survival: "In 1884 half of the Southern Ute children sent to boarding school in Albuquerque died," writes Ute historian Sondra G. Jones.[95]

In his statements, Kem neither comments on the cruelty of the situation nor acknowledges the coercion at play (Jones writes that Ute leaders, presumably other than Ignacio, were "pressured relentlessly" to agree to removal).[96] That said, in keeping with the Dawes Act, he does recommend that Utes who agree to "sever" their relation to the tribe be offered allotments of 160 acres in exchange.[97]

Evidently, the committee was divided. A second report, presented by the minority, flatly opposes Ute removal on the grounds that the "agreement" does not "fairly represent the real wishes of the Utes." The minority report recognizes the coercive nature of the plan; the Utes' comments, this report says, were "reluctantly given, and under stress."[98]

H.R. 67 did not pass (Utah's white residents and cattle industry were against it). And four years later, in another debate about Indian land, Kem repeats his condemnation of whites who appropriate Indian land, accusing white men of marrying Indian women in order to control the women's allotments.[99] His stated positions are not consistent, nor clear, though actions for sure will always speak louder. But that's not the main point I want to make. It is this: Kem, the other committee members, and all of Congress—the law itself—has a job to do. That job is to decide where Indian children should go to school, how Indian people should make a living, where Indian people should live.[100] Indians themselves, not being citizens and not being respected as members of independent nations, have little voice in this body of men, no representation or true negotiating power in the biopolitical regime that orders their lives.

Just three years later, with the money he was paid for his work as a congressman, Kem purchased a large and inexpensive piece of formerly Ute land (the Uncompahgre band) near Montrose, Colorado.

And three years after that, he quit politics to raise cattle and fruit trees on that land. As Patricia Limerick puts it, the history of the West (of the entire United States) can be boiled down to a very simple equation: "Some people occupied land that other people wanted."[101]

Disorder

> There are ninety and nine who live and die
> In want, and hunger, and cold
> That one may live in luxury,
> And be wrapped in a silken fold.
> . . . .
> And the one owns cities, and houses and lands,
> And the ninety and nine have empty hands.
> —Populist song[102]

> I repeat, we have begged you for years for relief, but you would not, and having sown the wind, you must now reap the Whirlwind.
> —Omer Kem, speaking to the House of Representatives, 1893

We begin with a body (a legislative body, a national body), a body in a House. Like all bodies, this body has boundaries, skin. It also has holes, just as the house has doors and windows. And just as doors and windows can be broken, the body itself is vulnerable; it is, after all, alive. There is illness, pain, incapacity, rupture, or simply, there is *more*. Law's job, law's science, is to mark and underscore the boundaries around this body—to repair where there is fissure, to remove excess, to sew the body shut again.

Inside the House's chambers, the law's tools, the law's method, is language, while on the streets, the law's tools are batons, tasers, guns, and cuffs. The law as boundary "cannot help but be armed. . . . To those who transgress it, it replies . . . with absolute menace."[103] All vigilant efforts to protect a body from invasion will tend toward violence, one way or another. In other words, language has a violence of its own.

In the Congressional Library, these words were heavy, dusty, and I was embarrassed to be asking for them. After all, I had been treated with suspicion. And even after I had passed security, I could not access these words without help. The librarian seemed reluctant.

But he called down (I think it was down) and told someone on the other end of the line what I wanted. I sat at a little desk and waited, like a child waiting for her lunch.

When the librarians arrived with their cart full of books, I was embarrassed again. The volumes were so massive, and there were so many of them. They knew and I knew that I wasn't going to actually *read* them. I was playing at being a historian, a scholar. A real historian would be online, using the search function. Or a real historian wouldn't need these books; they would already know what was inside.

But weight, heft, dust—this impossible glut of language—is the point. Online, the words are only light, they come and go in an instant, they hardly seem to be there at all. Here, the labor and the time it took to produce this torrent were palpable. Only an unremitting force of language (roll call, petition, debate, objection, joke, bill, vote) can make a body whole, where wholeness means less-ness, a repair by way of exclusion, an anorexic logic.[104] The law's game is border control.

But Omer Kem and his cohort of "dirt farmers" saw themselves as other than this border law; they were a *counter*-political force waged against a system of exclusion. Those who were born poor and laboring in the earth to drain it, to extract from it (corn, silver, or coal), those who were forcing out of the earth or the factory the products that would make capital flow—Kem saw these people as *other* than law; they were the ones who had had to beg. "I repeat, we have begged you for years for relief, but you would not, and having sown the wind, you must now reap the Whirlwind." Rural, white, and indebted—they entered the House as a destructive force meant to break those walls that had been closed against them.

They got in, but once inside, it was not just that they failed, stuck as they were in their Populist corner; it was also that they succeeded too well. Having arrived as the unhoused, they were absorbed into the House, fused in a fusion politics of Democratic Christian white supremacy. For in 1896 the Populists endorsed Democrat William Jennings Bryan for president and southern Populist Tom Watson for VP. Watson had once been a powerful advocate for interracial solidarity, but after his electoral loss, he, like many white Populists at the end of the decade, embraced full-blown white supremacy: "In the South, we have to lynch [the Black man] occasionally, and flog him, now and then, to keep him from blaspheming the Almighty, by his conduct, on account of his smell and his color," Watson later said.[105] As historian William Chafe argues, "In its finer moments populism represented a powerful ideal—the belief that men of different races but common interests could join together to secure economic and political justice." But in the decision to endorse the Democrat Bryan, the white Populists signaled their abandonment of their Black colleagues, for of course, the Democrats were "the very instrument of Redeemer rule."[106] (Bryan himself would later be lauded and honored by the Ku Klux Klan as a "man who always championed the cause of righteousness.")[107]

By the late 1890s white Populists in the plains and South had by and large abandoned the third party, while Black Populists, and Black people generally, had been legally or practically disenfranchised—their votes uncounted, violently stolen, or bought. (Black votes fell 62 percent across the South from 1890 to 1900.)[108] There would not be another large show of interracial class-based solidarity until the radical Industrial Workers of the World of the nineteen-teens (and then again with the interracial southern communists of the 1930s).[109] The collapse of interracial Populism *is* the failure of the Populist Party. As Stephen Kantrowitz writes, "A true interracial alliance required . . . white men to surrender their own monopoly on power," and to be clear, there has not even yet been much evidence of that.[110]

Bryan lost terribly to Republican William McKinley, whose legacy would be the annexation of Hawai'i and the Spanish American War—the beginnings of U.S. overseas imperialism.[111] Du Bois underscores the symbiotic relationship between this moment of Black disenfranchisement and the rise of American imperialism: "The increased political power of the South based on disfranchisement of black voters, took its place to reenforce the capitalistic dictatorship of the United States, which become the most powerful in the world, and which backed the new industrial imperialism and degraded colored labor the world over," he wrote in *Black Reconstruction*.[112] When the white Populists sided with white supremacy, and in this way capitulated their most radical goals, they made space for anti-Blackness to flourish, and not only in the American South.

Given all this, how should we feel about the flashes of possibility that the early 1890s Populists offer? It would be much too easy, at least for a white person, to take pride in these Populists. But then, it's another kind of easy to dismiss them. This brief and fragile history—these few years when poor, rural Black and white men and women struggled against capitalist monopolies, electoral fraud, unfair taxation, and resultant debt—might send a weak signal into the future, but it's a signal, nonetheless. Whether it lingers or fades will depend on how we respond to that flare.[113]

When I first met my cousin Chris Christensen, the one who had purportedly accused Creighton University's librarian of hoarding Kem's autobiography, he told me he wanted to run for office—as a populist, "the Omer Kem kind." I didn't know if the Omer Kem kind of populist, for Chris, was the kind who supports Indian sovereignty or the kind who administers and benefits from Indian removal. Was the Omer Kem kind of populist the kind who believed all working people to be deserving of justice and equity or the kind who sat silently complicit on the topic of anti-Black terror, considering Black people unworthy of protections and rights? Chris voted for Trump twice. But he also told me his political hero was Elizabeth Warren for how she had gone after the banks. This is the disorder of the populist movement, both then and now.

While the nineteenth-century populist uprising did not solve the problem of income inequality and certainly failed in any efforts individuals made toward racial justice or Indian sovereignty, for Kem personally it paid off. His three terms in Congress brought him previously unknown wealth. His salary was $5,000 a year, or about $160,000 today. He resolved his debts, bought land and cows, built himself a real house in Colorado, and returned to farming, this time emboldened by capital. In a period of twelve years, he had gone from being a widower under sod with three sick kids and no money to being the married owner of a thirteen-room ranch house with the land to match and father to seven. The Colorado chapter of Delloyd Guth's biography is titled "The Good Life."

4 Ghosts

We were a haunted country in a haunted world.
—Louise Erdrich, *The Sentence*

Thoughts Are Things
Tables tip and tables walk.[1] Chairs shift with no one in them. Doors swing open and will not stay shut. The curtains move, spread apart. A pillow flies through air. The mattress is folded in half, the chair upon the bed. When the body of the other stops playing with the furniture, it enters your body instead, moves through you, through your hands. The ghost speaks thoughts that are not your thoughts. The ghost is a body you did not see.

The boy was curled on the bathroom floor, a "ghost" or a "vision," an unseen seen thing, a being made only of air. This child did not speak but lay on the floor between the toilet and the bathtub, dressed in green shorts, a white shirt. In an earlier year, I'd heard my name spoken from a room I wasn't in, though I was the only person at home. Even earlier than that, I'd dreamed a man in a raincoat arriving at my grandmother Kathleen's door. She opens it for him, and then, as if struck, she falls. The next day, my father tells me that the man at the door was a neighbor; he had come to talk about her car, a pale blue Oldsmobile, which he was hoping to buy. It was raining in Salinas, California, that day. When she fell, the man in the raincoat was there to catch her.

Does dreaming one's grandmother's life constitute a haunting? We used to sleep together in her bed, her teeth in a glass beside us. She was the first to tell me about the séances her parents held in their dining room, how she and her brother Victor would spy through the window at Omer, Alice, and their friends, who were sitting, eyes closed, waiting for the spirits to write their messages in the precise purple of the asters in their vase. "All words are ghosts," writes KT Thompson, since they stand in for things not there.[2] Are all stories ghost stories, then?[3] All memories? If we invent these spirits that nonetheless alter our lives in large and minor ways, why do we invent them? What is it we want from our ghosts (our memories, visions, dreams, stories), and what do they want from us?

When Omer Kem was becoming a Populist at the end of the nineteenth century, ghosts were plentiful in America, as they are now.[4] Yet the spiritualist movement, such as it was, is famously difficult to define, its progression hard to track. It had (and has) no unified doctrine, no organized membership, no preachers (though it has celebrities), and no centralized church. Therefore, it gathered a large array of beliefs, practices, and supernatural occurrences under its umbrella, from noisy walls and walking tables to female bodies oozing plasma from their orifices, from trumpets sounding the voices of dead relatives to nightly visits from racial "others." Despite or because of this ranginess, nineteenth-century spiritualism was hugely influential and widespread. "It needs to be mentioned that this was not a fringe movement," writes James Mackay. "Hardcore Spiritualism certainly counted several hundred thousand adherents, while as many as eleven million people—out of a population of no more than twenty-five million—held at least some Spiritualist beliefs."[5] Mark Lause, who has extensively researched the movement, estimates five to six million adherents by the 1860s.[6]

Historians have long studied the crossroads between spiritualism and radical or progressive politics throughout the mid- to late nineteenth century. In her breakthrough book, *Radical Spirits: Spiritualism and Women's Rights in Nineteenth-Century America* (1989), Anne Braude argued that spiritualism's "principle of individualism" naturally corresponded with a rejection of hierarchical authority in various aspects of American social and political life: "They denounced the authority of churches over believers, of governments over citizens, of doctors over patients, of masters over slaves, and most of all, of men over women."[7] Others have followed Braude's lead in revealing spiritualists' involvement in a variety of progressive causes: children's rights, religious freedom, socialism, and abolitionism. Feminists Lucretia Mott and Elizabeth Cady Stanton, for example, wrote their "Declaration of Sentiments" on a table where spirits had also made their wills known. These women, who organized the country's first women's rights convention at Seneca Falls in 1848, were also leading abolitionists, having met at the 1840 World Anti-Slavery Convention in London. Other famous feminist abolitionists, such as Sarah Grimke and Susan B. Anthony, dabbled in spiritualism as well.[8] William Lloyd Garrison apparently went to séances, as did Frederick Douglass and Harriet Jacobs (though they were not necessarily believers).[9]

In the postbellum years, many of the white spiritualists who had taken up the cause of women's rights and abolition turned their energies to "Indian reform," though as I'll discuss below, the call to "reform" meant different things to different people. Populists, too, found their way to spiritualism, perhaps for many of the same reasons that other people had—it offered a rejection of the hierarchical order, especially that imposed by Christianity. But spiritualism, it seems, appealed to white Populists for other reasons as well, reasons having less to do with class and religion and more to do with race and nation.

The Soul within the Furniture

For Omer Kem, Populism and spiritualism went hand in hand. The people who introduced him to ghosts were all Populists, and he converted to both at more or less the same time. In 1891, when he was on the road campaigning for election to Congress, he visited the home of a Populist voter named Harris. Mr. Harris, who had known Kem's now deceased father and mother in Indiana when they were young, claimed to be mediumistic and offered to prove it. Kem, no doubt motivated by desire for contact with his parents, as well as for Harris's vote, was open.

After dinner Mrs. Harris goes out, leaving the two men alone. After a few ghost stories, Harris asks Kem to place his hands on the table. The men continue to talk, when "suddenly but quietly, one end of the table raised off the floor about six inches and then dropped back and this was repeated twice." Kem reports being a little frightened by this sentient piece of furniture (I would be a lot more so), but Harris assures him that a benign spirit is listening, ready to respond. Kem begins to think of his mother, asking her silent questions "about things in my past life that she and I only knew." Malinda Kem responds by lifting and dropping one end of the table—three times if the answer is "yes," and once if it is "no." When Kem leaves the Harris home the next day, his longing for more contact is primed.[10]

This was the first time Kem witnessed objects moving unaided, but ghost stories ran through his family, as they still do now. In the volume of his autobiography titled *Spiritualist Notes,* Kem tells us another story involving his mother, this one from when she was a little girl:

> She had retired for the night and soon after heard tappings on the walls as if someone were tapping with a pencil or a fingernail. . . . For some time she paid no attention, but at last it sort of got on her nerves, and she asked it, whatever it was, to take its departure and cease annoying her, but the raps kept rapping away. However, when it did not comply with her request (she talked to it just as if it were a person) she became angry, scolded it and threatened that if it did not leave she would get up, get a stick of wood and do dire and divers things to it. This seemed to have the desired effect noise seased [*sic*] and she never heard from it again.[11]

Malinda's childhood might well have been occupied by a variety of unseen beings. Her parents had both died before she was eight, and as mentioned before, the uncle who raised her sometimes hosted fugitives from slavery—people who would have been hidden, if not in the walls themselves, then possibly in rooms where Malinda didn't expect people to be. Maybe the spirit she spoke to (and threatened) "as if it were a person" was one. But this is conjecture.

Omer's father's side of the family told ghost stories too. In the mid-1850s, a number of aunts and uncles on the Kem side died in quick succession. The family reported witnessing various suspicious signs, such as doors that swung open and would not stay shut no matter how often the living tried to shut them. One day, Omer's grandfather was sitting on the porch arguing with friends about the validity of ghost tales. "If that table will walk across the kitchen floor while we sit here," he said, "I might believe these things you are telling me." As Kem relates: "The argument proceeded, but not for long, for their attention was soon attracted to the kitchen by the sounds as if someone with a wooden leg was stubbing across the bare floor. And, on casting their eyes in that direction, they saw coming toward them the table, hitching along first one leg then the other till it came to the door opening onto the porch where it paused for a moment, then hitched first one leg then the other up onto the porch till all were on a level."[12]

Something becomes someone, willfully (and comically?) in motion, crossing through the door to join the human gathering. What does it mean to be "on a level" with an object? What did it mean to this white family in the build-up to the Civil War to testify to the "spirits" in the furniture? More bluntly, is "the spooky dynamism of objects" (Fred Moten's phrase) a testament here to enslaved people who were, in the eyes and law of white America, approaching a transformation from "thing" to "person"?[13]

A ghost unsettles "propriety and property lines," writes Avery Gordon; this is especially true when an inanimate object suddenly reveals its inner life.[14] "Houses and laboratories, clothes and furniture, all have souls for the world beyond," asserts one popular text from the movement.[15] But even if, as I'm suggesting, spiritualism's fascination with dancing tables and spinning chairs was at times a kind of staging ground for abolitionists' curiosity about human ontology, it's beyond worth noting that for white spiritualists, the furniture didn't so much move on its own as respond to command: "The table, in its movements, was subordinate to man's will, directing itself to the right or left, towards any indicated spot or person, rising on command on one or two feet, knocking designated number of knocks, and beating or marking time," explains one author from 1865.[16] In this way, spiritualism shares common ground with that other nineteenth-century popular performance form: blackface minstrelsy, as with other forms of racial and cultural appropriation, as we'll see.[17]

"Is This for Me?": Necrophobia, Necrophilia, and the Desire to Be Healed

Just after he was elected to Congress, Kem went to Washington to prepare for his new job. Naturally, he met other DC radicals, especially those who wanted his ear. One day he received an invitation from Thomas and Cora Bland. The Blands were committed Populists, but the true focus of their activism was Indian rights. After the death of their friend and fellow activist, Alfred Meacham, they coedited the paper he had started, the *Council Fire and Arbiter*, and founded the National Indian Defense Association (NIDA), a far more radical reform organization than the better-known Indian Rights Association. NIDA included many Indian members, and in contrast with other "reform" groups, it actively opposed the Dawes Act and other forms of forced assimilation. Thomas Bland had also worked intensively with Lakota leader Red Cloud in his struggle for Indian sovereignty.[18] Because Kem had been placed on the Indian Affairs Committee, the Blands invited him to dinner, initiating what turned out to be a close friendship.[19]

Despite the clear purpose of this meeting, however, Kem records no conversations concerning Indians or Populism that night. Instead, having encountered his mother's ghost only months before, Kem turns the conversation away from politics and toward spiritualism, which, it turns out, the Blands know something about.[20] The Blands did not have children, but they lived with their niece, Maggie Davis, an eighteen-year-old clairvoyant. Though Maggie doesn't demonstrate her skills that night, her uncle explains the philosophy. After death, Thomas says, the body returns to the "original elements from which it came," while the spirit continues on, "retaining the same characteristics that it had when in the body." This spirit, with its "desires, hopes and fears," tends to hang around its friends and relatives, concerned for their well-being just as it was when embodied. Communications might be tapped out on the wall or table, blasted through a trumpet, or written out on a slate. In some cases, the spirit might speak through a medium, and in others, the ghost might simply appear. Kem finds this information more plausible than the

Christian belief in heaven or hell (for example), and the politically motivated Blands follow up.

Kem's next invitation to the Bland household includes the tempting line, "Mr. Kem, that little niece of mine is developing into a fine medium, both clairvoyant and slate writing and they [the spirits] want you to sit with us if you care to." Kem accepts, and at some point in the evening, Maggie begins to shade her eyes and squint, as if the light is bothering her. "There is a lady standing just to the left of you," she tells Kem, describing a woman who resembles Kem's dead (and beloved) sister Ellen. Then another spirit makes herself known: "Now I see what looks like an oval ball of electric light, very brilliant," says Maggie, "and it is resting on your right shoulder. Now it seems to be opening and there is the face of another lady appearing." This electric orb holds within it, as per Maggie's description, the face of Kem's mother.

After these preliminary encounters, Kem begins to experience touch: "It was as if someone had touched my thumb with the tip of the finger in a sort of caressing way, and gradually extended to different parts of the entire hand." Another time, a "lady's hand materialized through the curtain . . . and then, when fully developed, reached up and caressed one of my hands three or four times. The sensation was not different from that of a fleshy hand." And then he goes deeper still, coming into contact with his dead little boy, Omer Albert (Bert), who had been buried in Broken Bow in 1888 at just under two years old.

Bert first appears, it seems, a few months into Kem's association with the Blands, at which point Kem has grown so close to the family that he's taken a room in the house for the months when Congress is in session. For a while, the group had been practicing their spirit encounters in dim light. But as things advanced, as the spirits manifested in stranger and more concrete ways, the lights were turned all the way off. It was dark when Bert showed up, first as a glowing orb and then gradually as a speaking child:

> We also had the materialization of a light which began to show as an ill-defined feeble glow about the size of an apple. This contin-

ued to grow and develop till it assumed the dimensions and shape of a little lad about four or five years old. . . . For several evenings after the figure had reached the full size of a child of that age, it would emit odd little sounds, till one evening the exclamation "hello papa" came from it suddenly and quite distinctly. I replied "hello, is this for me?" and the reply was "yes, Bert."

Bert's spirit grew, in size and strength, lingering for longer periods each evening, though he always stayed close to Maggie. As Kem explains, he drew energy from her body. One evening Bert is sitting by Maggie on the couch. Kem says, "Bert, can't you throw me the pillow?" The pillow comes flying and hits Kem in the face. After that, Bert and Kem play catch for a while, "Bert giggling the whole time." On another occasion, Bert comes to dinner. He's not visible, but he sits in the chair next to Kem, tilting it toward his father as if to lean close to him. During the meal, Bert climbs under the table to untie Maggie's shoe.

Next, Kem invites Bert to his bedroom (in the Blands' house). On their agreed upon evening and time, Kem sits in the dark, waiting. Bert arrives, though Kem never sees him. Instead, he listens as Bert plays, jumping on the bed and rustling the blankets. After Bert leaves, Kem lights the lamp to discover that Bert has folded the mattress in half and set the rocking chair on top of it.[21]

Ellen shows up often—Ellen who had rocked Omer to sleep when he was a baby, singing the "Old Bachelor" song—always as a glowing light hovering near Maggie. She sometimes speaks but never materializes fully as a body. In an attempt to see his dead without Maggie around, Kem invites Ellen to visit him while he is traveling overnight by train. As he tells it, he is awakened at one in the morning. "I felt a sensation just as if someone had laid a heavy hand on my left ankle with such weight I was startled." Kem sits up, afraid he's being robbed, and is met with a vision of a brightly lit room with Ellen "standing sidewise to me with her head turned so she could look straight in my eyes." Ellen smiles and nods in recognition, and then she is gone. "I was still pounding over the rails in Virginia at about forty miles an hour," writes Kem in his loneliness.[22]

Who would not want to be so caressed? Who would not want to see the faces of one's dead? This desire is ordinary, repetitive, endless, and as I retell these tales, I grow tired. Is it Kem's need, his longing, that exhausts me? Or am I tired because nothing in these stories will satisfy that longing, a longing I also share? (I admit to another feeling, too, and that feeling is scorn, as if I would not be so fooled. And then I hear myself say, "Hi, Mom," out of nothing, to the trees, or the window.)

Kem's need is so strong, in fact, that he entirely dismisses the possibility that the Blands might be fraudulent. "Here was just the opportunity I was looking for. It was a condition in which fraud and deception of any sort would be as precluded as in my own home."[23] Why he feels such blanket trust in these people is hard to say. Like Kem, the Blands originally came from Indiana and were descendants of Quakers. It would not have been hard for them to gather information about him, about the people he had lost. And the Blands' political agenda was overt from the start of their friendship. Nonetheless, Kem believes them guileless. One evening Kem is asked to give up his handkerchief, to place it on the table. The lights are dim. Minutes pass. Three knocks on the table means the spirits are done with it—the handkerchief is now embroidered with his mother's favorite flower, a morning glory, and her name. He is astounded, painfully so.

But in some ways these sweet if strange encounters with lost beloveds are easy to accept, whether or not we believe them. To half dream, half feel the presence of the dead, is, after all, common. Harder to understand is the development of a new relationship that proves to be even more intimate than Kem's relationships with his dead mother, sister, or son ever were.

Avery Gordon writes that haunting "is an animated state in which a repressed or unresolved social violence is making itself known."[24] If this is so, then we cannot really call Kem's encounters with Bert, Ellen, and Malinda "haunting"; they're more like plaintive recalls. But Gordon's definition certainly fits the other form of haunting that grabs hold of Kem in 1897 and remains with him until his death in 1942.

Though in his first year of Congress, Omer Kem, possibly inspired by the Blands, had admitted to his settler guilt—*We have taken possession of the land of the Indian; we have dispossessed him of his home*—rather than attempting to redress this injustice, to heal this wound, he imagined the spirit of an Indian healer, "Fleet Wind," entering and moving through his own body to heal *him* and his loved ones of whatever illnesses befell them. In this blatant act of appropriation, this ongoing indulgence of "red-face" lies the settler's guilty desire for forgiveness. But it's more than that. Populism arose out of a condition in which the settler-farmer was deeply insecure in his relation to the land, which was nonetheless the foundation of his identity (and his survival). Indians, as people like Omer knew very well, had a legitimate claim to that land, which no settler could ever duplicate. "Playing Indian," then, was one way to get closer. As Philip J. Deloria puts it, "Indianness has, above all, represented identities that are unquestionably American."[25] But if the Indian-within became a proxy for legitimate belonging, it also provided the white "medium" another opportunity for power and control.

Fleet Wind and Bright Eyes: Appropriation and Property

> The ghosts that emerge from and haunt settler colonial contexts radiate from their roots in the moral, intellectual, and legal logics developed to legitimate, as necessity, the great violence of empire.
> —Danika Medak-Saltzman, "Empire's Haunted Logics"

A vision of a generic "Indian chief" first appeared to Kem, "squat[ting] by the campfire in the evening twilight," when he was still living in DC with the Blands. But it wasn't until the following year when he and his family moved to southern Colorado that Fleet Wind first entered Kem's body. This spectral presence was not frightening; rather, it was comforting, and useful: "One of the children became ailing with something, the nature of which I do not remember, but not serious, when I felt Fleet Wind's presence for the first time since leaving Washington. I not only sensed his presence but he seemed to want to control my hands which were laid on the child."

Kem finds his hands in motion, massaging and caressing. When the child gets better, Kem attributes this healing to the spirit. From then on, if any of the children are sick, Kem calls on Fleet Wind, whose "sole mission seems to be that of healing."[26]

In another instance (after a gap of a few years), Fleet Wind appears to heal my great-grandmother, Alice: "Mrs. Kem had been in bed three or four days suffering with aches and pains in her back and lower limbs, which the doctor failed to give a name and which medicine failed to relieve," writes Omer. A spiritualist is called in to help, and when this woman arrives, Kem instantly feels Fleet Wind's presence in his own body again: "I at once stepped to the bed, laid back the covers, and placing my hand at the nape of her neck, slowly passed it down the spine and one limb to the foot, and then repeated, passing the hand down the other limb, and repeated the entire movement three or four times when the pain was all gone, and the next day she was about her household duties, fully restored."[27]

In this familiar trope, the racial "other" is granted magical (and perhaps erotic) powers that the white man, by way of proximity, somehow manages to make his own.

Decades later, in a letter to his grown daughter, Iris, Kem explains that Fleet Wind had now directed his healing powers to Kem's own body. "Saturday my vitality had run low and I was feeling quite punk. Fleet Wind had not been with me for several days when, suddenly, as I was lying on the davenport, I sensed his presence and he began to flex my leg muscles vigorously and in five minutes I was relieved. . . . He is a good old friend."[28] Writing to my grandmother Kathleen during the same period, Kem says that his leg "has improved wonderfully" for "Fleet Wind treats it twice a day." He is, he says, "profoundly thankful to my good old friend of 40 years, Fleet Wind."[29]

Despite this persistent friendship, this precise example of the "return of the repressed," Fleet Wind was not present for the illness that killed the Kems' three-year-old daughter, Marie, in 1898, nor for the mental and physical illnesses that plagued their second daughter, Linda, who died in 1907. He was not available for Alice's broken ankle, Omer's appendicitis, or Kathleen's broken thigh at age three, and he was not there when the whole family got sick from arsenic applied to the apple trees. Fleet Wind did no healing work during the flu epidemic of 1918, which killed members of Kem's extended family though no one in the immediate. Nonetheless, for more than forty years—half of Kem's life—whenever someone did get better, Fleet Wind got the credit for entering and working through Kem's body.

However odd or disturbing this may seem, Indian spirit guides were common for white spiritualists in the nineteenth and early twentieth centuries, and they still are.[30] Omer and Alice's youngest son, Huxley Darwin, took his father's lead in this. When he was twelve, he would often wander the house, possessed, he said, by the spirit of an Indian boy who had drowned in New Mexico. The family didn't much believe in this spirit (or, as Omer puts it, "were not particularly interested in him") until one day, a possessed Huxley guided them to a map on the wall and pointed to the body of water that had taken the Indian boy's life. Apparently, this was confirmation enough for Kem and affirmation enough for Huxley, who, having had his spirit guide recognized, never entertained him again.

Historians Renée Bergland and Kathryn Troy have each traced the history of Indian spirit guides in white American spiritualism, coming to different conclusions about the politics of the phenomenon. For Bergland, the presence of Indian ghosts is yet another "technique of removal." As white spiritualists rendered Indians as spectral presences, they participated in a national imaginary that associates Indians with "melancholy and loss, homelessness and death." In this way, suggests Bergland, spiritualists can turn away from the "tenacity of Indian survival" and avoid having to communicate with actual, living Native people whose demands for justice extend far beyond spectral solidarity.[31]

Troy pays more attention to the progressive politics of many spiritualists who spoke through the voices of Indian spirits. Spiritualists in general were sympathetic to the struggles of Native people, Troy argues. They made use of the voices of their imagined Indian controls to garner support for Indian policy reform (even though, as Troy acknowledges, "reform" generally meant coerced assimilation through allotment and the Indian schools). U.S. spiritualists, she writes, often pointed to "the most common sins committed by

Americans against Indians—namely, greed, dishonesty, murder, corruption, and the victimization of Indian women and children as well as men." In a generous interpretation of this appropriative genre, Troy concludes, "American Spiritualists utilized the Indian spirits they claimed to encounter as sources of political empowerment—as agents of peace between whites and Indians . . . and as guides to spiritual progression for both races."[32]

But Kem's case offers an example of just how distorted this form of social justice work was. For while his friendship with the truly radical Blands and his own statements on the congressional floor in February of 1892 reveal him to have been profoundly (or at least performatively) aware of how murderously Indian people had been treated, of how brutal the centuries of invasion and land theft had been, he nonetheless used his power on that same floor, and in his life as a settler, to serve his own interests and those of other white people.

In the summer of 2019, on Swans Island, Maine, the traditional territory of the Wabanaki, where my extended family owns a house, I met a woman who told me she was a spiritualist. Since seeing a vision one night by the lighthouse, she had gotten involved with a community at a place called Camp Etna, where spiritualism has been practiced since 1876.[33] I asked what spirits she had encountered there. Mostly, she said, she felt the presence of her nephew, a ten-year-old boy who had died in a snowmobile accident a few years before. Sometimes she also felt her grandmother nearby. When the mediums spoke in trance, they shared lessons of spiritual wisdom from people of earlier eras, she told me. I asked if any of these spirit controls were Native, and she said that they were. I asked if any of the mediums were themselves Native. She did not think so.

As it turned out, my husband, Tim, and I were driving south along the mainland the next day. We arranged by email to visit Camp Etna, to hear about its history from one of its members, a woman named Diane. Camp Etna is just a few miles from Belfast, the town where, for a few very painful years, my mother and stepfather tried to live with her dementia before it became impossible to do so. For this reason—because, one could say, the town is haunted by my mother's most miserable ghost—we did not linger there but picked up sandwiches and headed for Etna.

Etna's entrance is off a small road with not much else on it but an old gas station where we ate our lunch, sitting on some tires in the sun. When we entered the camp, clouds had gathered, threatening rain. Diane came to greet us, dressed in costume—a black floor-length dress with a brooch, a white kerchief on her head. She led us to a little cabin filled with knickknacks from the past: utensils, books, framed portraits of famous spiritualists and, for some reason, a large collection of *O* magazines. A dad with three girls were there too; one of the girls had been reading Tarot cards lately. Two other women, a couple from Germany, completed the audience.

Diane's history lesson traced the movement through a wide range of historical and mythological figures known to be mediumistic, beginning with the Buddha and including the mythical Greek Sybil, Christ, Joan of Arc, the Salem witches, and Abraham Lincoln. Much of what she said was familiar to me from the pages of *Banner of Light* and other spiritualist journals, as well as from Omer's own writings (Joan of Arc was a favorite of his). But then Diane pointed to a portrait on the wall: a woman with dark hair and a disapproving frown whose name was Mary Scannell Pepper Vanderbilt. Mary had been the president of Camp Etna for ten years—1909–19—and remained the camp's spiritual mother, buried just outside.

Mary's story was an instructive one. Her mother had died in birthing her, and Mary had been raised at first by her father—a broom maker in Western Massachusetts—and then later by her aunt and uncle. In 1882, when she was fifteen, she had a vision—a spirit of a dead relative entered her room. When she described the ghost to her aunt and uncle, they proclaimed her mediumistic. Mary spent the next three months holed up, practicing her skills. When she emerged, she was speaking in the voice of an Indian "maiden," a spirit control she called Bright Eyes.

But this name did not appear out of nowhere. "Bright Eyes" is the English translation of *Inshata Theumba*, the Omaha name of Susette La Flesche, the woman who had participated in Ponca chief Standing Bear's 1879 and 1880 speaking tours, advocating for Indian land and civil rights. Through these tours, La Flesche had become famous, especially in and around Boston. She spoke to audiences in the thousands all across the region. She shared stages with Wendell Phillips and Oliver Wendell Holmes. She was revered by Helen Hunt Jackson and Longfellow, who wrote a poem for her. She was the first woman in history to speak publicly, to a standing-room-only audience, at Faneuil Hall in Boston. She had even been to dinner at the White House, where she spoke to President Hayes about the struggles of the Poncas. The teenaged Mary would certainly have heard of her if the family followed newspapers at all.[34]

Diane did not know that Bright Eyes was an actual historical person. When I almost jumped out of my seat to say so, she showed me a photo of a little girl with dark hair, claiming that *this* was Mary's Bright Eyes—a Kickapoo child, nobody famous.[35] But even if Mary's version of Bright Eyes was based on this girl, or no particular girl at all, she had nonetheless made good use of a famous name, for Mary became quite well known herself. She traveled all over Europe and even to Russia to perform her mediumistic skills, which went beyond speaking in the voice of Bright Eyes to include answering questions sealed into envelopes that she pressed unopened against her forehead. In 1904 she was named pastor of the First Spiritualist Church in Brooklyn.[36]

Diane told us that in the beginning, Bright Eyes "spoke" only in a dialect that was "half African, and half Indian and wholly ungrammatical," but after Mary performed in this dialect a few times, ex-judge Abram H. Dailey of New York volunteered to train the dialect out of the "Indian's" mouth. (It seems that even imaginary Indian spirits must assimilate.) "That the assistance of this generous-hearted and scholarly man was effective was indicated by the fact that in later years Mrs. Pepper's platform utterances were not only free from jargon, but were formed in flawless English," writes one of Mary's biographers.[37] The real Bright Eyes actually had no problems with English; languages were one of her greatest skills. She had gone on Standing Bear's tour originally as his interpreter but had surpassed him as an orator. In 1887 La Flesche and Thomas Henry Tibbles (who were married in 1881) toured Europe, where, unlike Pepper Vanderbilt,

La Flesche spoke in her own voice. Not only was La Flesche a prominent speaker, but she was also a journalist, writing about the Ghost Dance and the Wounded Knee Massacre in Tibbles's Populist paper, the *Independent*. In 1896 La Flesche was the only woman working as a reporter at the Populist Convention where Populists, including Omer Kem, put forward the Bryan/Watson ticket.

Later in Mary's career, after her first marriage to George Pepper ended in divorce, she met Edward Ward Vanderbilt, a wealthy lumber mogul from Brooklyn. The two married in 1907, at which time Vanderbilt was sixty-six and Mary forty. His adult daughter from his previous marriage, a woman named Minerva, took her father and new stepmother to court when Vanderbilt, persuaded by none other than Mary's Bright Eyes, willed Mary a large portion of his property. The trial was something of a sensation. Minerva's lawyers demanded that Mary invite "Bright Eyes" into the room to read the contents of a sealed envelope, but Mary pleaded unfavorable conditions and refused.[38] Minerva won the case; the jury declared her father mentally incompetent for believing in the "little Indian spirit," as the *New York Times* put it.[39] But later, Mary and Edward appealed, the ruling was reversed, and poor Minerva was disowned.[40]

And so, as I sat in the little cabin listening to this story with Tim and the others, rain now pouring down on Mary's grave outside, I thought about the real Bright Eyes and her significant accomplishments as a writer and activist. I thought about Mary Vanderbilt and her financial success, a success that led directly to the longevity of the very community I was visiting. And I thought about how white people had managed to make use of what they thought of as Indian authenticity, or what they thought of as Indian power, and how they had managed to use their imaginary Indians to feed their own power, to build their own wealth. And I wondered if the real ghost of Bright Eyes were present, what she would want, what she would say. Perhaps she would repeat what she'd said to her rapt Boston audience 140 years ago:

> The question, I believe, is "what shall be done with the Indian?" One part of the American people try to solve it by crying, "Exter-

7. Susette La Flesche, "Bright Eyes," ca. 1900. Author's collection.

minate him!" The answer to such people is, that he has a creator that will avenge his extermination. The other part cry, "Civilize him." Forthwith they go to work, tell him that his land shall be his "as long as the grass grows and the water runs." We all know that "the grass grows and the water runs" only as long as it pleases the Secretary of the Interior. They say to him, "You must not pass beyond this line without the permission of this man, your agent, whom we place over you." . . . This, you see, is a lesson in freedom and liberty. . . .

When the Indian, being a man and not a child or thing, or merely an animal, as some of the would-be civilizers have termed him, fights for his property, liberty, and life, they call him a savage. When the first settlers in this country fought for their property, liberty and lives, they were called heroes. When the Indian in fighting this great nation wins a battle it is called a massacre, when the great nation in fighting the Indian wins, it is called a victory.[41]

What Does the Body Want?

When I was a child, I thought Fleet Wind was real. I thought Omer Kem had an actual Native friend whose massage techniques healed his terrible arthritis. This didn't strike me as particularly strange; I had no idea how common or uncommon it was for settlers and Native people to be friends in Colorado at the turn of the century (and to me, a child in 1970s Boston, Colorado was a mythic place anyway, still the land of "cowboys and Indians"). At the same time, I think I was proud of this story, as if it stood as proof of some goodness in Kem, a goodness, therefore, in me. I think this is how my whole family felt about it, including Kem's children and grandchildren, the adults who knew that Fleet Wind was imaginary. For even if the friendship was made up, even if the gestures of care went only one way, it seemed as if Fleet Wind proved Kem's open-mindedness, his respect for Native people, his longing for connection across racial barriers. For these reasons, I was both disappointed and embarrassed when I learned that Fleet Wind was spectral. But this, too, was revealing. If I was disappointed, then I must have been aware of how badly our family needed to address our settler history.

For of course, a long-held belief in a healing "friend," one whose imagined powers you take into your own body, one who represents the very people whose suffering underwrites your success, is a pernicious form of sublimated guilt that leaves the settler conscience clean. This example of "going native" might be, as Shari Huhndorf writes, an attempt to "resolve . . . anxieties about the terrible violence marking the nation's origins."[42] But if so, Kem's attempts at a resolution entirely ignore the harmed party, "healing" only the guilt and shame of the one who has harmed. At least, one could say, he knew that he was ill.

The healing didn't work though. Not only because like everyone else, Kem eventually grew sick and died but also because the guilt had clearly not been expunged. The final pages of Kem's *Spiritualist Notes* were written in bed. He was seventy-five and in physical pain. Probably for this reason, his previous essayistic style breaks down into fragmented diary entries in which he describes two new "spirits" who now speak to him inside his head. Fleet Wind is neither seen, heard, nor felt at this time.

Both of these new visitors are the ghosts of white men who seem to be vying for "control" of Kem's mind. The more insistent of these voices is torturously garrulous, crude, pornographic, and violent. This spirit, whom Kem calls his "Munchausen friend," tempts him with salacious tales, such as one about "a fellow who had four wives, sleeping with two at a time." This "fellow," Kem tells us, was "mean" to his wives, "beating them at times, on the head, breasts, abdomen, and other parts of the body where there were not so many bones." The ghost's misogynistic tale bothers Kem, but he can't shake it. He reports unsuccessfully begging the spirit to leave him alone. "Aw, be a good sport," says the voice. "One can't be serious all the time." Months later, this character is still dominating Kem's mind with his "interminable gabble . . . running full blast and indulging, as usual, in his tattling twattle."

The second visitor is more reasonable, concerned less with sex and violence than with the Kem family's financial recovery (it's 1930): "Business will revive . . . you will be able to pay your doctor bills. Victor will regain his old job or a better one . . . Claude will pull through all right." However, this reassurance falls short. In the final paragraphs of the document, Kem tells us that the visitor promised "some additional good news" (assumed financial) based on information he was trying to "secure." He returns several times with further hints of information, but he never delivers, despite how faithfully Kem waits. Kem forgives him this betrayal, concluding his *Spiritualist Notes* with the obsequious line, "He has left with me a most favorable impression."[43]

Perhaps this second spirit is the voice of capital itself, dangling wealth and security, holding out promises it can't make good on, leaving its adherents stranded but still faithful. If so, he speaks for an aspect of American life that Kem, as a Populist, had at one time tried to challenge but that (as will become clear) in the end he submitted to. At the very least it seems that in his final years, Kem's spiritualism had moved far beyond the longing for lost kinship relations, and even beyond a desire for racial or political healing, had instead become a way to explore his complicated relationships to sex, violence, and money—showing him to be guiltily desirous of all three.

Desire for boundary crossing, for contact zones between bodies and spirits from diverse worlds, can take many forms and can show up in all sorts of arenas: political, social, artistic, racial, national, and so on. For this reason, it's not hard to see why Populism and spiritualism overlapped; both movements actively (and unevenly) challenged boundaries between different kinds of people—class and racial boundaries, gendered boundaries, or more generally, political boundaries, even if in challenging these boundaries, they also sometimes reinforced them. Around the time that Kem was sick in bed, receiving visits from the disturbingly crude "Munchausen friend," he was also writing letters to his oldest friend, James Ream. In the middle of an almost-essay on the topics of poverty, crime, and world economics, Kem writes the following request: "I read the abridged version of your annual address to the Grange, but that is only a taste that makes me hanker for more. . . . I want to see your insides exposed clear down to the lower end of the colon, there may be something hanging there around the region of the appendix that ought to be clipped off. . . . I have turned my insides out to you, and now you come across with yours, a fair exchange of guts is no robbery."[44]

A few months later he writes again, continuing in this vein: "I hope you have all of your fixins fixed, for only in this hope can I base any expectation of ever getting to the bottom of your colon as I've been trying to do all winter."[45]

One doesn't want to make too much of jokes like these, but one doesn't want to make too little of them, either. Kem and Ream were Populists and homesteaders together. They had supported one another through the loss of wives and children, through debt crises and terrible drought. The wish for deeper contact that Kem expresses in his jocular tone is not so different, in the end, from the desire to be touched by the dead or the desire to find within oneself a lifelong healing friend.

In one way of talking about it, spiritualism is a manifestation of the aspirational desire to enter and to be entered, to dissolve the rigidity of the individualized body, to find some way toward a deeper communion with others. Witnessing furniture moving on its own, opening their mouths to voices from elsewhere, writing thoughts they didn't think they were thinking, what the spiritualists refused was the boundary—between the living and the dead, first of all, but also between different categories of people, and even between things and beings. The taste of this refusal is addictive and sweet and lingers still. For this reason, though this is a strange and sometimes disturbing legacy, it's not one I'm able to entirely reject.

What private, perverse, or political cravings for boundary crossings of all kinds do we still look to ghosts to gratify? Perhaps in haunting, there's not only a memory of injustice, as Avery Gordon argues, but also a new kind of rupture, one perpetrated by the spirit and the living at once—an antagonism, then, that seeks a new reality structured out of dream.[46]

The ghosts, as plasmatic, aural, luminous, or merely energetic non-matter, offer evidence, to those who need it, of the tenuous borders between selves. There's a beauty to these cravings, but there's violence there too, for the yearning for a dissolve of political, social, or personal boundaries can look a lot like the settler's claim to the land—appropriative, aggressive, unjustified, and uninvited. And as such, haunting is like populism: a terrible demand and a radical invitation at once. A violent and utopian vision.

5 Water in Relation

The economic greatness of the United States is the fruit of a policy of peaceful conquest over the resources of a virgin continent.
—William E. Smythe, *The Conquest of Arid America*, 1899

Water is life. Water is the giver and sustainer of life. Water is a sacred and spiritual element to the Tribes of the Partnership. The Creator instilled in the First Peoples the responsibility of protecting the delicate, beautiful balance of Mother Earth for the benefit of all living creatures.
—Mission statement of the Colorado River Ten Tribes Partnership

Mother
My mother was often thirsty. Overheated and coughing. Sometimes she'd cough so hard she'd vomit. I was also thirsty, drawn toward pools, ponds, and quarries. More than once I tried to drown. Or I just stopped swimming, falling slowly beneath the surface. Why I did this, I don't really know. I was probably just curious. I think I wanted to know what it would feel like to give up. I can still see the way the light slanted toward me, how that changed as I sank deeper. I did and did not want her to pull me out.

All thoughts of water begin and return to the mother, to the water in the womb, the water that breaks (like an ocean wave), that had to be broken for the children to come. In a dream, my mother walks toward me from out of a lake. She is wearing only underwear and a purple T-shirt and is smiling benevolently, in a way she sometimes smiled. In my father's dream, he is walking along the shore with me and my brother as children. A large dark shape is moving slowly through the water, growing closer. My father is afraid, tries to shield us from this darkness, but we are fascinated, running toward it.

Father

And now I must talk about water on the father side, the water that the Coloradan ranchers and farmers pulled through a canyon wall so they could grow corn, wheat, potatoes, apples, plums, and peaches and raise cows. It required an enormous effort, many years, dynamite and drilling, one hundred serious injuries (including blinding and broken necks), and twenty-six lives.[1] It was a kind of work they had not done before, not to that scale. Imagine the celebration when the water poured through the hole in that rock wall, the cheering and the eager hopes.[2]

This story of blast and rush is preceded by other stories in which both Indians and settlers irrigated the land more modestly, in which hand-dug ditches marked the land as property and in good use. In some of these stories, irrigation is techno-democracy, a way to spread the wealth of water. In other stories, irrigation is violence.

Tunnel

In 1897, when Omer Kem arrived in southwest Colorado to survey the land he had bought—160 acres on Spring Creek Mesa about three miles from Montrose—he camped in his wagon. The previous owner of this particular homestead had mortgaged the land, just as Kem had done a decade earlier. Unlike Kem, who paid off his loan with the salary the U.S. government paid him, this owner had been unable to pay his debt, and so the mortgage company foreclosed on the loan. At $15 an acre, Kem bought the land from the lender. A not unimportant detail about the previous owner is that he was Black. "The farm I bought was one that a colored man by the name of Anderson had taken under the Desert Act," Kem explains.[3]

Anderson had planted about one hundred fruit trees (that's a lot of labor, as anyone who has tried to plant anything in the hard, dry, rocky soil of Colorado knows), and now Anderson's orchard was Kem's, along with two buildings: a two-room house and a stable. Kem writes that the land and buildings were abandoned when he arrived. And yet a paragraph later, he describes the following encounter:

> The prairie dogs were very plentiful there at that time and it is said that the young ones are very good to eat. There was an old darkey batching in the house at the time and one day, while at work there he invited me in to have dinner with him, saying as an inducement I presume, that he was going to have beans and dog for dinner. I thanked him but excused myself on the ground that I had lunch with me and as I did not care to carry it home I thought I had better eat it.[4]

One question is whether the man offering dinner is Anderson himself, living in his own home until forced to move. Another question is whether Omer declines the invitation because of what is for dinner or because of who is cooking. Either way, Omer says nothing more about it. He moves on, and he moves in—hoping to profit off Anderson's fruit trees, fed by the one canal Anderson likely dug by hand.

Peach, apricot, nectarine; apple, plum, pear, and sweet cherry surrounded the thirteen-room house they eventually built. In 1999 my grandmother Kathleen, Omer's second youngest daughter, wanted cherry pie for her hundredth birthday. My sister-in-law Kim pitted the cherries herself.

Many things happened after the Kem family arrived to live in Anderson's house while they built their own, and most of these things were hard. The hardest by far was the death of the three-year-old Norma-Marie in May of 1898. Marie, as they called her, suddenly fell ill. The ghost of Kem's mother spoke to the family, telling them to let the baby go. Less than a day later, Kem was left "with nothing but the shell in my arms." Marie's grave, he writes, is "on a little Mesa on the west side of the Uncompahgre River about a mile south of where the wagon road crosses the river at the edge of town," a description so precise I feel Kem imploring me to go find her.

The next especially hard thing that happened that year was that Kem's second daughter Linda, at about age twenty, began exhibit-

8. Norma-Marie Kem, 1895–98. Author's collection.

ing signs of mental illness. Kem calls her first episode a "nervous breakdown," surmising that it was brought on by bladder trouble and altitude (he doesn't consider the death of her baby sister as a catalyst).[5] She suffered untreated and was never really well again, not even when she moved to sea-level Portland.

Within a year of beginning to farm, Kem started making noise about the Uncompahgre valley's water problem. The valley was irrigated by a canal that drew water from the Uncompahgre River. But this single canal carried only enough water for the first half of the season. By mid-July there wasn't much left, and late-summer crops withered. Given Kem's devastating experience of drought in Nebraska, it's easy to see why he was worried—he didn't want to fail for the same reason twice.

The Gunnison River was about ten times the size of the Uncompahgre, but between the Gunnison and Montrose was sixteen miles and a formidable barrier—the Vernal Mesa Mountain at the western side of Black Canyon. According to Montrose lore, a man named Francoise "Frank" Lauzon was the first to present the idea of blasting through the mountain for water, after seeing the image of the tunnel in a dream.[6] Kem claims that honor for himself:

The thought occurred to me that if that water could be brought under the mountain through a tunnel into the valley, it would settle our water troubles for all time, for there was ample water to supply every acre in the valley. . . . I at once began to talk about it. However, it met with no encouragement on the start, it seemed to scare people and they met my advances with the assertion that it would cost a million dollars to bring that water through, I countered by pointing out that it would be cheap at most any price for it would enable every tillable acre in the valley to produce to capacity for all time.

He might have been right about the cost-benefit of the project; he was dead wrong about its duration.

Omer had been voicing his interest in large-scale public irrigation long before arriving in dry Colorado. He spoke at length on the topic during his first year in Congress in 1892. Like other Populists, he saw public irrigation as a line of defense against the tyrannical greed of capitalists, for under the then privatized system, individuals and companies owned the irrigation ditches and tunnels, charging what they could for their use: "The water necessary to irrigation, like every other necessity of the people, is fast passing under the control of corporations, and if not checked in a short time the water supply of the West will be completely in the hands of a few individuals and the millions will be at their mercy, for he who controls that supply is monarch of all he surveys, and the people will be compelled to pay him whatsoever greed or avarice dictates."[7] A farmer without riparian rights, Kem complained, was forced into dependency on the "water owner," while "eking out a miserable existence in his own home."[8]

As we've seen before, while Populists believed in the value and security of home ownership, they also mistrusted markets and fought for more equitable distribution of resources through "the principle of Governmental control." Kem in the 1890s wanted to see the "railways, telegraph and telephone lines, finance and irrigation" *all* nationalized: "We should abolish the present system by which private corporations control these great public necessities and build up colossal wealth for a few while robbing the many," he declared, sounding a lot like Bernie Sanders in 2020. (Once he became an owner of a private electric company, Kem reversed these positions.) Anticipating arguments against the "paternalism" of big government, Kem made clear what is even more clear today: the federal government already practices "paternalism" in its treatment of wealthy corporations—its "favored sons," as Kem called them. In the 1860s, he reminded his congressional colleagues, the federal government had handed out millions of acres of free land to the railroads, practicing what has come to be called "socialism for the rich."[9]

After a long process of public agitating and lobbying, Congress finally passed the Newlands Reclamation Act of 1902, named after its primary sponsor, Representative Francis Newlands (D-NV).[10] Newlands was an avowed white supremacist and anti-immigrant crusader. His 1909 letter to the state legislature of Nevada, "A Western View of the Race Question," offers a clear position: "Blacks are a race of children, requiring guidance, industrial training, and the development of self-control." He was perhaps even more insistently, if more subtly, anti-Asian. Though he claimed to respect both China and Japan, he warned that the mere presence of what he called "yellow" people in the United States would lead inevitably to race war. He joined other white supremacists in arguing for a complete shut-down of immigration from Asia and all countries where people were not "of the white race" (at that time, this included Italians and Jews).[11] The Reclamation Act contained a provision: "No Mongolian labor shall be employed thereon."[12]

I bring this up not to ogle at the common racism of the era but to draw attention to the ways that infrastructure development and white supremacy interact. One of the key winning arguments for the 1902 Reclamation Act was that an irrigated West could provide a "safety valve" for impoverished immigrant workers in the cities, reviled and feared by many for racial, political, and economic reasons. (After anarchist Leon Czolgosz assassinated President McKinley in 1901, fears of immigrant radicals intensified.)[13] Kem took this line in 1894 when he argued that a properly irrigated West would take care of the "surplus of humanity which is accumulating as it never did before."[14] By playing on easterners' concerns about urban crowding, worker revolts, and racial others, the irrigationists successfully forged an unlikely coalition of labor unions, farmers, Populists, eastern manufacturers, and railroad tycoons, all who had come to believe they would benefit from a developed "Great American Desert."[15] Irrigation was far more than a system to move water. It was an answer to the problems of immigration and urbanization. In other words, land engineering and social engineering went hand in hand.

Historian Laura Lovett points to a conflicting way that race was used in pro-irrigation propaganda. Irrigationists, as she describes, often employed an "ideology of the home" in their arguments, temptingly describing an irrigated West dotted with wholesome Anglo-Saxon families running small farms.[16] "Homemaking was perceived to strengthen the nation racially by encouraging the proliferation of Anglo-Saxon families," writes Lovett.[17] Apparently, reclamation would whiten the cities, prairies, and deserts all at once. Racism is a flexible tool.[18]

On the ground in Montrose, however, the issue was less about enticing people away from cities and more about enticing crops from dry soil. Sometime during the year of Marie's death, Omer and a few other farmers got together to organize a survey of the Gunnison. A four-man expedition—the Pelton Expedition, which did not include Omer—started out in two boats, the *City of Montrose* and the *John C. Bell*. Within a day, the *John C. Bell* was dashed to pieces. Three weeks later, the group abandoned the *City of Montrose* to a rapid they named the Falls of Sorrow. Nonetheless, they climbed out alive, garnering considerable attention from both state and national politicians. The next expedition was organized by the United States Geological Survey and was taken up by just two intrepid men, Abraham Fellows and William Torrence.[19] These two managed their survey in ten days, during which they abandoned their rafts and leaped into the crashing rapids, as rumor has it, seventy-six times.[20]

Meanwhile, Kem's group, now called the Uncompahgre Water Users Association, had petitioned the state legislature to appropriate

$25,000 to begin blasting a tunnel through the canyon wall. Nine hundred feet in, the project was abandoned; the prison laborers they had "employed" were simply impractical to surveille.[21] But at this point, the plan had momentum. Colorado senator John Bell spoke eloquently in Congress about the "dry, parched valleys" of southern Colorado that, with enough water, could be transformed into "ideal homes for many of our homeless people choked up in the great cities."[22] When the Reclamation Act passed in 1902, the 5.8-mile-long Gunnison Tunnel was its very first project.[23]

Of Omer Kem's many legacies, the Gunnison Tunnel, with almost all its original construction still in use today, has arguably had the most lasting structural, social, and environmental impact on the West. At 30,650 feet, it was for many years the longest irrigation tunnel in the world. It completely altered the nature of the Uncompahgre valley, delivering water at approximately 1,300 cubic feet per second to irrigate seventy-six thousand acres of land, land that now produces over $81 million of mostly hay and other forage crops per year.[24] "If there were nothing else in his life worthy of regard, his efforts on this behalf would entitle him to be enshrined in the loving remembrance of the Western people for all time," reads one tribute to Omer Kem.[25] Since I live here in Colorado, there's no way I don't benefit from his irrigationist dream. That puts it mildly.

But of course, this legacy of inventiveness and abundance is also a legacy of destruction and immanent decline. The Gunnison River feeds into the Colorado River at Grand Junction, sixty miles northwest of Montrose. As the tunnel draws down the Gunnison, it sucks water from the Colorado as well. I met with Steve Anderson, the current manager of the Uncompahgre Water Users Association, in a Denver hotel lobby. I wanted to know what today's Montrose farmers felt about the tunnel and about large-scale irrigation in general. Steve and I sat in a dim corner that had a kind of speakeasy feel. (Steve's striped overalls would have stood out there if we were in any major city other than Denver.) Steve told me, rather proudly, that the tunnel is the state's *largest* diverter from the Colorado, drawing more water from that desperately depleted river—currently running at about half capacity—than the entire state of Nevada.[26] The Colorado River rarely makes it to the ocean anymore. Instead, it "disappears into its sandy bed" eighty miles from the shore.[27]

And depletion is not the Colorado's only problem. Excessive irrigation also increases a river's salinity, for after the water has been drawn off and used, it returns to its source having run through, and picked up, the mineral salts in the ground. Meanwhile, flood irrigation will increase a soil's salinity, pulling the natural minerals up to the surface as waters evaporate. In California's Central Valley (fed by the Colorado), the extreme salinity of the soil is "reducing crop yields by 8 million tons a year—to the tune of about $3.7 billion in lost revenue."[28]

The Gunnison Tunnel did not only generate crops; it also created a "hydraulic public," an economy and community entirely dependent and attached not to the land itself but to an aggressive, expensive, federally supported, and deeply unstable infrastructure, one that threatens the very future of this vast region.[29] Reclamation, as it was imagined and practiced in the early twentieth century, with its "miracles of engineering," remade the West. And yet, irrigation in the West was and is also a form of environmental violence that reaches far into the future to waste it.

But to truly understand the impact of irrigation in Colorado, before we look ahead to that precarious future, we must look even further back.

"The Great Utopian Promise of Irrigation," 1870–78

In 1870, twenty-five years before Omer Kem bought land in Colorado and 135 years before I did, a utopian-minded poet named Nathan Meeker, unable to piece together a decent living from his work as a journalist, asked his editor, Horace Greeley, to invest $30,000 in a twelve-thousand-acre stretch sixty miles north of Denver.[30] Meeker, by all accounts an annoying man, had read some translations of French socialist Charles Fourier that had been published in Greeley's *New York Tribune* in the 1840s and had subsequently tried out communal living in a doomed socialist community, the Trumbull Phalanx of Ohio.[31] Now he was seeking a new way to manifest his communitarian (and prohibitionist) ideals while solving his money problems. Greeley, who was similarly attracted to semi-communal living and egalitarian structures and who was enamored of the West though he had hardly ever been there, put up the money to buy the "cheap land," which was then sold piecemeal to those ready to join the "utopian" colony.[32]

Within six months of the project's founding, five hundred colonists had signed on to live in what was then called Union Colony and what is now Greeley, Colorado. The speed with which Meeker and Greeley were able to convince people to drop everything and "go West" reveals something about Greeley's celebrity and also something about the mood of northern and midwestern whites just after the war—opportunistic and on the move.[33] By spring of 1871 the colony included about 1,200 people and five hundred buildings.[34]

The colony followed a hybrid economic model; colonists owned their own small pieces of property while holding resources and infrastructure in common. The sawmill, a dairy herd, several manufactories, the church, school, library, and town hall—all were owned and run collectively.[35] Because of Colorado's arid climate, the success of the community hinged on successful irrigation; there could be no crops without it. "Providence is not bankrupt," announced Greeley. "The time is to come when every foot of desert is to bloom. It only needs water, and this can be had by systematic irrigation."[36] And irrigation was more than just a necessary infrastructure; it was also the key to the colony's ideological goals. "The great utopian promise of irrigation," this "ecological foundation for communal living," as Donald Worster puts it, lay in how it could (literally) spread out the power of rivers.[37]

For Greeley himself, however, it seems that irrigation's promise was more aesthetic than political. Based on two years of letters between Greeley and Meeker, it appears that Greeley's main interest in the colony was arboreal. From the start, he was insistent that the colony be seeded "thick with trees."[38] In letter after letter he expresses ample anxiety for the well-being of his evergreen, acorn, and hickory and none for the people he'd convinced to buy in. By June of 1871 the first trees were dying of thirst. In September Greeley commands Meeker to plant more. "Have I *any* evergreens living?" he whines.[39] In nearly every letter sent to Meeker between July of 1871 and October of 1872, a month before his death, Greeley mentions the trees; sometimes he mentions *only* the trees. To be sure, there is something both horrible and wonderful about a utopian community that is, in the end, really just a dying man's irrational forestation fantasy.

Despite these hoped-for trees, nightly lectures, debate societies, theatrical performances, dances (including dressing up as Indians for a "war dance"), despite utopian visions of a fair economy set far from the glaring injustices of urban life, things did not go well for Union Colony.[40] For one thing, irrigation in the colony proved far more difficult, costly, and complicated than hoped. The initial cost of the ditches came in twenty times higher than expected and never carried enough water for the necessary yield. Moreover, from the very start there was a good deal of infighting and general unhappiness about the climate and farming conditions. "Many of the experiments undertaken were rendered abortive by grasshoppers and insufficiency of water. Many bright hopes of the early days . . . had been blasted," wrote one member reflectively.[41] Fair enough. Colorado is dry and rocky and its weather unpredictable, sometimes maddeningly so. But the folks who signed on to the project seem *especially* petulant. By August of the first year, some members, whom Greeley referred to as "lame duck" "grumblers," had to be bought out of their $150 down payments.[42] By February of 1872 even Meeker was jockeying to leave.[43]

Greeley died at the end of that year, and after a few more years, Greeley's daughters were threatening to sue Meeker for debt payment.[44] Union Colony would go on without him, leaving its socialist-utopianism behind. The town became Greeley in 1886, the county seat of Weld County. As the top producer of beef cattle in the state, it smells like blood.

Meeker's own legacy was another thing altogether. As it turned out, his utopianism, like much utopianism before and since, carried flavors of inflexibility and superiority, both of which led to disastrous outcomes once he moved to his next location. For after much lobbying of influential friends, he managed to get a new job: Indian agent for the White River Ute Indian Agency in northern Colorado, where irrigation, far from being a utopian technology, becomes a potent and dangerous weapon.

Inevitably—*Chinatown*

It seems one cannot talk about water in the West, or water and powerful men, or water and environmental injustice, without mentioning Roman Polanski's last American film, *Chinatown* (1974). A lot of people know what they think they know about irrigation in the West from watching this movie, although it is fiction. Whenever I mention that I've researched this topic, people talk about the movie; even water historians mention it, and some spend pages refuting the plot.

My father lived part of his childhood in the LA of *Chinatown*. He and my grandmother Kathleen lived on the edge of an orange grove, much like the one where Jack Nicholson's character, the detective Jake Gittes, is beaten nearly to death by farmers. In the winter, says my father, the farmers burned crude oil in little "smudge pots" underneath each tree, trying to keep the baby oranges from freezing, poisoning the air in the meantime.

In the film, as in Polanski's life, there's a side story and a main story. The movie's main story (or so it seems) is about the stealing of water. Powerful men running the Los Angeles Department of Water and Power send LA's irrigated water into the sea to exacerbate a punishing drought. This middle-of-the-night draining trick will pressure farmers to sell their dried-up valley lands cheap. The same group of men then secretly buy up this cheap land, hiding behind the names of dead or nursing-home-ridden old people. Their plan is to reirrigate the valley they'll then own, turning it into valuable property to sell to developers, making a mean profit. A comparable story happens every day in America's poor neighborhoods, which are parched for resources until the developers, in collaboration with the city that wants the tax revenue, buy what is cheap and prep it for sale.[45] (The farmers' attack on Jack, who they think is a developer or a city planner, thus offers a sharp warning.)

Chinatown's side story is about incestual rape. The same man behind the water theft, the ironically named Noah Cross, also raped and impregnated his daughter, Evelyn, when she was fifteen. Evelyn's daughter, Katherine, who is thus also her sister, is now fifteen, cared for in a separate house by Evelyn's servants. We see Katherine only four times in the film, and in each appearance, she wears only white, indicating that she has not yet been raped, though her grandfather/father is after her. Once Cross has murdered Evelyn's husband and protector, Hollis Mulwray, Evelyn desperately hopes to escape to Mexico, where she and Katherine will presumably be safe. This story about incest is strange in a movie that is primarily about infrastructure and corruption. Without her, without the violated woman, *Chinatown* would only be a man's movie—a movie about rich men stealing resources from poor men in the dead of night. And yet at one point, she simply takes over the plot.

You could say that the violated white woman's body is a distraction, diverting our attention from other violations running through the film. She diverts our attention from the violation of the poor by the rich and from the racial structures that underscore that violence (farm workers are Mexican, domestic workers Chinese). The violated white woman's body diverts our attention also from the violated treaties that allowed these white men to control and manipulate the land and water of Los Angeles in the first place. In this sense, the story of incestual rape is like an irrigation ditch sending our attention elsewhere.[46]

And yet in another sense, the violated woman's body is not ever a side story; it is a central and unending event within all stories of extraction, exploitation, manipulation, and thievery. Inasmuch as water is life, inasmuch as the maternal body depends on the health of the planetary body, and inasmuch as the maternal is the original commons, the stealing of water—which treats life itself as a commodity—and the raping of the daughter/mother are one.

"Father Meeker" and Ute Expulsion, 1878–81

> No Indian treaties, no Interior department regulations, no Indian Bureau contrivances can stop the onward flow of white emigration or prevent Anglo-Saxon civilization from occupying every foot of land on the continent.
>
> —Rep. William Springer, 1879

In 1868, just as the Great Sioux Reservation was being formed in the Dakotas, the federal government (represented by Kit Carson) signed a treaty with seven of the Ute Indian bands, people whose ancestors had been living in what is now called Colorado since at least the fifteenth century.[47] The treaty reduced Ute-controlled territory by two thirds and promised to keep settlers off the remaining Ute lands. But in a pattern that is repeated throughout the West, it took precisely five years for the 1868 treaty to be renegotiated, for in the early 1870s, settlers had found gold in the San Juan mountains. Under the new Brunot Agreement, signed in 1873, the Utes ceded another four million acres—most of the San Juan mining area.[48] And nonetheless, less than ten years later, nearly all the Ute people were forcibly removed from the state.

The expulsion of most of the Ute people from Colorado was thus both harsh and swift. And while the call for removal, or genocide, rang loudly through the territory from its inception in 1861, in the story of how that goal was nearly accomplished, irrigation plays a central part.

In May of 1878 Nathan Meeker, the aging utopian poet, arrived at the newly established White River Agency near the Wyoming border. The agency's location was selected in part because of the "great abundance of water for . . . irrigation [and thus farming] purposes."[49] At that time, the Northern Utes—the White River, Yampa, and Grand River bands—owned approximately four thousand horses; hunting and horse racing had been crucial aspects of their culture for over three hundred years.[50] And yet horses were not only a deterrent from the more "civilized" work of farming; they also made it possible for Utes to leave the confines of the reservation, which treaty stipulations allowed but that white settlers did not like.

Insisting on the moniker "Father Meeker," Meeker acted energetically from the start. His first move in the spring of 1879 was to relocate the agency fifteen miles downriver. By doubling rations (which he controlled), Meeker induced a group of Ute men to dig a mile-and-a-half-long irrigation canal from the White River. The canal ran near a pasture and racetrack designated for horse grazing, but Meeker disregarded the pasture's uses and ordered it plowed.[51]

That summer, as it grew clearer that the Indians were not interested in conforming to his vision of the good life, Meeker's strategies of persuasion grew increasingly abusive. In an effort to "convince" the Utes to give up their equestrian culture, Meeker threatened to withhold government rations and to trade away their horses. In this way, he would starve them into submission. These threats would not have rung hollow to the Utes. As Meeker's own son Ralph had reported in the pages of the *New York Herald*, Indians on reservations across the West were starving. Agents often withheld or illegally sold off food rations—those rations themselves frequently inadequate or spoiled—and corruption of all kinds ran through the Indian Bureau.[52] Despite his son's journalism, Nathan Meeker participated fully in this necropolitcal endeavor, writing letters of complaint to Colorado senator Teller and Governor Pitkin and publishing editorials in the *Greeley Tribune* (the paper he'd started in Union Colony). In one of these editorials, Meeker publicly threatened the Utes with land theft: "If you . . . won't work, white men away off will come in and by and by you will have nothing."[53]

Meanwhile, off-reservation forces were violently anti-Ute. Governor Pitkin had been elected in 1878 on a "Get the Utes out of Colorado" platform.[54] This will not surprise anyone who has read accounts of the public celebrations following the Sand Creek Massacre of 1864. When the murderers of up to 150 Arapaho and Cheyenne people, mostly women and children, returned to Denver parading body parts—genitalia, scalps—as souvenirs, they were cheered in the bars as heroes.[55] *Denver Tribune* editor William Vickers, the leader of the media campaign against the Utes, stoked that fire, published editorials proclaiming "The Utes Must Go!" and accusing the Utes of the "disgusting habit" of ranging all over the state and stealing horses.[56] Pitkin gave speeches and Vickers wrote letters to the Indian Bureau also accusing the Utes of starting forest fires.[57] In one of his many attacks, Vickers refers to the Utes as "actual, practical Communists" who were lazily living off the "bounty" of the Indian Bureau, concluding his paragraph with the familiar taunt, "The only good Indians are dead ones."[58]

Back at the agency, animosities between Meeker and the Utes were only deepening. In September Meeker began to plow the irrigated horse pasture. When Ute leader Canella (sometimes referred to as Canavish) confronted Meeker about this infringement, Meeker mocked him. Shoot your horses and be done with it, he reportedly suggested. A physical encounter followed (accounts vary), which left Meeker shaken and calling on the military for help.

And troops came.[59] On September 28, 191 soldiers rode down from their quiet, remote outpost in Fort Steele, Wyoming, led by Major T. T. Thornburgh. The troops had been bored; this rescue mission was at least something to do.[60] About fifty Utes met the approaching troops at Milk River, prepared to stave off an invasion. (The Utes were well-aware of what had happened in Sand Creek in 1864.)[61] It's unclear who fired the first shot, but in the end, thirteen U.S. troops were killed. A siege followed, with Ute leader Nicaagat and his followers holding a strong defensive line for six days.[62] At the agency, things turned gruesome; Meeker's head was bashed in and a barrel stave "driven through his mouth."[63] Eleven other employees met their deaths, while three women and two children, including Meeker's wife, Arvilla, and grown daughter, Josephine, were taken hostage. As Josephine describes it, the hostages were dragged through "a deep, wide ditch that father had caused the Indians to dig for the purpose of irrigating some fields." Josephine reports that the Utes took a certain pleasure in forcing the women into the ditch "because this ditch was for agriculture, and they abominated it for that reason."[64]

This sensational event was soon blasted in newspapers across the nation.[65] Governor Pitkin sounded the alarm, warning Colorado settlers that they were in danger of attack and calling for the total extermination of the Utes, a desire he had been voicing for years.[66] Pitkin also called on the state militia and nearby army troops to be ready for further battle—and they were. "At one point," writes Robert Silbernagel, "fully a third of the country's active-duty army units were in the state or near the Colorado border."[67] Meanwhile, Chief Ouray of the Tabeguache band and his sister Tsashin urged peace, fearing that the actions of the White River Utes would have disastrous consequences for all Utes in Colorado. After former Indian agent Charles Adams intervened, the hostages, who had been captive for twenty-two days, were let go.[68]

Three weeks after their release, the women reported having been "outraged" (a euphemism for rape) by their captors, though when they were first interviewed, they claimed to have been treated well. Josephine Meeker quickly publicized her ordeal, writing and touring her book brazenly subtitled *Brave Miss Meeker's Captivity and Her Account of It*, in which she refers to herself as "the handsome young woman, who by her indomitable heroism and determination had saved the lives of the whole party."[69] Like her original testimony, the book makes no mention of sexual assault and instead highlights some of the Utes' kindnesses. This does not mean, of course, that the women were not raped. While Muscogee scholar, Sarah Deer, points to "significant anti-rape sentiment in most tribal cultures," and asserts that in general, "Native men did not rape war prisoners," religious studies scholar Brandi Denison, situating the event within the Southwest "captivity culture," writes that it is likely "that the women had been adopted into the tribe as spouses," which plausibly could have included forced sex.[70] As Denison puts it, "Both nineteenth-century Ute culture and the United States cultures placed women within a position that limited sexual agency, even as the United States devalued and demonized Indian men and women."[71] There is no way, of course, to ascertain the truth; and what matters more at this point is how the story was understood by those in power. "It was the same as if a black man had been accused of assaulting a white woman," as Silbernagel writes. Much of the public believed the women's later testimony and demanded Ute removal or extermination with increased intensity.

"What became of Josephine Meeker when confronted by those savage Utes?" asked the *Rocky Mountain News*. "They did not give her a choice between death or rape, or she would have gladly preferred the former. . . . They raped her. They bound her and outraged her person."[72] Papers in Kansas, Wisconsin, Nebraska, Minneapolis, Nashville, and Chicago all pushed the same story, demanding "vengeance" and lynching, adding lurid details and often accusing Secretary of the Interior Carl Schurz of a cover up. Josephine's brother Ralph, who had previously written articles exposing the corruption of Indian agents, wrote a letter to the *Chicago Tribune* calling for the "hanging" of all Utes who were at the reservation at the time.[73] In the 1880 congressional hearings that followed the event, the story of the rape became the furnace that fueled the demand for total removal, "a central means for reasserting the right for white men to retain and expand power through land ownership," as Denison writes.[74]

Once again, as in *Chinatown* and countless other narratives, the white woman's body functions as a foil, drawing attention away from all other forms of violation. The "innocence" of her body stands in for the supposed innocence of the (white) nation that thereby is justified in whatever abuses it perpetrates against those whose land or labor it wants. Moreover, violation of such "innocence" becomes a seductive rhetoric: "thrilling and intensely interesting," as Josephine's jacket copy advertised. The white woman's body, as if always already raped, displaces the invaded land and people and justifies the expulsion of those now deemed "trespassers."[75]

And so, after the congressional hearings, the White River incident led decisively to the 1881 relocation of all White River, Yampa, Grand River, and Uncompahgre Utes to the Uintah Reservation in Utah and the containment of the Mouache, Weenuchiu, and Caputa bands on the relatively tiny reservation in southwest Colorado—120 miles long and 15 miles wide.[76] After the expulsion, the federal government opened six million more acres of Ute land for homesteading in Colorado: "Once the Utes were gone, the rush began."[77]

In fact, the two events were simultaneous. Sondra Jones quotes an American trooper who took part in the forced expulsion in the Uncompahgre valley: "Our task . . . was to hold back the civilians. They followed us closely, taking up and 'locating' the Indian lands thrown open for settlement." Within three days after removal, the valley "with its rich soil and wonderful opportunities for irrigation" was fully occupied by settlers.[78]

You will remember that 1881 was also the year that Omer Kem arrived in Broken Bow, Nebraska, to take advantage of *that* "free" land. And the expulsion of the Uncompahgre Utes from southern

Colorado meant that fourteen years later, the Kems would be able to purchase their second, and much more successful, plot of soil.

My three children were educated in Denver's public schools. None was ever taught this story.

"At Trail's End": Worlds within Worlds

We often think of settler-colonial hungers for land, oil, gas, or metals as the immediate causes of Indian displacement and genocide, but many dramatic twentieth-century displacements have had to do with water, for in the West, hunger for land and thirst for water are one and the same. The Fort Peck Dam project in Montana (completed in 1940) displaced 289 Sioux and Assiniboine families.[79] The Garrison Dam in North Dakota (1953) flooded 150,000 acres on the Fort Berthold Reservation, displacing 300 families.[80] And the Fort Randall Dam in South Dakota (1956) displaced 151 families from the Yankton, Rosebud, Lower Brule, and Crow Creek Reservations.[81] All these projects were part of the Pick-Sloan dam project, designed to control the Missouri River's natural flood cycles, to generate hydropower, and to aid irrigation. Nick Estes refers to this period as a "twentieth-century Indigenous apocalypse" and reads it as a chapter in the larger story of Indian dispossession in which the U.S. government destroys Native lifeways in its efforts to "develop" (control and monetize) the lands.[82]

"'Mni Wiconi': water is life, or, more accurately, water is alive. You do not sell your relative. . . . This is the practice of Wotakuye (kinship), a recognition of the place-based, decolonial practice of being in relation to land and water," write Estes and Jaskiran Dhillon.[83] In contrast to extractive capitalism's practice of treating water as simply a resource for human-centered development and growth, "water protectors"—such as those who gathered at Standing Rock in 2016 to protect the Missouri River from the Dakota Access Pipeline and those who are gathering now (in 2022) to "Stop Line 3" in Minnesota—assert an ethics of relationality between water and both human and nonhuman beings.[84] In this epistemology, it's less a question of who gets to control the water, of who has "rights" to it, or even of how best to use it, and more a question of how water is understood in the first place. As scholars Craig Howe (Oglala Sioux) and Tyler Young write, "Under the guise of fighting for and protecting their water rights, [the water protectors] are being good relatives. In traditional Lakota thought, relatives include more than persons. They also include all living things like plants, animals, stars, and the earth herself."[85] Or in the words of Indigenous feminist Joanne Barker, "Water teaches us to be mindful of our relations with one another. . . . It decenters human exceptionalism when considering issues of life and well-being, requiring practices of responsible care in understanding the world and its varied, place-specific ecosystems that extend beyond the centrism of humans."[86]

I did not go to Standing Rock. That same spring, I started a community garden at Counterpath, the community art space my husband and I run in Denver.[87] As I hauled dirt and built beds with Jessica, Mission, Matt, Sam, H.R., Mathias, Jeffrey, Isaac, Don, and others, as we seeded that ground with zucchini, cucumber, spinach, lettuce, radish, peas, and pumpkin with the goal of feeding ourselves and any number of people who made use of the free farm stand we donated to, we followed #standingrock and #NoDAPL and thought about driving up to South Dakota to what we did not quite know. Some friends went, bringing blankets and coats, books and diapers. They came back and spoke about the transformative possibilities of this Native-led resistance. I carried coats and blankets to the Four Winds American Indian Council in Denver and listened to the people who knew that struggle well, witnessing the fierce anger of two young women who were leaders in the movement.

One Native friend cautioned me against going unless I was sure of what I had to offer. No tourism. No photos. But I wasn't sure, having already donated coats, blankets, diapers, and dollars. What would my presence add, other than my own pride, or shame? In the end, I couldn't figure out my motives. I was concerned about my curiosity. I stayed home and seeded ground in the long shadow or bright light of Omer Kem, who seeded ground he also thought his.

I didn't go. And even now I feel unsure of my decision (not that it would have mattered much to anyone but me). But even if I had gone, I would not be the person to describe the force of that movement or the depths of that epistemology; there are those who can and do—Estes, Dhillon, Barker, and many other Indigenous scholars, historians, poets, and novelists.

Here's Diné poet Sherwin Bitsui, in his 2009 book *Flood Song*:

> as you inhale earth, wind, water,
> through the gasoline nozzle
>   at trail's end,
>   a flint spear driven into the key switch.
>
> You think you can return to that place
> where your mother held her sleeves above the rising tides

Bitsui's work is hard. In compressed language, it refuses fantasies of return and gives no sure way forward. What Bitsui gives instead is brutal truths that matter—the enmeshing of worlds, the "thud" of song "under the weight of all that loss."[88] What good is poetry in a time like this?[89] It's a way to break what you think you know, a way to begin.

Fathers, Mothers, Sons, and Daughters

> Faceless, nameless, innocent,
> Blameless and free,
> What's that like to be?
> —Natalie Merchant, "Motherland"

In *Chinatown*, Jake/Jack spends half the movie with a bandage on his nose. My father doesn't remember how the movie ends, but he remembers this: early in the film, Roman Polanski, playing a hired thug, sticks a knife up Jake's nostril and slices. From then on, the bandage is prominently featured—awkward and homely, it's a metonym for the head it's on. Like Jake, the bandage tries and fails to block an improper flow.

In the movie's opening scene, a cuckolded man is crying in Jake's office; his sobbing moans are the first sounds we hear. With smoke pouring out of his mouth, Jake tells the man to stop, get over it, "Enough's enough." In the movie's final scene, blood pours from a dead woman's head, her daughter weeping beside her, and Jake, who

9. Jack Nicholson in *Chinatown*, directed by Roman Polanski, 1974.

has tried from beginning to end to stop wasteful and misdirected spillage, not just of irrigated water but of semen, tears, and blood, can only whisper, "as little as possible."

Chinatown is set in 1937. This is the same year that Polanski's parents moved from Paris to Kraków, fugitives from the Nazis. Two years later, they were taken, leaving six-year-old Roman an orphan, hiding under false names. Evelyn, *Chinatown*'s mother, hunted by the Nazi-like Noah Cross, never makes it out. She dies in the getaway car.

Evelyn's murder clearly references Polanski's own mother's murder, and Katherine, screaming in horror, is Polanski himself, the orphaned child. Thus, the improper flow that the protagonist tries and fails to block stands in for the bloodletting of the holocaust itself, the six million Jews and others—shot, starved, tortured, and gassed to death while Polanski was precariously sheltered by a lie.

Chinatown is also the last film that Polanski made in the United States before he went fugitive in France, escaping the charge of stat-

 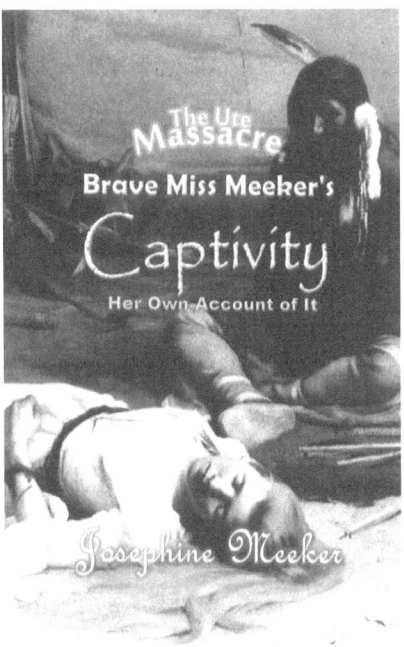

10. Belinda Palmer in *Chinatown*, directed by Roman Polanski, 1974.

11. *The Ute Massacre*, by Josephine Meeker, 1959, jacket cover. Author's collection.

utory rape. After photographing thirteen-year-old Samantha Gailey in a hot tub, this once and future fugitive, "the toast of the industry," raped her in Jack Nicholson's house on Mulholland Drive. All art is autobiographical—and so often in ways the artist cannot anticipate or control. Thus, any raped girl or woman in this and any of Polanski's films is also his victim; Polanski is the one with the camera, the one with the knife that slices.

This confusion of victim and perpetrator is a problem in U.S. history too. Innocence, emblematized so often by white girls (dressed in white), can never be "pure" in a nation built on crime. When bodies, land, and water are stolen, are treated as objects to be owned, sold, or traded, are forced to work until exhausted or depleted, innocence is simply unavailable. The land itself, the mother(country) herself, is contaminated.

Polanski creates a self-reflection in the child rape at the center of *Chinatown*, but the power of the movie is the mirror it simultaneously holds up to America: a tainted land. It's not LA's Chinatown that is the problem (and one cannot ignore the movie's racism in locating intractable violence there); it's all of California, which is only a metonym for the West, for the "frontier," for the birth of a nation—a nation that carries and will always carry the memories of its origins as settler-colonial forced penetration, of rape.

"There's Not a Lot of Water out Here"

The Jeffersonian ideal of the independent farmer was an impossible and violent imposition to force on a seminomadic culture that had thrived in Colorado and successfully managed its climate for centuries. Similarly, mass-scale irrigation was a dangerous demand to place on that climate itself. One hundred years of this demand has delivered us to a continuing and unimagined population boom, a thriving agriculture-and energy-driven economy, and, especially since the introduction of centrifugal pumping, a dangerously depleted water system. One study has predicted that the Ogallala Aquifer, one of the largest water tables in the world, will be 70 percent depleted within forty years under current irrigation practices.[90] Despite some governmental action, the depletion is not slowing. Rather, it's speeding up exponentially; in the past six years, the Ogallala shrank twice as fast as in the previous sixty.[91]

"American's breadbasket," as the plains are sometimes called, will not last. If it were truly producing grain for bread, though, it might. Instead, "America's butcher," a more accurate nickname, uses close to 90 percent of all its irrigated water to grow the grain that prepares cows and hogs for slaughter.[92] The American-led Livestock Revolution of the 1970s vastly increased meat consumption in the United States and across the world, with grave consequences for planetary health.[93] Meat production is now *the* major user of water in the United States and the fifth largest emitter of greenhouse gases.[94] (Just for comparison, fracking uses approximately one hundred billion gallons of water per year; raising livestock consumes thirty-four *trillion*.)

Large-scale irrigation, no matter how needed, no matter how productive, moves the life force into forced pathways and in this sense disregards and eventually or immediately damages the integrity and longevity of both land and water. Given that massive irrigation has been necessary for the feeding of millions of people and for the development of entire cities with their economies, technologies, creativity, and all the rest, it constitutes a kind of nonsense, an absurdity, to say it wasn't worth it; it would be like wishing never to have been born while wanting, very much, to keep on living. Regardless, under current practices, this is not a long-term bargain. Flooding riparian lands, sucking rivers dry, and dragging salts into the soil, the "utopian promise of irrigation" has led us to uneven developments with uncertain or doomed futures.

Nebraska, Kansas, and California are three of the top ten states for industrial agriculture in the United States. And yet from 2002 to 2008, Nebraska experienced 348 consecutive weeks of drought. A 400-week drought hit California in the following decade, and Kansas experienced 248 weeks of drought from 2010 to 2015.[95] The first twenty years of the twenty-first century has been, for the region, the driest twenty-year period in two millennia.[96] As a result of this extended, semipermanent drought, with consistently diminishing snowpack, Lake Mead and Lake Powell, reservoirs in the lower Colorado River basin system, have been, at the time of writing, reduced to about 35 percent capacity.[97] For the first time, Arizona's farmers, who often grow water-greedy alfalfa and cotton, will see a sharp cut in their water supply in 2022, with further cuts promised.[98] In an ouroborial cycle, the changing climate, brought on in part by the carbon dioxide and methane generated by the animal agriculture industry, diminishes the land and water available for agriculture.

Farmers know they need to save more water, and some are doing so while also building soil resiliency with techniques of regenerative agriculture, many learned from Indigenous farmers.[99] But deep conservation and climate mitigation would require more radical shifts, not just in farming techniques but also in agricultural scale and, most importantly, in *product*.[100] But when I asked Steve Anderson, whose family has been farming in Montrose County since 1809 (the year after the Kems left), what he saw as the long-term solution to the problem of diminishing water supplies in the state, he described his dream: a new dam and reservoir in southern Colorado. The Rams

Horn project would dam Cow Creek, which feeds the Uncompahgre just south of Montrose. "The main use for the water rights would be to supplement irrigation of 100,300 acres of mostly hay pastures," reports *Telluride News* in one of the few published articles about this project.[101]

The environmental group Save the Colorado, run by a taciturn environmentalist named Gary Wockner, lists the Rams Horn project as one of twenty-two proposed water projects it deems "irresponsible" for how they will deplete the Colorado River even more. But Gary didn't tell me much about what the region's farmers and ranchers, whether Native or non-Native, whether running small or enormous farms, should do about their dry lands; I could feel him shrugging over the phone. Similarly, Steve—whose deep concern for Native and non-Native water-users is palpable—brushes off the environmentalists. "For some people," he says, "dam is just a four-letter word."

There are many groups whose policy suggestions and actions fall between the two poles I've set up here, including the Bureau of Reclamation itself.[102] "Ten Strategies for Climate Resistance in the Colorado River Basin," for example, collaboratively generated in 2021 by seven environmental and conservation groups, presents strategies designed to at once "strengthen economic resilience in communities" *and* "reduce pressure on existing water supplies."[103] Ten Tribes Partnership brings together the Chemehuevi, Cocopah, Colorado River, Fort Mojave, Jicarilla, Quechan, Southern Ute, Ute, and Ute Mountain Ute Indian tribes and the Apache and Navajo nations, in collaboration with the Bureau of Reclamation, to produce a study of tribal water use and to advise future development within the context of climate change. The Indigenous Environmental Network, an umbrella organization in the United States, draws economic and environmental justice together as a single project of Just Transition.[104] There is progress, but most of this work is in the planning stage. And we are running out of time.

The dream of a fully irrigated West once seemed a pathway toward the larger American dream—a nation powered by home ownership more or less equally distributed across land and people. But now most of irrigation serves a different project altogether: the bloated, unnecessary, and environmentally destructive beef and hog industries. Meanwhile, the failures of the home-ownership project have only delivered us here: to the MAGA dream of locked-down borders, guarded riches, and reinvigorated white masculinist supremacy.[105] And in this new/old dream, this *nightmare*, a hot waterless climate, this crisis of human and planetary life, can, like so many things, be weaponized, as in the following warning, delivered by Donald Trump in 2019:

> And we've all seen the pictures of young people climbing walls with drugs on their back—a lot of drugs. I mean, they're unbelievable climbers. This wall can't be climbed. This is very, very hard. . . . And what the panel does on top, as I said, is structural, but it's also very hard to get by panel. Plus, it's designed to absorb heat, so it's extremely hot. The wall is—you won't be able to touch it. You can—you can fry an egg on that wall. It's very, very hot. So if they're going to climb it, they're going to have bring hoses and waters—water. And we don't know where they're going to hook it up, because there's not a lot of water out here.[106]

There's not a lot of water out here. He's right about that. But a weaponized climate, like all weapons, can and will turn on the one who wields it.

The mother is thirsty, and yet we are still sucking her dry. A thirsty mother cannot nurture; a thirsty mother will rage. And the mother who rages—she is not other than us. "If water is in us and we are in water, the link between human and other-than-human beings, the earth and other-worlds, is profoundly intimate and visceral," writes Barker.[107] The legacy of the great irrigators of the early twentieth century, that legacy that I carry as Omer Kem's great-granddaughter but also just as a person living in the western United States, is a legacy of unsustainable growth in which water is not a relative to be protected but, as an early twentieth-century California engineer put it, "a beast—to be shot down and dragged out by the first brute that came in sight of it."[108] This is not a battle we can win. As the rivers deplete, as the water table shrinks, as the temperatures rise, the

12. Kem family house after the fire, Montrose, Colorado. Author's collection.

forests, dependent on both ground and surface water, grow brittle and dry. And a dry and brittle forest is a forest that will burn.[109] It's almost fire season in the dried-out West again; it hardly ever isn't anymore. We have to find another way.

In 1923, fourteen years after the Kems had left it, the house in the Uncompahgre valley caught fire, leading Kem to wonder if it had been cursed.[110]

Interlude

"A Real Everyday Feeling,"
Portland, February 2020

My cousin Chris and his then girlfriend, Leise, took the day off work so we could drive from Portland to Salem to meet our other cousins, Randy Kem and his son Ely, for the first time. A Thursday morning, a light winter rain. I sat in the backseat with a toolbox filled with family photos and a grocery bag of documents from Chris's large and unwieldy collection.

I wanted to know more about all of them, but I was especially interested in Mary. Mary was Chris's grandmother and the Kems' middle son, Huxley's, daughter, and when she was a girl, Huxley got his hands on a movie camera and started to film her. These were not ordinary home movies, though. Huxley wanted to be a film director. He was the first president of the Southern Oregon Cinema Club, and he made narrative films in the style of the era with Mary as the star. Thanks to Chris, who had tracked down and digitized this archive, Huxley's movies are posted on YouTube, where you can watch them if you want. That morning, before our drive, I had watched them all.

Even when she was very small, Mary was a precocious actress—charismatic, funny. I liked her, especially in one scene in which she plays an orphan who runs off from an abusive orphanage and sleeps in an alley. When she wakes up, she rubs her eyes and swipes her nose like she's been studying for the role of Oliver forty years too soon. Later, when she got older, Mary got behind the lens, too, and made movies of her own. One of Mary's films, *The Haunted Camera* (1930), which she both directed and starred in at thirteen, is archived at amateurcinema.org.

The Haunted Camera has erotic undertones; Mary and another girl take shelter in a house haunted by escaped convicts. The girls get out unscathed, but the convicts set the house on fire. From a distance, the girls watch it burn.

She had wanted to be a movie star, just as her dad had wanted to be a filmmaker. But things didn't go that way. For a while, the family lived in a little house in Hollywood. Hollywood, Portland—a middle-class neighborhood then and now, shrouded by rainclouds.

Huxley wasn't just an amateur filmmaker; he was also an artist and an inventor. He invented an automated silk-screening machine and sold it to sign companies around the country. He invented a better paint for cars. When he was twelve, you might remember, he also invented a Native spirit, a boy he said had drowned in New Mexico and was now inhabiting his body. He had a droll sense of humor like his father ("sand, swamps, tourists and real estate men are the things of which Florida is made," he wrote while on business in Jacksonville).[1] In the absolutism of his racism, he followed the inventive mind of his namesake, Thomas Henry Huxley ("Darwin's Bulldog"), who created faux charts and diagrams linking African people to apes. T. H. Huxley's fake morphological skull sequences landed a Mbuti man named Ota Benga in the monkey house at the Bronx Zoo—and more than that, so much more.[2]

That morning, after I watched all of Mary's and Huxley's movies on YouTube, I returned to the letter Huxley wrote to Omer in 1925, the letter about Mary's seventh birthday that first alerted me to the family's eugenic racism and that I had not reread since encountering it in the Creighton University library in 2017. It was far worse than I remembered. My notes were inadequate; I had turned away.

> Mary had a birthday and got about $30.00 worth of presents. Yes, more than that I guess. All the kids in school and all the grown folks that knew her gave her something, and instead of getting five and ten cent store stuff, like they should, they got expensive things.
>
> One little n—— kid at school that Mary of course couldn't invite, gave her four presents that cost at least five dollars. The

13. Film capture of Mary Kem. *The Kem Story, Part 2*, by Huxley Darwin Kem, 1925. Chris Christensen personal archive.

poor kid looks perfectly white but her father is a mulatto. She is crazy about Mary. That is what is wrong about this business of going to the same school. This poor little kid wants to be white so bad, and when she really is white as this kid is, it is downright cruelty. The way they do across the line in Kentucky is the only way, separate schools, separate places in the trains and street cars. The northern cities where the negroes are flocking in large numbers will breed trouble of the most violent kind. An arrogant Negro is an animal without sense or reason. Pushed by a white man's civilization hundreds of generations ahead, he hadn't the brain development back of it to keep him mentally balanced. . . . I'm firmly convinced that the whites and the blacks must not mix, so much as even a drop of black in an ocean of white.

Huxley might have presented his ideas in scientific terms (brain development, mental balance), but his emotions are chaotic. Regret, guilt, self-justification, fear, rage. His need to defend the choice that he and his wife, Happie, had made—barring the one girl from the party because her father was, as he explains further on, one-eighth Black—is overpowering.

I wanted to know more about Mary, not only because I found her charming, charismatic, and funny and not only because of her birthday party but also because her daughter, Chris's mother, Valerie, now in her eighties, had told me that Mary was a cold and distant mother. They had not been close. Valerie had unceremoniously given Mary's jewelry to Leise. (But Leise, as she admitted from the front seat, likes puppets better than jewels.)

As we drove through Portland, Chris told me more about his grandmother Mary. An early marriage to a man named Verne Campbell had ended her Hollywood dreams. She became a mother almost immediately—Chris hinted at a shotgun wedding—and then Verne went off to Saudi Arabia to work for Standard Oil. (It was the beginnings of U.S. involvement in the oil fields of the Arabian Peninsula. So many riches and wars to come.) In fact, there was more to Verne and their unhappy marriage than even his departure to Saudi Arabia indicates, as I discovered when I found some photos of Verne from various times in his life. He looks sexy and happy in a skirt and halter top in one. In another, he is wearing a bikini, sprawled out on a beach towel with another man. Evidently, no one in the family sought to hide or destroy these hints of another life. For this, I give them credit.

I wanted to understand why the girl that the camera had loved, whose birthday party was a stage for her parents' aggressive racism, had become a bitter woman. Now it seemed I had answers—maybe a mismatched marriage, a thwarted career. But how deep does a culture of vicious racism cut? How does it infect the psyche, turn it "cold," "bitter"? "White people in this country will have quite enough to do in learning how to accept and love themselves and each other, and when they have achieved this—which will not be tomorrow and may very well be never—the Negro problem will no longer exist, for it will no longer be needed," wrote James Baldwin.[3] Mary had not, it seemed, learned how to accept or love herself. Or maybe she once had, and then there had been a forgetting.

About halfway to Salem, Leise took out her puppets. A chef, an old woman, an old man, and Polly-Anne, a constant companion in a feather hat. The puppets spoke to me from the front seat of the car in their various voices, sent through the corner of Leise's mouth. The old man wore a MAGA pin and asked me on a date. The woman was voting for Bernie. "A puppet speaks. A puppet is mute. A puppet is suggestive. A puppet is spooky. A puppet is pathetic. A puppet is hapless," writes Catherine Taylor. "Everything is said better with puppets," said Leise.

Chris, like Mary and Huxley, is dreaming up movies. One is based on Fleet Wind. I only half-hear the plot, though I get that it involves a totem pole. Fleet Wind was also, I suppose, a kind of puppet, though an invisible one, dwelling inside the body instead of on the lap of the puppeteer. "A puppet is a surrogate. A puppet is a proxy. A puppet is a disembodied self."[4] As Chris describes his imagined film, I am distracted by a photograph of my teenaged grandmother who wanted to be a singer. So many thwarted dreams in the backseat archive.

When we get to Salem, there's a protest going on. The loggers and others in the timber industry, under the name Timber Unity, have

14. Jenny Kathleen Kem, ca. 1919. Author's collection.

convoyed to the Capitol to protest the carbon cap-and-trade bill up for debate in the state legislature. A year ago, Oregon's Republican members of Congress had crossed state lines to avoid having to vote for this bill, shutting it down by their absence. Chris says, "The loggers don't want their emissions taxed." I sense by his tone that he's in agreement with the Democrats on this one. But it's confusing later when he defends Trump's climate policies, saying, "Trump didn't invent global warming" (true). He's strongly pro-border-control, a topic we don't get into. He also wonders aloud if he's a white nationalist. "I'm white," Chris says. "That's not anything I can do anything about. And I guess I'm a nationalist since this is my country." I don't know if he's just goading me or if he's sincerely unsure about the term.

Randy Kem, our other cousin, is a quiet man. He looks like the middle-aged saxophonist he is in just about every way, from his forest-green turtleneck to his slicked-back thinning hair. He's the grandson of Huxley's younger brother, Victor, who was by far the best looking of the Kem sons and the only one young enough to have enlisted in World War I. During the Depression years, Vic barely worked as a day laborer, drying prunes or picking them, driving trucks or not, and was, with his wife, homeless and itinerant, sometimes dependent on his parents.

Despite having grown up in a temperance household, Victor became an alcoholic—according to Randy, an abusive one. His wife was similar. Fifteen minutes after we met, as we were walking to a café for lunch, Randy told me that when his father, Charley, was a boy, his parents would tie him to the toilet with a rope every morning until he emptied his bowels—an image that will not soon leave me. Victor did other things to his son, said Randy, but he didn't tell me what they were.

When Randy's father grew up, he didn't have much to do with these parents, so I got no further stories from Randy about Victor or Omer and Alice Kem, but I got another sense of the family, a darker swath of fabric you could say.

Driving back to Portland with Chris and Leise, the conversation grew a little wilder. I was tired, watching the Willamette River run by. Chris did most of the talking. He said he wants to start a company to study the moment, the instant, that life begins. "Everything has a beginning," he says, "but when is it?" Chris wants to understand origins. I do too. This was when he told me he might run for city council as a populist, the kind that Omer Kem was.

Chris's feelings about our shared ancestor are different from mine. He's more admiring, and I'm more skeptical. This is a function partly of our personalities and partly of how we live—our politics, our work lives. Chris says that at one time, he had a lot of money. Now he has very little, but he's okay with that. What he's not okay with, he says, is his current job at a call center. Omer is an inspiration to him but also a challenge. "I feel like he's pulling me somewhere, but I don't know what I'm supposed to do," he says. "I sit in a cubicle with a phone strapped to my head making money for some corporation. Shouldn't I be doing a lot more?" I'm quiet and so is Leise. "That's a real everyday feeling," Chris says into that silence.

After I read one of Omer's long poems out loud from the backseat, we promise to collaborate on a poem of our own. Chris will set it to accordion music, and Leise will perform it with her Polly-Anne. But I'm also thinking about what puppets have to do with anti-immigrant fervor, with the sadness of the call center. At a rest stop there's a man in a little cap. In his arms, an enormous rabbit, bigger than a lot of dogs. He sets the rabbit down, and it doesn't hop away. Then I see its collar and leash—pink. Suddenly, I'm unsure whether the rabbit is a real animal or a toy. Polly-Anne and the old couple are in the back seat with me now, slumped against each other. "The immigrant is a puppet," my friend—himself an immigrant—tells me later, "a prop or a toy, not considered fully human."

In 2020 Chris ran for representative for Oregon's First Congressional District on a pro-border-control, pro-police, pro-gun, and anti-antifa platform. He won 35.2 percent of the vote. Now he's running for senator. His inspiration: Omer Madison Kem and Woody Guthrie.[5]

I made a GIF of Mary waking up over and over. I keep it on my phone.

6 Daughters

Because the reader has room to realize that the future may be different from the present, it is also possible for her to entertain such profoundly painful, profoundly relieving, ethically crucial possibilities as that the past, in turn, could have happened differently from the way it actually did.
—Eve Sedgwick, "Reparative Reading"

Love and Shame

I did not know Omer or Alice. But I knew their youngest daughters, my grandmother Kathleen and my great-aunt Thelma, and I loved them both. In their old age, they were close, living in the same neighborhood in Salinas, California, which smelled like dust. They lived, it seemed, to tease one another, lobbing barbs back and forth that occasionally or in the aggregate got mean. Maybe this was a form of pushback, a way to live in the world without bemoaning it. Or maybe it was something else, something harsher. Late in life, Thelma became a painter, but my grandmother, as far as I knew, didn't do a lot. When we visited her, my brother and I would walk downtown to watch the highriders and lowriders race each other along Salinas's main drag. Once, we bought condoms at the drug store, though we were both too young to use them. We bought them because, far from home, we could pretend to be older than we were, and we bought them because, in a small town in northern California in about 1980, two kids could buy condoms without condemnation or shame.

Another indelible memory from that time involves my grandmother looking out her window at a couple of men walking by. She said they were Mexicans and that they were lazy, or criminals, or both. I don't really remember what she said, but I remember the feeling of hearing and not wanting to hear, a kind of thud in my stomach. In this memory, I for sure felt shame, the shame white people feel so often and so often ignore.

It will not be enough to talk about Omer and all that he did, said, and believed. It will not be enough to note the power and property he gathered as defense against the vulnerabilities he, as a once poor laborer, had felt. And it will not be enough to discuss how those defenses turn, as they eventually do, into weapons. In the history of white America, the women cannot be ignored. They don't deserve to be, of course, but also, and more emphatically, they—we—do not get to be.

Death and Marriage

Despite how they had finally built themselves a real house on property that might yield profit, 1898 was a bad year for the Kems. Omer called it "the year of trouble." It was their first full year in the Uncompahgre valley of Colorado, and it led him to wonder if he had made a terrible mistake in moving there. Three-year-old Marie's death and Linda's mental breakdown were followed by a horse accident that left Alice with a badly broken ankle. After that, as if bad luck were addictive, a rush of illnesses and accidents befell the whole family:

> After hay harvest all of us except the little ones were either ailing or sick in bed, at times there were not enough well ones to take care of the sick. Linda came down again with her old trouble and I had something like an attack of appendicitis and Bert Lockhart, Allie's brother, who was working for me, had something similar and the rest of the women broke down waiting on the sick. Mrs. K. [Alice] was still ailing from her runaway and Linda was desperately ill for about four months. We tried everything we could think of to give her relief, including the service of a Christian Science practitioner, but nothing seemed to restore her health. After a time she got up and about again but was never well after.[1]

But alongside all this illness and loss, the Kems experienced fecundity and growing wealth. They had two hundred branded cows and dozens of fruit trees, watered by the meandering Uncompahgre, a modest river for a modest population. By their second year there, Alice had birthed her seventh child. Omer's influence on the community was immediate and strong; he joined the school board almost on arrival. I have already detailed his influence on the land, how he aided the movement of water through the Black Canyon's wall. Nine years after their arrival, Kem even took a dip back into politics; in 1907, he was elected as the district's representative at the State House in Denver, where he served just one not very eventful term.[2]

Still, after ten years of mostly successful farming, the settler's restlessness and rootlessness overcame them again, and in November of 1908, Alice and Omer sold their fruit farm and their thirteen-room house (at boom prices, given the future irrigation promised by the Gunnison Tunnel) and followed their two oldest daughters, Maude and Linda, to Cottage Grove, Oregon.

The April after this final migration, their third daughter, the nineteen-year-old Iris, got married in Linda's bedroom. Linda had been bedridden since Christmas, too sick to get up, so they brought the wedding to her. After a decade of mental illness, she was dying of tuberculosis (and perhaps also cancer—she had a tumor removed from her abdomen the year before). Between 1908 and 1910, 164,000 Americans died of tuberculosis. The only other disease that came even close to killing that many was heart disease, which took about 40,000 fewer per year.[3] Tuberculosis is highly contagious, passing from person to person through the air. The family of ten crammed into the bedroom for the ceremony.

Death by tuberculosis is death by drowning. The lungs become balloons for blood.

I read of Iris's wedding and Linda's death while I was quarantined with my family in Denver. It was April of 2020. A pool of exhaustion and terror seemed to surround me and at other times to fill me. It was the time of year when tulips bloomed and that was all, and that was enough. Daffodils and crocuses had had their short bright lives, and now their petals shriveled inward and faded to brown. The flowers for which Iris was named were yet to even fatten at the bud. COVID-19 took life after life in Colorado, the United States, the world—red bars or wavy lines climbing and spiking across graphs. Obsessively, I watched the numbers rise in our state and in Massachusetts, where my parents lived. As obsessively, I returned again and again to the passages Omer wrote about Linda and her death, hoping to understand something about grief, as if to prepare. But there was very little there, and what was there wasn't really about her:

> I have been clairvoyant for a good many years and frequently, see forms and faces, sometimes of those I knew in the body, but more often they are those of strangers. On the Monday of the week in which [Linda] left her body, I had an impression that sometime during the week she would pass on. That night after retiring . . . I saw a house whose entrance was reached by several steps to a porch or balcony, and on this porch . . . I saw standing a man—a stranger—as plainly as I ever saw anyone in the flesh. He was of medium size and light complexion . . . face covered with about two weeks growth of a reddish beard, but with all, a pleasant face. He was in his shirtsleeves, standing with his arms folded across his chest and had a faraway look as if he was pondering something. I asked, mentally, if Linda would pass on during the week and, in a very dignified manner, he inclined his head forward in an affirmative bow and was instantly gone. . . . In a few moments . . . I saw another man of just the opposite type . . . dark complexion with a two-weeks growth of black beard. . . . I asked the same question as to Linda's passing out. He . . . turned toward me and very gravely bowed in confirmation as did the other man, and just then, his whole face lit up with that sort of light the sun frequently casts on objects when it breaks from under a cloud. . . . I interpreted this to mean that she would pass during the week, just about sun down.

All this was entertaining, but like Huxley's amateur films—a little corny and contrived—it was also irritating. I wanted to know about the daughter, who she was, how she suffered, what her death meant to her family. Instead, I was learning more about her father's propensity to invent male figures with whom to converse. The actual event, the moment of her passing, Omer conveys only curtly. "She died on October 8th, 1909, aged 30 years 10 months and 1 day. We took the body back to Sellwood where it was cremated within a few blocks of where she had lived with Maude. I will say here that I think all dead bodies should be cremated, and that is what I want done with mine when I can no longer use it."

Immediately after this brief mention (which even in its brevity turns back toward himself), Omer drops Linda altogether and returns to the daughter who most readily resembled him—Iris: "Iris had graduated from the Montrose High school in 1908 and in the same class was a young man from Olathe, a little town 12 miles north of Montrose, by the name of, Gardner Brooks Corey.... [I]n April of 1909 he came to Cottage Grove and they were married the 29th of that month, and as Linda could not leave her bed, the ceremony was performed in her room."[4]

Perhaps I learned what I needed to know about Linda's illnesses and death by how her father treated them; her illnesses meant that she was long disabled and her death a long time coming. And when it arrives, it seems more a clearing than a calamity. She was loved—that much is clear—but no grieving is recorded. Instead, in the narrative's unfolding, her death makes a space for Iris to flourish.

When my father was a child, he lived briefly with his grandparents in Cottage Grove. A portrait of Linda hung on the wall. He tells me he was infatuated with this dead aunt whom he had never met. She was a beauty, it was true; everyone said so. But she held a different allure for me. She was the one daughter who, you could say, in not being well, escaped the family.

But Iris, too, managed an escape of sorts; after the wedding, she and her husband, Gard, returned to Colorado, where they opened a movie theater and ran a successful farm, irrigated by the water now drawn through the Gunnison Tunnel, which still today makes a brown land green. On her well-irrigated acres, she grew food enough to sell for

> I have my canning about done for this year. It has been pretty strenuous, evrything seems to come at once. Fruit is awfully cheap. Got perfect large sized peaches delivered at my door for 50¢ a basket(bushel size) and thousands of boxes at Palisade were thrown away, no market for them. Don't know how they are faring at Paonia. Haven't heard from Aunt Lilla lately. Laurance, Jay's boy, stayed all night with us not long ago.

15. Iris Kem letter of September 29, 1931. Omer Madison Kem Papers, 9:99.

profit; even during the Depression, she managed to sell cabbage and celery. And she raised four children, all girls, into adulthood.

Far from her parents and siblings, Irish flourished in another way as well: she became a writer. Long letters, spanning decades, describe her daily life, her politics, her keen intellectual curiosity, her longing for a family far away. In line after line, she conjures the labor of her body, the importance of the weather on her mood, her time, even her language—as the wind in the branches and the snow melting in the hills seem to make her sentences run: "We have been having some windy weather lately but it was nice and sunny today. There is lots of snow in the hills so I suppose there will be high water instead of no water this year. I haven't planted my sweet peas yet but want to next week and am in hopes I will have better flowers this year as I haven't so many trees."[5]

These letters are preserved, not in their original, but because they were painstakingly retyped by her father's hands.

More than to any of the other women, I am drawn to Iris. Like her, I am the mother of daughters. Like her, I like to read and write. Like her, I grow food (a comparatively tiny amount). Her "ideal church," she tells Omer, would be "a community gathering place where everybody is welcome and a free exchange of ideas is allowed."[6] This would be my ideal church too. And Iris was close to her father, as I am close to mine. It was only when I began to read Iris's letters in earnest that I found myself yearning for these relatives I had never met. One could even say I loved her.

Hers is the voice that most clearly articulates the passions of motherhood and daughterhood, that most poignantly expresses what kinship means, what belonging is. But then, in the 1920s and '30s, as her writing and thinking matures, Iris is the one family member,

16. Iris Kem, ca. 1907.
Author's collection.

besides Omer himself, who directly reveals the kinds of distortions kinship with and belonging to a white property-owning family in America can foster.

The wedding at the deathbed, as it turns out, provides a clear metaphor for the biopolitical imperative that the Kems, and much of America, came to adopt: some should marry, thrive, and breed, while others should simply die.[7]

Depression and Cure

In July of 2020, in the midst of the pandemic, we drove down from Denver to the Uncompahgre valley, knowing we would see no one, interview no local historians, visit no libraries, museums, or archives. In that strange hot silence, I could hope only to find traces of the Kems—of Iris, Linda, my grandmother Kathleen, and baby Marie—in the land. We slept near the rim of the colossal Black Canyon, called so, we surmised, because its walls are so high and steep that sunlight only fleetingly reaches its floor. In the morning, we drove down the hairpin road to immerse ourselves, for seconds, in the icy Gunnison. We walked through the cemetery where the dust of Marie has been absorbed into the earth. I tried and failed to find that baby's grave marker, while our daughter Lucy, who was twelve, walked alongside me, cheerfully describing the gravestone she'd like, should I have to bury her.

One afternoon, we drove down a bumpy dirt road to find the green expanse where the Kems' house once stood. A boy on a bike wobbled past suspiciously as I took pictures of the irrigation ditch and tall grass. And we drove the silent streets of Olathe (the name means "beautiful" in Shawnee), the still tiny farm town where Iris packaged her cabbage and celery, her popping corn.[8] Small wooden houses line those unpaved streets, sheltering farm laborers from the oppressive sun. Each time I stepped out of the car, I begged the land to feed me, just as Iris had, and Omer before her.

Nearby Montrose, where Omer had wielded his influence, was ghosted—nearly all the shops shut down. The two that were open—a high-end clothing boutique and a junk shop—were so desperate for customers that their proprietors ran to their doors to greet us. Of course, we didn't know when or whether the country would recover from the financial devastation the virus brought. At Counterpath in Denver, over forty families were showing up for the foodbank twice a week. In Montrose, we saw no foodbanks, but no families either. It felt like the end of the line.

In August of 1931 a twister tore through Iris and Gard's farm, knocking down trees and destroying sheds. Just before the cyclone came, the air got very still. It was hot, 6:30 p.m. The sky blackened. The wind picked up. Gard and their oldest daughter, Elaine, got into the house, and then "things began to crash, and every crash was harder." Twenty-three trees broke off at the trunk. Anita, their fourteen-year-old, had been trapped in the cellar alone. She came out screaming.

The cyclone and its havoc: a meteorological metaphor for the economic destruction that raged through the country, including the Kem family, in those years. Everyone suffered, and not just financially. Claude's pharmacy slumped when another sawmill shut down; Thelma got very sick and had to take time off school; Myrtle was also ill, so ill she could not work. Alice's eyes clouded with glaucoma; she needed surgery to save them. Then Alice's brother Robert died, and the Kems covered doctor and funeral expenses. Omer suffered numbness down his right side (from "nose to thumb"), and severe pain in his legs kept him bedridden for months. The family entered a maze of lending and borrowing—Claude is in debt to Omer and Alice, Omer borrows from Iris, Kathleen lends money for Thelma's schooling, everyone pledging to pay everyone back with plaintive, shame-filled promises.

But no one suffered more than the Kems' youngest son, Victor, who, having been in the war, was never able to get on his feet. "We sure are broke after paying our bills and making payment on our old debts. Am trying to save $10.00 to buy license for my car but am having a hard time doing it," he wrote, just before Shell Oil laid him off, leaving him jobless for years.[9] "Vic came back and raked the leaves off the yard," writes Omer to Iris. "Time has begun to hang heavily on his hands and he is beginning to realize that about the Hardest job on earth is in doing nothing." "The poor kid is getting it in the neck," she responds.[10] It's after midnight when she writes this. She's been canning all day. She goes to bed, then picks the writing back up in the morning: the price of popcorn, the poor yield of potatoes, the failed businesses in town. How she doesn't like packing celery (she'd lost most of it to heart rot anyway), how she wants to get to the sewing.

"This winter is going to be fierce for millions," writes Omer a few months later.[11]

This winter is going to be fierce for millions.

And of course, it was. By January of 1933 one out of every four working-aged people in the United States was out of work (approximately fifteen million), hundreds of thousands were homeless, including Victor and his wife, who moved from job to job, or more accurately, job search to job search, storing their belongings in a friend's attic, rarely writing home.

But Omer, forever a believer in progress, had a solution for all this suffering, a solution to the scarcity his family and the rest of the country were facing: "There are very pronounced ear marks that indicate strongly that we are tending toward dissolution and that our civilization is doomed to go the way of all civilizations that have gone before," he writes to Iris. "The only thing that will save it is a change in our method of thinking and acting, and the most noted of these, in my judgment, is Birth Control."[12] Birth control, which had for both Omer and Iris's entire reproductive lives been functionally illegal, was the modern bio-techno-political cure for a civilization that was otherwise failing.

On this point, father and daughter fully agree.

Anarchy and Control: The Early Birth Control Movement

The reproductive body, its hormones, organs, fluids, desires, behaviors, its joys and pains—what we do with our mouths, our vaginas, our penises, our anuses, breasts, hands, and arms—with what level of consent or under what duress, with which technologies, in what spaces, and with whom we do these things—how we stroke one another, penetrate one another, suck, lick, or kiss one another, how and where and how often we, some of us, give birth to, carry, and nurse those who grow inside us or grow inside others, how or whether we care for these others, feed them, protect them, or hurt them: all this is political. This is a truism. But what, really, does it mean? For even if, by now, just about everyone knows that the personal, the bodily, is political, we still also hold onto the feeling that what comes upon us as sex or birth, or motherhood or fatherhood, is a world apart from the kinds of powers that decide, for example, who gets to vote, or how to structure the economy, or whether to go to war and against whom. My orgasm, or your orgasm, or my baby or yours, can seem to stand outside of, or to the side of, these overt forms of power. "Always Orgasm," said the revolutionary strikers of Paris, May 1968, as if constant sex could set you free. But couldn't it? If the body itself, like the earth itself, has no preemptive claim on life, then there's truly nothing outside of (racial, patriarchal, and class) power, and this, of course, is intolerable. The history of the American birth control movement, then, like the history of the environmental movement, is the story of this dynamic: the anarchic energy of sex, or life itself, sometimes resisting and sometimes collaborating with and always entangled within the disciplines imposed by power.

Though in Omer and Iris's America—the America of the late nineteenth and early twentieth centuries—the distribution of birth control materials and information was criminalized, this hadn't always been the case. Some women, white married middle- and upper-class women, had always had access to these materials. But in the mid-nineteenth century, as poor rural people, immigrants, Black people, and many unmarried women flocked to cities, such materials were marketed to them also: "Everywhere one looked . . . contraceptive information, ads, and other materials were visible."[13] The industrialization and mass migrations of the postbellum years brought many more married and unmarried women into contact with the commercialization of contraception and the freedom from patriarchal control that it allows.

The inevitable backlash against all these frankly displayed signs of sex was codified in 1873, when "purity" crusader and guilty masturbator Anthony Comstock, though not a legislator, wrote a national "anti-obscenity" bill to criminalize the circulation and sale of such "obscene" information and materials (drugs, gels, diaphragms, condoms).[14] In 1873 teenaged Omer was still digging ditches in the Indiana mud, though his first wife, Nan, was already pregnant with their first baby, a boy named Edwin, who died before turning one. Over the next seven years, Nan would endure four more pregnancies, just about as many as one *can* have in that amount of time. She was either nursing or pregnant or both right up until her death at twenty-nine. It seems that in those years, "obscene" materials, legal or not, had not been available to a poor rural woman like her.

The year of Comstock's crackdown, 1873, was a pivotal year for other reasons as well. Just eight years after the war, and following a panic on the banks, the country faced its first Great Depression. The "panic of 1873," wrote Du Bois, "altered the face of society" by leading to a four-year depression, followed by a consolidation of wealth in the hands of the few and a shift in the labor movement away from interracial class solidarity toward craft-based unionism.[15] In the northern cities, the streets were flush with the jobless poor, while in the Midwest, miners and factory workers faced wage reduction or sat idle. In the South, meanwhile, Reconstruction was attacked by "Redemption," with its swelling waves of anti-Black terror.[16] In Colfax, Louisiana, for example, where Black men had briefly made up the majority of the electorate and the state assembly, a group of white paramilitary terrorists attacked the Black state militia with guns and cannons, killing (or later executing) up to 150 Black men.[17] What Comstock's crackdown on "obscenity" might have had to do with this inflection point in racial capitalism is something I've not seen explored, and I can't explore it here either. But without a doubt, Reconstruction, immigration, and urbanization inspired great fears in white people in the South and North, fears having to do with racial "contamination" and the status of white workers. And racial anxieties, as can be observed in present-day America, seem always to inspire concurrent anxieties about the sexual lives of women.

At any rate, when Comstock presented himself to Congress, senators, whom you'd expect to be preoccupied by more serious dangers, expressed universal feelings of "indignation and disgust" about all materials pertaining to sex and contraception. Thus, the Comstock Act passed easily, with Comstock himself appointed its chief and energetic enforcer.[18] Thousands of people were arrested during the law's first decades.[19]

The dawn of the new century brought a crackdown on free speech from another direction as well. After Leon Czolgosz assassinated President McKinley in 1901, anarchists, socialists, and especially members of the radical wing of the labor movement, the IWW, found themselves frequently thrown in jail for speaking their views in public. In response these same groups waged an intensive defense of the First Amendment in the streets—staging protests, filling jail cells, publishing diatribes. The early birth control movement, which included free-speech, free-love anarchists like Emma Goldman, aligned itself with this truly valiant struggle for freedom, a struggle that led to the arrest and torture of hundreds, if not thousands, of people.[20]

Thus, in the early twentieth century, the worker-led free-speech movement and the woman-led birth control movement emerged almost as one, responding to and resisting the same oppressive and reactionary forces waging war against their voices, their bodies, and their hopes for more just futures.[21]

Margaret Sanger, who was not the birth control movement's only leader, though she was its most visible, was herself early on a labor activist and advocate for the poor. Having grown up poor, she had seen firsthand how lack of birth control destroyed women's lives; her mother had eleven children and died at fifty. The inspiration for Sanger's crusade against "involuntary motherhood" was her experience as a nurse, attending to impoverished immigrant mothers in New York City who were dying prematurely from botched self-inflicted abortions and suffering physically, materially, and psychologically from raising more children than they wanted.

In the early years (around 1912–20), Sanger saw birth control not only as a feminist issue but also as an anti-capitalist strategy, a way to deny the capitalist his abundant and therefore cheap labor pool (she was a member of the Socialist Party until joining the more militant and racially inclusive IWW in 1912).[22] "Scarcity of labor results in good wages for all," she wrote, and better-paid workers are better equipped to assess and resist exploitation.[23] "No plagues, famines or wars could ever frighten the capitalist class so much as the universal practice of the prevention of conception."[24] In this she was aligned with Emma Goldman, who put it this way: "Who would create wealth? Who would make the policeman, the jailer, if women were to refuse the indiscriminate breeding of children?"[25] Before, during, and after World War I, Sanger and her comrades presented birth control as anti-war and anti-imperialist as well: with fewer babies made, fewer soldiers would be available for battle.[26]

In 1914 Sanger began to publish the *Woman Rebel*, an "anti-capitalist soap box oratory" as she called it, from her Greenwich Village apartment.[27] "The aim of this paper will be to stimulate working women to think for themselves," she announced.[28] NO GODS NO MASTERS, the anarchist slogan dating back to the 1880s, blazed just under the journal's title. In each issue, she reprinted the preamble to the IWW's constitution: "The working class and the employing class have nothing in common. There can be no peace so long as hunger and want are found among millions of the working people and the few, who make up the employing class, have all the good things of life. Between these two classes a struggle must go on until the workers of the world organize as a class, take possession of the means of production, abolish the wage system, and live in harmony with the Earth."

Why did she launch the *Woman Rebel*? She answered the question herself on the first page of the first issue:

> Because I believe in the offspring of the immigrant, the great majority of whom make up the unorganized working class to-day.
>
> Because I believe that this immigrant with a vision, an ideal of a new world where liberty, freedom, kindness, plenty hold sway, who had courage to leave the certain old for the uncertain new to face a strange new people, new habits, a strange language, for this vision, this ideal, certainly has brought to this country a wholesome spirit of unrest which this generation of Americans has lost through a few generations of prosperity and respectability.
>
> Because I believe that on the courage, vision and idealism of the immigrant and the offspring does the industrial revolution depend.
>
> Because I believe that through the efforts of the industrial revolution will woman's freedom emerge.[29]

Immigrant workers and their children were the key to anti-capitalist revolution, which was itself the foundation for women's full liberation. But only if freed from compulsory motherhood could immigrant women find and wield their power. Birth control was the first step in transforming the world.

Militantly anti-capitalist, pro-worker, pro-immigrant, pro-woman, and sex-positive, Sanger took the latter positions into further action when she wrote and published her pamphlet, *Family Limitation*, also in 1914. The pamphlet offered enough direct contraceptive advice to send her into a two-year exile in England and land her husband in jail for distributing it. *Family Limitation* was "dangerous" not only because it informed women all over America, and far beyond, about contraception (it was translated into more than a dozen languages) but also because it was explicit about sex itself. She cautions against the withdrawal method, for example, because of how it makes women's orgasms unlikely. And women who have sex without orgasm, implies Sanger, are essentially prostituted by their husbands. Condoms, she says, can be useful here, since they tend to delay male orgasm—not

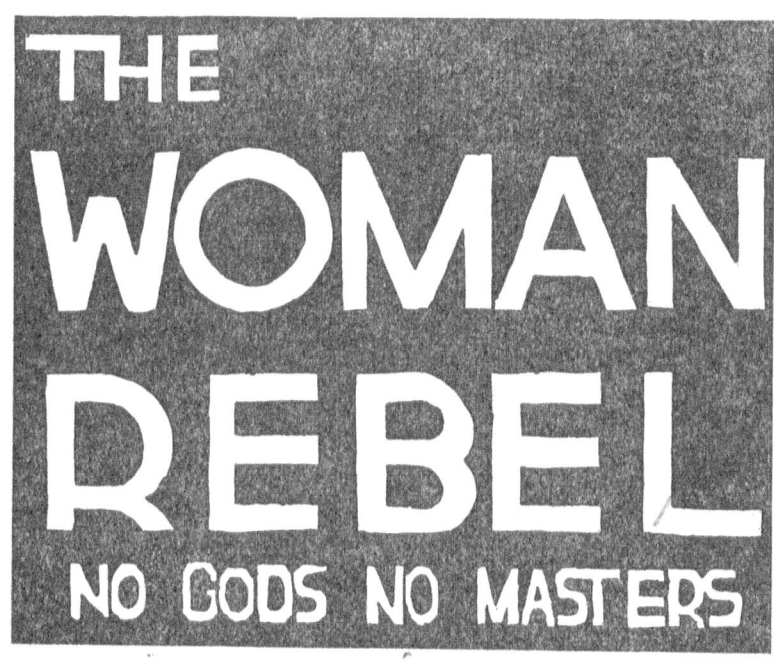

17. Front page of the *Woman Rebel*, March 1914.

the sort of advice generally circulated in 1914. "Nothing as practical and as revolutionary in its capacity to transform women's lives had been so widely circulated in the United States or anywhere in the world," writes one historian.[30] After its initial printing of one hundred thousand copies, the pamphlet went through eighteen printings in the United States alone. Each edition encouraged its readers to copy it by hand and pass it on, so there is no way to know how far it really spread.[31]

In September of 1919, through her third publishing venture, the *Birth Control Review*, Sanger extended her vision for the liberation of immigrant and poor white women to center Black women as well. The first of three special issues on Black women and birth control was titled "The New Emancipation: The Negro's Need for Birth Control, as Seen by Themselves."[32] The issue includes a one-act play by Harlem Renaissance playwright Mary Burrill in which a Black mother of eight dies from overwork, a note of endorsement and short poem from Du Bois, and an interview with Black socialist, economist, and cofounder of the *Messenger*, Chandler Owen. Owen, like Sanger at this time, saw birth control as a mode of resistance to capitalist exploitation, though Owen emphasized the particular experiences of Black women who were facing an epidemic of rape by white "masters" in peonage camps. "On the military field, a surplus of men is needed for soldiers, on the industrial field, laborers are wanted. . . . During slave days, Negro women often had as many as 20 or 25 children. . . . Even today, Negro girls have large numbers of children—forced by their masters in peonage camps in the South."[33]

"I firmly believe in birth control," wrote Du Bois in the BCR.[34] Three years later, in his own magazine, he embellished his position. In a 1922 editorial published in the *Crisis*, Du Bois calls for sensible birth control as remedy for the "crime" of high Black infant mortality rates: "Birth control is science and sense applied to the bringing of children into the world, and of all who need it we Negroes are first."[35] Systemic racism in housing, employment, and health care meant that the infant mortality rate for Blacks was twice that for whites in the 1920s.[36] (In the United States now, and for the same reasons, the Black infant mortality rate is *more than double* that of white infants: 11.4 per thousand births vs. 4.9.)[37] Du Bois believed, as did Sanger, that fewer babies meant healthier babies.

Other Black leaders and groups, Marcus Garvey and the UNIA most prominently, saw birth control as a genocidal tool. "It is unfortunate, if true, that any Negro should practice Mrs. Sanger's project. If the white people are not satisfied about the millions they slaughtered in the last war, they should confine their birth control to themselves," wrote one UNIA member in 1925.[38] But for Du Bois, Owen, Burrill, and others, birth control was a strategy of resistance to the brutal abuses of Black women's fertility.

And yet, as is now commonly known and often decried, in around 1920 Sanger shifted her movement away from its radical roots. Under her leadership, the movement began to align itself instead with the growing eugenics movement and its anti-immigrant, racist, ablest, and classist ideology (of which much more will be said in the next chapter).[39] In her 1919 essay "Birth Control and Race Betterment" (and here, *race* refers to the human race, not to any particular racialized group), Sanger announced herself in favor of the voluntary sterilization of the "feeble-minded, the insane, and the syphilitic"— all conditions thought to be hereditary.[40] In 1920 she organized the first American Birth Control Conference in New York to purposely follow directly after the Second International Conference of Eugenics, hosted by eugenicists Fairfield Osborn and Madison Grant, author of the stupendously fascistic *The Passing of the Great Race*.[41] (Notably, Sanger's conference, unlike the conference organized by Osborn and Grant, was violently raided by the police and shut down on its second night; Sanger and another woman were dragged off while the crowd of mostly women sang "America (My Country 'Tis of Thee)" in protest.[42] As we see so often, subjugated people demanding bodily sovereignty are considered more dangerous than those who announce their intention to control, even eliminate, others.) Alongside her own first voicings of eugenic ideas, Sanger also made space in the *Birth Control Review* for leading voices in the eugenics movement, some of whom, like Paul Popenoe, Havelock Ellis, and Guy Irving Burch, advanced venomously racist and nativist beliefs and policies.[43]

But clearly Sanger herself was conflicted. Her 1922 book, *The Pivot of Civilization*, reveals this conflict as it swings wildly from a rejection of eugenics as ethically wrong to full-throated endorsements of eugenic principles and back again. Early on in its pages, Sanger asserts that birth control "is not aiming to interfere in the private lives of poor people, to tell them how many children they should have, nor to sit in judgment upon their fitness to become parents." She rejects eugenic *laws* because, as she writes, all women's fertility decisions "must come from within," and she warns that "an idealistic code of sexual ethics, imposed from above . . . can never be of the slightest value in effecting change in the customs of the people."[44] Toward the book's end, she calls out the massive ethical problem at the heart of eugenics: "We should here recognize the difficulties presented by the idea of 'fit' and 'unfit.' Who is to decide this question?" Efforts to "breed" for "fitness" would risk weeding out radicals and geniuses, she argues, such as (her list) Nietzsche, Dostoevsky, Poe, and Schumann.[45]

On the other hand, in the book's middle, Sanger tells us that the solution to "the great problem of the feeble-minded" is "to prevent the birth of those who would transmit imbecility to their descendants." For support, she quotes the racist eugenicist Charles Davenport as he complains that "the feeble-minded" are too "protected from mortality." Feeble-minded women's "always numerous progeny," Sanger writes a page later, "run the gamut of police, alms-houses, courts, penal institutions, 'charities and corrections,' tramp shelters, [and] lying-in hospitals." One of her key examples of a "feeble-minded" mother is a Black woman from Kansas whose sixteen children all had trouble with the law, one way or another. The implication is, of course, that none of these children should have been born.[46]

Then in 1934, as the compulsory sterilization law of Nazi Germany was coming into action and as similar laws were being debated across Europe, Sanger put out a press release on the issue. Rather than denouncing the Nazi law, she concurred that mentally disabled people, some who were deemed "insane," and those with certain inheritable diseases should consent to be sterilized.[47]

Perhaps, as many scholars have argued, in the throes of her single-minded vision, it made strategic sense to embrace these "progressive" ideas, which in 1920 were becoming mainstream.[48] Or perhaps the betrayal of her movement's early radicalism was simply a matter of survival. By 1919 the Red Scare was clamping down on political radicals of all types. Her early allies—Chandler Owen, Eugene Debs, Elizabeth Gurley Flynn, Bill Haywood, and Emma Goldman—had all been arrested or deported, and many of their publications banned.[49] But whatever the reasons, the disappointment remains and is bitter.

I got a little obsessed with the young Sanger, I admit. I wanted her to somehow survive her later self. But that's not really how it works. And if I had hoped that the birth control movement's anarchic origins had been as attractive to Omer and Iris as they were to me, I would be disappointed again. By the time father and daughter were avidly discussing the project of birth control in the 1920s, it was fully "grafted" to the eugenics movement.[50] Indeed, had it still been associated with anarchism or socialism, they would never have embraced it.

The (White) Reproductive Body as the New Frontier

Iris's advocacy for birth control can best be found in two speeches she gave to the Olathe Women's Club in 1924 and 1925, just around the time that Sanger was establishing the country's first long-term birth control clinic, Birth Control Clinical Research Bureau, in New York City. In the first of these speeches, "Birth Control as I See It," Iris's opening sentence is telling: "My purpose in coming before you today to discuss this question is not because I believe you, as individuals, are in particular need of birth control."[51] Rather, she goes on to explain, birth control is a matter for *other* women—poor women, immigrant women, urban women—a way of "doing away with misery and crime" through "controlling the birthrate" of the poor.

Iris gathers professional support by naming a series of male doctors, including some from Montrose, who support legalizing contraception, "reliable persons" all. Iris's final point pertains directly to the West, the frontier that once functioned as a "safety valve" for what Omer (and many others) called "surplus populations": "There are no more vast unoccupied territories to send our young men to," she observes. While once we might have been able to send them off to colonies, like Britain had done, these colonies are also rapidly filling up, as was the rest of the non-Western world: "China is terribly overcrowded, so is Japan, India is even more so." What's more, Iris goes on, in these countries, people are not dying of famine and disease like they used to. "These countries are now learning how to take care of their babies and cure their sick. India is saving thousands who died before." Faced with all this excessive life, there is only one answer: birth control.[52]

A year later, in another speech to the same body of women, Iris goes beyond this neo-Malthusian argument. "Pioneer Life in Olathe as Seen by the Coreys" is a mostly nostalgic talk, in which she traces the early experiences of both the Kem and the Corey families after their arrival to the Uncompahgre valley. When she was a child, she tells her listeners, she and her siblings would play "Indian": "Our play was always most realistic because we found so many evidences of former Indian occupation" (here she complicates her earlier depiction of "vast unoccupied territories"). As an adult, Iris did some research—mostly talking to old-timers—to better understand the pattern of dispossession she and her family took part in. Perhaps surprisingly, Iris describes the events leading up to Ute removal in much the way that I did in the previous chapter: "Because of the Meeker massacre at White River and other minor troubles the whites in Colorado became incensed at the Indians, and also being covetous of the fertile lands they occupied brought about their removal, which was accomplished by another treaty in 1880, by which the Indians ceded this land away, believing they were to have other land near Grand Junction. Instead they were taken to Utah Territory, where they didn't want to go."[53]

Like Omer in his congressional speeches from the 1890s, Iris makes clear how Indian removal was forced and coerced, how under threat of military attack the Utes were driven out by "incensed" white settlers who simply wanted their land. As the speech continues, Iris emphasizes her gender-based empathy with Ute women: "This must have been a sad Journey, as sad as the departure of the Arcadians. This had been their home and they were certainly exiles. Chipeta, Ouray's wife, must have been near heartbroken at leaving her home [when] so short a time before [she'd been] made desolate by the death of her famous husband."

And yet despite this sad journey, this heartbreak, Ute removal makes a space that is quickly filled: "The morning after the departure of the Utes, came the rush of settlers to occupy the land," she acknowledges.[54]

These first settlers include Iris's in-laws, the Coreys, and then, sixteen years later, the Kems. After admitting to this opportunistic land grab, Iris shifts gears to describe some of the difficult challenges the early settlers faced. For twenty-two paragraphs, she details their clothing, their food production, and their struggles to develop transportation and education. And then, at the very end of her speech, Iris takes a rather abrupt turn, as if she's just then remembered that she is speaking to women, that she has a message particular to them:

Those women suffered hard-ships and achieved many things, but we women of today have hard things to do and much to conquer if we would leave the world a better place than when we came into it. We have the vote, which our pioneer mothers didn't have, and with it we can do much if we will. Assisting at the birth of new babies can safely be left to the doctors of today, but who dare say that it shouldn't be in the hands of women to say what kind of babies shall be born and when they shall be born. May women soon awake to their opportunities and use them for the betterment of the race.

In his mind-opening book *The End of the Myth: From the Frontier to the Border Wall in the Mind of America* (2018), Greg Grandin argues that the frontier didn't "close" with the Wounded Knee Massacre in 1890 or with white settlement in Oklahoma, as the Census Bureau, and then Frederick Jackson Turner, had made doctrine. Rather, the "expansionist imperative" kept America moving far beyond its physical borders into the twentieth and twenty-first centuries. Ballooning imperialist projects echo and reignite the logic of early America's wars of western expansion. From the Spanish American War in 1898 to early twentieth-century occupations in Latin America and the Caribbean, from the First World War, the Korean War, and Vietnam to the so-called war on terror—all this functions much the way the western frontier did: uniting (certain) Americans under a shared aggressive ideology. The "spread of democracy" justifies all these wars, just as the "spread of civilization" justified Indian genocide and the annexation of Mexico. But while aggression is spun as progress, Grandin argues, "the promise of boundlessness" keeps us forever distracted from the racism and inequality that has always given the lie to the mission.[55] (Until now, that is. Grandin's thesis is that Trump's border wall and the explosion of white supremacy and corresponding rise of anti-racism in our public discourse are signs that the frontier myth might finally be dying. His book predates the U.S. withdrawal from Afghanistan, but this event adds evidence to his thesis.)

Grandin's argument is powerful, and everyone should read his book. But there is yet another frontier in America that he doesn't mention, one that can never close: the white woman's reproductive body. Iris's narrative of the pioneer woman's journey is one of progress, despite the "sad" story of Indian dispossession and genocide that made that progress possible. Through white women's struggles, lands have been cultivated, children educated, and democracy expanded. And now, says Iris, there are other lands to "conquer." No modest proposal, Iris tasks "we women" with the role of curating the human race itself.[56]

White women (and she is explicitly speaking to white women here), are uniquely and newly positioned to be the arbiters—through the vote—of the awesome power of reproduction. For Iris's generation, women are no longer just breeders; they are now also deciders. And as white women decide "what kind of babies shall be born and when they shall be born," we make the world, the whole wide world, "better."

Toward the end of her earlier speech, Irish unleashes the truly supremacist nature of her passion. "If we can make laws to exclude undesirable people from the shores of our country," she reasons, "can we not make laws excluding the undesirable among the unborn?"[57] Who are these "undesirables"? They are the many children of impoverished mothers, the "poor little disgusting mites who have just 'growed' and whose influence is a menace to all other children."[58]

It was just a joke, of course, an attempt to spice her warnings, as Omer so often did, with a laugh. And yet humor is often the repository for undercurrents of anxiety and violence, especially of the racist category. Iris's joke is not very funny, but it does beg a question, one we can direct both to 1924 and to 2022. As reproductive justice is so unevenly distributed across race, citizenship, and class, who, really, is being menaced, and by whom?

Love and Violence

> Love's full of uncorrected error.
> —C. S. Giscombe, "Two Directions"

I started having sex at sixteen; not that young, but way too young to be a mother. I didn't know that much about Sanger during the years when I carried my diaphragm in my backpack, kept condoms in my pockets, but I knew enough to be grateful.[59] History didn't really start, in my mind back then, until women had been freed from constant breeding.

Omer and Iris admired Sanger, and I've wanted to keep admiring her too. It wasn't only that Sanger had fought so hard and so endlessly for the reproductive and sexual freedoms of people like me; it was that she started out with such a powerful vision of freedom for *all* people. In 1913 Sanger envisioned "a new society . . . a new psychology, new literature, new art," where "all symbols of . . . slavery" would be relegated to the "junk heap."[60] Her faith in the transformative power of women-led social movements is a gift. But how do we accept gifts from the mothers who disappoint us, or even from those who terrify us? Or more fundamentally, what is love and how much can it hold?

I wanted to write about Omer's daughters not because I needed to honor them but because I needed to understand them and thereby better understand myself. Above all, I needed to understand one thing: how their struggles *as white women*—their efforts to liberate their gender, to secure the vote, to win reproductive freedom, education, and economic independence—how all these struggles were tied up with their racism. They had failed, we had failed, I had failed to understand and help generate justice even within our righteous struggles *for* justice, for so often, it was the position we claim as women, as mothers, that allowed us to wield the cruelty of our imagined superiority. When I was writing this chapter, I had a dream in which I was screaming at another white woman in the alley—but I was both of these women.

When I woke up from that dream, I held it in my body for a long time, thinking about violence and about love, and especially about motherhood—how in a society scarred by inequalities and antagonisms, that most "selfless" love can readily become an occasion for the brutality of disregard, neglect, or even active harm, not necessarily of one's own children (though sometimes that) but of other people's children. Women—and white women most of all—play hard at the brutal biopolitical game in which some children are protected and supported and others are underfed, unhoused, and exposed to violence and imprisonment. How selfless, really, is our love?

I could just forget about Sanger, erase her name and with it, Iris's name too. But in the end, it's not enough—or it's not right—to leave wounds festering unattended. And anyway, I hadn't anticipated longing. "Love them through their loves," my friend had said, suggesting that even while my ancestors disappointed or even enraged me, as I learned how they had loved each other, my heart would soften. And that has proved a little true.

And so, allow me to dwell just a bit longer on the central fact that draws me to Iris: her love for her father in a precarious time. Throughout 1930 and '31, with Omer often bedridden and falling into debt, they wrote to each other about once a month. When he was up, he was too weak to even mow the lawn, as he lamented, but he could write from bed with a pencil, and on better days, he could use his typewriter for short spurts. Iris's intense activity stands in contrast to Omer's lethargy: she's making sausage, or she's sewing dresses, or she's hauling rocks, or she's selling cabbage.

But despite her good marriage, her four daughters, and all her frenetic activity, Iris's loneliness is keen. She misses her father and her siblings (rarely, it seems, does she miss her mother); she's not there for the wedding, the birthday, Mother's Day, Thanksgiving. "I wish I might live across the way again. It is so far even when one has the money with which to go." "I see you had another birthday, Papa, about a week ago Sunday. I thot of writing you then but something prevented. Am wondering how you all are, all of you so close and me so far away."

So many of her sentences open with a sigh: "Well, I suppose the next big event will be Xmas"; "Well, I suppose Marie and Vic's baby is due"; "Well I suppose Julian is married now"; "Well, this isn't much of a letter"; "Well, good night and love to you all." Well. A strange and melancholic word. She uses it as a breath, a hesitation before giving in to the longing. She can't really know what's happening to her kin, and she's never really reaching them, despite all her efforts in letters.

"I see the fates have decreed that you be the isolated one," Omer offers by way of sympathy.[61]

Though it would be twelve years until Omer finally dies, in 1930, when he is quite ill, father and daughter attempt to prepare. "I'm going to ask you now what I probably wouldn't ask you if I could talk to you," writes Iris in December of that year:

> If you should go over into the unknown spirit realm, before I do, if you won't try to communicate with me some way. . . . You speak (to quote from your letter) of feeling that it isn't going to be long before you slip your earthly cable and saying that, knowing death to be inevitable, you are approaching it in the same spirit as a pioneer does in approaching a new country with the added incentive of finding old and long unseen friends there. . . . But . . . I can only see the rest of us standing on the shore with hands outstretched watching you go out of sight and hearing of this earthly life. So, if you can make yourself known to any of us or to me, it will help take the place of the letters you can't be writing any more.

For Iris, the request for afterlife contact is a long shot, but at least she thinks it worth making. She's not mediumistic, has had no prior contact with the dead, but she doesn't believe in heaven, so what else can she hope for? And then she tries to calm herself, to remind herself that the day of Omer's passing has not yet arrived, may not arrive anytime soon: "But you are still here . . . so I won't borrow trouble. . . . I am coming home before long to see you all . . . and when you do pass on I am going to try to believe that your hand is going to be on mine helping me to guide my plow and I hope to be a little better for it, as I believe I have been in the past and am now, from your example and guidance."[62]

I came upon this letter during the second month of the stay-at-home order in Colorado. My own father was eighty-four and two thousand miles away. I knew, as all children of elderly parents knew at that time, that it was possible I would not see him again.[63] Of course, this was always possible, but now it was possible in a new and sharper way. Those who were dying of the disease were dying alone, attended by only health-care workers in full protective gear.

These were not gentle deaths. As I read Iris's words, a sob rose in me. I stopped reading and looked away. But Iris was beseeching me not to turn away, to look at death, the inevitability, head on, which I, and everyone, needed to do.

Iris dreamed of an America in which her children were freed from the "menace" of the "disgusting mites" of others, and I can't forgive her even as I can't not love her. That is the complicated truth that I can express in no other way. Omer didn't teach me how to grieve when Linda died. But Iris *was* teaching me how, even before my father died, even before he was born. The ancestors demand that we love with courage. Love is sorrow and love is healing. *Tikkun olam.*

7 Blood

> Everyone should be free, cause if we ain't we're murderous.
> —Nina Simone, 1976

Party, 1925

"I was that girl," my friend Ruth said after I told her about Mary Kem's seventh birthday party and the one girl who was not invited. We were sitting in a little restaurant near our place of work when she said this. Ruth is Black and biracial and grew up in a white community in the 1970s and '80s. One day we will write something together about our childhoods, we promise—we keep promising. It's in part because she said this, said, "I was that girl," that I keep returning to Mary's party, as if I could somehow shift the story by telling it over again.

But Mary's seventh birthday party is of course only a very minor example of the segregationist fury that gripped white America in the 1920s.[1] This party, where children ate cake and presented evidence of their parents' relative wealth, in which a mother and a father in the small city of Cincinnati were congratulated for their reproductive success while another family down the road was given to understand their unworthiness, was surrounded by countless other cruelties, many of them violent, all of them designed, as this one was, to protect and promote a narrow and increasingly threatened idea of whiteness.[2]

It was one year after Congress passed the most racially restrictive immigration law in U.S. history, one year after the militarization of the southern border. In the aftershocks of Red Summer (1919), when throughout the country—Maine, Georgia, California, Missouri, Texas, Nebraska, Florida, New York, DC—anti-Black violence had run wild, whiteness was on lockdown.[3] Not that the rampages had ended. The

Tulsa Massacre, in which white people murdered hundreds of Black people in a single night, was in 1921. Closer to the party, and just a few months before it, seven hundred Black laborers at the Dix Dam construction site had been driven off in the dark of night by a mob of white workers, many of the Black men shot or beaten, their entire neighborhood, "Shacktown," destroyed.[4]

What happened at the birthday party thrown by Huxley and Happie Kem for their seven-year-old daughter might seem worlds apart from such overwhelming mob violence, but small and large acts of brutality reinforce one another, relying as they do on the same exclusionary logic. ("Every form of dominance signals [a] lethal conclusion," writes Judith Butler.)[5] What must be noted, therefore, is less the cruelty surrounding the party, since such cruelty was commonplace, and more the reasoning through which both father and son justify humiliating a small child. The one girl not invited was perceived by the Kems to be dangerous.[6]

In his letter to Huxley about the party, Kem senior puts it this way:

> It's a sad thing for both races, when the whites and blacks are mixed. The greatest mistake that was made as a result of the civil war, is that the races were not segregated then. . . . The times coming that, when a white couple get married, they will not know for sure, whether their children will be white, black, ringed, streaked, striped or spotted.
>
> Take the little girl you speak of as an illustration, she seemingly, is white, and where she is not known, would pass for white without question. Her mother is white, her father a mulatto, and yet, if she marries a white man, some of her children may be as black as the ace of spades, which shows that the old southerner was right when he said that "one drop of negro blood contaminates the whole." We have not come to the real grief yet as a result of freeing the slaves without providing a safeguard.[7]

A safeguard. Omer had bragged about his abolitionist ancestors who had been active in the Underground Railroad. His "political heroes," the only politicians who wrote him letters from beyond the grave, were Abe Lincoln and Radical Republican Benjamin Wade. Clearly, Kem's pride in these heroes, as far as it went, did not rest on any convictions about the humanity of Black people.[8] Rather, as we can see in his joke about "white, black, ringed, streaked, striped, or spotted" children, he tied Blackness with extreme otherness—with animals. "An arrogant Negro is an animal without sense or reason," Huxley had written, and was not, by his father, contradicted. A kind of terror about the instability of race requires a firm line, not just between racial groups but around the category of "the human," which, for these people, was indivisible from whiteness. For both men, Blackness is a biological threat, and "black blood" is an astonishingly resistant contagion. The "disease" that Blackness carries is the disease of no longer being a person.

Thus, when Omer Kem was in his fifties, and for the remaining three decades of his life, he became nearly obsessed with the dangers of blood mixing—the problem, and the promise, of genetics. Over and over, in letters to family, friends, and newspapers, Omer promoted firm racial segregation and a eugenic program aimed at first defining, and then "weeding out," an ever-increasing list of subhuman types: the idiot, the imbecile, the feebleminded, the moron, the criminal.[9]

Eugenics—most simply the science of better breeding as applied to humans—was embraced by scientists, academics, physicians, criminologists, politicians, welfare professionals, and ordinary people all across the United States from around 1907, when the first eugenic sterilization law was passed in Indiana, to around the mid-1930s. Believing that controlled breeding could promote healthier babies and fitter (smarter, more moral) genetic strains in the population, eugenicists advocated a range of practices and policies, from birth control to marriage laws, from the institutionalization of the physically and mentally disabled to severe immigration restriction, to, finally, the elimination of "undesirable" people through the forced sterilization of those deemed dysgenic. As a prime aspect of biopower, eugenics sought to steady racial, class, and gendered hierarchies by at once controlling sexuality and pathologizing racial and sexual minorities, disabled people, and the poor.[10]

In Oregon, where the Kems lived, after a prolonged back and forth, a surgical sterilization bill was signed into law by Governor Withycombe in 1917 (it was deemed unconstitutional in 1921 but was adjusted and reinstated two years later). Dr. R. E. Lee Steiner, superintendent of the state hospital in Salem, where most of the state's early sterilizations occurred, reported having sterilized sixteen people by 1918: "All of the 12 males who were operated upon in his institution were castrated. In all four female cases the ovaries were removed. All of the 16 cases, both males and females, were flagrant masturbators or sex perverts," writes lead eugenicist Harry Laughlin. A few years later, the pace picked up and Steiner reported "no untoward or unfavorable results" from the "great many" operations performed.[11] While the state's early victims were mostly men, the progressive physician Bethenia Owens-Adair, Oregon's most avid eugenics crusader, offers the following descriptions of "feeble-minded girls who have become pregnant" and who should, in her opinion, be sterilized:

> Mary—About 30 years old . . . cannot learn to read or write. Has 1 child, a girl, now ten.
> Angie—Her child was a monstrosity. . . . Was a ward of the Boys and Girls society, was put out to work, and became pregnant.
> Velma—Velma is a most repulsive degenerate.
> Ella—Feeble-minded, staggering gate. . . . Her brother was the father of the child.
> Paulina—16 years. . . . Sweet, loveable disposition. . . . Her mother was a working woman.
> Etoila—16 years old, incorrigible. Sexual perversions of the worst type.
> Bertha—"Mentally dull." . . . Her uncle was the father of her children.
> Laura M.— . . . Was put in the family home of a man with three children to do the work and became pregnant there.[12]

Like Owens-Adair herself once was, these girls and women are poor, illiterate, and abused. Nonetheless, she views them as a poison and believes sterilization to be "the only means by which to purify the river of life."[13] In 1911 a Kansas doctor with a similar philosophy described the physical effects of sterilization on the women under his care: "One girl has become obese. Menstruation ceased in all cases with atrophy of uterus. . . . Breast atrophy noted in all cases. All desire for sexual intercourse and, all erotic fancies apparently removed. . . . Skin more fair."[14]

Skin more fair—a seemingly uncalled for side effect—takes its place alongside the de-sexing of the mind and body as motive-cause of the eugenical project writ large.

By 1942, when Omer Kem died, thirty-two states had sexual sterilization bills on their books, for the constitutionality of the practice had been settled by the 1927 Supreme Court decision in *Buck v. Bell* ("Persons are undone in the sanctity of the courtroom," writes Colin Dayan).[15] The practice slowed once the Nazi eugenics program came to light, but it did not stop. In 1945 American physicians had forcibly sterilized approximately 38,000 people; by 1980 that number had nearly doubled.[16] Oregon did not abolish its Eugenics Board until 1983, at which point the state had sterilized at least 2,500 people designated as "insane," "habitual criminals," "moral perverts," or "sexual deviants." Sterilization abuse continues today; in California, Tennessee, and elsewhere, prisoners have been sterilized without their consent or coerced into sterilization in exchange for release as recently as 2017. In 2020 a whistleblower revealed that detainees in a privately operated detention center in Georgia were being sterilized without their knowledge or consent.[17]

And while eugenics in the United States did not single people out specifically by race, as we see in Kem's reasoning about his granddaughter's birthday party, eugenics and racism were indivisible. It's not only that the leading eugenicists also happened to be aggressive white supremacists or only that coerced and compulsory sterilization tended to target people of color; it's that vigilant racial segregation—including racist immigration restriction—was justified by eugenics.[18]

A party to which you must be *invited* and to which you can thus be *excluded*, a party in which life itself is the celebrant and class and race the measure of life's success is one way to describe white America in 1925. The party's theme was purity, and like all things supposedly pure, it was only precariously so. For only an insecure and always already violated identity could require such strict protections.

They kept the little girl out of the party not because they didn't like her, and not even because she looked different from the rest, but because her blood was "contaminated" and could therefore, in some slippery slope of racial mixing, spoil their own "pure" blood. In another way of putting it, racial segregation *was and is* eugenics.

I didn't fully enter the eugenic dreams of my great-grandfather until my third visit to the archive in the summer of 2017. Bea, a student from that spring's poetry workshop, accompanied me to Omaha, where the then still undigitized archives were housed. She would explore the city, take pictures, while I read. Bea had gone out to search for the nearly fifty-year-old Great Plains Black History Museum, which, it turned out, was located at that time in boxes stored in a nearly abandoned mall.[19] I stayed behind in the reading room, where the abhorrent language of "fit" and "unfit," of "race purity," "contamination," and "race suicide" rose up from Omer's hand-typed lines. I texted my husband: "He was a eugenicist." "They were all eugenicists then," he texted back, a response that only prompted further questions.

But that day I could read very little. Feeling dizzy and nauseous, I put my head down on the desk, waiting for Bea. When she finally returned with her disappointing report, I said, "Let's go. Let's find something to do."

Populist Eugenics
In 1911, when Kem first began entertaining eugenic ideas, Alice Kem had just given birth to her eighth child (Omer's thirteenth)—my great-aunt Thelma. The family had been living in Cottage Grove, Oregon, for three years, where Omer and his son-in-law, Charles Shinn, were quickly expanding their electric company. As new members of the community, the Kems were invited to attend the local Methodist church. In declining this invitation, Omer wrote a lengthy letter to Reverend Robert Sutcliffe.

As always when discussing Christianity, Omer was scathing. Though he was a firm believer in the presence of spirits, a believer therefore in "immortal life," he found the notion of an all-powerful God to be ridiculous, if not offensive. "No one thing has caused so much crime, misery, tears and suffering, both physical and mental . . . as religion," he once wrote.[20] I don't know what Alice felt about Sutcliffe's invitation or about the church in general, because Omer never tells me. I don't know much about Alice at all. She is mentioned so briefly, and almost none of her writing is recorded. Her physical body, except in that it gave birth to eight children and suffered some accidents and illnesses, is nearly, in Omer's autobiography, erased. So are her politics and her religion if she had one.

Omer's opinions, however, are both clear and forceful. Responding to the Christian concept of being "born again," Omer declares, "Let the battle cry of the church be 'Ye must be born right' instead of 'Ye must be born again.' One born right cannot well go wrong and one born wrong cannot well go right, and, just so long as we continue our present methods of reproducing our kind, just so long will we continue to increase the facilities of our alms houses, our jails, lunatic asylums and penitentiaries."[21] Omer explains that morality, such as the church claimed to promote, was not teachable: "Morality cannot be taught the moral idiot any more than sense can be given the mental idiot; yet moral idiots are being born every day, and no steps taken to prevent it."[22] The church was wasting its time trying to achieve what could only be managed through science and law.

It was a little early in 1911 for a non-specialist like my great-grandfather to be drawn toward eugenic theory. Before that year only four states had eugenic sterilization laws on the books: Indiana, California, Washington, and Connecticut. The wave of popular support was just getting going—"better babies" contests didn't really take off until 1913, for example.[23]

As a Populist in Congress, Kem had once argued that a man "with a family of ten . . . struggling to feed, clothe, and educate his children" deserves governmental support, paid for by taxes on the rich.[24] Now, just over ten years later, he clearly sees poverty as a function not of bad policy but of bad genes. While in one sense, Kem's shift in thinking simply follows Progressive Era scientific trends, the eagerness with which he grabs hold of bio-fatalism prompts me to ask whether his

Blood 165

Populist past, despite its egalitarian principles, had in particular ways prepared him to ever-more precisely partition "the human" into categories of relative worth.[25]

The first documented case of compulsory sterilization in a U.S. institution was not in Indiana, as is often thought, but in Kansas—a hotbed of Populism. In 1893, at the peak of the Populist uprising, Dr. F. Hoyt Pilcher, the Populist director of the Kansas State Home for the Feeble-Minded, cut off the testicles of forty-four young men and performed hysterectomies on fourteen women to control their masturbation and other sexual activities.[26] Though the surgeries were illegal, Pilcher had the support of Kansas's Populist governor, Lorenzo Lewelling (like Kem, the grandson of abolitionist Quakers). Public outcry against the sterilizations cost Lewelling and Pilcher their jobs, but just two years later, with the election of another Populist governor, John Leedy, Pilcher was reinstated.[27]

As historian Mark Largent has shown, in the 1890s eugenic thinking was running through the medical and criminological literature in other Populist strongholds as well: "There is as much evidence to prove that vice and crime are hereditary as there is to prove any disease to be so," writes one Nebraska doctor advocating for castration in 1894.[28] In a meeting of medical doctors in Colorado, there was general agreement that castrating criminals "would benefit society because there would thereafter 'be no further propagation of [their] kind.'"[29] Another Kansas doctor in 1897 called for the "asexualization of criminals and defectives" to prevent the "over-production" of such people.

Of course, as Largent points out, "judges, juries, medical authorities, and vigilantes" hadn't exactly needed legal or institutional approval to perform castration as punishment and/or eugenic "solution" against certain men accused of rape.[30] Castration—often referred to simply as "mutilation"—was a common component of "lynchcraft," and "rape" a common excuse for it.[31] In fact, one could say, as Largent implies, that the lynching epidemic that followed Reconstruction and ran right through the first few decades of the twentieth century provided an ongoing model for the compulsory sterilization of "undesirables" throughout the nation.[32]

Whether Omer was exposed to these ideas through the medical and criminological literature of his region (and from his archive, I can't tell), when he and ten other Populists entered Congress in 1892, they found hereditary arguments dominating another biopolitical sphere: immigration. And here it seems clear that the Populists, despite their loud promotion of fairness and equality, found such ideas compelling.[33]

The Blood of America

> The success of democracy depends upon the quality of its individual elements. If in these elements the racial values are high, government will be equal to all the economic, educational, religious and scientific demands of the times. If, on the contrary, there is a constant and progressive racial degeneracy, it is only a question of time when popular self-government will be impossible, and will be succeeded by chaos, and finally a dictatorship.
> —Harry Laughlin, 1922

> Why do we want all these people from shithole countries coming here?
> —Donald Trump, 2018

By the 1920s the perceived threat to white American purity seemed to flow from all directions, including from overseas. With the passage of the 1924 National Origins Act (also called the Johnson-Reed Act) influential eugenicists achieved a long-sought goal: limiting such "pollution" by prohibiting the entrance of those deemed racially unassimilable or undesirable to the national body. Prostitutes, beggars, epileptics, alcoholics, the insane, the "feebleminded," political radicals, and even the illiterate had already been barred from entry by 1917; what made the 1924 bill different from earlier twentieth-century law is that at the peak of eugenics' popularity, it openly delineated "dysgenic" populations by "blood or race" rather than individualized characteristics or traits.[34]

However, long before this date, legislators had used hereditary arguments in their efforts to restrict immigration to whites.[35] Just as Jim Crow laws claimed to protect whiteness from the contagion of

"Black blood," immigration barriers from the 1880s on defended native-born Americans (understood as white) from the genetic infiltration of unworthy racial others.

In 1882 western senators introduced the first nation- and race-based immigration law in the United States: the Chinese Exclusion Act. Presumed biological difference (and not jobs) was their primary reason for barring "these strange people come to occupy the land."[36] Chinese racial traits were presented as character traits, intractable and threatening to "Anglo-Saxon civilization." Senator Miller of California spelled it out: "These two civilizations which have here met are of diverse elements and character, both the result of evolution under different conditions, radically antagonistic, and as impossible of amalgamation as the two races who have produced them."[37] Because of "a heredity as old as the records of man," the Chinese, says Miller, are biologically indisposed to democracy and are therefore menacing to the very foundation of American life. For Miller, the Chinese were not only genetically un-American; they were also not quite human, at once "beasts" and "machines."[38] The Chinese Exclusion Act barred Chinese immigrants from obtaining citizenship, fined the owners of vessels found to carry Chinese immigrants ($500 per laborer), and criminalized the immigrants themselves by fining and imprisoning those who defied the ban. (With this, the concept of the "illegal alien" was born.)[39]

As is common, street violence accompanied legal violence. In San Francisco in 1877, in Denver in 1880, in Washington and Wyoming in 1885, and in Wichita, Kansas in 1886, Chinese immigrant-owned properties were razed and hundreds of Chinese people beaten or murdered.[40] Much of this violence was perpetrated by members of the Knights of Labor, an organization that Kem belonged to in the 1880s and that was allied with (and a precursor for) the Populists. Knights leader Joseph Buchanan publicly described Chinese workers as "so many leeches sucking our blood" and encouraged members to "butcher every thieving infernal Chinaman in the country" (1883).[41] Some followed this suggestion.

In 1892, when Kem and his Populist colleagues were first-term representatives and senators, the Chinese Exclusion Act was set to expire. Arguing in favor of its extension (as the Geary Act), Senator Charles Norton (R-CA) bluntly disclosed the purpose of the law. Again, the emphasis was not on jobs: "It is a question of civilization, and we of the Pacific coast would preserve ours, the Western type, and not submit to the Eastern. To preserve ours we must exclude the other—the Eastern." Senator Felton (D-CA) (a former banker and soon-to-be prison director) developed Norton's argument in biological terms. "The Chinese," says Felton, "are without conscience, without charity, devoid of sympathy and gratitude."[42] Drawing on prevailing hereditary theory, Felton suggests that this unassimilable racial group is dysgenic not because they are "less fit" (weaker) than Anglo-Saxon Americans but because they are "simpler" and therefore more racially stable, *and* potentially more numerous: "Races so dissimilar cannot assimilate and hence cannot exist together in unity, peace or prosperity—one or the other must survive and the older, the simple, will exhaust the newer and more complex. This is the law of nature, and China, with from six hundred and fifty to seven hundred and fifty millions of people to draw from, if permitted, will possess this land."[43]

Felton concludes his speech with a standard eugenic metaphor: the threat of poison in the pure fluid stream. "Mr. President," he says, "we would not permit the purity and sweetness of our national waters to be contaminated or polluted by the mingling of its pure streams with the impure from any source whatsoever."[44]

The Geary Act won full-blown support from the two Populists in the Senate and the nine in the House and thus, we can assume, from their thousands of constituents who were overwhelmingly from the plains. (In 1892 three Populist congressmen were from Nebraska, five were from Kansas, one each were from Minnesota and South Dakota, and one was from Georgia.) The law they voted for did not merely extend the Chinese Exclusion Act; it made it harsher. There would be no further Chinese immigration; all Chinese immigrants would now carry papers. The act suspended the writ of habeas corpus for Chinese immigrants, disallowed Chinese witnesses in court, and sentenced anyone of Chinese descent deemed unlawfully present to imprisonment in hard-labor camps prior to deportation.

The Geary Act was not without opposition. In the House, after an impassioned speech from Mississippi's Charles E. Hooker, who decried the bill's racism, forty-two members of Congress voted no. The no votes came from all over the country except the Pacific Coast—New York, Alabama, Kansas, Illinois, Wisconsin, Texas, North Dakota—and included both Democrats and Republicans. Only the Populists were unified in supporting total Chinese exclusion.[45] After all, as first-generation settlers from western states, they had benefited from ethnic cleansing already.[46]

This was two decades before Calvin Coolidge—in a passage circulated by the far right in 2019—underscored the theory of ethnic nationalism, asserting that "quality of mind and body suggests that observance of ethnic law is as great a necessity to a nation as immigration law."[47] It was two decades before eugenicist Madison Grant—whose obsession with "big blond" Germans and their "pure Nordic blood" would have been only bizarre if it weren't so murderously influential—warned that new immigrants, at this point mostly Italians, Slavs, and Jews, "adopt the language of the native American, they wear his clothes, they steal his name and . . . take his women," but can never assimilate to "American ideals."[48] And it was more than three decades before the National Origins Act defined legitimate American identity through a racialized concept of blood. But as we see, already in 1882 and again in 1892, Americanness is presented as an elusive and vulnerable quality, forever out of reach for certain racialized groups *and* deeply threatened by their presence. Anti-Chinese racism and Chinese exclusion are central to America's white supremacist past and present and to the anti-immigrant fervor that stands always in opposition to our myths of inclusion. Democracy, as legislators in 1882, 1892, and 1924 argued, is in the blood.[49]

There's an ongoing debate in the Populism historiography about how nativist the white Populists of the 1890s really were. It's not a very satisfying debate, since there's not a lot of concrete evidence to draw from; the Populist project was oriented toward domestic economic concerns. Even the Populists' endorsement of the Geary Act doesn't supply proof of their ethnic nationalism, for while racism was fundamental to proponents' arguments, the Populists in Congress didn't actively participate in these debates. Scholars Joseph Gerteis and Alyssa Goolsby have recently tried to answer some of these lingering questions by analyzing language from the Populist press, concluding that for Populists, "Americanness" was a crucial and insecure identity but was not directly tied to whiteness per se: "White identity was by no means a given or universally meaningful category for them."[50] Perhaps this was true, if we take published newspaper articles as the measure, but the indisputable fact remains: Populists in the plains were surrounded by and part of a culture that marked some people as intrinsically worthy of freedom, democracy, and bodily autonomy and others as congenitally and dangerously worthless. The racialization of these categories might have been fluid (or might have varied according to region), and certainly not all Populists, not all people of any party, were drawn to that worldview, but in my great-grandfather, Populism finds expression of its most anxiously vigilant side.

Jus Soli / Jus Sanguinis

Blood was the symbolic marker of value (class, race, and strength), but blood in its propensity to spill and pour from the cut or wound is also a sign of bodily vulnerability. Menstruating people are, of course, especially bloody; blood flows without even a breach of skin. The menstruating or maternal body provides proof of how porous our boundaries are. And so, while contaminated blood was the dominant metaphor for genetic mixing, because the vehicle for contamination was thought to be heterosexual sex, racism and sex hysteria often go hand in hand (as we see today).

As racial others "invade the land," land that had only recently been invaded by the very people now defending it, their supposedly overactive birthrate (if women) or sexual virility (if men) will lead, nativists and white supremacists fear, to an intolerable demographic shift. For this reason, many eugenicists of the 1920s advocated so-called positive eugenics—or pro-natalism—as well; they urged white middle-class women to produce more babies and were often against birth control for this reason.[51] (Pro-natalism was also a favored ideology/policy of European fascism.)[52] Today's far-right obsession around birth-right citizenship and so-called anchor babies is just another iteration of the fear that as non-worthy immigrants "flood" our shores and borders, they'll flood our maternity wards too.

The Nazis, inspired by the American effort, replaced birthright citizenship (*jus soli*) with citizenship based on blood or race (*jus sanguinis*).[53] Many Americans now, like the "legal scholar" John Eastman—who was a key player in Trump's effort to turn back the 2020 election and who was employed in 2020–21 by the University of Colorado, where I work—are promoting a similar project. Just after Joe Biden picked Kamala Harris as his running mate, Eastman published an op-ed in *Newsweek* in which he questioned Harris's citizenship, though she was born in Oakland, California. Eastman's controversial and long-held opinion is that people who are the children of "merely temporary visitors" do not qualify as citizens under the Fourteenth Amendment (at the time of Harris's birth, her parents were in the United States on student visas).[54] In his op-ed as elsewhere, Eastman argues that the Fourteenth Amendment, despite stating "All persons born or naturalized in the United States, and subject to the jurisdiction thereof, are citizens of the United States and of the State wherein they reside," meant to exclude children born on U.S. soil whose parents, for one reason or another, still "owe allegiance" to a foreign government and so are not *exclusively* "subject to the jurisdiction" of the United States. (The logic is immediately skewed—the phrase "and subject to the jurisdiction thereof" applies to the child and not its parents—but no matter, Eastman has built a career on this sleight of hand.) At the end of a 2019 talk sponsored by CU Boulder's Benson Center for the Study of Western Civilization, Eastman bragged that President Trump, having read his articles on the subject, was prepared to revoke the citizenship of all U.S.-born children of "illegal immigrants" by executive order, a move that Eastman said was entirely within Trump's "authority" and "obligations," despite being potentially unfair to those who have been "treated as citizens" and despite being politically risky.[55] No one in the audience that day, affiliates of the Benson Center, openly questioned these assertions.

I was enraged by Eastman. I guess I went on a kind of rampage; I helped craft a petition to have him removed or sanctioned, I advocated for changes to campus rules around hiring visiting professors, I complained about him (and the Benson Center) obsessively, then, as if on a hunt, I asked him to talk to me over Zoom and was surprised when he immediately agreed. As we talked, I tried to get him to admit his endgame, told him I already knew his arguments, wanted to know their reasons.[56] How calmly and logically, how good-naturedly, he promoted a complete revisioning of the Fourteenth, one that would target Central and South American migrants and their children almost exclusively, all the while denying any racist motivations. There was no endgame, Eastman insisted, other than the race-neutral goal of simply getting the Constitution right.

Maybe my rage was outsized; some thought he was just a buffoon (later revelations suggest I should have been far more concerned, not less). But I suppose he reminded me of Omer—when most bombastic, brutal, and wrong—and as such, I felt personally implicated by his arguments, even more by his attitude. Hidden in his faulty reading, his research, his quotes from legal dicta, his etymologies and jokes lay the image of a monstrous mother—her brown or Black pregnant body like a Trojan horse carrying invasive, unworthy life.

"You will not replace us," chanted marchers in the Unite the Right rally of August 2017, just before one of their members murdered Heather Heyer with his car. This hyper-violent fear of being "replaced" has only grown hotter since Donald Trump left the White House. In April of 2021 Fox News host Tucker Carlson warned his viewers about docile voters from "third-world countries" "disenfranchising" those already here.[57] Representative Scott Perry (R-PA) lent the theory a bit more authority: "For many Americans, what seems to be happening . . . is we're replacing national-born American—native-born Americans to permanently transform the landscape of this very nation."[58] That same month, Representative Marjorie Taylor Greene (R-GA) announced that she and others were launching a new America First Caucus, though there is nothing new about it. Included in the caucus's policy statement was this claim: "America is a nation with a border, and a culture, strengthened by a common respect for uniquely Anglo-Saxon political traditions. History has shown that societal trust and political unity are threatened when foreign citizens are imported *en masse* into a country."[59] For all these people, whether they carry a torch or a microphone, wield a weapon, write a law, or teach a seminar, the effort is the same: to settle American identity firmly in the blood, blood imagined as white.

Populism versus Populism: "No, No, Honey, They Shan't Touch Ye"

In 1926 the *Oregonian* printed the terrible story of an impoverished woman named Edna Fuller, a mother of five, who gassed herself and four of her children in their beds. In response, Kem writes one of his many "Letters to the Editor," in which he includes the following: "The blind, the lame, the idiotic, the criminal and the insane come unrestricted. True, a few sporadic efforts have been made to head off these undesirables, but the general public is so ignorant or indifferent that it has amounted to but little if anything."

Fuller's husband, a night watchman, told the press that the landlord had nearly doubled their rent in an effort to get the family out. Kem, uninterested in the landlord, asserts that a person with only the income of a night watchman "has no right to bring children into the world." It is high time, Kem goes on, that we began to consider breeding "thoroughbreds" instead of "criminals."[60]

This letter earned Kem an admiring response from a man named Mr. Schuman, a member of a Portland-based fascist organization, the Nordic Aryan League of America, who addresses Omer "with Aryan greetings." Kem finds the writer a little batty but does not hesitate to respond, noting that he and his interlocutor are in general agreement about the value of the "Great White Race" (with this phrase Omer makes me wonder if he'd been reading Madison Grant).[61] Repeating the joke he had made a year earlier in his letter to Huxley, Omer writes, "The time will come when so-called white couples marry, they will not know whether their children will be black, white, ringed, streaked, striped, bronzed, or spotted. The only way now left by which this calamity can be averted, is to sterilize all participants in these mixed marriages."[62] Clearly, barring one girl from a birthday party was not nearly safeguard enough.

During this period, Kem was suffering from poor health and maybe loneliness too. In 1923 he initiates what turns out to be a decade-long debate with his old Populist friend, Jim Ream. Ream is still in Nebraska, still running a farm. Their lives have diverged and so have their politics. Jim has moved further to the left, Omer further to the right. But while it seems Jim is content to leave this difference alone, to focus their correspondence on less volatile subjects, Omer demands greater intimacy.

On March 30, 1923, in a letter of thirty-five hefty paragraphs that primarily address the foolishness of Christianity, Omer turns to assess American "progress": "We are merging into the future when we will be taught to do right, not for Christ's sake, but for right's sake, when the mental and moral idiot, the sexual pervert and the hereditarily diseased will not be allowed to reproduce their kind, then we will be in a position to make real progress."

This letter, despite its rejection of religious orthodoxy, has a confessional vibe: "I will say to you Jim, that you are getting a deeper insight into my insides than any man ever has."[63]

Jim delays responding for months. His silence is so deafening that Omer writes a nervous follow-up to check in. When Jim finally does respond, it's with a very brief note—he claims he's been busy—but he does include the following:

> Your change of viewpoints as the years have gone by reminds me that I too have drifted quite a little in relation to the here and now, but never before have I been quite so sure of having a sure foundation to work from. . . . Here it is very briefly; All life, vegetable or animal, is endowed with a spark of divinity that is ever clamoring for an opportunity for greater individual development. Evidence of this truth can be found on every side. Here lies the secret motive power, that, through what we term evolutionary processes, has lifted man above the brute, and only to the extent to which this spark of divinity, man's conscience, is developed, is man divine.

With that, Jim signs off. It's a rebuke, a gentle one, but its message is not lost on Omer. He is hurt and tells Jim so: "You say you haven't time to write. Darn poor excuse brother," he complains.[64]

Seven years later the stakes of their argument have grown more urgent. What might have been an abstract discussion about American "progress" in 1923 was as serious as it gets in 1930. Jim reminds Omer of their Populist days, when they were trying to "push back against those who would monopolize the whole earth." The crisis now, he tells Omer, is far, far worse. Jim and his wife, Annie, had been out to Oregon to visit the Kems. The visit was pleasurable, and yet, says Jim, "what surprised me most when I met you a year ago was the complacency with which you viewed the future." Risking offence, Jim tells Omer to "wake up."[65]

Omer defends himself, of course, but their differences become clear. For Jim the problem is American capitalism itself. The rich grow richer, accumulating factories, now across the globe, in which the poor produce goods they cannot afford to buy. Capitalism, says Jim, has proven itself incapable of bringing the blessings of the machine age to "all the people of the earth." Instead, it enriches the very few while exploiting the many. Jim, it seems, has read his Marx, or his Eugene Debs; his egalitarian ethics have delivered him to "socialism."[66] On the question of eugenics, Jim is at first equivocal. Conceding that "the really unfit" should not be allowed to breed, he quickly shifts to sarcasm; the unfit, he says "of course wouldn't include such fellows as O.M. and J.D."[67]

Omer spills a lot of ink over the next year begging Jim to explain "the practical side of socialism." The word by itself, he says, "is as clear as mud." Not hearing enough detail, not enough of a "plan," he accuses Jim of having "Utopian" ideals. Without details, socialism is nothing but a "beautiful theory," he says.[68] And it's true; Jim keeps avoiding the question, worrying instead about Omer's health—entreating him to eat well, to speak directly to his body, to practice deep breathing, and to get a massage. He wants Omer to get well, to "live for a thousand years," so that he might "do as in the past a lot of good." He begs him to "stay here and help work out this greatest of all problems: *What are we here for, what should life mean to me, to us?*"[69]

18. James D. Ream, ca. 1925. Institute of Agriculture and Natural Resources, University of Nebraska–Lincoln.

In lieu of a plan, Jim offers an ethics: "Each and all are entitled to all the blessings of life that anyone is entitled to enjoy." "Thugs, thieves, liars, and murderers" are the natural result not of bad genes but of the entire "capitalistic system of business," which he seeks to "modify if not annihilate."[70] Factory, farm, and mine production should be directed toward the goal of "adding to the comforts and blessings of all the people of the earth." "Give the people an opportunity to be human," he concludes, "step by step . . . in one long series of cooperative efforts."[71] It's the kind of longing that breaks your heart.

But Omer laughs at him: "Now, you long legged specimen of the genius hobo, get a hike!" "Improvements" must be made, he agrees—but not to the systems of production and distribution. It's high time we "take the weakness out of man himself," he writes, "by giving him both brains and moral character or, perhaps I had better say, weeding out those who have neither."[72]

As the correspondence goes on, Omer digs deeper into this genocidal point of view, as if daring Jim to abandon him. In 1931 he insists that "criminality" is an immutable character trait, independent of any crime committed. ("Once the mechanism of a biocriminal was called upon . . . criminality was conceptualized in racist terms," writes Foucault.)[73] Then later, "Bad government is the product of bad people, the only remedy is to get rid of them."[74]

Jim tries in vain to convince Omer otherwise. He sends Omer socialist pamphlets and books; he tries persuasion and sometimes silence. Occasionally, he grows sardonic: "Isn't it funny how an old kid who is too old to do anything should want to fix the younger kid so he couldn't do anything, hay ha, hum."[75] When Omer promotes an ever more expansive list of those whose reproductive lives should be cut off—"thugs, thieves, liars, murderers and libertines, the idiotic, the lunatic, moron and incompetent"—Jim's response is to note that under Omer's proposed sterilization project, there'd be "no breeding stock left." Omer quickly reassures him: "Poor old feller, did you think for a moment that I would sterilize good people like you and me? No, no, honey, they shan't touch ye."[76]

Gas

> Racism is contempt for life.
> —Martin Luther King Jr., "Where Do We Go from Here?"

Once again, Kem's belief that criminality and other social problems are largely caused by hereditary traits, and further, that isolating and/or sterilizing people thought to be dysgenic would cleans the nation of these ills in just a few generations, was shared by much of the scientific community and vast numbers of lay people in the 1920s and '30s.[77] Bizarre and painful to us now, these ideas were commonplace then. Nothing is less impressive to a historian of this era than the news that someone was a eugenicist (and to the general public, it seems, nothing is more shocking). But what *is* astonishing, at least to me, is the fact that my great-grandfather dared to believe himself genetically pure.

Poverty was thought to be a sign of degeneracy, and Kem had been devastated by poverty, so much so that only a massive government handout could save him. Even after that he had to give up his children for a time to survive. Mental illness, Linda's "trouble," was another key "dysgenic" trait. Homosexuality, or sexual "perversion," was an excuse for sterilization, and Kem's daughter Myrtle lived with her "female companion" (as she was referred to) in the family home for years.[78] Homelessness and alcoholism marked some people for sterilization; Kem's youngest son, Victor, an alcoholic, was itinerate and mostly jobless through the 1920s and '30s. Kem's own chronic disease, arthritis, kept him bedridden for months and was believed to be hereditary. And yet Kem bluntly insists that his own bloodline is untarnished: "In all four of my ancestral branches, I have not found nor do I know of one who went to prison, to an insane asylum or to the alms house. There may have been some but I never met any or heard of them. For this reason, although none have been wealthy above the average, I am proud of my ancestry. Yes, I thoroughly believe that what is back of one has more to do with what is in front of them than anything else. This is why I am a stickler for sterilization."[79]

Of course, one can be a stickler for sterilization (especially if one is a parent of thirteen) only if one believes oneself pure. However, once again, nothing pure is ever really pure enough; the threat of "invasion" is always present, regardless of boundaries, borders, and laws (and it seems the more such laws, the greater the perceived threat).[80] Eugenics is a "technology of sex" aimed at establishing "biological rigor."[81] And like other forms of bio-necro-politics, it responds to a felt weakness and vulnerability in the dominant population.[82] Thus, the eugenicists—like the anti-immigrant crusaders and the segregationists (often the same people)—both built upon and required an exclusionary attitude steeped in paranoia.

Plains Populism arose out of a condition in which settler-farmers were deeply insecure in their relation to the land. They had been granted the land as remedy for poverty and as path to independence, but when the land didn't yield or when unregulated industries exploited their need, the lie of "independence" was laid bare. If the land is hostile, if the land runs out, if the land can't provide, then where are you, and what? Humans don't float about the world; we are not abstract beings but outgrowths of soil, water, sun, and all else that these elements bring forth, astonishingly. It makes sense, then, that given the unstable circumstances in which they struggled—given the need, nevertheless, for security—some settler-homesteading Populists like Kem would seek to relocate the source of their legitimacy from *where* they lived and *what* they did to *who they thought they were*, that is, from the land to the blood.

But Populism, it seems, could go another way, and that "other way" was there all along. The populist concern for justice and equity, for "the love of the whole people for each other," might, if followed like a current, carry one toward a widening ocean of inclusion. "All the people of the earth" are deserving of life and its blessings, Jim Ream had insisted, and then, further, "*All life*, vegetable or animal, is endowed with a spark of divinity." This too is populism, an eco-inclusive populism that believes, to borrow from the IWW (an organization Kem despised and Jim admired), "an injury to one is an injury to all."[83] For why else would Jim make note that under Omer's plan, he too would be subject to the knife? Jim Ream's fundamental faith in the value of all beings on earth proves too unwieldy, too expansive for Kem's self-defensive populism, in which walls must be built to exclude the undesirable from the category of the living.

And in the end, that is where it went. The final pages of Kem's autobiography are something of a jumble. Included are the last letters he and Jim exchanged before Jim died in May of 1933. Their exchange had grown more strained, with longer and more bellicose arguments from Omer and shorter and more distant responses from Jim. In Omer's penultimate letter, he points out (rightly) that Stalin's Russia had become a despotism in which personal liberty was eclipsed and food shortages were endemic.[84] Taken to task for not responding to the letter, Jim says he had misplaced it. I imagine that for Jim, as for so many on the American left, the failures of the Bolsheviks were just too painful, too confusing, to address. So Jim gets quieter, but Kem gets louder and also messier. Inserted into his retyped copies of their letters are newspaper clippings about eugenics, some that he had sent to Jim and others that postdate their correspondence.

One stands out. In March of 1936 the head of both sociology and economics at Willamette University, Dr. S. B. Laughlin, made a public recommendation that, in Omer's words, "all helplessly insane infants should be painlessly and mercifully exterminated."[85] Laughlin defended his scandalous remarks in the *Oregonian*, using the same talking points that Omer had been repeating since 1911: "At present according to government figures, there are more than 100,000 feebleminded in the United States and more than 350,000 insane. Figures show that 75 percent of all mental diseases and afflictions are hereditary, yet critics claim that my proposal is impractical and impossible." Omer has clipped Laughlin's defense, noting that it demonstrates "the necessity of prompt and vigorous action." Oregon's governor went further: the *Corvallis Gazette Times* reported that Governor Martin openly defended Laughlin, saying he was "right in principle" when he advocated the chloroforming of feebleminded infants.[86]

Of course, by drawing attention to this event, Omer is not necessarily endorsing the gassing of "insane" children. But he's not condemning the idea either. Indeed, what the Nazis named as euthanasia but is actually just murder is the logical development of Omer's position, as history has shown.[87] The Nazis murdered hundreds of thousands of mentally and physically disabled children (and later, adults), including those deemed mentally ill or chronically "criminal" in hospitals and "clinics" *outside of the camps* beginning in 1939. In her 1922 book, *Human Sterilization*, Bethenia Owens-Adair was explicit about the racist genocidal logic of eugenics. In a private letter she makes public, she writes, "Our nation cannot exist another century if the black race, the insane, or the feebleminded, are permitted to propagate to their own sweet will."[88] And then, a bit later, she suggests a solution: "Should the time come that the black race became a menace to our nation, a remedy could be found without resorting to war. Congress could pass a law requiring the sterility of the female."[89] Genocide, for Owens-Adair, was not, it seems, limited to Black people, for in 1921 she hinted at a similar "plan" to address Japanese immigrants.[90] Omer Kem never references Owens-Adair, but he shared at least some of her views.

I found it strange and intensely sad that Omer's oblique reference to eugenical infanticide was jammed in with his final letter to his oldest and dearest friend. Still fighting with Jim's ghost, he could not let their argument go. But at the same time, it seems he didn't quite want to win.

Jim died shortly after he claimed to have lost Omer's longest and most combative letter. He never wrote to Omer again. Omer could have silenced Jim, buried their letters in the past. Instead, he copied more than a hundred pages of correspondence into his autobiography, preserving Jim's expansive, visionary faith for me to read. He was explicit about this: "I warn you now" he told Jim in 1930, "that part of you that comes to me in your letters will go on record for future generations to read."[91] There is no denying the love these two men had for each other. And because of that love, Omer meticulously typed up all Jim's words, even when in great physical pain. And so it was that Omer gave me Jim, Jim who believed in the value of *all* life, "animal and vegetable"—a foundation on which to build.

Party, 2017

> I felt that without a common bond uniting men, without a continuous current of shared thought and feeling circulating through the social system, like blood coursing through the body, there could be no living worthy of being called human.
> —Richard Wright, *Black Boy*

> In our dreams our spirits meet in places we can't see
> and live where the future has begun
> —Alice Roberts, great-great-granddaughter of Omer and Alice Kem

"The circle around my father's people and my mother's people was tightening," I wrote in one version of this book's introduction. My mother was Jewish. Far-flung members of her family, originally from Ukraine, had been murdered for the eugenic cause called Nazism (I know nothing more about them). The young Omer Kem once threw a hard crust of bread into the face of a Jewish girl for no reason other than that she was there and a Jew. He referred to the bankers he hated as "Shylocks," and even as he once respectfully quoted a rabbi describing the trauma of antisemitism, he also wrote that "the old Jews" were "an ignorant, self-centered, savage, brutal people."[92] This ordinary (but why should it be ordinary?) and intermittent antisemitism can feel personal when I remember how my mother so often wore the face of fear, especially after she had ridden in a crowded subway car. But there's more to it than a personal insult. American eugenicists (and white supremacists more generally) strongly influenced Nazi policy; the authors of the Nuremberg laws found guidance in the genocide and containment of Indigenous people, in Jim Crow and anti-miscegenation laws, in restrictive immigration, and in U.S. sterilization laws.[93] Hitler, having been inspired by Madison Grant's *The Passing of the Great Race*, followed the model provided by the Americans in his "Law for the Prevention of Defective Progeny," through which over four hundred thousand Germans were forcibly sterilized.[94]

U.S. sterilizations laws, which my great-grandfather so passionately championed, didn't only deeply harm thousands of Americans; these laws also provided one seed and model—according to historian James Whitman, the *primary* seed and model—for the policies that wiped many of my maternal ancestors out. But this tension lies in all of us—all of us, if we look hard enough, carry the ghosts of victims and the ghosts of perpetrators, and sometimes these are the same people.

Still, there are moments when the history of American eugenics seems almost banal. If nearly everyone agreed that some form of controlled human breeding was at least plausibly useful, then why present it as a moral crisis, a crime?[95] As many scholars point out, we practice a *kind of* eugenics in currently accepted ways all the time: choosing our partners, planning our families, managing our resources, raising our children. Some of us even undergo genetic testing and choose to abort pregnancies based on the results of these tests.[96] And we do all these things toward the goal of some articulated or implied idea of "progress" or "success."[97]

But at other times, reading this material, the dizzy nausea of my first encounter returns full force. It's when I'm with my own children, or really, anyone's children, that it hits me the hardest: the opportunity for this profound experience of human love was stolen from thousands—would have been stolen from thousands more if the eugenicists had had their way. And of course, it wasn't just about reproduction (as if that were somehow a minor aspect of life). American eugenicists and their ordinary followers, of which there were millions, clung to their supremacy and cultivated it. With this supremacy came disdain, disgust, hatred, and an even more brutal dismissal. Believing themselves superior (believing themselves white) meant that the eugenicists claimed the right and the duty to decide who deserved to live and who did not. In the end, it's as simple and as horrible as that.

"What is genealogy?" I asked my students. "Genealogy is the physical, inherited archive that we carry in our own bodies," said one.[98] Another pulled her collar down to reveal a long scar running just beneath her collarbones. My mother's face of fear is sometimes my face of fear. And the questions she carried to her grave are also mine: What is evil? Where does hate come from? How can we unlearn violence? But Omer Kem's proud-boy shoulders are also mine, and so are his questions: How are we haunted? What do we inherit? How might we outlive ourselves? What, therefore, do we owe the past and the future both?

In this way, a central confusion arises. For as much as I reject Omer's hereditarian fatalism, I also feel him in my body. As much as I want to say no, every person is born free, at the same time I am saying we are not. We are born with our ancestor's crimes on our conscience, as much as we might carry their traumas, their achievements, and their loves.[99] And it might take us half a lifetime to learn what these crimes or traumas are, to find the scars and know them as our own, and another half to try to respond and to repair.

Bea and I left the library that summer night in Omaha to drive around without purpose. We kept mostly silent. I was thinking about Mary's birthday party and the project of race purity that, as much as any dream of Populist egalitarianism, was my inheritance. I didn't know what Bea was thinking about as she aimed her phone's camera out the window. Maybe about the histories of Black Nebraskans that had been stored inside boxes in a mall. And then, up on a grassy hill, there was a party.

In the non-worded language of the dance, under evening clouds amassing and dispersing to a different rhythm, I felt we had found

19. Hector Rosado y Su Orquesta Hache, Jazz on the Green, Omaha, Nebraska, 2017. Image modified by Joel Swanson. Author's collection.

a future. I got caught in the grassy scent, a man's wrist floating from his seat on the lawn, a girl's ponytail swaying in syncopation with the beat. Bea moved toward a woman in a red dress who taught her a new step. For us to arrive there, in that dance, it seemed we had had to leave the reading room behind. The words had told one story, but the dance told another. Through the blood in motion—the blood that is not other than the breath, the breath that is not other than the air, the air that is not other than another's air, another's blood—we were not pure. Like the mud that clung to Omer's memory and made him anxious then made him rage, we were unsettled.[100]

The desire to locate some essential beingness, some essential selfhood, in the blood was a hysterical response to the always compromised relation between the colonizer and the land he staked his claim on. But the blood is not the metaphor they hoped it was. The blood does not speak of difference and distinction, of purity and separation; the blood speaks only the language of contamination, which at its root means to come into contact, to comingle.

To dance in the presence of others we did not know, to feel their breath and sense their blood, to be among children and aged people moving in their ways in the apparitional night, was a slipping gesture, a slide to the side of the forms of power that nonetheless still held us tightly. Such fantastic escapes might not translate into the daily, but they do linger on in the sense-memory of the body. The dance is not the day, but it is a protest, a desire, an unbalanced act of devotion to the unknowable, circulating, common blood—with all its gravitas and all its air.[101]

8   Power

Power can be invisible, it can be fantastic, it can be dull and routine. It can be obvious, it can reach you by the baton of the police, it can speak the language of your thoughts and desires. It can feel like remote control, it can exhilarate like liberation, it can travel through time, and it can drown you in the present. It is dense and superficial, it can cause bodily injury, and it can harm you without seeming ever to touch you. It is systematic and it is particularistic and it is often both at the same time. It causes dreams to live and dreams to die.
—Avery Gordon, *Ghostly Matters*

It is the language that drinks blood, laps vulnerabilities, tucks its fascist boots under crinolines of respectability and patriotism as it moves relentlessly toward the bottom line and the bottomed-out mind.
—Toni Morrison, "Nobel Lecture," 1993

Breath

Perhaps it's now time to leave Omer Kem behind. Certainly, his failure to condemn the murdering of so-called insane children would merit an abandonment. If only his ghost were willing to comply. But that, as he understood well, is not how haunting works. The spirits return—that's what they do. They return, or they never left; and in never leaving, they take many forms—generating crowds, directing intimacies, forcing confrontations, crying out for justice.

I hadn't believed in Omer's spirits, hadn't believed he played catch with his dead child or felt his dead brother's hand on his wrist, his dead sister's touch on his shin. I had especially disbelieved the Native spirit he thought he carried in his body for half his life.

But after five years of encountering his ghost, I could no longer pretend not to believe in haunting. His spirit lived on, not just in me or in my father or brother or our children; his spirit lived on in people I did not know. And this spirit, this ghost, in insisting on being known and believed, by drawing me into the past, was also guiding me forward, even if he himself, the person of Omer Kem, had gotten lost.

In Cleveland in the summer of 2016, a man on his knees wept for Tamir Rice. He was surrounded by what felt like hundreds of police. They stood in their trained imperviousness—their faces immobile, their eyes looking past or through him. The man spoke directly to them: "You killed him," he said. "You killed our child." He wore a bloodied shirt, his family gathered nearby; it was a form of street theater, but it also was not. Black Lives Matter had been in action since 2013, but this was a different sort of protest. The man was not chanting, marching, or stopping traffic. He was alone, he was crying, and he refused to be subdued by their silence.

The man, the police, the few and far between protesters, and the thousands of people in red MAGA hats; we were all there in downtown Cleveland because this was the day that the Republican Party, a full half of America's electorate, formally endorsed a presidential platform built on the rhetoric of race purity only thinly disguised. We were all there for the same reason, and we had to confront each other on those streets. But that day, despite the stalking police, the men with their rifles strapped to their backs, the micro street protests and performances, the convention hall filling with wildly excited delegates and party operatives, it was as if nothing moved, as if there was that day no breath.

Within the first minute of Trump's acceptance speech (which we watched later on TV), the crowd was chanting our country's initials. "We" would be "a country of Law and Order," he assured them, recycling the Klan's relentlessly recycled slogan (all racism is mimicry, repetition, stasis). I was invited to identify with this "we," invited into that cheering crowd. I was invited into the folds of the law. The man on his knees outside the convention hall was not. Tamir Rice could not *be* invited, for he, a twelve-year-old child, had been killed by Officer Timothy Loehmann—who was never indicted—in that city two years before.

Trump did in fact implicitly acknowledge this murder, and so many like it, in his next sentence: "The attacks on our police and the terrorism of our cities threaten our very way of life," he says. "We cannot afford to be so politically correct anymore!" At this the crowd leaps to its feet, fists in the air. In the next moment, tightening another plank in the platform, Trump warns of the immigrants "roaming free." He's going where white people have long gone when we want to demonize and thereby dominate others, to the death of an "innocent" (as he calls her) white woman. Sarah Root had died in Nebraska in a drunk-driving accident. The driver was a nineteen-year-old undocumented immigrant named Eswin Mejia.[1]

In that moment, as both Trump and his audience indulged in a dramatic display of white innocence, which is white resentment, which is white power, these two untimely deaths—the police shooting of a Black boy and the accidental death of a white woman—were horribly, almost inevitably, allegorized. It was in so many ways an ordinary day in America.

"Are we not touched by the same breath of air which was among that which came before? is there not an echo of those who have been silenced in the voices to which we lend our ears today?" wrote Walter Benjamin toward the end of his life.[2] To breathe with others is to breathe in the past, no matter how it might catch in the throat or burn. To breathe is to move, and we have to move. The ghosts in the room, the hall, the street, the forest or field—they *are* the breath, no matter how they might make us rage, weep, or feel ashamed. To refuse them is to stagnate in more violence. I want to know about your great-grandfather, your great-grandmother, whoever you are, so that one day, maybe, we can breathe together.

I could end this book there, on that perennial wish for connection and for life, but there is one more story that I've leaped over and left behind. If I've been unable to move smoothly along in a linear narrative, it's because haunting is anti-linear. I find myself returning again and again, regathering—like sweeping the floor while a hard wind blows the dust around.

Rope

In February of 2020, just before the pandemic took over, Randy Kem and I were walking down a wet sidewalk in Salem, Oregon. Though we were cousins, we'd known each other only fifteen minutes. This was when Randy told me, as if it were the most ordinary thing in the world, that Victor Kem, Omer and Alice's youngest son, had roped his own son, Charley—Randy's father—to a toilet every morning of Charley's childhood. *Abusive* was the word Randy used to describe his grandfather, though he did not elaborate further.

Charles Kem was born on December 9, 1933. He was Victor and his first wife Marie's only child, coming along a little late in their marriage. In the few letters from Victor that Omer transcribed, Victor barely mentions his son, though to be fair, he was not much of a writer. Writing "sure is about the hardest task for me to do," he confessed in 1930. "My only excuse is that it's just one of my many failings."[3]

I wanted to know more about what had happened to Charley. I wanted to know more about Victor too, where the maliciousness came from. When I tried to follow up with Randy, sending emails and leaving phone messages, he did not respond. 2020 was a painful year; anything could have happened. Or nothing. He could have been just busy, or maybe, like his father, Randy didn't want anything more to do with the family.

And so I went back to look again for Victor in the archive. And when I found him, I found something else too: I found the war. Somehow, in all my thinking about land, ghosts, and blood, I had almost managed to ignore it, as if war's logic wasn't at the heart of all that ails us.

Power

By the time Omer Kem was fully and obsessively voicing the urge to cleanse the population of the "unproductive" and "contaminating" types, he had been living in Oregon for a decade, having moved there, as I said, in 1908. With this final move (farther and farther west), he

20. Brown sawmill on the left, Cottage Grove Electric and Light on the right. Curtis Irish Collection, courtesy of the Jay Swofford archives.

had left farming behind and joined the ranks of the business class. His business was power.

Omer bought Cottage Grove Electric and Light with his oldest daughter, Maude, and her husband, Charles Shinn. They bought it outright with money from the sale of the Montrose ranchhouse.[4] The plant was stationed across the street from a sawmill, since its energy source was wood waste—sawdust and scraps—the leftovers from the booming timber industry.[5] As the old trees went down, the furnace was fed, transforming water to steam, steam to motion, motion to current, and current to heat and light.[6]

Theirs was the only electric company in town. They could charge whatever the customers would pay.[7]

But despite what looks like a successful move into the capitalist class, Kem was not happy in his new line of work. In 1915, just five years after production began, Kem and the Shinns tried to sell their plant. No one wanted it. But if, as is likely, there were financial troubles behind their discontent, Omer discovered a way out of them.

Omer's older sister, Sophronia Mellett, was living at that time with her two adopted daughters, Lottie and Louise, on her Indiana farm. Sophronia's husband had long since died, and Sophronia's own health was failing. The sisters, who had been adopted when they were five and seven by the otherwise childless Melletts, were now in

21. *Left to right*: Alice Kem, Lottie Mellett, Thelma Kem, Louise Mellett, Sophronia Mellett, Omer Kem, ca. 1916. Author's collection.

their twenties, and their relationship with their adoptive mother had turned sour. In letters to Omer, Sophronia accuses the young women of abusing her, of refusing to work, of reading her mail, and of stealing her money. (In the only other story of Sophronia in the autobiography, she is a small child with cataclysmic premonitions.)

In December of 1915, just after failing to sell the electric company, Omer determines to take charge. Leaving the company in Charles Shinn's care, Omer takes his family to Indiana, hires a lawyer, and ousts the young women from the house—and from their inheritance. When Sophronia dies later that year, the house is Omer's.[8] Within a month or two, Omer sells the house for $5,500 and immediately transfers that wealth to his business. With this sudden infusion, Kem and the Shinns buy a bigger furnace to burn twice the wood, and in this way, they double the reach of their power.[9]

But if I seem to be making a moralistic tale out of a little family drama, it's because this common story of capitalist accumulation and expansion, this story in which (as it seems) a brutal solution is found for an economic problem, provides something like a model-in-miniature for the vast crisis unfolding just then on the national and international stage.

War

> Security was commerce, commerce was prosperity, prosperity was power, power nurtured virtue, virtue was freedom, and freedom had to be extended to be secured and secured to be extended.
> —Greg Grandin, *The End of the Myth*

> Wars begin with language.
> —Mariana Oliver, *Migratory Birds*

The U.S. economy had been in recession since the Panic of 1910–11. With domestic markets sagging, both production and income levels were on the decline.[10] As Woodrow Wilson put it in his acceptance speech at the 1912 DNC Convention, American companies "will burst their jackets if they do not find a free outlet to the markets of the world. . . . Our domestic markets no longer suffice."[11] World War I provided an answer to this problem, for it energized the international market for American farm, mine, and factory products—steal, copper, weapons, explosives, clothing, and wheat.[12] "Nearly every sector of the economy had grown as a direct result of wartime contracts with the belligerents," writes Michael Nieberg. "Between 1914 and 1917 American exports to Europe increased exponentially from $1.4 billion to $4.3 billion."[13] Because of wartime blockades, this robust international market was restricted to neutral and Allied countries, especially to Britain.[14] When Wilson returned to his "jacket bursting" metaphor in 1915, it was to exclaim that there was now "no straightjacket" that could confine America's business. "We . . . have to be the reserve force of the world in respect [to] economic power," he announced to a gathering of American businessmen, urging them toward "the spirit of conquest!"[15]

Three years into the war, with French, British, and German armies stagnating in trench-war stalemate—their soldiers choking on mustard gas or rotting in the scorched earth of No Man's Land—America's farms and factories, but even more importantly, America's banks, were doing well indeed, selling the British alone $75 million worth of goods per week while lending them the money to pay for it all.[16] The "vehicle for this transatlantic operation" was one bank: the House of J. P. Morgan.[17] In 1916, reports Adam Tooze, the Allies' debt to the House of Morgan (now JPMorgan Chase & Co.) was around $2 billion; by 1921 it was five times that amount.[18] Through this tight system of economic dominance—make the products, expand the market, offer credit to impoverished customers—the United States became, for the first time in its history, a creditor nation—*the* creditor nation.[19]

Wilson, who had been reelected on the slogan "He kept us out of the war," struggled to maintain political, if not economic neutrality, but eventually, German aggression, or desperation, forced his hand. In February of 1917 Germany, nearly starved into submission by the Allies' U.S.-funded power and the blockades, announced a return to unrestrained submarine warfare against even neutral or merchant ships.[20] Meanwhile, the intercepted "Zimmerman Telegram" revealed that Germany had offered to help Mexico invade the southwestern United States in exchange for Mexico's alliance (there is no evidence that Mexico was agreeable).[21] When Wilson finally abandoned "neutrality," he denied self-interested or aggressive aims, claiming only moralistic ones: "The world must be made safe for democracy. Its peace must be planted upon the tested foundations of political liberty. We have no selfish ends to serve. We desire no conquest, no dominion," he announced to Congress.

"Safety" is always a dangerous concept; "It can turn justified acts of defense into preemptive acts of tyranny. It can turn defenders into predators," as Catherine Taylor writes.[22] Moreover, the "end" of economic conquest had already been "served" and now demanded both expansion and protection. Were the Allies to collapse, so would their credit.[23] In April of 1917 the United States got ready to sacrifice

```
                      ENLISTMENT RECORD
Due travel pay
To Muncie, Indiana C JM
Name: Victor R. Kem               Grade:    Private 1st class
Enlisted, or inducted, April 18, 1917, at Jefferson Bks Mo
Serving in  First           Enlistment period at date of discharge
Prior service:         None

Noncommissioned Officer:          Never
Marksmanship, gunner qualifications or rating:  Not qualified
Horsmanship:   Not mounted


Knowledge of any vocation:  Laborer        (should have been mechanic)
```

22. & 23. Victor's enlistment papers. Omer Madison Kem Papers, 3:36, 37.

what would eventually be more than a hundred thousand young men to the cause.[24]

Precisely sixteen days later, Victor Kem—nineteen years old, aimless, and recently uprooted—enlisted. Had he not done so, he would have been taken anyway. By mid-May Congress had imposed a draft.[25]

A look at Victor's enlistment papers, as copied over by Omer, is revealing:

None. Never. Not qualified. Not mounted. Laborer.

The parenthetical note, "should have been mechanic," was added by Omer. I don't know whether he means here that Vic should have *written* "mechanic" or should have *been* one. Either way, though, even if proud of his soldier son, it seems Omer was ashamed of Victor's self-assessment. While "mechanic," carrying a sense of independence, skill, and artisanship, might have been preferred in a son, Vic was only being truthful; he was then and for many years after a laborer. He laid pipes and drove trucks for oil companies, he picked plums and dried prunes for farmers, he served drinks to golfers when he was thirty and too broke to pay rent and get his teeth fixed both.[26]

Power   195

Whether proud, ashamed, or a little of both, one thing is clear: as the war ground on with Victor in training, Omer was afraid (and so, I assume, was Alice). Victor's cousin Roger was killed in France in 1917. The names of the fallen, the "Pershing Reports," were published in the papers—by spring of 1918, hundreds of names each day.[27] When finally, in early fall of that year, Victor was sent to France, the family's anxiety ran high. Omer channeled his fear into a poem.

Even though, or because, I am a poet, I've avoided sharing Kem's poems (they tend to be jingly, witty, and long), but this one demands to be read. Didactic, jovial, and above all, patriotic, the poem offers justification for the righteousness of the war and encouragement to Vic to do his "small" part well.

> Remember my son, when chasing the Hun
> Some say it is wrong to fight.
> I'll say, however, it depends altogether
> Whether you're fighting for the right.

But as it goes on, Omer's poem shows a deep uncertainty about the nature of this "right." Despite all the propaganda, the hyperpatriotism of the era, the war's causes remained (and remain) abstract.[28] After declaring that it would be wrong to fight for wealth and power alone, Omer writes:

> But it is always right to battle with might
> For the things that ought to be.
> Otherwise the things that righteousness brings
> Would perish, as you well can see.

What are these "things" that ought to be? What "things" are in danger of perishing? Omer doesn't say.

Wilson had declared war for the sake of democracy. But even if the international spread of democracy was Wilson's genuine cause, others of his domestic policies before, during, and after the war presented a problematic vision of what that meant.[29] As governor of New Jersey (1910–12), he passed progressive labor and election reforms while signing that state's eugenic sterilization law, which targeted criminals as wells as "defectives."[30] As president, even as he successfully promoted key progressive economic reforms—the New Freedom—many of which had been proposed by Populists, including Kem, in the 1890s, he applied Jim Crow laws to federal employees, resegregated the military, and remained resolutely silent when up to one hundred Black people were murdered by white mobs in St. Louis in 1917.[31] Wilson emboldened the Klan by adopting their slogan—100 percent Americanism—and allowing his own racist language to be repurposed in the 1915 Klan-emboldening film, *The Birth of a Nation*, written by his friend Thomas Dixon, which he then screened at the White House.[32]

Wilson's concept of democracy-for-some meant that he was vehemently against federal protections for disenfranchised Black voters in the South. He refused to support women's suffrage until jailed suffragists went on a hunger strike and bent his will.[33] He signed the most anti-democratic attacks on free speech in the nation's history, the 1917 Espionage Act and the 1918 Sedition Act, which criminalized speech that was perceived to be in any way anti-American (including anti-conscription speech), and which led to vigilante violence and the arrest, torture, and deportation of pacifists, conscientious objectors, labor leaders, socialists, Wobblies, and other left radicals.[34] In 1918 Wilson signed a revised Anarchist Exclusion Act; now, any naturalized citizen who adopted anarchist ideas or participated in "acts of sabotage," even five years after immigrating, could be stripped of citizenship and deported.

"America must now make peaceful conquest of the world," Wilson announced in 1915, just before he sent troops to occupy Haiti (a "reign of terror" as Du Bois called it, which lasted for twenty years).[35] In 1917 Wilson directed his secretary of state, Robert Lansing, to lead the American annexation of the Virgin Islands, while his military also maintained control of both Costa Rica and Cuba.[36]

Wilson's domestic and foreign policies were rooted, then, in a shared ideology: white supremacy. "Just as he never questioned the South's system of racial segregation and disenfranchisement of African Americans, Wilson never called for an end to Europe's colonial empires," writes Ross Kennedy.[37] Mutually respecting sovereign nations did not, in practicality (or even, really, in theory), include the colonized nations of Africa, Asia, the Pacific Islands, the Caribbean, or Latin America. Wilson held to the colonizer's conviction that such nations required "tutelage of a 'civilized' power" before they could achieve self-determination.[38]

While America's involvement in the war thus leaned on the language of freedom, democracy, and sovereignty—language that ordinary citizens like Kem echoed and amplified—the war had other far more practical aims; to win the war was to ensure the continued reach of America's economic power and influence. In a sense, U.S. involvement in the war was less Woodrow Wilson's project than it was J. P. Morgan Jr.'s. And so, Omer Kem's patriotism ironically served a war that further enriched America's foremost banker, the son of J. P. Morgan, the railroad mogul and founder of U.S. Steel—the kind of man (in a sense, the *very* man) Kem had spent most of his life despising.[39]

In this way, each American who lost his life, a limb, his eyesight, or his sanity fighting in that war lost it for the sake of American global capitalism.[40] Maybe you think this a worthy cause—or would have thought so in 1917. Regardless, a person should know what they're being asked to die for.[41]

War at Home

> Patriotism is surely the most revolting emotion people go in for.
> —Martha Gellhorn, 1940

In September of 1917, with the war in a critical stage and Victor in training, the underpaid, overworked, and severely under-housed shipbuilders and boilermakers up and down the Oregon coast planned a strike. Demand for military production was high, especially after "the most dramatic naval expansion plan in American history" was signed by Wilson in 1916.[42] For once, labor had the upper hand.[43]

The carpenters and metal trades unions struck first, followed by all workers across the shipping and shipbuilding industries in both Oregon and Washington. By the time the strike was resolved, with workers winning small concessions, the U.S. government had been forced to all but discontinue use of wooden ships in the military. In this way, the strike "contributed to the demise of an entire industry."[44] But another effect of the strike—and others like it during the war—was to turn middle-class people like Kem, who might once have been allies to the working people (or been among them), flatly against them.

"I have been a laboring man all my life and was one among the first to advocate publicly [for] better conditions for the laboring classes, and especially for the wage earner," Kem asserts in one of several letters he wrote to Oregon senator Charles McNary and to the *Oregonian* on the issue of wartime strikes. But now, he continues, in the context of war, the strikers' demands are trivial—even worse, *treasonous*: "The very lives of our boys in the trenches are absolutely dependent upon this shipping and the man who will deliberately desert his job under these conditions hasn't a drop of loyal blood under his miserable hide." The tools of copper miners, sawyers, or shipbuilders, Kem says, are "instruments of war"; to "throw them down" is to "desert in the face of the enemy."[45]

To strike, writes Omer, is an act of aggression, not against the bosses but against the soldiers whose survival depends on the products of factory and shipyard. "When [a worker] throws down his hammer and refuses to work it tends to destroy the boys in the trenches, as effectively as if he were to take the hammer and knock them on the head," he says rather dramatically.[46] For Kem, the worker had become merely an "animated tool" (Martin Luther King Jr.'s phrase) whose own basic needs—for the eight-hour day, for adequate housing and pay, for safer working environments—were irrelevant.[47] "I do not know Senator, whether you have a boy in the army or not," he adds, bringing his argument home. "I know I have, and for this reason, this favoritism to labor is beginning to get under my hide as it is getting under the hide of many others who have given their best to their country."[48] He signs this letter with the Populist slogan "Equal Rights for All, Special Privileges for None!"

This is an example of what Judith Butler calls "the phantasmagoric inversion of aggression," in which a vulnerable person or group's protest against inhumane treatment is itself considered an act of violence, often against the state.[49] Voicing the aggressive militarism of the time (and the opinions of the president), Kem calls for "prompt action" against the strikers' "disloyal, unlawful, criminal, acts."[50]

But this seemed only fair. As he had argued, the "boys in the trenches" had no choice but to fight: "The Government places a gun in the hands of these boys and commands them to get into the muddy trenches not for eight hours . . . but for twenty-four hours . . . their lives are in danger every minute . . . if they were to throw down their guns and desert their post, as the hammer thrower has done frequently, they would have to face a firing squad, and they ought to."[51]

This was in fact true. Under Article 85 of the Uniform Code of Military Justice, any soldier found in military court to have deserted during wartime would face execution by his superiors at dawn. The law was absolute on the matter; in the fall of 1917, two men, ages nineteen and twenty, were convicted of desertion for having briefly fallen asleep while standing sentinel "in correct military position" during an all-night watch.[52] War logic makes animated tools out of everyone.

But had Omer wanted to resist the situation in which the government demanded the potential sacrifice of his youngest son in order to protect its markets and grow its international power and influence, he would have found many friends in that struggle, some of whom, like the anti-imperialist Jim Ream, were also aging Populists.[53] Those who refuted Wilson's decision to enter the "Great War" included another of Omer's one-time political allies, Wilson's first secretary of state, William Jennings Bryan. Bryan was a pacifist with a sustained critique of "power politics," which, he argued, "presupposes the existence of an enemy who must be hated until he can be overcome."[54] Bryan opposed J. P. Morgan's initial request to lend money to France on the grounds that the debt would inevitably draw the United States into the war.[55] "Money," he said, is "the worst of all contrabands because it commands everything else."[56] In June of 1915, after Wilson threatened to retaliate against Germany's U-boats, Bryan resigned in protest and, for a time, joined the anti-militarism movement in earnest.[57]

In the lead-up to America's entrance into the war, the American Union against Militarism and the Women's Peace Party both staged powerful anti-war demonstrations and marches, including a silent march of 1,500 women down New York City's Fifth Avenue. Two thousand women from twelve countries, including forty-six Americans, met in a conference for peace at the Hague in the spring of 1915. Eighty thousand people marched in an "anti-preparedness" parade in 1916. That same year, *War against War*, a satirical anti-war exhibition, attracted five to ten thousand visitors a day in New York and then toured nine other cities. The Socialist Party held an emergency convention in the spring of 1917 where they condemned the war as a "crime against the people of the United States." The People's Council of America for Democracy and Peace brought socialists, unionists, feminists, and religious leaders together to oppose the war on moral grounds, arguing that militarism only begets more militarism, with the outcome being at best an unstoppable and ever more dangerous arms race.[58] Anarchists Emma Goldman and Alexander Berkman formed the Non-Conscription League in 1917; eight thousand people showed up to their first meeting.[59] Feminist pacifists Alice Paul, Jane Addams, and Fannie May Witherspoon, labor activist and feminist Crystal Eastman, IWW leaders Bill Haywood and Elizabeth Gurley Flynn Black socialists A. Philip Randolph and Chandler Owen, and the progressive governor of Wisconsin, Robert La Follette, all actively and publicly resisted the war.[60] It was "the largest, most diverse, and most sophisticated peace coalition at that point in U.S. history," as historian Michael Kazin writes.[61]

"How can profits be made out of the war," Randolph and Owen asked in the pages of their paper the *Messenger*? "By selling to the government those things which are needed to keep the war going.... Now, Mr. Common-man, do you own any of those things? If you don't, then you cannot profit from the war."[62] Rabbi Judah L. Magnes, speaking at a 1917 People's Council rally in New York, denounced the war as a "riot of power in the hands of a few overlords."[63] Indeed, as Populists had long known, rising tides did not lift all boats; the wartime boom economy led to a rise in cost of living with no corresponding rise in wages: "It was the American worker who was paying for business war-profiteering," writes Tooze.[64] But Kem directed no rage against the profiteering owners of banks, mines, shipping companies, or factories; instead, he turned on Mr. Common-man himself. Too old to fight the "Hun," Kem sided with the "capitalist class" and went to war against the workers.

This situation can be understood, of course, solely through the lens of class; Kem had become a businessman and so had shifted his alliance from the workers to the owners. But that doesn't tell the whole story. His turn against workers' rights was not driven by economics; it was driven by fear and aggression—which is really what being a patriot in wartime is all about.

War, that ultimate expression of power, a power that values the state more than the person, that understands the person as a "tool," a weapon, or a source of revenue primarily, will always strive to mask a nation's internal political and cultural antagonisms under a forced or forged unity. In arguing in favor of mandatory conscription, one representative in 1917, for example, referred to military training as "a melting pot which will . . . break down distinctions of race and class and mold us into a new nation . . . of Americans."[65] But for this alchemical magic to work, groups with legitimate grievances and claims—Black people, Native people, immigrants, working people, women—would have to bury their needs and merge their cries with the nation's own vengeful voice.[66] No "unity" grounded in such violent and repressive patriotism is sustainable.

Troops came home in late 1918 to joyous parades. Famously, Black soldiers, the Harlem Hellfighters, were cheered on their return by largely white crowds in New York City.[67] But just months after Armistice Day, the smoldering class and race antagonisms in the country, which had never "melted" away, ignited. In January of 1919 the International Workers' Defense League pledged a national strike in defense of AFL leader Tom Mooney, who had been sentenced to life in prison for allegedly bombing a 1916 Preparedness Parade.[68] In February the city of Seattle went silent for six days as workers in all sectors—waitresses, candymakers, butchers—struck in solidarity with the shipbuilders.[69] Hundreds of thousands of coal workers walked off their jobs that year, and a nationwide steel strike dragged on into the winter of 1920.[70] In Chicago, at a three-week-long IWW conference, the Wobblies, though significantly weakened, demanded the end of capitalism, and then, in Centralia, Washington, engaged in armed struggle with Legionnaires. Anti-capitalism went a huge step further on June 2 of 1919, when the anarchist Carlo Valdinoci bombed the home of Attorney General A. Mitchell Palmer. Though Valdinoci succeeded in blowing up only himself, his was one of at least seven bombs set off by Italian anarchists across America that night.[71]

Wartime violence proved an addictive infusion, an "almost animal craving" as war resister Max Eastman had written.[72] Throughout the summer of 1919, white people from sea to sea, enraged by the presence of Black men in uniform, as many have argued, exposed the limits of unity by burning and even bombing Black neighborhoods and businesses and beating and lynching Black people with an extreme brutality not seen since Reconstruction. At least thirty-eight riots or massacres led to hundreds of deaths. Tens of thousands of people lost their homes. As historians Cameron McWhirter and Adriane Lentz-Smith detail, Black people did not take such violence passively: "African Americans on the ground in riot-besieged districts did not wait for government protection that might never come; they fought back."[73] In New York the NAACP, which had been expanding its reach and power tenfold under Black leadership, led the first ever national conference on lynching, attempting (and failing) to push Congress to pass the Dyer anti-lynching bill.[74]

And the government fought back too, with vengeance. Attorney General Palmer and the twenty-four-year-old J. Edgar Hoover, drawing a direct line of connection between anarchists, Russian Bolsheviks, and Black activists (or just Black people), used their wartime powers—the Espionage and Sedition Acts—to raid, deport, and jail as many activists as they could.[75] "By April 1919 almost all the first- and second-line IWW leaders were in federal prison," writes Melvyn Dubofsky.[76] Socialist leaders Eugene Debs and A. Philip Randolph were both imprisoned, and by 1919, Goldman and Berkman were deported. Hundreds of ordinary Americans on the left were silenced, beaten, or thrown in jail for speaking out in public or private against the war, as the federal government's aggression went viral.[77]

The rise of the 1920s anti-Black, antisemitic, anti-Catholic, and anti-immigrant KKK, the increases in legal and illegal anti-Black terrorism across the country, the racist and nativist immigration policies, and the national embrace of eugenics—all were energized by the logics of war through which we are reminded that some lives are valuable and others simply fuel or trash.[78]

Neighbor

> O, let my land be land where Liberty
> Is crowned with no false patriotic wreath,
> But opportunity is real, and life is free,
> Equality is in the air we breathe.
> —Langston Hughes, "Let America Be America Again"

> The impossible world is the one that exists beyond the horizon of our present thinking—it is neither the horizon of terrible war, not the ideal of a perfect place. It is the open-ended struggle required to preserve our bonds against all that in the world which bears the potential to tear them apart.
> —Judith Butler, *The Force of Nonviolence*

During the Vietnam War, my mother became a committed anti-war activist, organizing marches, rallies, and study groups in Cambridge, Massachusetts, where we lived.[79] In 1967 she spearheaded a campaign to get an anti-war referendum on the city ballot. Presenting her petition to the city council, she spoke forcefully and bluntly, as she generally did. "The Vietnam war is brutal, senseless and wasteful," she told them. "People hate this war."[80]

I was an infant then, and my brother was a toddler. We went to the protests in a baby carriage. She used to say, "It was not politics that got to me. What did I care about politics? It was thinking about the neighbor's son." In fact, she cared a lot about politics, but she understood politics to begin with a turn toward the neighbor. The neighbor—the person you might not even know but whose kinship bonds you can nevertheless hold in your mind—might call you toward a life you did not plan but cannot refuse. That is how I understand what happened to her: as the mother of two small children, she could and did imagine what it would be like to have a child at war. And because she could imagine that terror, she fought against it.

I want Omer of the nineteen-teens and twenties to be able to imagine the neighbor's son when that son is working in a shipping yard

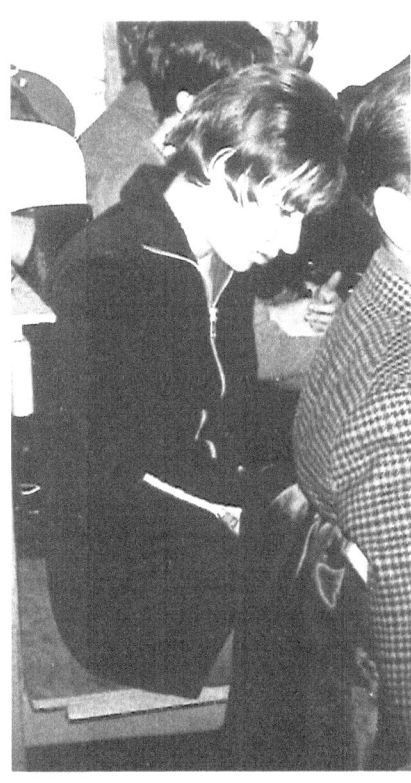

24. Carolyn Carr, anti-war meeting, Cambridge, Massachusetts, 1967. Author's collection.

for twelve hours a day with nowhere to sleep at the end of it. I want him to imagine the neighbor's son or daughter when that son or daughter is Black in any city in America in 1919 or before that date, or after, when hostile white people and their police murderously rage. I want Omer to be able to imagine the neighbor's child as an infant in an asylum or a migrant at the border.

But if I want Omer to be able to extend his imagination, and his concern, to all these children and their families, then I need to be able to do the same, and I so often fail. Imagination is powerful, and imagination is fragile and weak. Imagination, through which we can expand our sense of responsibility and care beyond our immediate friends or family, beyond our neighborhood, city, our country, and even our species, is not the work of an individual mind but of an entire community. The wider that community, the wider the imagination of its members and the wider the circle of care.

"A new imaginary is required—an egalitarian imaginary that apprehends the interdependency of lives," writes Butler. "All kinship, in the end, is imaginary," writes Ruha Benjamin. Which does not mean it isn't real.[81]

And so I come to this: I need also to imagine what it might feel like if the state were to take my child and send him into battle for reasons abstract at best. I need to understand how given the option of futilely resisting the state, or translating that outrage into personal pride and power, I might choose the latter. And I need to understand how, having chosen the latter, having fully internalized the logic of war as a force for "right," I might find myself turning that war logic against other people's sons and daughters, not only on the battlefield but also at home, as if to create a shield of vengeance around my own child.

Despite having lived almost all my life in a country at wars both overt and covert, I have no first-hand knowledge about it. Or that's what I tell myself. Part of this ignorance is gendered, of course—military history is boy stuff, as my bibliography for this section can attest to. But claimed ignorance is also a product of a willed and fabricated American "innocence." If I know nothing, I can't be blamed.

But though no one in my close family fought in the Korean War, the Vietnam War, the first Gulf War, or the wars in Iraq or Afghanistan, what I do know, so well that it's almost like not knowing it, is what war does to those of us who live far from battle sites or drone targets while the most powerful country in the world rages on in our name, seemingly without end. This experience of war power is an acute psychological reality, though it's so ordinary in America that it might feel like nothing. Living in a country at near constant war means that there is always something held up as more important than life, than *anyone's* life, and that something is power. War might be demanded, might be provoked, but no matter its causes, it imparts a logic of annihilation. (Even the so-called good war, we must never forget, ended with the United States obliterating over one hundred thousand Japanese lives in an instant, an event the entire world is still living.)[82] War—through which nations, *this* nation, often in the name of peace or self-defense, performs, protects, and expands its influence—divides the world and

25. Victor Kem, 1917. Author's collection.

all the people in it into two categories: the valued and the valueless, even as those categories constantly shift. This is what I know of war. Victor, though he did not kill and was not wounded, knew more.[83]

I tried to imagine Victor as a child and not as the damaged and abusive man he became. Omer gives me little. I know the date of Victor's birth, November 28, 1897, and I know he was, like his father, a redhead. But Omer tells me no more of Victor's childhood. Victor was born the year the family moved to Montrose, Colorado. With seven children between eighteen months and twenty-one years old, a new home, farm, and ranch to get going, it is perhaps not surprising that Omer says little about him. Within the first two years of Victor's life, his older sister, Linda, suffered her first mental health crisis, and his youngest sister, Marie, died. This is all I know of Victor's childhood before he entered the war.

But if I have trouble visioning Victor's boyhood, I have even more trouble imagining what soldiers and their families went through then or go through now. But I *have* to be able to imagine these things. "The neighbor's son" includes the one who has been drawn into war, even, or especially, if that war takes from him the possibility of an empathic life. *Blue with all malice*, the violence went after him too.[84]

<pre>
                    ADDED ADENDUN

                     MARCH 1934

TO THOSE FRIENDS WHO MAY ATTEND THE CEREMONY INCIDENTAL TO THE

                   DEATH OF MY BODY

                       GREETIBF
</pre>

26. "Added Adendun," March 1934. Omer Madison Kem Papers, 11:200.

Afterlife

> As flowers turn toward the sun, by dint of a secret heliotropism the past strives to turn toward that sun which is rising in the sky of history.
> —Walter Benjamin, "On the Concept of History"

> Run to it, run to it. It's an "afterlife."
> —Dream voice, June 3, 2020

At eighty, when he was anticipating his own death, Omer Kem wrote a letter to his future survivors: ADDED ADENDUN. GREETIBF. It was difficult for him to type it, but it was important. He believed he would live on without his body, but nonetheless, there were three things he needed to impart before the transition: first, his ashes must be scattered in the Oregon hills; second, there must be no minister of any denomination invited to his funeral; and finally, "the only source of salvation lies within one's self."

His body hung on for seven more abysmal years. World War I, which had turned Omer into a "patriot," had bled toward a future in which the genocidal fantasies of Americans would be realized by their enemies. By the time Omer died, Mussolini had invaded Ethiopia, the Nazis, in the name of race purity, had sterilized hundreds of thousands of people, and the mass slaughter of six million Jews and thousands upon thousands of homosexuals, communists, people with disabilities, and Roma and Sinti people had begun. There is no way to cleanly divide these atrocities from the American genocide of Native people or from Jim Crow or from the American eugenics movement. "You tell me that hitler / is a mighty bad man. / I guess he took lessons / From the ku klux klan," as Langston

Hughes put it.[85] European fascists had studied America and learned what worked.

The stories my father and grandmother told me about Omer Kem—how he had crossed the country in a covered wagon, how he had stood for ordinary farmers and laborers, how he had fought against political corruption and capitalistic greed—these stories made me a little proud and were an inspiration. At a time when 9 percent of American families owned 71 percent of the country's wealth, when the average industrial worker lived on $406 a year, and when striking workers were routinely beaten and shot at by hired thugs, he had actively and energetically sought justice for the working poor—he did far more than most for that cause.[86] He was a passionate man, an adventurous man, sometimes a funny man and—most important to my father—he was adored by his children.

All of this was true, but it was a partial truth.

For during the roughly twenty years that Omer Kem lobbied and legislated on behalf of poor farmers and laborers, he simultaneously excluded those whose labor and land the country had most aggressively appropriated and exploited, people who often suffered the worst poverty in the nation, from the category of the worthy. Having been granted stolen land on which to build his wealth, Omer actively tried to strip Native people of even more of it, even while calling out the injustice. He refused admission and thus opportunity for people from Asia (nearly half the world's population), while having no concerns about immigrants who were white. He saw Black people as a biohazard and supported Jim Crow barriers. As if his racism had primed him for general disregard, when he moved into the middle class, he left his struggle for working people behind and became the opportunistic capitalist that he had once railed against. During the war and after, he turned against workers' legitimate demands for justice, safety, and even bare survival. Throughout the teens, twenties, and into the thirties, Omer became fluent in what Toni Morrison called "the lethal discourse of exclusion," drawing an ever tightening circle around those he considered deserving, in the end, of life itself. Finally, it seemed that the settler's view of the natural world—that it was his to exploit, subdue, and control, a resource over which the white man had dominion—applied to people too. No one in the family had ever mentioned these aspects of the legacy.[87] Our legend, like all legends, was selective. But Omer led me directly to this fuller story of himself by meticulously documenting the development of his eventually fascistic ideas. It was as if he were offering himself as a warning, a blueprint of what was to come.

In some ways, none of it was surprising. The oscillating tension between egalitarian ideals and racist classist exclusion is as old as America. Like the power grid with its lethal charge, this tension is sometimes starkly visible and sometimes hidden in the walls, but it is always there, feeding everything we do. "It is this paradox which allows in America the most rapid advance of democracy to go hand in hand . . . with increased aristocracy and hatred toward darker races, and which excuses and defends an inhumanity that does not shrink from the public burning of human beings," wrote Du Bois with acerbic clarity in 1915.[88]

An obsession with whiteness, a proudful self-reliance that barely masks the shame of dependence, an aggressive assertion of patriotic belonging that obscures the trespasser's guilty relation to the land, and an inflamed sense of personal rightness and strength, even purity—these qualities might be particular to white settler Populists like Omer Kem, but they are also fundamental to so much of white America. And to find such qualities in another does not mean they do not reside in the self.

But the other strand of that current was right there too, in the founding document of the Populist Party. The Omaha Platform is credited to white Minnesota farmer and novelist Ignatius Donnelly and was adopted by the new party in 1892, just after Kem was elected to Congress.[89] But we know that the Omaha Congress was made up of both white and Black and men and women, including prominent Black Populists William Warwick of Virginia, H. D. Cassdall of Missouri, and L. D. Laurent of Louisiana. The writing of the party platform was a collaborative effort.[90] And so, as we read that document, we must try to imagine all those people's voices coming together in shared outrage and shared hope.

"The conditions that surround us best justify our cooperation," they begin. Corruption in all institutions, an unfree press, extreme inequality, "homes covered with mortgages, labor impoverished, and the land concentrating in the hands of capitalists": these were the conditions under which they struggled. "The fruits of the toil of millions are boldly stolen to build up colossal fortunes for a few," and politicians, indebted to the corporations, simply do not, *cannot* within this structure, care. Instead, these politicians "destroy the multitude in order to secure corruption funds from the millionaires."[91] Here in this document lies one seed for the resistance we desperately need now when once again (or, as always) massive corporations—oil and gas companies, pipeline companies, chemical and coal companies—use their vast wealth to direct politicians at every level into helping them perpetrate ongoing and heinous crimes against the human and nonhuman worlds.

While some of the solutions the Populists propose are particular to their time (the re-monetization of silver, for example), others sound as relevant in 2022 as their distress does. The Populists call for the full unionization of labor, for worker-owned factories and farms, for the nationalization of transportation and communication, for a fair, graduated income tax, for worker protections, for free and fair elections, and for the end to land speculation so housing can be available for all. Perhaps, in the context of American capitalism, these proposals are perennially relevant.

But as crucial as these complaints and demands are, their foundation is perhaps even more so, for the Populists based their cries for justice and equity on the principle of love: "This Republic can only endure as a free government while built upon the love of the whole people for each other." And though this word *love*, like the phrase *the people*, has so often been cheapened, distorted, and mobilized for violent ends, I still want to ask: What if we took them at their word?

What could it possibly mean for a "whole people" to love each other? The Populist platform begs this question, asking us to consider the feeling we attach to our children or parents, our siblings or partners, our friends—this profound desire for our beloveds' survival and well-being, the overwhelming drive to secure their happiness when possible and to provide comfort and care when not—and it asks us to extend these fierce and tender feelings to *all* the people, those we see and those we do not see but know to be there, to be *here*, even to those who are elsewhere, even—or especially—during wartime. Because a population is not and never can be a stable entity, because a population is a shifting, growing, migrating, living, and dying motility, the "love of the whole people for each other" is by definition an anarchic, limitless love that resists boundaries and borders wherever and whenever they arise.

This is the impossible dream that the Populist platform holds out, and it's the only one worth believing in. Salvation does not "lie in one's self" but in the improvisatory ongoing movement between and among all people when we are oriented toward one another's care and toward the care of the earth that sustains us. For what is the alternative? Perhaps this is not a politics but, as Jim Ream said, a *foundation*, an orientation, a vector to follow.

On that terrible day in July of 2016 in Cleveland, as the GOP celebrated, I made a private vow. I would dig down into this American story, get to something buried underground, some original seed of violent exclusion, of bitter rage and barrier; I'd dig it out and maybe eat it, as if I were a demon or a dog.

The image of digging for answers in the dirt came to me suddenly—and as suddenly, I knew it was wrong. That drive to root out a mystery and subsume it into the self, this fantasy of eating the secrets buried in the earth, carries a hint of aggression, even of hubris, for not all knowledges are for me. But the image was wrong for another reason too; the thing that seemed to be buried underground was not in the least buried. It was right here in the open, everywhere I looked. When I asked my father for memories of his grandfather, he told me of lying in the grass in Omer's backyard, gazing up into the branches of a fir tree. Omer is not in this memory, but he is.

My memories of my father also include lying down on the earth. I am maybe ten, we are on our backs, holding hands, feeling the world spin, watching leaves shift and flutter. I can still smell the scents of soil and grass. I can still feel his hand, which holds me in place as I fall.

Omer is also in this memory. So is Iris, Linda, Huxley, Victor, Alice, about whom I still know so little, and Kathleen, whose life I saw in my dreams. So too are the people whose lives their lives intersected with, people they disregarded and harmed, and people they loved and tried to protect. History dissipates through the air, enters our bodies, makes us who and what we are. But we might not see it unless we see how it makes things move, might not feel it except in moments of great duress or quietness, when we sense ourselves to be breathing.

Five years into the writing of this book, I found a new image. It came to me in a dream. I was walking toward a group of young people, maybe my children, maybe other people's children. I was holding something small and hard in my hand, like a stone. It's my manuscript, I said; I was looking for a safe place to put it. But they laughed at me. Don't you know you don't need that thing anymore? It's in your whole body now.

That summer, 2021, I had hoped to go to Oregon. I wanted to see Chris again, to look through his family photos one more time. I wanted to talk to people who live in Cottage Grove now, and I wanted to walk in the forests where the trees that powered Omer and Charles Shinn's furnace once grew, to breathe that forest's air so that I might breathe in Omer's ashes. But the pandemic was spiking in Oregon. The state was facing its highest hospitalizations since March of 2020. It seemed brazenly foolish and also unfeeling to fly there under these conditions. At the same time, in a sense I was already there, breathing in those trees and that ash.

All that August, wildfire smoke had been flowing east from Oregon and California. It entered my lungs in Denver and dulled the skies all the way to Maine. As I breathed those toxins in my sleep and in my waking hours too, my blood was altered with the land.[92]

We are not other than the histories that move through us, not other than the futures we make. And so, in the end as at the beginning, there is really only one question, here written by Jim Ream and retyped by Omer's hand: *What are we here for, what should life mean to me, to us?*

Notes

Introduction

1. *Harvard Magazine* Archive, no page, accessed August 2021, https://www.harvardmagazine.com/sites/default/files/html/1997/03/biblio.3.html.
2. Wilkinson, *Caste*, 4.
3. The term *populism* has been used to refer to a wide range of political groups from Latin America, Europe, Asia, and the United States. In this book, when I use the capitalized terms *Populism* and *Populist*, I am referring to the southern and western U.S. farmers who formed the People's Party in the 1890s. Some scholars refer to the actions of the Farmers Alliance also as "Populism." When I use the lowercase terms *populist* and *populism*, I am referring more generally to a bottom-up politics, which can be embraced by the right or the left. Useful to me for cross-national comparisons have been Dix, "Populism: Authoritarian and Democratic"; Mouffe, *For a Left Populism*; and Gandesha, "Understanding Right and Left Populism." Paolo Gerbaudo's *The Great Recoil: Politics after Populism and Pandemic* offers an analysis of both right and left populism as an almost inevitable response to globalization, neoliberalism, and (for the right) increased migration in the twenty-first century.
4. In 1962 a Creighton University master's student named Delloyd Guth defended his thesis, "Omer Madison Kem: The People's Congressman." Guth praised Kem as a radical bent on preserving his agrarian "birthright" against the rising tide of industrial capitalism. Guth had corresponded with my grandmother Kathleen and great-grandmother Alice. He had interviewed Omer and Alice's oldest son, Claude, who was the holder of Omer's eleven-volume memoir. Because of Guth's interest, Claude eventually donated the volumes to Creighton University's library.

5. Wikipedia, s.v. "Stephen Blumberg," last modified March 25, 2022, https://en.wikipedia.org/wiki/Stephen_Blumberg.
6. Congressional Research Service, "U.S. Income Distribution." See especially figure 3 on page 10.
7. Center on Budget Policy and Priorities, "Fact Sheets." The University of Colorado, where I work, receives just 4.5 percent of its budget from the state. The cost of attending CU Boulder in 2021 was $54,296 for out-of-state students and $28,478 for in-state.
8. Crenshaw, "Looking Back to Move Forward," timestamp 7:50. PEN America has been tracking these "educational gag orders," some of which also ban the teaching of communism and socialism, or police language around gender and sexuality. So too has *Education Week*. See Sachs, "Steep Rise in Gag Orders."
9. Roediger, *Wages*, 20.
10. Whiteness, as Cheryl Harris writes, was "an exclusive club whose membership was closely and grudgingly guarded." Harris, "Whiteness as Property," 283.
11. *Plessy v. Ferguson* (1896). Plessy was also considered "seven-eighths Caucasian and one-eighth African blood." "Legal reasoning manipulates the fictions that sustain idioms of servility." Dayan, *The Law*, 4.
12. Kem, 4:67–68, OMKP. Huxley became an artist and filmmaker, winning awards for his amateur films, made with Mary in the 1930s. He was a commercial sign maker and patented a form of commercial paint. He was also deeply enthusiastic about family history and made a genealogy of his own (now lost).
13. Kem, 7:4, OMKP.
14. Giscombe, *Prairie Style*, 5.
15. Celan, "The Meridian," 49.
16. Stephen Carr, now retired, designed parks and other public spaces through the architectural firm Carr, Lynch, Hack and Sandell, and, with Kevin Lynch, advocated for, wrote about, and practiced participatory design.
17. Burch, "Bibliomania," 9.

1. Mud

1. Daniel Sayers argues that the term *Underground Railroad* "feed[s] and sustain[s] a kind of 'feel-good' (or apathetic) and facile historical

awareness." He prefers to discuss the process of *marronage*, which centers activity on the "maroon" rather than on the person supplying aid in transitory movement. Sayers, "Marronage Perspective," 142.

2. Narratives of rescues performed by white Quakers tend to omit the work that free and enslaved Blacks did as leaders, organizers, and foot soldiers in the Underground Railroad. LaRoche, *The Geography of Resistance*.

3. Regan-Dinius, "With Bodily Force and Violence." "In the spring of 1822 Samuel Todd of Kentucky sent two agents to Wayne County, Indiana, to capture a fugitive slave who had left him about four years before. The agents, after vigilant search, found him in the person of one George Sheldon." Bulla, *Biography of Thomas P. Bulla*. See also C. N. Fassett, "Man Sacrificed for Principle," *South Bend Review*, July 16, 1921, 12.

4. Bulla, *Biography of Thomas P. Bulla*, 18; O'Brien, "The Stationmaster."

5. The 1884 *History of Wayne County* states the following: "Thomas Bulla, came to America from Ireland, when a young man, and settled in Chester County, PA, where he married Esther Widows, by whom he had twelve children. In 1784 he moved to Randolph County NC. He owned six or seven slaves, but set them free in his will" (769).

Kem's *Genealogy* lists three slaves who were not freed in Thomas Jr.'s will but sold upon his death to Gray. The *Genealogy* includes a corroborating copy of Thomas Bulla Jr.'s will. "All of the whites who were not able to own slaves were looked upon as 'poor white trash' and not considered quite as good as the Negro," writes Kem. *Genealogy*, 49, OMKP.

6. *Johnson v. M'Intosh*, whose precedent still stands, is considered the cornerstone of U.S. property law to this day. Banner, *How the Indians Lost Their Land*, 179–88.

7. *Johnson v. M'Intosh*; Barker, "Sovereignty," 6–9.

8. As Mary Hershberger describes, women led the anti-removal movement, "flood[ing] Congress with antiremoval petitions." Hershberger, "Mobilizing Women," 15. For more on the passage of the Indian Removal Act, see Bowes, "American Indian Removal."

9. Bowes, "American Indian Removal," 72–73. The forced removal of the Potawatomi from the Yellow River area of Indiana in 1838 is referred to as the Potawatomi Trail of Death. At least forty people died in the two-month journey from northern Indiana to Kansas.

10. Campion, "Indian Removal Northern Indiana," 38–39.
11. "Even after completion of the Wabash and Erie Canal, which ran through the swamp, Indiana's reputation as a haven for dangerous diseases retarded settlement. The state's first wave of settlers were relatively poor people from the Carolinas and Kentucky, not the more affluent settlers from New England and New York who established Illinois and Ohio." Pisani, "Beyond the Hundredth Meridian," 475.
12. Kem, 1:19, OMKP.
13. LaRoche, *The Geography of Resistance*, 57–70.
14. Later, my cousin Chris found it for me: www.youtube.com/watch?v=BjxZntflKrM.
15. Conklin, "The Underground Railroad in Indiana," 66.
16. Fehrenbacher, *The Slaveholding Republic*, 212–13.
17. Du Bois, *Black Reconstruction*, 13.
18. "No person held to service or labor in one state, under the laws thereof, escaping into another, shall, in consequence of any law or regulation therein, be discharged from such service or labor, but shall be delivered up on claim of the party to whom such service or labor may be due." *Constitution of the United States of American*, Article IV, Section 2, Clause 3. For a detailed narrative of the event and ruling, see Finkelman, "Sorting Out *Prigg v. Pennsylvania*."
19. As legal scholar Paul Finkelman notes, according to this ruling, the violent capture of previously enslaved persons, or their descendants, is *not* considered a breach of peace. Finkelman, "Sorting Out *Prigg v. Pennsylvania*," 637.
20. According to Finkelman, the court's decision was not unambiguous. Though the leading opinion, written by Justice Story, upheld the constitutionality of the 1793 Fugitive Slave Act, there were seven opinions written in total. Only one of these (from Justice McLean) was a clear dissent, but four of the others disagreed with portions of Story's opinion. Indeed, long before his ruling in *Dred Scott*, Taney had been a member of the anti-kidnapping society in Maryland. As a lawyer in 1806, he took up the case of a free Black man who'd been kidnapped in Pennsylvania and manumitted eleven enslaved people. Huebner, "Roger B. Taney and the Slavery Issue," 17–38; Finkelman, "Sorting Out *Prigg v. Pennsylvania*," 630.
21. *Prigg v. Pennsylvania* (1842).
22. Hambly, *Argument of Mr. Hambly*, 6.

23. Finkelman, "Sorting Out *Prigg v. Pennsylvania*," 656. Italics added.
24. Murphy, *The Jerry Rescue*, 20–23.
25. Even before this law, it was a crime in Indiana, punishable by fine, to help free a recaptured slave. The new law ups that punishment significantly and vastly increases the number of commissioners required to oversee recaption efforts. Pinsker, "After 1850," 99.
26. Prior to this law, in Indiana a person suspected of being a fugitive from slavery was given a trial by jury.
27. Farrow, Lang, and Frank, *Complicity*, 3–45.
28. These numbers are derived from Campbell, *Slave Catchers*. For Du Bois's discussion of how the Fugitive Slave Law motivated abolitionists, see Du Bois, *Black Reconstruction*, 32–54.
29. Minnesota Board of Water and Soil Resources, "Carbon Sequestration in Wetlands"; Sarah Almukhtar et al., "The Great Flood of 2019," *New York Times*, September 11, 2019; Sarah Bowman and London Gibson, "'Last Line of Defense': New Bill Would Strip Protections for Many of Indiana's Wetlands," *Indianapolis Star*, January 25, 2021.

    The drainage of wetlands has also contributed to water crises in the western states. Restoration projects seek to mitigate this loss. See Martin & McCoy et al., *Ten Strategies*, 24–25.
30. "Swamps contained great natural wealth . . . and in most places they served as a vast commons. Standing and downed cypress and cedar trees attracted lumber companies, but they also permitted poor farmers to supplement their income by splitting shingles. In addition, the extensive grasslands bordering swamps beckoned to those who wanted to raise cattle and hogs." Pisani, "Beyond," 476.
31. Pisani, "Beyond," 477. "For a state to move forward, it not only had to tame wetlands but also to banish the impoverished human beings who clustered around the swamps." Pisani, "Beyond," 476.
32. Mosier, "The Settling of the Grand Marsh of the Kankakee River."
33. Pisani, "Beyond," 475; Strausberg, "Indiana and the Swamp Lands Act," 194; Prince, "A Marsh-Land Chronicle," 3–22.
34. States that were granted swamp lands were LA, AL, AR, CA, FL, IL, IN, IO, MI, MS, OH, MO, and, in 1860, MN and OR. Dahl and Allord, "History of Wetlands."
35. M. Bogue, "Swampland Act and Wet Land Utilization in Illinois," 170.
36. Sayers, "Marronage Perspective," 137, 138. A growing field of *marronage* studies addresses this history of resistance and solidarity across

the Western hemisphere, employing a variety of research methods, including, in this case, archeology.

37. Diouf, *Slavery's Exiles*, 131. Diouf also discusses "borderland maroons," those who took refuge in undeveloped lands just beyond the limits of the plantation, often motivated to do so by proximity to family members: "The only places that were close to their loved ones and also relatively safe were the forests and swamps that bordered the plantations." She stresses that all maroon communities, no matter how brief or long, small or large, close or far from white control they were, managed to forge some degree of "autonomy, mobility, enterprise . . . physical security, freedom from scrutiny, [and] control over their time and movement." Diouf, *Slavery's Exiles*, 175, 8.
38. Sayers, *A Desolate Place*; also see R. Grant, "Deep in the Swamps."
39. Indiana's whites had enslaved both African and Indigenous people from the time of their earliest arrival until at least the 1820s. McDonald, "The Negro in Indiana Before 1881."
40. S. Taylor, "Fletcher's Swamp and Bacon's Swamp."
41. "So, after all, Mr. Fletcher's favorite bird, and a very unpopular one too, in that day was the blackbird," this writer concludes. "The Swamp with a History," *Indianapolis Journal*, December 15, 1889, 13.
42. A. Gordon, *Hawthorn Archive*, 33.
43. Carlson, "Drain the Swamps for Health and Home," 4.
44. Carlson traces such theories to Comte de Buffon's late eighteenth-century *Histoire naturell*: "Buffon insisted that North America, just prior to its discovery, began to recover from a transcontinental flood. As a result, long stretches of marshes and swamps, towering forests, impenetrable undergrowth, and a frigid and miasmatic atmosphere predominated. . . . The chilly and wet climate produced an indolent, sickly, and unimpressive natural order." Carlson, "Drain the Swamps for Health and Home," 28–29.
45. Waring, *Draining for Profit, Draining for Health*, 11–12.
46. Today when a city embarks on a large-scale development plan or creates an "opportunity zone" for developers, it first has to locate and label the markers of "blight" in a neighborhood—areas of decay or overgrowth, often described as "cancerous," generally unhealthy or "unsafe." Now as then, once an area is deemed "blighted," it becomes an "opportunity" not so much for the people who live there but for those who seek their removal.

47. "Deforestation [and] the drying of the swamplands for agriculture and urbanization were among the factors that led to the fading of large [maroon] communities." Diouf, *Slavery's Exiles*, 38.
48. Carlson, "Drain the Swamps for Health and Home," 32.
49. Less than 3 percent of the swamplands of Indiana remain. McCorvie and Lant, "Drainage District Formation," 22; "Indiana, Surveyor's Note," quoted in Strausberg, "Indiana and the Swamp Lands Act," 191.
50. Prince, *Wetlands of the American Midwest*, 147, 205.
51. Strausberg, "Indiana and the Swamp Lands Act," 200.
52. Strausberg, "Indiana and the Swamp Lands Act," 201. See also McCorvie and Lant, "Drainage District Formation," 27–28.
53. "Counties offered swamplands for sale at less than the government minimum price, some for 50 cents, some for as little as ten cents an acre, in the hope that purchasers might undertake improvements. Most of the land was acquired by speculators who added to their large holdings." Prince, *Wetlands*, 204–5.
54. McDonald, "The Negro in India," 291–306. Almost all discussions of Article 13 that I've read emphasize that it was poorly enforced.
55. Fletcher, *Diaries*, 4:238.
56. Indiana Constitutional Convention, "Report of the Debates, 1850," 458.
57. McCorvie and Lant report that "absentee speculators and large landowners captured as much as 56 percent of the [drained] lands." McCorvie and Lant, "Drainage District Formation," 28.
58. "The Swamp with a History," *Indianapolis Journal*, December 15, 1889.
59. Kem, 1:40, 47, OMKP.
60. Across the corn belt, 95 percent of wetlands have been drained. McCorvie and Lant, "Drainage District Formation," 22–25.

2. Sod

1. Kem, 1:69, OMKP.
2. Kem, 7:42, OMKP.
3. Kem, 1:69, OMKP.
4. W. Webb, *The Great Plains*, 489.
5. Wishart, *An Unspeakable Sadness*, xiii. The *Nebraska Blue Book* estimates that in 1800, there were as many as forty thousand Native people in what is now Nebraska as a whole, including Cheyennes, Arapahos, Winnebagos, and Teton Sioux.

6. Quoted in Frymer, *Building an American Empire*, 151. See Banner, *How the Indians Lost Their Land*, chapter 7, for a detailed narrative of the policy shift from removal to the reservation system.
7. Cozzens, *The Earth Is Weeping*, 17. See also Wishart, *Unspeakable*, 47. For a history of Pawnee dispossession in Nebraska, see Karuka, *Empire's Tracks*, chapter 6. For discussion of the decimation of the buffalo populations in the nineteenth century, see Cunfer and Waiser, *Bison*; Hamalainen, "The First Phase of Destruction."
8. Treuer, *Heartbeat*, 94–95; Estes, *Our History*, 93–108. The Great Sioux Reservation also included the Black Hills region of South Dakota and Wyoming, an area that proved rich with gold and so was quickly repossessed by the U.S. government. This land-claim dispute between the Sioux nation and the United States is ongoing. Estes, *Our History*, chapter 3, 222, 245.

   KT Thompson points out the confluence of the Compromise of 1877, which ended Reconstruction, and the Black Hills Agreement also of 1877: "The year 1877, then, marks a shift to support white (settler) supremacy both on the Plains and in the South with legislative actions to subdue Plains Indians and freed African Americans." Thompson, "Stock Histories," 11.

   Among the few white Americans who decried the land grab in the plains were spiritualists writing in *Banner of Light*. Troy, *The Specter of the Indian*, 134. The most recent battle regarding the area is over proposed uranium mining in the Black Hills. Friedler and Frazier, "Get the Hell Off."
9. Mathes and Lowitt, *The Standing Bear Controversy*, 11. Poncas had been living along the Niobrara since around 1750. For details on the traditional homelands and migrations of Nebraska Indians, see Wishart, *Unspeakable*, 4–14.
10. "Indian workers did not dare venture more than one-quarter mile from their village; agency workers always kept their guns by their sides. . . . Every year in spring, as soon as the grass had nutrients to support their horses, Brule raiders renewed their attacks, stealing ponies, killing stock, and scalping Ponca. The raids were a 'weekly occurrence' during the summer months and they continued right up to the Poncas expulsion to Indian Territory." Wishart, *Unspeakable*, 205.
11. Wishart, *Unspeakable*, 205.

12. The forced march happened in two stages. The first group of about 170 people (largely of so-called half-bloods) began in early April of 1877. These were followed by over five hundred more resistant Poncas a month later. Mathes and Lowitt, *The Standing Bear Controversy*, 34–38; Wishart, *Unspeakable*, 210.
13. Wishart, *Unspeakable*, 209–10.
14. Mathes and Lowitt, *The Standing Bear Controversy*, 36–38.
15. Mathes and Lowitt, *The Standing Bear Controversy*, 38.
16. Nebraska Studies, "Standing Bear Arrested."
17. Wishart, *Unspeakable*, 209; Mathes and Lowitt, *The Standing Bear Controversy*, 23, 39.
18. The Omahas of Nebraska were long-time friends and family to the Poncas. Susette La Flesche and her father, Joseph, traveled to meet the Poncas during their forced expulsion to offer support. Mathes and Lowitt, *The Standing Bear Controversy*, 37; D. Wilson, *Bright Eyes*, 138.
19. Mathes and Lowitt, *The Standing Bear Controversy*, 54. Tibbles, *The Ponca Chiefs*, xii.
20. National Park Service, "A Complex Prairie Eco-System."
21. "A century and a half after the initial colonization of the region, the ecosystem has been remade to support the cattle industry, 'from feed crop monoculture to feedlots, from underpriced public permits (a holdover from old reservation leases) to drawdown of the aquifers, agricultural runoff, and soil erosion,' destroying the biodiversity, and much of the life, in the largest community of plants and animals on the continent." Karuka, *Empire's Tracks*, 31.
22. Frymer, *Building an American Empire*, 10. Frymer makes a convincing case for the Homestead Act's racial goals, but homesteads were available to Black people as well, and some did take advantage of them. A University of Nebraska study estimates that 3,500 Black Americans successfully staked claims under the Homestead Act. See National Park Service, "African American Homesteaders on the Great Plains."

In 1933 Nazi Germany introduced the Hereditary Homestead Law and the Law for the New Formation of the German Farmerstock. These laws "provided more than 100,000 new home-steads for families of 'good stock' and subsidized 'hereditarily valuable' farmers" in Germany. It seems likely that these laws, like the Nazi eugenic laws, were influenced by the American model. See Kühl, *The Nazi Connection*, 29.

23. Grossman, *Unlikely Alliances*.
24. For Indian property rights, see Banner, *How the Indians Lost Their Land*, 257–90. Estes writes, "Private ownership . . . is seen, in U.S. law, as the highest possible form of ownership, while Indigenous occupancy is seen as temporary; thus, collective Indigenous ownership and use could be dissolved for private ownership, but not the other way around." Estes, *Our History*, 108. Treuer quotes John Oberly, the commissioner of Indian affairs in 1886, stating that "the Indian 'must be imbued with the exalting egotism of American civilization so that he will say "I" instead of "We," and "This is mine," instead of "This is ours."'" Treuer, *Heartbeat*, 144. Barbed wire was invented by farmer J. F. Gidden in 1874. Martinez discusses how barbed wire "guaranteed the colonization of the United States." Martinez, *The Injustice Never Leaves You*, 12.
25. Kem, 1:74–75, OMKP.
26. Kem, 1:74–75, OMKP.
27. Kem, 1:75, OMKP.
28. Reisner, *Cadillac Desert*, 106.
29. Hicks, *The Populist Revolt*, 31.
30. "Wheat is a thirsty crop, and every wheat seed they sowed contributed to the desiccation. . . . They had changed the climate, the ecology, the land itself. . . . Weather patterns may be among the most complex phenomena to analyze and explain, but studies have conclusively established that agriculture clearing promotes dryness." Fraser, *Prairie Fires*, 154.
31. See Treuer, *Heartbeat*, 123. Kem never mentions Tibbles in his autobiography, but it is possible that they met at the Populist Convention in 1896, or before.
32. Mathes and Lowitt, *The Standing Bear Controversy*, 51–55. The Poncas had had other white supporters before Tibbles. See Mathes and Lowitt, *The Standing Bear Controversy*, 30–33.
33. Treuer, *Heartbeat*, 124; Starita, *"I Am a Man,"* 136. Estes refers to Crook as "a veteran Indian fighter" who was instrumental in later convincing the Sioux at Standing Rock to agree to the Dawes Bill, which "left the western divisions of the Oceti Sakowin [Sioux] deeply divided and in disarray." Estes, *Our History*, 121, 122.
34. Starita, *"I Am a Man,"* 7.
35. Quoted in Starita, *"I Am a Man,"* 6.

36. Mathes and Lowitt, *The Standing Bear Controversy*, 64. Racialization in the United States is clearly a disciplinary process that divides humanity into "persons" (or humans), "not-quite persons," and "non-persons," where the category of the human person belongs first and foremost to whites. See Wilderson, *Black White and Red*; and Wang, *Carceral Capitalism*, 262.
37. Treuer, *Heartbeat*, 139.
38. Quoted in Starita, *"I Am a Man,"* 6. "The law in general tends to recognize the humanity of racialized subjects only in the restricted idiom of personhood-as-ownership." Weheliye, *Habeas Viscus*, 4.
39. Tibbles, *The Ponca*, 80.
40. Mathes and Lowitt, *The Standing Bear Controversy*, 65. Dorothy Wilson writes that Standing Bear's "skill at adapting himself to each situation was almost uncanny." D. Wilson, *Bright Eyes*, 230–31. Following Michelle Raheja, we can read Standing Bear's speeches as an example of "visual sovereignty," a way to manipulate white audiences by seeming to adhere to white expectations. Raheja, "Reading Nanook's Smile," 1161.
41. Quoted in Mathes and Lowitt, *The Standing Bear Controversy*, 66.
42. Judge Webster had also appealed to the Christian feelings of patriarchal piety when he referenced Standing Bear's desire to bury his dead son's bones at home: "Such love of home and native land may be *heathen* in origin, but it seems to me that they are not unlike *Christian* in principle." *Standing Bear v. Crook*, 25. Tibbles's book offers insight into the version of Indian personhood deemed acceptable. It opens on a scene of church-going, school-attending Indians with "nice houses and farms." Tibbles, *The Ponca*, 5.
43. Crying often seems to represent a certain kind of sympathy, a sympathy based on an understanding of the other as a victim, or a child.
44. This freedom, it must be underscored, was the freedom to no longer be Indian. Dundy asserted the plaintiff's "clear and God-given right to withdraw from his tribe and forever live away from it, as though it had no further existence." *Standing Bear v. Crook*, 25.
45. The La Flesche siblings include Susan La Flesche Picotte, who became the first Native woman to earn a medical degree, graduating as valedictorian from Women's Medical College in Pennsylvania in 1889. After practicing medicine on and off the Omaha Reservation for twenty years, in 1913 La Flesche opened a hospital in the reservation town of Walthill.

The hospital, which had become dilapidated, is now being restored to become a museum. National Institute of Health, "Dr. Susan La Flesche Picotte"; Bonderson, "Old Hospital in Walthill Being Restored."

Francis La Flesche became an ethnographer at the Smithsonian, writing books on the history, music, and language of the Omaha and Osage people. American Indian Relief Council, "Francis LaFlesche."

46. "I had to devise a case and a method . . . that could recast our nation's whole Indian Policy." Tibbles, *Buckskin and Blanket Days*, 199.
47. "Prospective Justice to the Poncas," *Boston Evening Transcript*, February 18, 1880, 2.
48. Chapman, *The Otoes and Missourias*, 51.
49. There are many reasons that some Indians were in support of allotment. Besides the security and value of private property, there was also the fact that the allotment program could free Indians from the control of abusive Indian agents. Warren, *God's Red Son*, chapter 8.

The trial was not without other dire consequences: Standing Bear's brother, Big Snake, was murdered by a U.S. soldier while Standing Bear was on tour. According to the secretary of the interior, Carl Schurz, the Indian agent had called for Big Snake's arrest because of the general apprehension following the "Meeker Massacre" in Colorado, which will be discussed in chapter 5. Standing Bear saw the murder as an act of terror, a punishment for his resistance. D. Wilson, *Bright Eyes*, 226, 230; "The Ponca Question: Reply of Secretary Schurz to Senator Dawes," *Boston Evening Transcript*, February 10, 1881, 2.

50. Mathes and Lowitt, *The Standing Bear Controversy*, 1.
51. Wishart, *Great Plains Indians*, 103.
52. P. Wolfe, "Race and the Trace of History," 280.
53. "The Indian is a man, and being a man, is a brother," said Representative Marriott Brosius (R-PA) as he argued for assimilation through the forced and permanent removal of Indian children from their families. 24 Cong. Rec. 1522 (1892) (statement of Marriott Brosius).
54. "The erasure of the sovereign is the racialization of the 'Indian.'" Barker, "Sovereignty," 17. Barker goes on to explain how in the years after World War II, Indigenous nations made important claims for sovereignty, most impactfully in the adoption of the *Declaration on the Rights of Indigenous Peoples* by the United Nations. However, the use of the European concept of sovereignty is not without its complications in this context. Barker, "Sovereignty," 17–26.

55. "Home embodied all the gendered and racialized assumptions of American republicanism and the American economy. . . . The threat to the home—from industrialization, great wealth, and urbanization—became a threat to the entire society. Farmers and workers mobilized the home in defense of their interests. Those who failed to secure proper homes were cast as a danger to the white home—as happened to Chinese, blacks, Indians, and to a lesser degree some European immigrants. They became the targets of horrendous violence and repression, which the perpetrators always cast as self-defense." White, *The Republic*, 5.
56. I wrote about this dream also in *Climate*, a book of epistolary essays co-written with Lisa Olstein and published by Essay Press in 2022.
57. Denver Homeless Outloud, "Myths and Reality of Homelessness."
58. "Denver has at least 3,445 people experiencing homelessness (a known undercount) and not quite 2,000 spaces at shelters." Shelters are often not viable options for people who work at night or early morning, do not want to be separated from partners, for disabled people, people with more than two bags of belongings, or for trans people, and so on. Denver Homeless Outloud, "Press Release."
59. Hartman, *Scenes of Subjection*, 20. Kyla Schuller describes this dynamic as foundational to sentimentalism: "Sentimentalism stimulates the moral virtuosity and emotional release of the sympathizer and her affective attachment to the nation-state at the expense of the needs of the chosen targets of her sympathy, typically those barred from the status of the individuated Human: often the impoverished, the racialized, the conquered, the orphaned, and/or the animalized." Schuller, *The Biopolitics of Feeling*, 2.
60. In 2018 alone, two million additional people became homeless in the United States. Stein, *Capital City*, 4.
61. Sy, "Texas Homeless Suffer." Sy interviews Chris Harris, an advocate for the unhoused, who explains how arresting the unhoused makes their problems far worse and that when encampments are out of sight (hidden from police), there is less public incentive to address the problem of homelessness.
62. Guth, *Kem*, 14. The U.S. government confined the Otoe-Missouria tribes to the Big Blue River Reservation in 1855. The reservation was frequently encroached upon by white settlers even before the Otoe-Missouria people were removed to a new reservation in Oklahoma.

Six years after this relocation, with the passage of the Dawes Act, the Otoe-Missouria people lost half of that land as well. Otoe-Missouria Tribe, "Who We Are."
63. Kem, 1:49–50, OMKP.
64. Kem, 1:55, OMKP. The Custer County website includes the following under "History": "The first white men to enter Custer County in its recorded history were ranchers who drove their immense herds of white-faced cattle up from Texas as early as 1869. As happened in so many other Nebraska regions, the ranchers were later driven out by migrations of homesteaders, who found Custer County's land suitable for raising crops as well as cattle. It was these permanent settlers who built up the country's resources until today its agricultural product totals more than those of any other Nebraska county." Indians are only mentioned three paragraphs later in the context of white fear. Custer County, Nebraska, "County History."

3. Law and Order

1. "Memorial Address on the Life and Character of John. R. Gamble," 24 Cong. Rec. 2025–6 (1892).
2. For a discussion of the massacre and the process of statehood, see Youngkin, "Prelude to Wounded Knee." For a narrative of the massacre and its aftermath, see Treuer, *Heartbeat*, 1–6 and throughout.
3. The end of Reconstruction had nearly eliminated Black representation in Congress. In 1892 one Black representative was present: Henry P. Cheatham of North Carolina's Second. In 1877 there had been seven Black representatives in Congress. For the next fifteen years, that number unevenly declined. Then from 1892 to 1901, there was only ever one Black representative. From 1901 to 1929, there were none. In all of U.S. history, there have been only eleven Black senators.
4. Butler, "Violence, Mourning, Politics," in *Precarious Life*, 20 and throughout; and Butler, *The Force of Nonviolence*.
5. Limerick, *Legacy*, 27.
6. Goldsby, *A Spectacular Secret*, 43–44. Calvin McDowell's face was entirely ravaged by bullet holes. Moss was left shoeless with his "face in the ground." "The Mob's Work," *Appeal-Avalanche Memphis*, March 10, 1892, 4. In the aftermath of the lynching, "a judge issued an order for the Sherriff to shoot any Black demonstrators who seemed to be

'causing trouble' and prohibited the sale of guns to Blacks." Giddings, *When and Where I Enter*, 18.

7. 23 Cong. Rec. 4222–4225 (1892). Micaela Cruce and I both searched through the year's record using search terms *lynch*, *murder*, and *negro*. We found only the one mention of lynching discussed in this paragraph, though we were limited to what we could find by our search terms.

8. *United States v. Cruikshank*.

9. In contrast, there were approximately 668 petitions regarding the taxation of lard during the first session of 1892.

    Investigations into the actions of white mobs, including the Klan, were left to the states. According to Du Bois, from 1870 to 1897, 5,046 suites brought against the Klan were dismissed, 1,432 convicted, and 903 acquitted. Du Bois, *Black Reconstruction*, 684.

10. "Cruel as it was, segregation paled in horror next to images of people who were tied to a stake while their skin was sometimes peeled away in patches: their fingers, ears, noses, tongues, toes, and genitals sliced off; their eyes gouged out; and their bodies roasted alive over fires made deliberately slow. Always, some whites would probe through the smoldering embers to take fragmentary remains as relics: teeth, bones, slivers of the heart." Williamson, "Wounds Not Scars," 15.

11. J. Goldsby, *A Spectacular Secret*, 33.

12. The first anti-lynching legislation was presented to Congress in 1900. Representative George Henry White of North Carolina, the only African American in Congress at the time, introduced H.R. 6963 to the Judiciary Committee, where it languished. No anti-lynching bill passed either House until the 1922 Dyer Bill, which, after considerable efforts by the NAACP, including a national conference on lynching, passed in the House but not the Senate. After 240 failed attempts to pass anti-lynching legislation, the House finally passed the Emmett Till Antilynching Act in 2019. Because of opposition from Senator Rand Paul (R-KY), the bill (H.R. 35) was stalled in the Senate for two years. H.R. 35 was eventually passed and signed into law by President Joe Biden on March 29, 2022. www.congress.gov/bill/116th-congress/house-bill/35.

13. Terrell, "Lynching," 571.

14. There is one exception. During the debate about the Pinkertons discussed above, white Populist senator Jerry Simpson of Kansas said,

"Congress has investigated the lynching of negroes in the past." I am assuming he means during debates around the passage of the Ku Klux Klan Act, but I am not sure. Regardless, his comment was ignored. 23 Cong. Rec. 4225 (1892).
15. Benjamin F. Foster, *Topeka Weekly Call*, August 9, 1891, quoted in Chafe, "The Negro and Populism," 409.
16. Ali, *Lion's Mouth*, 21, 26. Black Populists supported the Lodge Bill of 1890, which would have required elections of state representatives to be federally regulated. White Populists largely rejected the bill, which did not pass. Ali, *Lion's Mouth*, 88. "The two races joined the Populist movement for different reasons: the white man was concerned with economics, the Negro with prejudice and protection from violence," wrote historian William Chafe in 1968. Chafe, "The Negro and Populism," 404.
17. Ali, *Lion's Mouth*, 98. In 1898 Lytle became the first Black female law professor in the country when she joined the faculty at Central Tennessee College. Connolly, "Attorney Lutie A. Lytle," 10–12.
18. Ali, *Lion's Mouth*, 19, 74, 84–95.
19. A white delegate enthusiastically announced (to cheers) that the party had the support of "upwards of 400,000 African Americans." Ali, *Lion's Mouth*, 91–93.
20. Giddings, *When and Where*, 19.
21. Wells-Barnett, *Southern Horrors*, "Preface," 10.
22. Wells-Barnett, *Southern Horrors*, 14. Three years later, Wells-Barnett published her monumental work, *The Red Record: Tabulated Statistics and Alleged Causes of Lynching in the United States*.
23. Wells-Barnett, *Southern Horrors*, 16.
24. "If the dead and dying are the archival and asterisked cosmogonies of blackness, within our present system of knowledge—a system, to paraphrase Frantz Fanon, where the subhuman is invited to become human on terms that require anti-black sentiment—scraps and bits of black life and death and narrative are guaranteed to move toward, to progress into, unlivingness and anti-blackness." McKittrick, "Mathematics," 18.
25. Hartman, *Scenes*, 22.
26. Vasudevan, "Brown Scholar, Black Studies," 44.
27. 23 Cong. Rec. 1258 (1892)
28. Guth, *Kem*, 113–14.

29. Kem, 1:115, OMKP. 23 Cong. Rec. 5631 (1892). Income tax was restored (after it had been repealed in the postwar period) as part of the Wilson-Gorman Tariff Act in 1894. A year later, the conservative Supreme Court ruled income tax unconstitutional. The United States had no graduated income tax again until the ratification of the Sixteenth Amendment in February of 1913.
30. Guth, *Kem*, 25–26.
31. "They all got used to breathing and biting the desiccating grist of windblown sand," continues Guth. Guth, *Kem*, 2.
32. Because of the combined forces of drought and debt, the late 1880s and early '90s show a massive reverse migration, with many families returning east. As Hicks puts it, "Within a few years whole districts in this region were almost totally depopulated. . . . Fully half the people of western Kansas left the country between 1888 and 1892. . . . In the single year of 1891 no less than eighteen thousand prairie schooners crossed from Nebraska to the Iowa side of the Missouri River in full retreat from the hopeless hard times." Hicks, *Populist Revolt*, 32.
33. Kem, 1:72, OMKP.
34. Kem, 1:88, OMKP.
35. Hicks, *Populist Revolt*, 23.
36. Cashman, *America in the Gilded Age*, 292.
37. Falling crop prices were also a function of European protective tariffs against imported grain. Cashman, *America in the Gilded Age*, 314.
38. Canovan, *Populism*, 20.
39. Higgins, *Out of the West*, 110. Reports on the drought years vary. Seager and Herweijer suggest that the 1890s drought was partially responsible for the passage of the Reclamation Act in 1902. Seager and Herweijer, "Causes and Consequences."
40. Kem, 1:135, OMKP. Even before drought set in, lack of experience with dry farming, and what is now called "regenerative agriculture," played a part in farmers' struggles. Kem did not know, as the Pawnees did, that the land required periodic replenishment through the planting of legumes. Guth, *Kem*, 33.
41. Shannon, *The Farmer's Last Frontier*, 54. Lepore suggests that the percentage of failure was even higher: "Between 1889 and 1893, the mortgages on so many farms were foreclosed that 90 percent of farmland fell into the hands of bankers." Lepore, *These Truths*, 343. See also statistics offered by Olson, *History of Nebraska*, 166–68.

42. Edwards, Friefeld, and Wingo, *Homesteading the Plains*, 196–98. Edwards et al. consider Shannon's statistics to be simply wrong, referring to his work as a "poisoned tree."
43. "The whole trouble with Western Mortgages comes from the loan agents. . . . These fellows are the vampires that has brot all the discredit to Kansas." Letter from P. P. Elder to John Davenport, March 26, 1891, quoted in A. Bogue, "The Land Mortgage Company," 20.
44. Hicks, *Populist Revolt*, 21.
45. Many "wild cat" mortgage companies were not regulated; both fees and rates were levied at the lender's discretion. A. Bogue, "The Land Mortgage Company," 22, 25.
46. Hicks, *Populist Revolt*, 23, 24. Another Nebraska settler of the 1890s recalls, "In the year 1893 crops in Nebraska were almost totally destroyed by drought and hot winds. Then came the panic and financial stress, which paralyzed business. In 1894 Nebraska was doomed to have another crop failure. Farmers were obliged to ship in grain and even hay to feed their stock; many sacrificed their livestock by selling at very low prices. Some farmers shot their stock hogs to prevent their starving. Financial conditions grew worse and the entire state was almost in the grip of actual famine." "Timeline Tuesday."
47. Dunbar-Ortiz, *Indigenous*, 141. The "commutation clause" of 1891 provided that after fourteen months residence, a homesteader might "commute" for a cash sum and thereby avoid the residence requirement. Speculators could in essence "flip" the land, buying it outright for approximately $400 after the required short stay and selling it later for as much as double that amount.
48. H. Hughes, "The Abuse of the Homestead Law," 350–53. Edwards et al. do not deny that this sort of fraud existed, but they argue that claims for its prevalence have been exaggerated. Edwards, Friefeld, and Wingo, *Homesteading the Plains*, 198.

In his statistical analysis of indebtedness and agrarian unrest in the period, political economist James Stock concludes that the chief "cause" of such unrest was the general threat to property that debt created. Stock, "Real Estate Mortgages," 96, 105. The fear of foreclosure has led to political uprising in more recent years as well. In Occupy Wall Street and its sister movements, Occupiers shared a motivating critique of finance capital, "which endeavors to insinuate a creditor-debtor relationship into all aspects of social life and had

destabilized the lives, homes, and neighborhoods of tens of millions of people." Kautzer, "The Occupy Movement," 242–43.
49. Emery, "Demonetization of Silver," 52.
50. Nugent, *The Tolerant Populists*, 115. Postel writes, "The claims made by Hofstadter and other scholars that the Populists were an ominous source of anti-Semitism and intolerance have lost currency." Postel, *The Populist Vision*, 18–19. For a data-supported study on Populist antisemitism, see Gerteis and Goolsby, "Nationalism in America," 215–17.
51. Kem, 1:8, OMKP.
52. Kem, 140, OMKP.
53. Laura Ingalls Wilder describes the poverty of her settler childhood but not the considerable debt her family was in. Nor does she discuss the possibility that her father abandoned one of their homes to skip out on unpaid debt. Fraser, *Prairie Fires*, 64.
54. Graeber, *Debt*, 86. Graeber's book is an attempt to answer the question of why people (and nations) feel honor bound to pay their debts, even when doing so would create a humanitarian crisis on a small or large scale. Graeber argues that the presumption that one must pay one's debts is just that, a social presumption with moralistic weight that disciplines, humiliates, and sometimes seriously harms people.
55. Graeber, *Debt*, 120.
56. "Debt is social and credit is asocial. Debt is mutual. Credit runs only one way." Moten and Harney, *The Undercommons*, 61. Annie McClanahan points out that whatever concerns debtors have with honor, whatever humiliation-based rage they may feel about their debt, what debt really comes down to is state violence. McClanahan, *Dead Pledges*, 95.
57. The comparisons predate the Populist period: "From 'white slave' to 'free labor,' antebellum white workers could not begin to describe themselves without reference to the fact of slavery, and increasingly, to the ideology of race." Roediger, *Wage*, 20.
58. Kem, 1:88, OMKP.
59. 26 Cong. Rec. 8398 (1894).
60. Quoted. in Hicks, *Populist Revolt*, 180.
61. Quoted in Nugent, *Tolerant*, 96. In the South in particular, labor that had been performed by enslaved people was now often performed by the indebted, in some cases white women and children. Farmers Alliance leaders in the South "likened [white] women working in

the cotton fields to slavery," for while "black women had worked southern fields for centuries," the end of slavery meant that poor white women now often performed that stigmatized work. Postel, *The Populist Vision*, 87. For more on Populists referring to themselves as "slaves," see Gerteis and Goolsby, "Nationalism in America," 215.

62. In an interview with Ezra Klein, Noam Chomsky portrays the nineteenth-century Populists as anti-capitalist heroes and reinforces the comparison between wage earners, poor farmers, and slaves. Klein, "Noam Chomsky on Anachronism."

As an example of how wrong such comparisons can go, in 1917 San Francisco's IWW Local 173 "placed an anticonscription placard in the window of its headquarters at 403 Broadway Street: 'In 1861 Uncle Sam freed the blacks; in 1917 Uncle Sam enslaved the whites'—a doubly unfortunate statement that not only misstated the date of the abolition but also obfuscated the fact that a disproportionate number of African Americans were being drafted." Zimmer, *Immigrants against the State*, 139.

63. Du Bois, *Black Reconstruction*, 168–70. Hartman also discusses a kind of moral debt that was imposed on Black people after emancipation: "Emancipation instituted indebtedness" as Black people were made to feel "blame" for the Civil War and forced to "prove their worthiness." Hartman, *Scenes*, 130–34. For discussions of racialized debt today, see Wang, *Carceral Capitalism*; and R. Benjamin, "Black AfterLives Matter."

64. As Greg Grandin puts it, "The United States was a process of expanding a certain kind of liberty [through property ownership] by putting down people of color and defining that liberty in opposition to the people of color they put down." Grandin, Interview with Daniel Denvir.

65. Estes, *Our History*, 248.

66. Kem, 1:53, OMKP (emphasis added). The Proud Boys, the organization of white neo-fascist men founded in 2016 by Gavin McInnes, proclaims itself a "pro-Western fraternal organization for men who refuse to apologize for creating the modern world." See Stern, *Proud Boys and the White Ethnostate*. Stern pays special attention to the ties between the early twentieth-century eugenic movement and the Proud Boys and other white nationalist groups. See especially chapter 3.

67. White, *The Republic*, 518. See also Hild, *Arkansas's Gilded Age*. Statistics from Kazin, *American Dreamers*, 91.

68. The Farmers Alliance provided collective support and education for farmers. With national membership in the millions—including, by 1890, 250,000 women—its political influence was wide, powerful, and growing. Not all members believed electoral politics to be the best route toward progress, however, preferring to focus their efforts on education for farmers. Postel, *Populist Vision*, 14–15, 45–67, 76.

69. Hicks, *Populist Revolt*, 130.

70. Cashman, *America in the Gilded Age*, 322.

71. Kem, 1:91, OMKP.

72. The railroads routinely charged westerners three times what they charged those east of the Mississippi, and western farmers were dependent on the railroads for goods and for sales. Cashman, *America in the Gilded Age*, 315.

73. For a succinct description of Populism's national growth in the 1890s, see Postel, *Populist Vision*, 13–14.

74. Kem, 1:94, OMKP.

75. This performance of debt as political theater shows up 120 years later when members of Occupy Wall Street carried signs displaying their debt loads. McClanahan, *Dead Pledges*, 81.

76. Tens of thousands were placed in other government boarding schools, many with prison-like conditions. Child, *Boarding School Season*.

77. Dunbar-Ortiz, *Indigenous*, 161. Treuer, *Heartbeat*, 132–43.

78. 24 Cong. Rec. 1520 (1892).

79. Treuer, *Heartbeat*, 140.

80. W. Davis, "The Remains of 215 Indigenous Children Have Been Found"; Ian Austen and Dan Bilefsky, "Hundreds More Unmarked Graves Found at Former Residential School in Canada," *New York Times*, June 24, 2021.

81. "When the school is on the reserve the child lives with its parents, who are savages, he is surrounded by savages, and though he may learn to read and write . . . he is simply a savage who can read and write," said Sir John Macdonald, the first prime minster of Canada. Quoted in Treuer, *Heartbeat*, 139.

82. 24 Cong. Rec. 1522 (1892)

83. In this dialogue, we can hear the overlapping of colonization and rape culture that underscores the centuries of sexual violence that Native women have endured and continue to resist. See Deer, *Rape*.

84. Frantz Fanon's description of the colonized Antillean's relation to the French language is relevant here: "The Negro of the Antilles will be proportionately whiter—that is, he will come closer to being a real human being—in direct ratio to his mastery of the French language." But this new "whiteness," as Fanon explains, is equivalent to a state of permanent exile: "The fact that the . . . Negro adopts a language different from that of the group into which he was born is evidence of a dislocation, a separation." Fanon, *Black Skin, White Masks*, 14.
85. 24 Cong. Rec. 1258 (1892).
86. 24 Cong. Rec. 1257 (1892).
87. 24 Cong. Rec. 1257 (1892).
88. David Grann's *Killers of the Flower Moon* tells the story of that oil and how white settlers conspired to murder whole families of Osage Indians to get it.
89. Oklahoma Historical Society, "Land Run of 1889."
90. Kem, 1:118, OMKP. See Dunbar-Ortiz, *Indigenous*, 158–59.
91. Kem, 1:118, OMKP.
92. Kem, *Report to Accompany H.R. 67*. In this report recommending removal, Kem mostly quotes from the committee's report to the Fifty-First Congress, written before his appointment.
93. Jones, *Being and Becoming Ute*, 215–16.
94. By 1892 most of the Ute children were being educated at Fort Lewis, twenty-five miles away. Kem, *Report to Accompany H.R. 67*.
95. Jones, *Being and Becoming Ute*, 216.
96. Jones, *Being and Becoming Ute*, 218.
97. The issue of allotment divided the Utes on the Southern Ute Reservation. In 1895 Chief Ignacio led the Weeminuche Utes, who opposed allotment, to the western half of the reservation in protest. The reservation is still divided today into the Southern Ute and the Ute Mountain Reservations. Jones, *Being and Becoming Ute*, 219–23.
98. The minority's primary concern is not for the Utes' welfare but for the Mormons in Utah who were not welcoming to the Utes. Another influential lobby, the cattle industry, also opposed the formation of a new reservation in Utah. By this date, Congress had officially ended the reservation system in favor of assimilation, adding to the complexity of passing H.R. 67. Jones, *Being and Becoming Ute*, 218
99. 28 Cong. Rec. 1989 (1896).

100. In July of the same year, Kem submitted a committee report recommending the passage of Senate Bill 782, which supported debt relief for settlers who had purchased lands, through competitive bidding, in the former Otoe-Missouria Reservation in Nebraska. Kem, "Certain Lands of the Confederated Otoe and Missouria Tribes."
101. Limerick, "The New Significance," 64.
102. Quoted in Hicks, *Populist Revolt*, 81–82.
103. Foucault, "Right of Death," 266.
104. "Law enforcement, in whatever exclusionary attempt to ensure equilibrium, belatedly responds to what shows up as (de)generative dehiscence requiring suture and irregular wholeness in need of incision." Moten, *Stolen Life*, 1.
105. Woodward, *Tom Watson*, 432. Tom Watson had once gathered two thousand armed white Populists together to protect the life of Black Populist Henry Doyle and had proclaimed poor whites and Blacks as "political allies" in the fight against "financial despotism." Watson, "The Negro Question," 18–28. See Ali, *Lion's Mouth*, 79–80.
106. Chafe, "The Negro and Populism," 402; Ali, *Lion's Mouth*, 107.
107. "Klansmen End Capital Rally," *Lansing (MI) State Journal*, August 10, 1925, 3.
108. Cashman, *America in the Gilded Age*, 240.
109. Unlike the AFL, the IWW was open to Black, immigrant, and Asian workers. See Foner, *The Industrial Workers of the World*, 29. For Black southern communism, see Kelley, *Hammer and Hoe*, and Gilmore, *Defying Dixie*.
110. Kantrowitz, "Ben Tillman," 500; Chafe, "The Negro and Populism," 402.
111. "MicKinley's campaign raised more than ten times the $300,000 raised by Bryan's, and the election could be seen as representing the triumph of big business, banking, and industry over farmers, producerism, and antimonopolism." Hild, *Arkansas' Gilded Age*, 123.
112. Du Bois, *Black Reconstruction*, 630.
113. See W. Benjamin, "On the Concept of History."

4. Ghosts

1. "Thoughts Are Things" is from Henslow, *The Proofs of the Truths of Spiritualism*, 127.

2. Thompson, *Blanket*, xxii.
3. "All stories are ghost stories, if only because each word, each random collection of syllables, is intended to conjure forth an unreal reality, to embody and to animate a strange imaginary entity that is both there and not there, actual and not actual." Bergland, *The National Uncanny*, 6.
4. For an overview of contemporary and nineteenth-century spiritualism, see Cep, "Kindred Spirits."
5. Mackay, "Review of *Specter of the Indian* by Kathryn Troy," 169.
6. Lause, *Free Spirits*, 5–8, 14; McGarry, *Ghosts of Futures Past*, 3, 128n7.
7. Braude reveals how spiritualists' feminism went even beyond advocacy for equality by presenting ample and novel opportunities for young women to speak authoritatively in public: "Spiritualists became a major—if not *the* major—vehicle for the spread of woman's rights ideas in mid-century America." Braude, *Radical Spirits*, 56.
8. Braude notes some feminist spiritualists' "racist overtones" and argues that despite how spiritualism developed out of abolitionism, spiritualists after the 1850s proved more interested in speaking with the dead than in fighting for the living. Braude, *Radical Spirits*, 57, 73–81.
9. Braude, *Radical Spirits*, 16–17. Harriet Jacobs lived in the Post household for a time. Douglass was present at séances but did not believe in the ghosts, calling the "rappings" "atrocious." See Powalski, "Radical Transmissions," 10.
10. Kem, *Spiritualist Notes*, 5, CCA.
11. Kem, *Spiritualist Notes*, 6.
12. Kem, *Spiritualist Notes*, 6–7.
13. Moten, *In the Break*, 93.
14. A. Gordon, *Ghostly*, 63. Henslow relates a number of instances in which objects move unaided: a large heavy table suddenly begins to spin; a key passes through a window. Henslow, *The Proofs of the Truths of Spiritualism*, 84, 106.
15. Lawrence, *Spiritualism*, 6.
16. Kardec, *Spiritism in Its Most Simple Expression*, 4.
17. Kem reports visiting a medium who went by the name P. O. L. Keeler. Keeler's "spirit control" was famed blackface minstrel George Christy. Christy had been one of the original members of the Christy Minstrels (under E. P. Christy, his stepfather) and had been well known in the 1860s, especially for impersonating Black women. According

to Kem, once Keeler accessed his "control," he would sit to the side of the stage. The instruments of the minstrel show—banjo, bones, and tambourine—would play on their own, presumably activated by George Christy's invisible ghost. Kem, *Spiritualist Notes*, 17, CCA.

18. Genetin-Pilawa, *Crooked Paths to Allotment*, 123–24, 129–30.

The Blands' leading role in the Indian rights movement began in the 1870s, when they met Alfred Meacham in Boston. With the Blands' encouragement, Meacham started the paper the *Council Fire* in which he and others argued for Indian rights, including land rights. Meacham had protested the removal of the Uncompahgre Utes from the Uncompahgre valley in Colorado, where in 1895 Omer Kem bought land.

As editors of the *Council Fire*, the Blands frequently published writing by Native as well as white activists. Shortly after its founding in 1885, NIDA was as large in membership as the IRA. However, like many people and groups whose opinions did not win out, NIDA has, until very recently, received little scholarly attention. As Genetin-Pilawa points out, by ignoring NIDA, scholars have wrongly suggested that the passage of the Dawes Act was inevitable. See Cowger, "Dr. Thomas A Bland," 78; B. Johnson, *Red Populism?*, 21; Genetin-Pilawa, *Crooked Paths*, 116; Jones, *Being and Becoming Ute*, 203–4; Cashman, *America in the Gilded Age*, 298–99.

19. Kem writes, "Soon after my election I had a letter from a Dr. T. A. Bland of Washington D.C. saying that he was a member of the Indian Rights Association (an organization interested in the welfare of the Indian) and as had [*sic*] some Indians in my district, he would like to make my acquaintance, and gave me a very cordial invitation to visit him when I came to Washington." Kem is in error about the organization Bland belonged to—it was NIDA, not the IRA. Notably, this is the only mention Kem makes of Indians living in Nebraska's Third District. Kem, *Spiritualist Notes*, 8, CCA.

20. While the Blands have been studied by a few historians, none has yet written about the Blands' spiritualism, perhaps because this aspect of their lives was not well documented. Kem, however, focuses almost entirely on the ghosts that filled the Blands' house from 1892 to 1897.

21. Kem, *Spiritualist Notes*, 10–11, CCA.

22. Kem, *Spiritualist Notes*, 13.

23. Kem, *Spiritualist Notes*, 10.

24. A. Gordon, *Ghostly*, xvi.
25. Deloria, *Playing Indian*, 183. See also Gerteis and Goolsby: "Populism can be read as a reaction against what farmers and working people saw as a decline in their civic and political status. In short, it was an economic and political movement that was built around claims of American identity." Gerteis and Goolsby, "Nationalism in America," 205.

    Given the year of Kem's first encounter with Fleet Wind (1897), we might also wonder whether Fleet Wind provided a substitute for Populism, which was just then collapsing. Was Fleet Wind—this symbol of authentic belonging and radical, even magical, healing—an internalization of the Populist's failed aspirations?
26. Kem, *Spiritualist Notes*, 25, CCA.
27. Kem, *Spiritualist Notes*, 28.
28. Kem, 9:86, OMKP.
29. Omer Kem letter to J. Kathleen Carr, June 13, 1933, personal collection.
30. For further discussions of non-Indian appropriations of Indian culture, see Meyer and Royer, *Selling the Indian*.
31. Bergland, *The National Uncanny*, 3, 4.
32. Troy, *Specter*, xii.
33. Camp Etna is the subject of Mira Ptacin's *The In-Betweens*. See Caldwallader, *Mary S. Vanderbilt*, 43–44.
34. D. Wilson, *Bright Eyes*, 239–59, 309.
35. The photo plays an important part in Pepper Vanderbilt's story. It was produced as "proof" of the real Bright Eyes during a performance in New Bedford. Edward Vanderbilt purchased the photo (or a copy of it) as a gift for his first wife when they attended a Mary Pepper sermon in Brooklyn. Caldwallader, *Mary S. Vanderbilt*, 7–8; "Vanderbilt Clings to 'Bright Eyes,'" *New York Times*, August 27, 1907, 3.
36. Caldwallader, *Mary S. Vanderbilt*, 26–30.
37. Caldwallader, *Mary S. Vanderbilt*, 6.
38. "Bright Eyes Shy," *Plain Speaker*, September 7, 1907, 8.
39. "Vanderbilt Clings to 'Bright Eyes,'" 3.
40. Ptacin, *The In-Betweens*, 57.
41. Susette La Flesche, speech given in Boston, February 1880, available at https://edan.si.edu/transcription/pdf_files/8132.pdf.
42. Huhndorf, *Going Native*, 2. Huhndorf doesn't discuss Indian spirit guides in white spiritualism, but she does discuss other examples of

appropriation from the late nineteenth century to the 1980s. For Huhndorf, the process of "going native," whether at the 1893 World's Columbian Exposition, in popular films like *Dances with Wolves*, in Boy Scout handbooks, or in New Age texts, has generally two imperatives: to escape the "degenerative and corrupt white world" and to redeem American society by discovering in the Indian its "true" identity. In Fleet Wind, Kem does both—he finds a healing force that can cure his family and self of their ailments, and he finds that healing force to be one with his own body. Also see Deloria, *Playing Indian*, whose ideas Huhndorf extends. Huhndorf, *Going Native*, 5.

43. Kem, *Spiritualist Notes*, 29, 32, 35, CCA.
44. Kem, 10:8, OMKP.
45. Kem, 10:16, OMKP.
46. In Louise Erdrich's 2021 novel, *The Sentence*, the ghost of a settler tries to violently force itself into the body of a Native woman. Though this is a reversal of Omer Kem's fantasy of being inhabited by Fleet Wind, it provides an even more visceral example of appropriation, one that directly mimics the process of land appropriation in U.S. history. Erdrich, *The Sentence*, 309.

5. Water in Relation

1. McAdams and Wang, "Gunnison Tunnel."
2. At the Gunnison Tunnel dedication ceremony, President Taft opened the headgates by pressing a golden bell against a silver plate that then swung open. In fact, the tunnel was not yet complete at this time, so the river water could not flow. Workers had constructed a temporary dam inside the tunnel so that seepage water would back up. When the plate was opened, the dam was released and water gushed out, delighting the crowd. U.S. Bureau of Reclamation, "Uncompahgre Project," 8.
3. Kem, 2:28, OMKP.
4. Kem, 2:29, OMKP.
5. Kem, 2:33, OMKP.
6. Montrose County Historical Society and Museum, *Montrose*, 69.
7. 23 Cong. Rec. 4138 (1892). Today, water privatization is once again a concern in the United States and across the world. For overviews of the issue, see the Community Environmental Legal Defense Fund's website (https://celdf.org) and the Sierra Club, "Water a Public

Resource: How Privatization Happens," https://angeles.sierraclub.org/news_conservation/blog/2020/07/water_a_public_resource_how_privatization_happens.
8. 26 Cong. Rec. 8395–6 (1894).
9. Kem's comments from 26 Cong. Rec. 8395–6 (1894). For railroad financing, see Kammer, "Land and Law": "In all, agents of the federal government granted roughly 130 million acres to railroads from 1850 to 1871" (2).
10. The first legislative movement toward federal irrigation came with the passage of the Carey Act of 1894, under which millions of acres of public lands were ceded to western states. As with the Swamp Lands Act forty years before, states were tasked with either developing the projects themselves or selling the land to private developers. The Carey Act was a failure; projects were simply too complex and costly to be handled by individual states or by developers.
11. Newlands, "A Western View of the Race Question," 49–51. Ultimately, it was not so much the bill's sponsor but California water lawyer and lobbyist George Maxwell, the founder of the National Irrigation Association, who finally rallied enough support around federal irrigation to get the Reclamation Act through Congress. See Boime, "'Beating Plowshares into Swords.'"
12. Reclamation Act, June 17, 1902.
13. Czolgosz wasn't an immigrant, but many anarchists were, including Emma Goldman, named by Czolgosz as inspiration. In 1879 forty thousand people, many of them immigrants, marched in an anarchist parade. In 1886 the United States saw 1,400 separate strikes. For details on the buildup to the passage of the Reclamation Act, see Pisani, *To Reclaim a Divided West*, 273–325; and McCool, *Command of the Waters*.
14. 26 Cong. Rec. 8396 (1894).
15. "When the reclamation bill was introduced in 1901, an impressive and diverse array of interest groups endorsed it, including the National Association of Manufacturers, the National Board of Trade, the National Business League, the American Federation of Labor, the United Mine Workers, and many other businesses and labor associations." McCool, *Command*, 26.
16. This ideology enforced gender norms as well, encouraging women away from independent urban lifestyles and back toward home and motherhood. See Lovett, *Conceiving the Future*, 45–76.

See Grandin on how Anglo-Saxon racial theory, also called "germ principle," was fundamental to American exceptionalism and expansionism from the time of Jefferson forward. Grandin, *End of the Myth*, 23–24, 114, 117.

17. Lovett, *Conceiving the Future*, 54. Kim TallBear writes that the patriarchal heteronormative monogamous settler family structure "co-constituted with resource extraction and private property are integral to ongoing genocide in the Americas—of both human and other-than-human persons." Strathern et al., "Forum on *Making Kin Not Population*," 168.
18. Sara Porterfield has studied how the Reclamation Act followed models in India. Federal engineers George Davidson and Herbert Wilson traveled to India and studied, wrote about, and hoped to emulate the centralized irrigation systems they found there. "Overseas travels led Wilson to believe that managing the West's water efficiently through a central plan would allow the United States to become the dominant engineering and economic power in the world—one to rival imperial Britain." Porterfield, "Creating an American Nile," 11.
19. Torrence had responded to Fellows's call for an assistant who was "a good swimmer; strong and athletic" and unmarried, "with no one entirely dependent on him." McAdams and Wang, *Gunnison Tunnel*, 828.
20. I have lost the source for this assertion, and so it should be considered only a rumor.
21. Holleran, *Historic Context for Irrigation and Water Supply*, 42–43. For information on the use of prison labor, see Colorado State Board of Charities and Correction Biennial Report, vol. 6 (1903).
22. Senator Bell remarks, 34 Cong. Rec. 791 (1901).
23. The Reclamation Act was followed by other expansions of governmental reach in the Progressive Era, such as the establishments of the Pure Food and Drug Act, the National Forest Service, and the National Parks system. The other four first projects were the Milk River Project, Newlands Project, North Platte Project, and Salt River Project.
24. Census of Agriculture, "Montrose County, Colorado"; U.S. Bureau of Reclamation, "Uncompahgre Water Project."
25. Genealogy Trails History Group, "Omer Madison Kem."
26. U.S. Department of the Interior, "Drought in the Colorado River Basin."

27. Kammeyer, "Corporate Water Stewardship."
28. The Colorado River serves at least forty million people in the cities of Albuquerque, Tucson, Phoenix, Denver, Salt Lake City, Las Vegas, Los Angeles, San Diego, Mexicali, and Tijuana, as well as the agricultural region of the Imperial Valley of southern California. The soil of California's Central Valley is now so salty that at least 250,000 acres have been forced out of production. Ten Tribes Partnership, "Keepers of the River"; Abrahm Lustgarten, "Forty Million People Rely on the Colorado River. It's Drying up Fast," *New York Times: Sunday Review*, August 29, 2021, 1; Mike McPhate, "California's Soil Is Getting Too Salty for Crops to Grow," *California Sun*, July 19, 2018.
29. For the concept of a "hydraulic public," see Hanand, "Public Water."
30. Greeley to Meeker, 02.19.1870, HG.
31. For Greeley's opinions on Fourierism, see *New York Tribune*, November 20, 1846–April 28, 1847. Greeley not only published Brisbane and others on Fourier and presented at the Fourier Convention of 1843; he also published a series of articles edited by Karl Marx, beginning in 1848 and running for nearly a decade. The payment that Marx received from Greeley during those years was his primary means of support during the period when he wrote *Capital*. See Hale, "When Karl Marx Worked for Horace Greeley."
32. The first sentence of the colony's constitution states, "The object of the above named Colony shall be to settle on Government or other cheap land in the West, to the end that men may engage in various industries and pursuits, and that they may have homes of their own, and that schools and churches may be convenient." Boyd, *A History*, 427.
33. For statistics about the colony applicants, see Shaw, *"Yours for Colorado,"* 57–61.
34. "Systematic Emigration," *New York Tribune*, April 14, 1871.
35. The colony retained the centrality of private property. It hoped to enrich its members through pooling some resources while dividing others.
36. Horace Greeley, "Lecture before the L. I. Historical Society," *New York Tribune*, March 29, 1871.
37. Worster, *Rivers of Empire*, 83, 85.
38. Greeley to Meeker, 03.18.1871, HG. A Fourierist whom Greeley published in the *Tribune*, H. H. Van Amringe, included "the subjugation

and cultivation of the entire earth" as one of the most laudable tenets of Fourierism. *New York Tribune*, January 22, 1846, 1.

39. Greeley to Meeker, 09.01.1871, HG
40. Boyd, *A History*, 263.
41. Boyd, *A History*, 268.
42. Greeley to Meeker, 08.25.70, HG.
43. Greeley to Meeker, 08.25.70, HG.
44. Colorado Encyclopedia Staff, "Nathan Meeker."
45. Stein, *Capital City*.
46. Film scholar Amy Parziale sees it the other way around: "The 'water' plot serves as a distraction for viewers from the horrific knowledge of incest." Parziale, "'As Little as Possible,'" 60.
47. The Southern Ute Indian tribe website offers the following under "Early History": "The Ute people are the oldest residents of Colorado, inhabiting the mountains and vast areas of Colorado, Utah, Wyoming, Eastern Nevada, Northern New Mexico and Arizona. According to tribal history handed down from generation to generation, our people lived here since the beginning of time." https://www.southernute-nsn.gov/.

    Scholar Brandi Denison writes that the Ute Indians, descendants of the Numic-speaking people, lived throughout the Great Basin area since at least 1400 CE. Denison, *Ute Land Religion*, 28; Jones, *Being and Becoming Ute*, chapter 2.
48. The Southern Ute Indian tribe website refers to the Brunot Agreement as a "forcible relinquishment."
49. Denison, *Ute Land Religion*, 42–43.
50. Jones, *Being and Becoming Ute*, 190.
51. Denison, *Ute Land Religion*, 59. While one small group of Utes, led by Quinkent ("Douglas"), followed Meeker, a much larger group refused, following Nicaagat ("Captain Jack") in continuing to hunt. Nicaagat traveled to Los Pinos Agency in August of 1879, seeking help from the influential Chief Ouray of the Tabeguache band, and then on to Denver to beseech Colorado's first governor, Frederick Pitkin, to remove Meeker. He was ignored. Jones, *Being and Becoming Ute*, 189.
52. Sprague, *Massacre*, 32–33.
53. Quoted in Jones, *Being and Becoming Ute*, 188.
54. Jones, *Being and Becoming Ute*, 183.

55. Ethnicity, Race, and Migration, "Remembering the Sand Creek Massacre"; Whitacre, "The Search for the Site of the Sand Creek Massacre."
56. Jones, *Being and Becoming Ute*, 184.
57. Sprague, *Massacre*, 165. In 2020 an informational plaque on Cheyenne Mountain near Colorado Springs still maintains that forest fires in the 1850s were started by "warring Ute tribes." This same plaque subtly mocks the Indians for failing to understand that the "crazy white men" were mining stones for their silver. The plaque mentions nothing about forced removal.
58. Sprague, *Massacre*, 163–64; quoted in Jones, *Being and Becoming Ute*, 189.
59. "Frontier individuals' endless appeals for state protection not only presupposed a commonality between the private and official realms. . . . It also presupposed a global chain of command linking remote colonial frontiers to the metropolis." P. Wolfe, "Settler Colonialism," 394.
60. Decker, *The Utes Must Go!*, 128–30.
61. Denison, *Ute Land Religion*, 40.
62. The Utes maintain that they only shot in self-defense; the United States maintains the opposite. Silbernagel, *Troubled Trails*, 14.
63. Jones, *Being and Becoming Ute*, 194.
64. Meeker, *The Ute Massacre*, 8, 9.
65. Silbernagel, *Troubled Trails*, 96–101.
66. Jones, *Being and Becoming Ute*, 193.
67. Silbernagel, *Troubled Trails*, 99.
68. Jones, *Being and Becoming Ute*, 194; Decker, *The Utes Must Go!*, 143; Denison, *Ute Land Religion*, 64.
69. Meeker, *The Ute Massacre*, 1.
70. Deer, *Rape*, 20; Denison, *Ute Land Religion*, 75.
71. Denison, *Ute Land Religion*, 73.
72. *Rocky Mountain News*, January 6, 1880, 21:4.
73. "A Howling Disgrace," *Grand Island Times*, January 8, 1880, 2; "Lynching the Just Doom: The Horrible Treatment of the Women Captives," *Minneapolis Tribune*, January 9, 1880, 1; Ralph Meeker, "A Brother's Plea on Behalf of his Sister," *Chicago Tribune*, January 28, 1880, 3.

On December 30, 1879, Arvilla Meeker (Nathan's wife) published a letter in the *Pueblo Chieftain* claiming that she and other women had suffered "the sickening and most humiliating misfortune that can befall a woman." This letter was circulated widely. "The Hellish

Utes," *Tennessean*, January 10, 1880, 3; "The Fiendish Utes," *Great Bend (KS) Register*, January 15, 1880, 4; "Captive Women Outraged," *Eau Claire (WI) Argus*, January 15, 1880, 4.

The killings and hostage taking at White River were seen by some whites as acts of self-defense, or as crimes committed by individual men who could be held accountable. Jones points to articles in papers from New York and California that blame the White River incident on Congress's failure to honor previous agreements with Utes. Jones writes that "most newspapers outside of Colorado took the Utes' side" but does not offer statistics. Jones, *Being and Becoming Ute*, 196, 199.

74. Denison, *Ute Land Religion*, 77.
75. The raping of Native women was then and is now an ongoing trauma wrought by the extractive economy of settler-America wherever it forces its way onto or near reservations. Deer reports that one in three American Indian and Alaska Native women will experience sexual assault or rape in her lifetime, a rate double that for all other racial groups. Deer, *Rape*, 77–79 and throughout. See also *Violence on the Land Violence on Our Bodies*, created collaboratively by Women's Earth Alliance and Native Youth Sexual Health Network; and Rainn (website), "Victims of Sexual Violence."

Indigenous feminists make clear the ties between capitalism, colonialism, eco-violence, and gendered violence, arguing that to demand change in one of these areas means demanding change in them all. "Ultimately, neither labor nor gender roles can operate according to a logic of patriarchy, which is a violent ideology of gender that simply reinforces the violent ideologies of settler colonialism and capitalism." Yazzie and Curley, "Decolonizing Development," 152. See also TallBear, "Making Love."

76. Jones, *Being and Becoming Ute*, 195–207. The Southern Ute Reservation was diminished further after the Allotment Act in 1887 and in 1895 was divided in two. The 1937 Restoration Act returned 222,016 acres to the Southern Utes.
77. Montrose County Historical Society and Museum, *Montrose*, 7, 33.
78. Quoted in Jones, *Being and Becoming Ute*, 207; Emmitt, *The Last War Trail*, 292–93.
79. Thorson, *River of Promise*, 82.
80. Berman, "For the Taking."
81. Lawson, "'We Lost Our Way of Living,'" 136.

82. Estes, *Our History*, 134. For other statistics on flooding, displacement, and compensation, see Govinfo.gov, "Indian Issues: Damages and Compensation for Tribes at Seven Reservations Affected by Dams on the Missouri River."

The Pick-Sloan Dam project included five major dams designed for hydropower and irrigation and to control the Missouri River's natural floods that had killed two hundred people and displaced thousands between 1936 and 1950 alone. Sioux tribal leaders did reluctantly agree to the Pick-Sloan plan but at a time when the tribal resources were extremely low. Understanding that the project was inevitable, they hoped that the government would make good on its promise of direct benefits from the project, including "irrigation, low-cost electrical power, improved water supplies, and recreational and industrial development." However, as Michael Lawson documents, the government did not make good on this promise. Currently, the Fort Berthold Reservation is the center of oil extraction in North Dakota. Lawson, *Dammed Indians*, 39.

83. Estes and Dhillon, *Standing with Standing Rock*, 3.
84. Standing Rock was the largest pan-Indigenous movement in U.S. history, stretching far beyond the physical camps to include hundreds of thousands of supporters across the United States and the world, including 360 Native nations that rallied behind the Standing Rock Water Protectors through online campaigns, street marches, and donations of material goods. Despite an intensive surveillance operation led by the private security firm TigerSwan and aggressive militarized state and federal police actions—the use of dogs, pepper spray, rubber bullets, and water cannons shot in freezing temperatures—the camps were fully active, with thousands of participants, through the fall of 2016.

After considerable public pressure, Obama finally paused the DAPL project, demanding that the Army Corps of Engineers withhold Energy Transfer Partners' easement across Lake Oahe until they'd conducted a full environmental impact statement. But within a week of Trump's inauguration, in the flurry of his executive orders, Trump reversed Obama's decision, demanding that the project (and the Keystone Pipeline) move forward. Oil started flowing through the pipeline in June of 2017. During the six months left of that year, as 570,000 barrels of crude oil ran through the pipe each day, there were at least five reported oil spills from the pipeline.

Finally, in March of 2020 (following earlier losses) the tribes won their legal battle against the Army Corps. Judge James Boasberg of the U.S. District Court for the District of Columbia ruled that the corps must conduct a full environmental impact statement, a process that could take up to three years. Estes, *Our History*; Brown, Parish, and Speri, "Counterterrorism Tactics at Standing Rock"; Anderson, "Indigenous Rights to Water," 372–73; A. Brown, "Five Spills, Six Months in Operation." For "Stop Line 3," see www.stopline3.org/#intro.

85. Howe and Young, "Minisose," 59. Kinship relations between human and nonhuman beings are explored by all the contributors to Haraway and Clarke's *Making Kin Not Population*.
86. Barker, "Confluence," 6.
87. Counterpath is a nonprofit community and arts space, press, free bookstore, gallery, food bank, and community garden in the East Colfax neighborhood of Denver. Counterpath purchased a 1950s filling station in 2015 with donated funds, a large part of which were proceeds from the sale of the building that housed my father's architectural firm, Carr, Lynch, Hack and Sandell, for thirty years. For the first three years, we donated produce grown in the garden to a soup kitchen and a food bank in Denver. In year four, Counterpath, in collaboration with the East Colfax Neighborhood Association, started a food bank, which now donates produce and food from many sources directly to the people in the neighborhood who are in need, many of whom are immigrants and refugees. www.counterpathpress.org.
88. Bitsui, *Flood Song*, 9, 11.
89. "What good is poetry at a time like this?" Joron, *Fathom*, 15.
90. Buchanan et al., "The High Plains Aquifer"; Frankel, "Crisis on the High Plains."
91. Bruce Finley, "The Water under Colorado's Eastern Plains Is Running Dry as Farmers Keep Irrigating," *Denver Post*, October 8, 2017. See also Congressional Research Service, "The Federal Role in Groundwater Supply."
92. For an overview of the "Livestock Revolution" and an analysis of its impacts, see Sumberg and J. Thompson, "Revolution Reconsidered." For statistics on U.S. livestock industry exports, see U.S. Meat Export Federation, "Strong Momentum Continues."
93. In the 1980s and '90s, as producers of poultry, pork, and beef were rapidly bought up by large corporations, "the global production of

animals for consumption grew about one and a half times faster than the world population." More than 1.7 billion animals are used in livestock production worldwide and occupy more than one-fourth of the earth's land. Production of animal feed consumes about one-third of total arable land. Stanford Report Staff, "New Report Reveals the Environmental and Social Impact of the 'Livestock Revolution.'" Large-scale animal agriculture is also a breeding ground for zoonotic (species hopping) disease. See K. Brown, "The Pandemic Is Not a Natural Disaster." See also Centers for Disease Control, "Zoonic Disease." For the effects of the livestock industry on Kansas's water problems, see Bessire, *Running Out*, 78–79.

94. The livestock sector, including feed production and transport, is responsible for about 14.5 percent of all greenhouse gas emissions worldwide. According to the University of Michigan's Center for Sustainable Systems, "ruminants such as cattle, sheep, and goats produced 178 million metric tons (mmt) CO_2e of enteric methane in the U.S. in 2018." Food and Agriculture Organization of the United Nations, "Key Facts and Findings"; Center for Sustainable Systems, "Carbon Footprint Factsheet."
95. See Drought.gov for statistics for all states.
96. Williams et al., "Large Contribution from Anthropogenic Warming"; Ten Tribes Partnership, "Water Study." See also Henry Fountain, "How Bad Is the Western Drought?" *New York Times*, February 14, 2022.
97. U.S. Bureau of Reclamation, "Lower Colorado Water Supply Report." Martin & McCoy et al., *Ten Strategies*, 12–13.
98. Henry Fountain, "In a First, the U.S. Declares Shortage on Colorado River, Forcing Water Cuts," *New York Times*, August 18, 2021.
99. Martin & McCoy et al., *Ten Strategies*, "Regenerative Agriculture," 26. See Bessire, *Running Out*, especially 107–13, for a stunning narrative about how agribusiness moguls manage to block efforts to limit groundwater pumping on the plains while using "astonishing amounts of water" on their own ranches and farms.
100. "While well tested and widely implemented water conservation efforts are essential, they are developed and implemented with a focus on the management, movement, and use of water and therefore do not typically or sufficiently include or consider broader economic, environmental, and social risks from changing climate dynamics." Creating "new market pathways" at a meaningful scale would require significant

investment from federal and state agencies, not only in farmers but also in food processors, transportation, and marketing—the kinds of investments that went into creating the "Live-Stock Revolution" in the first place. Martin & McCoy et al., *Ten Strategies*, 19, 30.

See also Energy Futures Initiative, "From the Ground Up," for information about agricultural innovations that could enhance biological and terrestrial carbon dioxide removal and sequestration. https://energyfuturesinitiative.org/reports/from-the-ground-up.

101. Tanya Ishikawa, "First Steps in Developing Cow Creek Pipeline and Reservoir," *Telluride News*, January 29, 2020. See also Heather Sacket, "Ouray County Water Project Faces Opposition from State, Others," *Aspen Times*, August 29, 2021.
102. See the bureau's 2012 Colorado River Basin Water Supply and Demand study and 2015 Moving Forward report.
103. Martin & McCoy et al., *Ten Strategies*, 6, 19. For the vulnerability of Native communities, see Tom, Begay, and Yazzie, "Climate Adaptation Plan for the Navajo Nation." The Navajo plan lists water scarcity as the nation's number one climate concern.
104. "Just Transition is a framework for a fair shift to an economy that is ecologically sustainable, equitable and just. After centuries of global plunder, the profit-driven, growth-dependent, industrial economy is severely undermining the life support systems of Mother Earth. An economy based on extracting from a finite system faster than the capacity of the Earth to regenerate will eventually come to an end. Our Indigenous Nations must be ready." Indigenous Environmental Network, "Just Transition." On November 15, 2021, the Colorado River Basin Tribal Coalition sent an open letter to Secretary of the Interior Deb Haaland demanding that the tribes be consulted and included in future planning around drought mitigation in the basin.
105. The median price for a single-family home in 2021 in the United States was $375,000 and rising at a rate of 16 percent per year. The median family income in the United States is $65,000 for a family of four. https://fred.stlouisfed.org/series/MSPU.S.; www.census.gov/library/publications/2020/demo/p60-270.html.
106. Trump, "Remarks by President Trump during Visit to the Border Wall." This speech was delivered just six weeks after Patrick Crusius massacred twenty-two people in El Paso, Texas, because he believed they were migrants from Mexico.

107. Barker, "Confluence," 15.
108. William Hammond Hall, California's first state engineer, quoted in Pisani, *To Reclaim*, 36.
109. On September 10, 2020, the air quality index in Cottage Grove, Oregon, was 807. This is air that no mammal can breathe. The year 2020 was the by far the worst on record for wildfires in Colorado. The Cameron Peak fire burned over two hundred thousand acres. Before that, there had never been a fire that burned more than a hundred thousand acres in the state. See John Ingold, "Five Charts That Show Where 2020 Ranks in Colorado Wildfire History," "Five of the Largest Six Fires in California's Modern History Occurred in 2020," *Colorado Sun*, October 20, 2020; "Wildfires Linked to Groundwater Depletion," *Fluence*, September 20, 2018; Martin & McCoy et al., *Ten Strategies*, 13–14, 17.
110. Kem, 4:91, OMKP.

Interlude

1. Kem, 5:28, OMKP.
2. Charting and graphing the supposed proximity of some humans to animals was a justification for slavery and an early twentieth-century pathway to genocide.
3. Baldwin, *The Fire Next Time*, 33.
4. C. Taylor, *You, Me, and the Violence*, 15
5. In an October 18, 2020, interview with Steve Oatley on his *Wake Up America!* podcast, Chris states, "I call myself the anti-antifa candidate." In the 2022 Republican primary for U.S. Senate, Chris came in fifth with 8.2 percent of the vote. Jo Rae Perkins, an avid and very public QAnon follower, won that race.

6. Daughters

1. Kem, 2:34, OMKP.
2. In both the school board and state house, Kem maintained the rebellious attitude of the Populist; on the school board, he fought successfully against mandatory smallpox vaccinations for students. In the legislature, he opposed and exposed Republican corruption, especially in the election of Simon Guggenheim, "a man known solely and only because of his dollars," to the U.S. Senate. Kem, 2:44, OMKP.
3. Centers for Disease Control, "Mortality Statistics 1910."
4. Kem, 2:81, OMKP

5. Kem, 9:106, OMKP
6. Kem, 9:148, OMKP
7. Foucault, *Society*, 241.
8. Settlers named the town Olathe in 1896 after a town of the same name in Kansas. The land was Ute land, not Shawnee, and so, in a sense, is misnamed.
9. Kem, 9:3–4, OMKP.
10. Kem, 9:99, OMKP.
11. Kem, 9:129, OMKP.
12. Kem, 9:87, OMKP.
13. Solinger, *Pregnancy and Power*, 70. Whether the methods were effective or safe is another matter.
14. Comstock's masturbation habits are reportedly in his diaries, which I admit I have not read. D. Leonard, "The Life and Times of a True American Moral Hysteric."
15. Du Bois, *Black Reconstruction*, 595–96, 684.
16. Barreyre, "The Politics of Economic Crises."
17. Keith, *The Colfax Massacre*, xi, 88–110. Keith reports that in 1867, "Louisiana's 127,639 voters included less than 45,000 whites." The massacre was designed to restore "white supremacy and home rule." Keith, *The Colfax Massacre*, 54, 110.
18. *Congressional Globe*, February 20, 1873, 1436. One of Comstock's greatest supporters was the abolitionist and Radical Republican Vice President Schuyler Colfax. D. Leonard, *Neither Snow nor Rain*, 54–55.
19. Solinger explains how "sexual purity" was understood as a condition of white privilege. Solinger, *Pregnancy and Power*, 71–72.
20. See Foner, *The Industrial Workers of the World*, chapters 7 and 8, for thrilling descriptions of the IWW free speech fights.
21. Engelman, *A History of the Birth Control Movement*, 24.
22. With IWW leaders Elizabeth Gurley Flynn and Bill Haywood, Sanger helped organize the 1912 Bread and Roses Strike in Lawrence, Massachusetts, and the 1913 Silk Strike in Paterson, New Jersey. After the failure of the Paterson strike, Sanger strongly criticized the IWW leadership for their tactics of passive resistance—their "hands-in-your-pockets" policy—because of which, she writes, "they were no longer feared." Sanger, *Selected*, 1:57.

    In the early 1910s Sanger and her husband, William Sanger, were active members of the Socialist Party and were involved in Goldman and Berkman's Ferrer Center and "Modern School," with its roster of now famous radicals and artists (Max Weber, Upton Sinclair, and Eugene O'Neil; Goldman taught classes). See Engelman, *A History of the Birth Control Movement*, 27–32; Sanger, *Selected*, 1:17, 39–40.

23. Sanger, *Birth Control Review* 1, no. 4 (June 1917): 7.
24. *Woman Rebel*, March 1914, in Sanger, *Selected*, 1:73.
25. Goldman, "Marriage and Love" in *Anarchism and Other Essays*, 243. In their theories of social reproduction, both women anticipate Foucault in his discussion of how biopower and capitalism interact. Foucault, "Right of Death," 263.
26. *Birth Control Review* 1, no. 4 (June 1917): 5. See also Mayer, *Beyond the Rebel Girl*, 141–56. Mayer discusses Marie Equi and the IWW's support for birth control.
27. Quoted in Engelman, *A History of the Birth Control Movement*, 39. Sanger was arrested in August of 1914 for distributing material that the U.S. District Court of New York referred to as "vile, obscene, filthy, and indecent." National Archives, "Margaret Sanger."
28. *Rebel Woman* 1, no. 1 (March 1914).
29. Sanger, *Selected*, 1:72.
30. Engelman, *A History of the Birth Control Movement*, 45. Sanger, *Family Limitation*.
31. At least one hundred thousand copies were distributed directly through the IWW. L. Gordon, *Woman's Body*, 276–77; and Mayer, *Beyond*, 144.

When Sanger returned to the United States in 1916, she opened the first, and short-lived, birth control clinic in Brownsville, Brooklyn. Immigrant women from Hungary, Italy, Poland, and Russia were among the first clients, 488 of whom were fitted with diaphragms in just over a week. The clinic was shut down and Sanger arrested after ten days of what must have been frantic activity. When another birth control activist, Sanger's sister Ethel Byrne, was arrested and jailed, she went on a hunger strike, creating a media storm for their cause. See McCann, *Birth Control Politics*, 61; Engelman, *A History of the Birth Control Movement*, 86–87.

For an example of how U.S. society thought of women's sexuality in the teens and twenties, McCann offers the following: "Throughout the 1910s, and particularly during the war, police powers were brought to bear on young women through active surveillance of their sexual activity. During the war an adolescent girl could be arrested for public flirting or consorting with military personnel. All young women who were arrested for any reason were given a medical examination; if they were found to have a venereal disease they were charged with prostitution and could be incarcerated without a trial for the war's duration." McCann, *Birth Control Politics*, 44.

32. *Birth Control Review*, September 1919. For discussions of the later "Negro Project," see Schuller, *The Biopolitics of Feeling*, chapter 5; and Schoen, *Coercion and Control*. Schoen writes, "Sanger envisioned a broad grassroots campaign under the direction of African Americans that would educate the members of black communities about birth control, allowing them to start their own services independent of potentially hostile whites." Schoen, *Coercion and Control*, 47–49.

33. Owen, "Women and Children of the South," 9. Another socialist leader, Eugene Debs, also wrote for *Birth Control Review*. "Freedom, complete freedom is the goal of woman's struggle . . . the struggle in which she must persist at any cost until she is absolutely free from man's insolent and debasing domination." Debs, "Freedom Is the Goal," 7.

34. Du Bois also included the last stanza of his "A Hymn to the Peoples": "Save us, World Spirit, from our lesser selves / Grant us that war and hatred cease, / Reveal our souls in every race and hue / Help us, O Human God, in this thy truce / To make humanity divine!" Du Bois, "A Word from Doctor Du Bois," 15.

35. Du Bois, "Opinion," 248. For discussions of Black women's leadership in the twentieth-century birth control movement, see Ross, "African American Women and Abortion"; Rodrique, "The Black Community and the Birth Control Movement"; Rodrique, "The Afro-American Community"; and Roberts, *Killing the Black Body*, 85–86.

36. McCann, "Introduction." The death rate in general for Black people was 42 percent higher.

37. "Reproductive Health," Centers for Disease Control, "Infant Mortality." For more on contemporary understandings of epigenetic health discrepancies across race, see Sullivan, "Inheriting Racist Disparities."

38. Benito Thomas, "Advocates of Birth Control Flayed," *Negro World*, April 4, 1925, 10. For more on Marcus Garvey and the UNIA's opposition to eugenics and all forms of birth control for Black women, see McCann, *Birth Control Politics*, 154–55.

39. Some of the earliest and loudest opposition to birth control came from eugenicists who feared that readily available contraception would only lower birthrates among middle-class whites while having no effect on the birthrates of immigrant, poor, Black, or brown women. Engelman, *A History of the Birth Control Movement*, 54.

   The shift in the white birth control movement toward more conservative (racist, ablest, and classist) values had to do in part with a division within the movement itself. With Sanger in exile in the mid-teens, a group of more moderate feminist reformers, led by suffragist Mary Ware Dennett, formed the National Birth Control League. Leagues were established in western cities—San Francisco, Los Angeles, Seattle, and Portland—growing the movement away from its radical New York base. Dennett worked to advance birth control through changes in the laws rather than through breaking them, and she divorced the project entirely from its anti-capitalist anti-Statist agendas. Engelman, *A History of the Birth Control Movement*, 104.

40. Some trace this shift to Sanger's friendship with Havelock Ellis during her exile in England (1914–16). Ellis was a socialist eugenicist. See H. Ellis, *The Problem of Race Regeneration*.

41. Engelman, *A History of the Birth Control Movement*, 121; Okrent, *The Guarded Gate*, 296.

42. Engelman, *A History of the Birth Control Movement*, 133–34.

43. For more on eugenicists in the pages of *Birth Control Review*, see L. Gordon, *Woman's Body*, 282–83.

44. Sanger, *Pivot*, 23–24.

45. Sanger, *Pivot*, 170–89. "We should here recognize the difficulties . . ." (181).

46. "Every feeble-minded girl or woman of the hereditary type, especially of the moron class, should be segregated during the reproductive period. Otherwise, she is almost certain to bear imbecile children, who in turn are just as certain to breed other defectives. The male defectives are no less dangerous. Segregation carried out for one or two generations would give us only partial control of the problem. . . . When we realize that each feeble-minded person is a potential source of an endless progeny of defect, we prefer the policy of immediate sterilization, of making sure that parenthood is absolutely prohibited to the feeble-minded." Sanger, *Pivot*, 101–2. In most other moments, Sanger advocates only voluntary sterilizations.

47. Sanger, *Selected*, 2:273. Sanger, who was married to a Jew, would almost certainly have known that the Nazi sterilization campaign targeted Jews. "Some have assumed that because American wartime propaganda did not emphasize the persecution of Jews, the American public didn't know the depths of Nazi terror until the Signal Corps footage of Buchenwald appeared in movie theaters in 1945. To the contrary, the American public was exposed to Nazi atrocity stories against Jews and leftists throughout the thirties." Vials, *Haunted by Hitler*, 38.

48. "Despite many disgusting ramifications of eugenics, eugenics language had crucially enabled the reproductive rights movement to unshackle birth control from physicians' reluctance," writes Joyce Berkman, summarizing the conclusions of many. Berkman, "The Question of Margaret Sanger," 478.

49. Kazin, *War*, 147–48.

50. Soloway, "The 'Perfect Contraceptive,'" 640.

51. Kem, 5:67, OMKP.

52. Kem, 5:73, OMKP. For more on the "safety valve," see Grandin, *The End of the Myth*, chapter 4. Contemporary environmentalists on the right and the left are again voicing concerns about population growth. See Haraway and Clarke, *Making Kin Not Population*, for perspectives on "the impacts and consequences of expanding numbers of humans on the planet" from Black, queer, Indigenous, and Asian feminist points of view.

53. Kem, 5:127, OMKP.

54. Kem, 5:128, OMKP.

55. Grandin, *The End of the Myth*, 7.

56. Kem, 5:131, OMKP. As Wendy Kline demonstrates, the idea that white mothers, by "controlling the racial makeup of future generations," would be the pioneers for the future was common in eugenic discourse of the 1910s and '20s. Kline, *Building a Better Race*, chapter 1. See also Carey, "The Racial Imperatives of Sex." Carey discusses the deep ties between white supremacy, eugenics, and the early twentieth-century birth control movement in the United States, Canada, and the United Kingdom.

57. Kem, 5:70, OMKP.

58. Kem, 5:71, OMKP.

59. See the CNN video of seventeen-year-old Paxton Smith delivering a clandestine valedictorian speech at Lake Highlands High School. In

response to the 2021 passage of the "heartbeat bill" in Texas, Smith makes an impassioned case for women's bodily autonomy. One year later, with the *Dobbs v. Jackson Women's Health Organization* decision, the U.S. Supreme Court opened the floodgates for many more anti-abortion bills across the Unites States. At the time of writing, so-called heartbeat bills, which ban abortions at approximately six weeks gestational age, have been signed into law in Ohio, Oklahoma, South Carolina, Tennessee, and Texas. States with near total abortion bans include Idaho, Missouri, Louisiana, Mississippi, Alabama, Kentucky, Indiana, South Dakota, and Wisconsin. Smith's speech can be seen at www.cnn.com/2021/06/03/us/paxton-smith-texas-valedictorian-speech-trnd/index.html.
60. Sanger, *Selected*, 1:58.
61. Kem, 9:130, OMKP.
62. Kem, 9:88–89, OMKP.
63. Because of medical and environmental racism and profound economic inequality, some elderly people—Black, brown, and impoverished—were far more at risk than my father, who is white and financially secure.

7. Blood

Epigraph: Nina Simone performing "I Wish I Knew How It Would Feel to be Free" at the Montreux Jazz Festival in 1976.
1. Jim Crow laws were in force since the later 1870s. I'm singling out the 1920s because of the rise of the second Ku Klux Klan and of eugenics during that decade. Thirty thousand Klansmen marched in Washington in August of 1925. Seventy thousand people attended Licking County, Ohio's, Klan conventions in 1923 and '25. Oregon, where Omer and Alice lived, and Colorado, where I live now, held the strongest Klan presence in the West. Ohio History Central, "Ku Klux Klan"; Lay, *The Invisible Empire*, 11, 162.
2. "It must be remembered that the white group of laborers, while they received a low wage, were compensated in part by a sort of public and psychological wage." Huxley and Happie Kem were not laborers, but they were struggling to make ends meet, and they were new to Cincinnati. The party was one way they were establishing themselves as worthy members of the community. Du Bois, *Black Reconstruction*, 700.

3. See Karen Sieber's Visualizing the Red Summer website at http://visualizingtheredsummer.com/?page_id=6ael.
4. White workers likely resented how the construction company, L. E. Myers, imported Black laborers from the South to keep wages low. Once the largest rock-filled dam in the world, the Dix created Lake Herrington, which now serves three counties of swimmers and boaters. Each of these counties is 95 percent white. "Troops Patrol Kentucky Camp after Negroes Are Attacked," *Cincinnati Enquirer*, November 11, 1924, 1–2; G. Wright, *Racial Violence in Kentucky*, 150.
5. Butler, *Nonviolence*, 189.
6. "Emphasis on blood as conduit for the stain of black ancestry became more necessary as bodies of color began to merge, losing the visible trait of blackness. The supremacy of whiteness now depended on a fiction threatened by what one could not always see but must always fear: through wanton *misalliance* black blood would not only pollute progeny but infect the very heart of the nation." Dayan, *The Law*, 50.
7. Kem, 6:71–2, OMKP. Many abolitionists and other white progressives were proponents of "colonization." See Kazanjian, *The Colonization Trick*, chapter 2.
8. "There is no outright assumption of black humanity in the world (the potency of 'Black Lives Matter' as an emblem confirms this), and indeed black humanity has to be argued over and again," writes Kevin Quashie in 2021. Quashie, *Black Aliveness*, 2.
9. "The human is a historically variable concept, differentially articulated in the context of inegalitarian forms of social and political power; the field of the human is constituted by basic exclusions, haunted by those figures that do not count in its tally." Butler, *Nonviolence*, 59.
10. Kevles, *In the Name of Eugenics*, 72–74; Foucault, *Society*, 245, 243.
11. Laughlin, *Eugenical Sterilization*, 89.
12. Owens-Adair, *Human Sterilization*, 18–19. The passage includes descriptions of other girls and women. For the sake of brevity, I have elided some while maintaining the original order. Owens-Adair, still sometimes celebrated today as a pioneering physician and feminist, wrote the eugenic sterilization law that eventually led to the forced sterilization of 2,500 Oregonians, and she strongly influenced a similar law in Washington State. In 2014 the anonymous writer of the *History of American Women* blog writes, "Her writing reveals that she was motivated by a genuine concern for human well-being."

13. Owens-Adair, *Human Sterilization*, 19.
14. F. C. Cave, MD, Winfield, Kansas, "Sterilization in Kansas State Home for Feeble-Minded," *Journal of Psycho-Asthenics*, 1911, 123, quoted in Laughlin, *Eugenic Sterilization*, 434.
15. Dayan, *The Law*, 12. Carrie Buck, who'd been raped at seventeen and had thereby become an unwed mother, was slotted for sterilization by Lynchburg, Virginia's, State Colony for Epileptics and the Feebleminded. Her fate was debated in the Supreme Court for one reason only: eugenicists used her as a test case. Buck's lawyer, Irving Whitehead (an active eugenicist and former board member of Lynchburg Colony), brought no witnesses in her defense. Justice Oliver Wendell Holmes wrote the infamous and near-unanimous opinion: "It is better for all the world, if instead of waiting to execute degenerate offspring for a crime, or to let them starve for their imbecility, society can prevent those who are manifestly unfit from continuing their kind." The only Supreme Court justice to dissent was Justice Pierce Butler, a Catholic. For a detailed narrative of *Buck v. Bell*, see Black, *War against the Weak*, 112–17.
16. American eugenics finds its roots in nineteenth-century genetics, evolutionary theory, race theory, criminology, medicine, and, as Kyla Schuller has provocatively shown, sentimentalism. The complex story of how and why early twentieth-century white middle-class Americans latched onto eugenic theory with such passion has been deeply examined by historians Daniel Kevles, Diane B. Paul, Edwin Black, Alexandra Minna Stern, Mark Largent, Nancy Ordover, Wendy Kline, Schuller, and others. These scholars discuss how urbanization, accelerating immigration, the growing independence of women, and rapid Black migration to the North generated anxiety about shifts in power dynamics, as well as concerns about the real problems associated with urban poverty. Most scholars interpret eugenics as a backlash against these demographic and hierarchical changes.

    For statistics on sterilizations, see Kaelber, "Eugenics." Kevles writes that before *Buck v. Bell*, "fewer than nine thousand people had been eugenically sterilized in the United States." Kevles, *In the Name of Eugenics*, 106.
17. For statistics on sterilization in Oregon, see Largent, "'The Greatest Curse of the Race,'" 205. For contemporary sterilizations, see Hunter, "The U.S. Is Still Forcibly Sterilizing Prisoners"; Rivas, "California

Prisons Caught Sterilizing Female Inmates"; Brigitte Amiri, "Reproductive Abuse Is Rampant in the Immigration Detention System," ACLU News & Commentary, September 23, 2020; Haraway and Clarke, *Making Kin Not Population*, 7; and Journeyman Pictures, *Sterilized behind Bars*.

18. The Sterilization and Social Justice Lab, a collaborative and multidisciplinary group of scholars, is tracking the demographics of coerced and forced sterilizations in the United States. According to group members' research, in California, where one-third of all state sterilizations were performed, ethnic Mexican women and girls were 59 percent more likely to be sterilized than white women. See Novak et al., "Disproportionate Sterilization of Latinos."

    Some Black professionals of the era promoted eugenic ideas, including Du Bois. For an in-depth look at Du Bois's eugenic theory, see Schuller, *The Biopolitics of Feeling*, chapter 5.

19. The museum was founded in 1975 by Bertha Calloway. It has since gained a permanent location at 2221 N. Twenty-Fourth St., Omaha.

20. Kem, 4:105, OMKP.

21. Kem, 2:86, OMKP. As Kevles writes, for some, eugenics provided "a secular substitution for religion." Kevles, *In the Name of Eugenics*, 68.

22. Kem, 2:86, OMKP. Kem sometimes emphasized that eugenics should target people based on "character" rather than class or race: "I surely would not apply eugenist remedies on class ground alone and would be guided entirely by personal worth and action, regardless of class." However, in other instances, it's clear that he did advocate eugenic "remedies" to the problem of poverty. Kem, 10:99, OMKP.

    As Kevles points out, "State sterilization laws applied only to the inmates of public mental institutions, whose residents were disproportionately from lower-income and minority groups. In Virginia the overwhelming majority of those sterilized were poor; perhaps as many as half of them were black." Kevles, *In the Name of Eugenics*, 168.

23. Okrent reports that "the number of articles on eugenics appearing in the popular press had tripled between 1909–1914." Okrent, *The Guarded Gate*, 241. For more on better babies contests and other forms of positive eugenics, see Stern, "Making Better Babies"; and Dorey, *Better Baby Contests*.

24. Omer Kem, "Speech on Income Tax," February 8, 1894, in Kem, 2:1–6, OMKP.

25. Gerteis and Goolsby argue that the Populist movement was always a nationalist movement, bent on defining and shoring up a threatened sense of Americanism, though "Americanism" was, for their subjects, as much a civic as it was a racial term. Americanness was conflated with whiteness infrequently in the Populist press they study, but this conflation was nonetheless "important." Gerteis and Goolsby, "Nationalism in America," 215 and throughout.

It should be remembered also that almost all Populists were farmers familiar with breeding techniques for both animals and plants. Their knowledge and experience in this area certainly encouraged some to apply the same principles to humans. See Kimmelman, "The American Breeders' Association."

26. Paul, *"Three Generations of Imbeciles Are Enough,"* 617. See also Derrell, *The Women of Reform*, 13–14.
27. "Kansas Populists apparently found Eugenics the answer to the projected 'flood' of degenerates that would swamp the nation," writes Julius Paul in one of the earliest studies of American eugenics we have. Paul, *"Three Generations of Imbeciles Are Enough,"* 618.
28. Quoted in Largent, *Breeding*, 15. Largent's research reveals that American doctors, especially in the West, were among the first to promote the practice of forced sterilization and in some cases illegally implement it. As early as 1849, Texas physician Gideon Lincecum presented castration as a useful tool against "depravities . . . recognized as transmissible by heredity," such as rape. Largent, *Breeding*, 13.
29. Largent, *Breeding*, 16.
30. "From the 1860s through the 1880s newspapers reported the castration of men who were convicted of rape . . . almost all of whom were African American." Largent, *Breeding*, 12.
31. After a Black man named Sam Holt, accused of murder and rape in 1899, was castrated and burned to death in Georgia, one commenter wrote, "It is better that a thousand such as Holt should burn at the stake than that one like his victim go shame-lashed and sorrow-haunted to her grave." "The Negro Question," *Herald and Advertiser* (Newnan GA), May 12, 1899, 1. Also see Dray, *At the Hands of Persons Unknown*, 81.
32. In an example of northern elites learning technique from lynch mobs, Simeon E. Baldwin, a Connecticut Supreme Court justice (and later governor), reportedly suggested in 1899 that the legalization of cas-

tration as punishment for sexual crimes might put a stop to lynching, satisfying the lynch mob's blood lust. See Dray, *At the Hands of Persons Unknown*, 144.

33. Some Populists and populist-leaning activists opposed sterilization for moral or religious reasons. For William Jennings Bryan's opposition to sterilization, see Gould, "William Jennings Bryan's Last Campaign," 428–30. For the story of Lora C. Little and the Anti-Sterilization League in Portland, Oregon, see Johnston, *The Radical Middle Class*, 197–206. For more on sterilization opposition, see Paul, *The Politics of Heredity*, 81–93; Kevles, 164–75; Stern, *Eugenic Nation*, 185–93; and Schoen, *Coercion and Control*, 103–5.

34. 54 Cong. Rec. 2621 (1917). At first, the eugenicists who formed the IRL were laser focused on so-called intelligence as a marker of value, lobbying for an immigration literacy test for decades. Once that goal was achieved in 1917, the group shifted their focus to race.

    The 1924 act based new national quotas—2 percent from each racial group—on the demographics of the 1890 census rather than the 1910. In this way, Congress purposely privileged older immigrant groups ("Nordics") while severely restricting immigrants from "races" or nationalities considered to be "dysgenic" (southern and eastern Europeans). The bill explicitly barred all future immigration from Asia (including Japan, exempted from earlier bans) and limited African immigration by excluding Americans of African descent from the quota altogether. See Okrent, *The Guarded Gate*, 165–91; Ordover, *American Eugenics*, 1–31; Ngai, *Impossible Subjects*, 27 and throughout.

    Ngai argues that the Johnson-Reed Act instigated two major shifts in U.S. attitudes to race, ethnicity, and nationality: 1) it generated a stronger sense of racial hierarchy, introducing new stratifications into that structure and "harden[ing] racial categories into law"; and 2) it re-defined and strengthened the idea of our national borders, "marked by unprecedented awareness and state surveillance of the nation's contiguous land borders." Ngai, *Impossible Subjects*, 7, 3.

35. Andrew Gyory writes that Chinese exclusion "set the precedent for . . . broader exclusion laws and fostered an atmosphere of hostility toward foreigners that would endure for generations." Gyory, *Closing the Gate*, 13. Ordover writes, "Eugenicists owed their influence over twentieth-

century immigration policy in large part to nineteenth-century legislation." Ordover, *American Eugenics*, xvi.

See Schuller, *The Biopolitics of Feeling*, chapter 5, for an overview of hereditary theory from a Lamarkian theory of impressionability to a more rigid theory of the gene, influenced by the resurfacing of Mendel's pea-plant experiments in 1900. In the early twentieth century, Schuller explains "theories and strategies of progress via impressibility gradually gave way to theories of immutable heredity." Schuller, *The Biopolitics of Feeling*, 33.

36. 13 Cong. Rec. 1482 (1882). See Paisley Rekdal's *West: A Translation* for a multimedia poetic engagement with the history of Chinese labor on the railroads and Chinese exclusion in the United States. https://westtrain.org.

37. 13 Cong. Rec. 1483 (1882). This rejection of what came to be called the "melting pot" was based in part in shifts in hereditary theory, as Schuller shows. Schuller also points out that contemporary geneticists are again studying the effects of experience on hereditary material (epigenetics). See Schuller, *The Biopolitics of Feeling*, "Introduction" and chapter 5.

38. 13 Cong. Rec. 1481–88 (1882).

39. For the passage of the bill in the Senate (including opposition), see Gyory, *Closing the Gate*, 210–26. Ngai locates the birth of the "illegal alien" in 1924, seeing the Chinese Exclusion Act as a precursor. Ngai, *Impossible Subjects*, 1–14, 18.

40. Wortman, "Denver's Anti-Chinese Riot, 1880"; Courtright, "A Slave to Yellow Peril." Both Wortman and Courtright stress that laborers in Denver and Wichita did not experience any competition from Chinese workers, since almost all Chinese workers ran or worked in laundromats, which white workers did not do.

41. Saxton, *The Rise and Fall*, 299. Saxton and Gyory both argue that Chinese exclusion was motivated less by actual economic competition between white and Chinese workers than by racism. Gyory stresses that this racism was drummed up by politicians seeking to motivate voters, while Saxton argues that anti-Asian racism was an offshoot from anti-Blackness. See Gyory, *Closing the Gate*, 13; and Saxton, *The Rise and Fall*, 311, 315, 322–23, 379.

42. 23 Cong. Rec. 3478 (1892).

43. See Gossett, *Race*, 48–49.

44. 23 Cong. Rec. 3478 (1892).
45. Populist senators at the time were Peffer (NE) and Kyle (SD). Populist congressmembers were Watson (GA), Clover (KS), Davis (KS), Owen (KS), Baker (KS), Simpson (KS), Halvorson (MN), McKeighan (NE), and Kem (NE).

    In the Senate there were voices of dissent, though few. Senator John Sherman (R-OH) argued that to "exclude the whole race of four hundred million human beings with an older civilization by far than we can boast of, with great wealth, great commerce, vast cities, with every sign of modern civilization" was, if not morally wrong, bad for business, as it would cause a breakdown in commercial relations between the nations. In the House Charles Hooker (D-MS) eloquently protested the bill's suspension of the writ of habeas corpus. Gyory provides some evidence that Hooker was motivated by the South's need for cheap labor. 23 Cong. Rec. 2911–2916 (1892); and Gyory, *Closing the Gate*, 312n55.
46. Gerteis and Goolsby demonstrate that Populists were more concerned with Jews as outsiders than with the Chinese. Jews were thought to control the British and European banks and to be land speculators who had contributed to economic crises for farmers. Gerteis and Goolsby, "Nationalism in America," 214.
47. Coolidge, "Whose Country Is This?," 13; J. Taylor, "The Racial Revolution."
48. M. Grant, *The Passing of the Great Race*, 91. Hitler reportedly read Grant when he was in prison and referred to *The Passing of the Great Race* as his "bible." Hoff, "Passing."
49. "If the principle of individual liberty, guarded by a constitutional government created on this continent nearly a century and a half ago, is to endure, the basic strain of our population must be maintained. . . . The question of immigration . . . has passed the stage where it can be considered entirely from an economic standpoint. . . . It has advanced to the question of who will inhabit the land of our fathers." A. Johnson, "Restriction of Immigration," 16, 26. For more on theories tying race to democracy, see Gossett, *Race*, 88; King, *Where Do We Go from Here?*, 76–78.
50. Gerteis and Goolsby, "Nationalism in America," 220.
51. Engelman, *A History of the Birth Control Movement*, 97.
52. "The entire white race, the Western race, can become submerged by other races of color which multiply at a rate unknown to ours.

Blacks and yellows are thus at the gates? Yes, they are at the gates, and not only because of their birthrates but also because of their race consciousness and their future in the world. Meanwhile, for example, the whites of the United States have a miserable natality rate. . . . The alarm is sounding and all who are able to see beyond daily contingencies (in my opinion, anyone who is unable to see at least fifty years ahead has no right to govern a nation) are worried." Mussolini, "Strength in Numbers."

53. Whitman, *Hitler's American Model*, 43–48.
54. Eastman, "Some Questions for Kamala Harris."
55. Eastman, "Born in the USA?," timestamp 33.6.
56. "Faculty Assembly Discusses Role in Hiring Professors, Including Visiting Scholars," *CU Boulder Today*, February 4, 2021, www.colorado.edu/today/2021/02/04/faculty-assembly-discusses-role-hiring-professors-including-visiting-scholars. After Eastman took the stage beside Rudy Giuliani just before the January 6, 2021, attack on the Capitol, he was removed from his responsibilities at the University of Colorado Boulder, though he was still paid a salary of $185,000 through the academic year.
57. Media Matters for America, "Tucker Carlson Gives Passionate Defense."
58. Cillizza, "How the Ugly, Racist, White 'Replacement Theory' Came to Congress."
59. "America First Caucus Policy Platform." After GOP outcry, Greene denied her role in the caucus plan. In April 2021 *Politico* reported that Greene had raised $3.2 million toward her reelection campaign. Beavers and Zanona, "MTG's Eye-Popping Fundraiser Haul."
60. The published version of the letter does not include the phrase "has no right to bring children into the world," but Kem includes it in the copy of the letter he typed for his autobiography. Omer Kem, *Morning Oregonian*, September 10, 1926, 8; Kem, 7:1, OMKP.
61. Kem, 7:3, OMKP. In this letter, Kem embraces the term *mongrel* because his ancestors could be traced to five European nations.
62. Kem, 7:3–5, OMKP.
63. Kem, 4:106, 100, OMKP.
64. Kem, 4:107, OMKP.
65. Kem, 10:2, OMKP.
66. For discussions of "prairie socialism" in the plains, see Kazin, *American Dreamers*, 109–18; and Burbank, *When Farmers Voted Red*.

67. These initials correspond to Omer Madison and James Donahue. Kem, 10:8, OMKP.
68. Kem, 10:21, 92, OMKP.
69. Kem, 10:16, OMKP.
70. Kem, 10:17, 40, OMKP.
71. Kem, 10:17, OMKP.
72. Kem, 10:22, OMKP. Taylor Greene's proposed "America First Caucus" used similar language in its policy platform: "These pauses [in immigration] have been absolutely essential in assimilating the new arrivals and weeding out those who could not or refused to abandon their old loyalties and plunge head-first into mainstream American society." "America First Caucus Policy Platform."
73. Foucault, *Society*, 258.
74. Kem, 10:35, 99–100, OMKP.
75. Kem, 10:93, OMKP.
76. Kem, 10:23, 66, OMKP.
77. Some form of eugenics was accepted by many on the left as well as the right, including American (and British) socialists and Marxists. See Paul, *Politics of Heredity*, 11–36.
78. In most documented sterilizations of homosexuals, the victims were men. Largent, *Breeding*, 20–21.
79. Kem, 9:149, OMKP.
80. "Reproducing white lives requires ongoing sterilization." R. Benjamin, "Black AfterLives Matter," 42.
81. Foucault, "Right of Death and Power over Life," 268.
82. See Popenoe, *Applied Eugenics*, 284, 306. Popenoe explains that the American dream, class mobility, is too fragile to survive infusions of "inferior" non-white people who frustrate the free movement across class by their presence.
83. IWW Constitution. Ni Una Menos, the contemporary women-, trans-, and queer-led movement organized in Argentina and across Latin America to protest and resist femicide and the exploitation of women and the poor, employed a similar slogan: "If they touch one of us, they touch us all!" Gago, *Feminist International*, 19.
84. Kem, 10:97, OMKP.
85. Kem, 10:105–7, OMKP.
86. "Governor Agrees with Dr. Laughlin," *Corvallis Gazette-Times*, March 14, 1936, 1. In *Human Sterilization*, Bethenia Owens-Adair includes

an article about Dr. Jean Zimmerman of Chicago, who advocated chloroforming "defective" children after they get to a "certain age." Owens-Adair did not advocate the killing of children. Instead, she argued that sterilizing defective parents would prevent these children from being born. Owens-Adair, *Human Sterilization*, 107.

87. Ost, "Doctors and Nurses of Death," 6. Ost also notes the racist motivations of many of the killings. Ost, "Doctors and Nurses of Death," 11–15, 24.
88. Owens-Adair, *Human Sterilization*, 194.
89. "Open Forum," *Capital Journal*, January 31, 1921, quoted in Antonovich, "Medical Frontiers," 234. Perhaps Owens-Adair had read R. W. Shufeldt's *The Negro: A Menace to American Civilization* (1907), which suggests castrating all Black men. See McWhirter, *Red Summer*, 60.
90. *Oregon Journal*, August 9, 1935, quoted in Antonovich, "Medical Frontiers," 234.
91. Kem, 10:8, OMKP.
92. Kem, 4:105, OMKP. Kem, 6, 52, OMKP.
93. Whitman, *Hitler's American Model*, 1–16. American eugenicist Charles Davenport traveled to Berlin to participate in the Fifth International Congress on Eugenics (1927). In the 1920s and '30s, the Rockefeller Foundation financed the study of race biology and eugenics in Germany. Kühl, *The Nazi Connection*, 20; Black, *War against the Weak*, 288.
94. U.S. Holocaust Memorial Museum, "Nazi Racial Science." See Whitman, *Hitler's American Model*, for ample archival evidence for this assertion. See Kühl, *The Nazi Connection*, "Introduction" and chapters 2–4, for an examination of the international collaborations among eugenicists, especially between Americans and Germans, before, during, and after the Nazi eugenics program. See also Vials, *Haunted by Hitler*, 21.
95. "In the first three decades of the twentieth century, eugenic ideas were politically influential, culturally fashionable, and scientifically mainstream." T. Leonard, *Illiberal Reformers*, 109.
96. See Paul, *The Politics of Heredity*, 173–86, on PKU screening. See Kevles, *In the Name of Eugenics*, 251–68, on genetic screening and postwar eugenics. For gene editing technology, see Davies, *Editing Humanity*.
97. To counter these arguments, eugenics was never about what a person does with their *own* fertility, their *own* children. Eugenics was always about other people's fertility, other people's lives.

98. Hennessey, "Home as the Uncanny Archive."
99. Advances in epigenetics point to the complex ways experiences and behaviors, including ancestral trauma, affect our genetic expression. As far as I've been able to discern, this science is still contested. See Sullivan, "Inheriting Racist Disparities."
100. In his one moment of concession to Jim, Omer wrote, "Generally speaking, we are all made out of about the same sort of human mud and the difference is largely the result of the condition of our surroundings and opportunity." However, in the very next paragraph, he argues that no "Eutopia" is possible unless there is "a vast improvement in the race," and he never repeated or expanded on this position in the autobiography. Kem, 10:20–21, OMKP.
101. The dance artist K. J. Holmes told me that blood is the heaviest fluid in the body, but as the conduit for oxygen, it carries and is carried by the air.

8. Power

1. Fred Barbash, "The Story of Sarah Root," *Washington Post*, July 22, 2016. In using Sarah Root's death as evidence for the need for a southern border wall, Trump echoes the pattern we saw in chapter 5, when the reported rape of Josephine Meeker added fuel to anti-Ute fury in Colorado. See also NPR, "Fact Check."
2. W. Benjamin, "On the Concept of History." In Benjamin's *Selected Writings*, the passage is translated by Harry Zohn as: "Doesn't a breath of the air that pervaded earlier days caress us as well? In the voices we hear, isn't there an echo of now silent ones?" W. Benjamin, *Selected Writings*, 4:389. For an excellent and brief summary of Benjamin's theory of history, see Vials, *Haunted by Hitler*, 28.
3. Kem, 9:3–4, OMKP.
4. Kem, 2:109, OMKP. Alice Kem had no shares in the company. Maude had a full third.
5. Wood waste is an example of biofuel, a semi-renewable energy source. The timber industry in the early twentieth century was ruthless in its appropriations of Northwest forests: "Between 1909 and 1929 . . . the timber industry in Washington, Oregon, and British Columbia cut more than 15,000 square miles of forest . . . the same area as Delaware, New Jersey, and Connecticut combined," writes Steven Beda. This is a rough estimate. It was a rough business too, especially once steam

power made clearcutting an attractive option. One in four workers suffered death or serious injury each year. See Beda, "Landscapes of Solidarity," 63–64. See also Pouty, *More Deadly than War*.

6. In a state that had encouraged only white settlers under the Oregon Donation Land Act (1850), that had (like all western states) moved its decimated Native populations into ever shrinking reservations, and that had, from 1844 until 1927, legally excluded Black people from settling and from owning property, it's clear that as the Kems generated electric power, they accumulated white power too. My cousin Chris remembers buying his first house in Portland in 1995. The deed included a (by then illegal) "restrictive covenant" barring Black people from ownership or occupancy. See K. Barber, "We Are at Our Journey's End."

7. At first, they based their rate on the numbers of appliances in a house or business. One local history describes Charles Shinn going door to door, trying to catch women in the act of unreported ironing. Cottage Grove Historical Society, *Golden Was the Past*, 169.

8. "I have made a rather detailed statement of my trouble with [my nieces], Lottie and Louise . . . in order that if, sometime in the years to come, anyone should accuse me of robbing two helpless orphan girls of their rightful inheritance, which is not at all improbable, this can be referred to as a refutation of it," writes Kem in his defense. Kem, 3:46, OMKP.

9. Kem, 4:52, OMKP.

10. Dubofsky, *We Shall Be All*, 168–69.

11. Floyd, *Abandoning American Neutrality*, 4, 15–16.

12. The domestic market shot up too as imports took a plunge. Neiberg, "Why the U.S. Entered the First World War," timestamp 24:24.

13. Neiberg, *The Path to War*, 99.

14. By late 1915, according to historian M. Ryan Floyd, U.S. companies "relied almost exclusively on the United Kingdom for their prosperity." Floyd, *Abandoning American Neutrality*, 5, 59–60. See Ross Kennedy's review of Floyd for a critique of Floyd's emphasis on the economic impetus for U.S. involvement in the war.

15. W. Wilson, "Address to Ohio Chamber of Commerce," December 10, 1915, PWW.

16. Tooze, "American Power," timestamp 7:56. "In all my dreams before my helpless sight, / He plunges at me, guttering, choking, drowning." Wilfred Owen, "Dulce et Decorum Est."

17. Tooze, *Deluge*, 38. See also Floyd, *Abandoning American Neutrality*, 13–14, 25; Horn, "A Private Bank at War."
18. Tooze, *Deluge*, 12.
19. "In a speech given on May 3 [1915], chief of the Bureau of Foreign and Domestic Commerce, Edward Pratt, noted that at the beginning of the war, the United States owed nearly $7 billion to European creditors, including $4 billion to Great Britain alone." Floyd, *Abandoning American Neutrality*, 165.

    For Tooze the rise of fascism is a direct response to the rise of the United States as a "novel kind of 'super-state'": "The leaders in Fascist Italy, National Socialist Germany, Imperial Japan, and the Soviet Union all saw themselves as radical insurgents against an oppressive and powerful world order." Tooze, *Deluge*, 7.
20. In this the Germans were violating the Sussex pledge of May 1916. They argued that this violation was justified by U.S. economic involvement in the war.
21. The February Revolution in Russia also meant that the United States could join the Allies without seeming to hypocritically support a nondemocratic government.

    In a 1915 letter to Wilson, Secretary of State Robert Lansing warned that a slow-down of U.S. exports to Europe would cause "industrial depression, idle capital, and idle labor." Lansing to Wilson, September 6, 1915, PWW; Floyd, *Abandoning American Neutrality*, 171.
22. C. Taylor, *You, Me, and the Violence*, 28.
23. Neiberg, *The Path to War*, 101.
24. In World War I, 116,516 American soldiers died. Of these, 63,114 died of disease. Byerly, "War Losses (USA)."

    For U.S. propaganda, see Dubofsky, *We Shall Be All*, 215–16; Kennedy, *Over Here*, 38–69. The propaganda came from across the Atlantic as well. In 1914 Britain cut the transatlantic telegram cable that connected the United States to Europe, thereby controlling the flow of information. London included an "American Ministry of Information" in its "War Propaganda Division" and employed prominent writers to create a flow of information for Americans. Floyd, *Abandoning American Neutrality*, 14–15.
25. Kazin, *War against War*, 197–212. By the end of 1917 the minimum draft age was lowered from twenty-one to eighteen.
26. Kem, 8:87, OMKP.

27. For examples of the casualty lists in the newspapers, see the anonymously compiled selection of newspaper clippings titled *World War I Casualties*. See also Wikipedia, s.v. "General Pershing World War I Casualty Lists," last modified May 7, 2022, https://en.wikipedia.org/wiki/General_Pershing_WWI_casualty_list.

28. Kazin references the lyrics to a popular African American song from the era: "Jined the army fur to get free clothes; What we're fightin' 'bout, nobody knows." David Kennedy writes that even in the spring of 1917, "the congressional debate on the war resolution . . . reflected the persistent confusion about America's stake in the fighting, and about the precise causes and purposes of American entry." D. Kennedy, *Over Here*, 38.

29. R. Kennedy, *The Will to Believe*, 15.

30. T. Leonard, *Illiberal Reformers*, 110.

31. Reforms under the New Freedom agenda include lowering tariffs, an end to child labor, an eight-hour workday, federal aid to farmers, a graduated income tax, the establishment of antitrust laws and of the Federal Reserve. And yet the postwar period brought a series of recessions, exacerbating poverty especially among poor immigrant and African American migrant communities. See Kline, *Building a Better Race*, 10.

    Wilson refused to meet with a delegation of Black leaders from Baltimore. The NAACP led thousands in a silent march of protest and mourning through New York. Even after this, Wilson rejected attempts by James Weldon Johnson and other leaders to meet with him. Rudwick, *Race Riot*, 133–35.

32. In Wilson's *A History of the American People* in 1902, he'd argued that Reconstruction "put the white South under the . . . negroes' heels." The phrase is repeated almost verbatim in the film, which Wilson watched at a private screening in the White House. Ambrosius, *Woodrow Wilson*, 65, 80–81.

33. Ambrosius, *Woodrow Wilson*, 67. See also Public Broadcasting Service, "Suffragist Alice Paul Clashed with Woodrow Wilson."

    In 1917 the novelist Djuna Barnes staged a performance of being force-fed to bring attention to the brutal experiences of Alice Paul and the other jailed suffragists. Almost one hundred years later, the actor and performer Mos Def (Yasiin Bey) exercised the same tactic, staging a force-feeding on YouTube to bring attention to force-fed hunger strikers at Guantanamo Bay. Wolcott, "Suffragists Used Hunger

Strike"; Ben Ferguson, "When Yasiin Bey Was Force-Fed," *Guardian*, July 9, 2013.

34. For Wilson and the Espionage and Sedition Acts, see Kazin, *War*, 147–48; D. Kennedy, *Over Here*, 198–99; and Preston, *Aliens and Dissenters*. For the crackdown on labor, especially the IWW, see Gregory, "Introduction," xvi–xvii; and Dubofsky, *We Shall Be All*, 243–54. For police raids of anarchists and the IWW, see Zimmer, *Immigrants against the State*, 147–52.

35. On Wilson, Haiti, and Du Bois, see Gilmore, *Defying Dixie*, 17–18 and 21–26. For Wilson's foreign policy in Haiti and elsewhere, see Tooze, *Deluge*, 44; Grandin, *The End of the Myth*, 126–28; and Hannigan, *The Great War*, 22–23, 85–87. For Wilson and Jim Crow, see Ambrosius, *Woodrow Wilson*, 75–79.

36. W. Wilson, "Address to Ohio Chamber of Commerce," December 10, 1915, PWW. Hannigan, *The Great War*, 22–23, 85–87. Ross Kennedy refers to the "paradox at the heart of Wilson's national security strategy—that of practicing power politics to end power politics." R. Kennedy, *The Will to Believe*, xiii–xiv.

37. R. Kennedy, *The Will to Believe*, 49. Hannigan calls him "the most antiblack president . . . since at least the time of Andrew Johnson right after the Civil War." Hannigan, *The Great War*, 215.

38. "Wilson's Secretary of State, Robert Lansing, wrote . . . that the principle of self-determination clearly did not apply to 'races, peoples, or communities whose state of barbarism or ignorance deprive them of the capacity to choose intelligently their political affiliations.'" Manela, *The Wilsonian Moment*, 28.

   For the exclusion of colonized countries from the League of Nations, see also R. Kennedy, *The Will to Believe*, 48–49; Gilmore, *Defying Dixie*, 21. Ambrosius asserts that Wilson's prewar and wartime policies "drew a global color line." Ambrosius, *Woodrow Wilson*, 1.

39. In 1915 Erich Muenter, a German American anti-war radical (and former Harvard professor), made an attempt on Morgan's life. "Because [J. P. Morgan Jr.] was so powerful as an individual, it was actually possible to believe that assassinating him could actually stop the war." Capozzola, remarks in *The Great War*, American Experience, PBS, 2018, https://www.pbs.org/wgbh/americanexperience/films/great-war.

40. "The United States relied on European markets and financing to ensure its economic growth, which meant that unless the U.S. business

community was willing to accept a shrinking share of the global market or immediately secure new overseas customers, policies enacted by their most important trading partners would affect the country and make tension unavoidable." Floyd, *Abandoning American Neutrality*, 29.

41. Wilson purported to believe that "prosperity in part of the world ministers to prosperity everywhere." This has not born out. As Du Bois put it in 1915, the nationalism of the European nations, as of the United States, "is no mere sentimental patriotism, loyalty, or ancestor-worship. It is increased wealth, power, and luxury for all classes on a scale the world never saw before. . . . Whence comes this new wealth on what does its accumulation depend? It comes primarily from the darker nations of the world—Asia and Africa, South and Central America, the West Indies and the islands of the South Seas." W. Wilson, "A Special Message to Congress," May 20, 1919, PWW; Du Bois, "The African Roots of War," section 2.

42. Tooze, *Deluge*, 35; Lentz-Smith, *Freedom Struggles*, 55. W. Williams writes that in early 1917, there were 50,000 shipyard workers in America; by 1918 there were 150,000, and by the end of 1918, 360,000. W. Williams, "Accommodating American Shipyard Workers," 51.

43. On housing shortages for shipping industry workers, see W. Williams, "Accommodating American Shipyard Workers," 51–59. For more on the 1917 strike, see "Tales from Pauling's Boyhood." See also Spitz, "'More Tons, Less Huns'"; and P. Webb, "Seattle Shipyard Workers on the Eve of the General Strike." Because shipbuilding was essential to the war—"More Tons, Less Huns!" was the slogan—the government got involved in trying to alleviate the housing crisis, passing a public housing bill in 1918 that eventually generated thirty thousand units for shipbuilders. But of course, this solution came only *after* the 1917 strike.

44. "Tales from Pauling's Boyhood."

45. Kem, 3:91, 92, OMKP. Because shipyard workers were considered war necessary, they were exempted from the draft. Many people assumed that some men chose this work to avoid fighting.

46. Kem, 3:79, OMKP.

47. King, *Where Do We Go from Here?*, 103. King is discussing Kant's categorical imperative in this moment.

48. Senator McNary wrote back, but only to dismiss Kem: "I do not care to become embroiled in a newspaper debate with you." Though McNary

had voted for war, he did not seem to care much about Victor, or any other soldier either, for in his response to Kem he said nothing on that topic at all. Kem, 3:79–80, OMKP.

49. Butler, *Nonviolence*, 121. Butler also refers to this process as "the inversion of violence and nonviolence," 63.

50. Kem, 3:92–93, OMKP. "No body of men have the moral right in the present circumstances of the nation to strike until every method of adjustment has been tried to the limit. If you do not act upon this principle you are undoubtedly giving aid and comfort to the enemy, whatever may be your own conscious purpose," wrote Wilson in reference to the shipbuilder's strike. In this same letter, he referred to striking workers as "lawless and conscienceless profiteering." Wilson to Hutcheson, February 17, 1918, PWW.

51. Kem, 3:79, OMKP.

52. A letter-writing campaign likely saved their lives. Indeed, there was so much public outcry against the verdict, Wilson's secretary of war beseeched him to stay the executions, which he did. Twenty-four American soldiers were given the death sentence for desertion, but none were executed. See Welch, "Military Justice"; Fantina, *Desertion*, 112. For the case in question, see Baker to Wilson, May 1, 1918, PWW.

53. Jim Ream writes, "You clearly understand without me telling you, that the surplus machinery of America is going into every land where it is possible to introduce it, not only this but American money and American genius managerial and otherwise is going into every country on earth and it is only a question of a short time when the whole world will be flooded to the same extent that America is flooded today with the necessaries of life that the people are unable to buy because of the enormous toll that is levied by the few who have control." Kem, 10:8, OMKP.

54. Bryan, "Peace Day," *Commoner* 14 (October 1914), quoted in R. Kennedy, *The Will to Believe*, 8.

55. Tooze, *Deluge*, 43.

56. Quoted in Floyd, *Abandoning American Neutrality*, 13.

57. Kazin, *War*, 94. Bryan had the foresight to note that unless there was a compromise between the two sides, Europe would erupt in another war before long. Floyd, *Abandoning American Neutrality*, 28. See also Tooze, *Deluge*, 43. On Wilson's own fears that peace would not last, see R. Kennedy, *The Will to Believe*, 11 and chapter 2.

58. Kazin, *War*, 48–57, 82–83, 214–23; Early, *A World without War*, 44–45; R. Kennedy, *The Will to Believe*, 54–56.
59. Zimmer, *Immigrants against the State*, 139.
60. "The pro-war forces were a minority in America even after the sinking of the *Lusitania*." Tooze, *Deluge*, 43. For the SP's position, see Kazin, *War*, 212–23. For the IWW and anti-militarism, see Foner, *The Industrial Workers of the World*, 36. The IWW was not officially anti-war. Philadelphia's Local 8, led by Black Wobbly Ben Fletcher, supported the war by loading ammunition on Philadelphia's docks. This did not protect them from attack when in 1918 the federal government arrested Fletcher and dozens of other members for sedition. Cole, *Ben Fletcher*, 16–21.

    Both Owen and Randolph were imprisoned for their anti-war views. After the *Messenger* folded in 1928, Owen went on to edit the *Chicago Bee* and got involved in the Republican Party. He supported U.S. involvement in World War II. Adams, "Chandler Owen."
61. Kazin, "The Rise of the Security State."
62. Randolph and Owen, "Who Shall Pay for the War?," 7–8. For the U.S. wartime economy, see National Bureau of Economic Research, "The Economics of World War I."
63. Quoted in Kazin, *War*, 218.
64. Tooze, *Deluge*, 46.
65. 55 Cong. Rec. 319 (1917), quoted in D. Kennedy, *Over Here*, 16. According to Grandin, World War I did not so much obfuscate anti-Black racism as mobilize and embolden it by drawing the unrepentant South back into the fold of a national project. Grandin, *The End of the Myth*, 143–45.
66. For anti-Black racism in the military during World War I, see Lentz-Smith, *Freedom Struggles*, 109–36 and throughout. In 1915 Du Bois argued in the pages of the *Atlantic* that despite the anti-Black Imperialist roots of the war, the war was the only hope for the spread of democracy in Africa and other colonized nations. Du Bois, "The African Roots of War," section 4. By 1918 Du Bois was calling for Black men to "close our ranks shoulder to shoulder with our own white fellow citizens" and join the war effort. Du Bois, "Close Ranks," 1.
67. Gates, "Who Were the Harlem Hellfighters?"
68. Friedheim, *The Seattle General Strike*, 84.

69. Gregory, "Introduction," vii–xxix. Gregory explains that Seattle's Central Labor Council was far more radical than the AFL, due in part to the strong presence of the IWW in the Pacific Northwest.
70. Dubofsky, *We Shall Be All*, 258.
71. For the Centralia incident, see Dubofsky, *We Shall Be All*, 277; Foner, *The Industrial Workers of the World*, 214–24; M. Brown, "Armistice Day in Centralia." For anarchist bombings, see Zimmer, *Immigrants against the State*, 149–51.
72. Quoted in Kazin, *War*, 213.
73. Lentz-Smith, *Freedom Struggles*, 194 95. Also see Gilmore, *Defying Dixie*, 36–37; McWhirter, *Red Summer*, 57; and Goldberg, "Unmasking the Ku Klux Klan."
74. McWhirter, *Red Summer*, 54–59; Lentz-Smith, *Freedom Struggles*, 184. James Weldon Johnson argued that the Dyer Bill was not unconstitutional because mob violence, which overcame the justice system, was essentially a takeover of the state and thus a federal, not state, crime. J. W. Johnson, "Lynching," *New York Times*, January 1924, 5.

    More militant Black resistance movements—the African Blood Brotherhood, with its focus on international Black liberation, and the League for Democracy, which advocated armed resistance—were also initiated in 1919. See Lentz-Smith, *Freedom Struggles*, 216–21; Gilmore, *Defying Dixie*, 60.
75. Wilson had confided to his doctor that returning Black soldiers would be "our greatest medium in conveying bolshevism to America," since being treated as equal to whites in France had "gone to their heads." From the Diary of Dr. Grayson, March 10, 1919, PWW; Grandin, *The End of the Myth*, 142. See also M. Ellis, "J. Edgar Hoover," 41.
76. Dubosky, *We Shall Be All*, 254.
77. Kazin, *War*, 245–45, 348n9, n10.
78. The death toll of World War I heightened fears of racial suicide among white supremacists. See T. Leonard, *Illiberal Reformers*, 111.
79. Carolyn Robbin Grace (then Carr) co-chaired the Cambridge Neighborhood Committee on Vietnam. CNCV spearheaded a ballot initiative in 1967, asking voters whether they supported full withdrawal from Vietnam. She also organized rallies and marches, such as the Cambridge Peace Fair on Cambridge Commons in 1967.

In his 1971 book, *Political Action*, Michael Walzer writes, "Community organizing, SDS-style, required us to find 'community people' and make them the leaders of the organization. This could be an inauthentic politics. . . . But that wasn't the case in CNCV. One of our early volunteers was a part-time film editor and young mother who turned out to understand more about organizing than any of the rest of us—and who went from the CNCV to law school and a distinguished career in civil liberties work." Walzer, *Political Action*, xv. Here, Walzer doesn't name my mother.

80. Carolyn Carr, speech to the Cambridge City Council, 1967, personal archive.
81. Butler, *Nonviolence*, 203. R. Benjamin, "Black AfterLives Matter," 64.
82. See Samet, *Looking for the Good War*, "Introduction" and 116–17.
83. In the end, Victor never made it to the front. He was close enough to hear the guns when Armistice was announced. The Kems did not know whether he was safe until the war was over. Kem, 3:37–38, OMKP.
84. "Let the boy try along this bayonet-blade / How cold steel is, and keen with hunger of blood; / Blue with all malice, like a madman's flash; / And thinly drawn with famishing for flesh." Wilfred Owen, "Arms and the Boy."
85. Langston Hughes, "Beaumont to Detroit: 1943," in *The Collected Poems of Langston Hughes*, 281.
86. Statistics from Cashman, *America in the Gilded Age*, 262. For comparison, in 2018 the top 20 percent of Americans owned 52 percent of the wealth. Schaeffer, "6 Facts."
87. In February of 2022, after attending a talk I gave from this book, my father texted me the following: "Omer's belief in eugenics came as a shock and put a big dent in my lifelong idol and has made me sad. That's not your fault . . . so please don't worry about my feelings. . . . Your talk and my reading his beliefs have caused me to gain a deeper understanding of myself and to recalibrate my relationship with Omer, or his ghost. A good thing."
88. Du Bois, "The African Roots of War," section 2.
89. Donnelly had been a Radical Republican. "At the St. Louis convention in 1892 Ignatius Donnelly, the leading white Populist from Minnesota, exclaimed, 'We propose to wipe the Mason and Dixon line out of geography; to wipe the color-line out of politics.'" Ali, *Lions Mouth*, 91.

90. Ali, *Lion's Mouth*, 92–93.
91. "National People's Party Platform (1892)."
92. For the adverse health effects of exposure to wood smoke, see Schwartz, Bølling, and Carlsten, "Controlled Human Exposure to Wood Smoke."

Bibliography

Archives and Manuscript Materials

CCA: Christensen, Chris. Personal archive. Portland OR.

Hennessey, Madeline. "Home as the Uncanny Archive." Unpublished term paper, University of Colorado, Boulder, 2020.

HG: Greeley, Horace, and Nathan Meeker. Correspondence. Typed transcripts of Horace Greeley's letters prepared by Steve Gates, 45 pages, 02.19.1870, box 1, folder FF2. Denver Public Library, Western History and Genealogy, Denver CO.

Johnson, Albert. "Restriction of Immigration." Report 350 to Accompany H.R. 7995 (1924). Harry H. Laughlin Papers, Special Collections and Museums Department, Pickler Memorial Library, Truman State University.

OMKP: Kem, Omer Madison. Papers. Vols. 1–11. Reinert Alumni Memorial Library, Creighton University, Omaha NE.

Paul, Julius. *"Three Generations of Imbeciles Are Enough": State Eugenic Sterilization Laws in American Thought and Practice.* Unpublished manuscript. Washington DC: Walter Reed Army Institute of Research, 1965. Accessed August 2021. https://readingroom.law.gsu.edu/buckvbell/95/.

PWW: Wilson, Woodrow. *The Papers of Woodrow Wilson Digital Edition.* Charlottesville: University of Virginia Press, Rotunda, 2017. https://rotunda.upress.virginia.edu/founders/WILS-01-47-02-0560.

TTP: Tibbles, Thomas H. Papers. Smithsonian Online Virtual Archives, "Susette La Flesche Speeches," box 1, folder 5. Smithsonian National Museum of the Native American, Washington DC. https://sova.si.edu/details/NMAI.AC.066?s=0&n=10&t=C&q=tibbles&i=0.

U.S. Congress. Congressional Record. Vols. 13, 23, 24, 26, 28, 34, 54, 55.

Published Works

Adams, Luther. "Chandler Owen." Black Past, January 18, 2007. https://www.blackpast.org/african-american-history/owen-chandler-1889-1967/.

Ali, Omar H. *In the Lion's Mouth: Black Populism in the New South, 1886–1900*. Jackson: University Press of Mississippi, 2013.

Ambrosius, Lloyd E. *Woodrow Wilson and American Internationalism*. Cambridge: Cambridge University Press, 2017.

"America First Caucus Policy Platform." *Punchbowl News*, accessed September 2021. https://punchbowl.news/wp-content/uploads/America-First-Caucus-Policy-Platform-FINAL-2.pdf.

American Indian Relief Council. "Biographies of Plains Indians: Francis La Flesche 1857–1932." Accessed September 2021. http://www.nativepartnership.org/site/PageServer?pagename=airc_bio_francislaflesche.

Anderson, Robert T. "Indigenous Rights to Water & Environmental Protection." *Harvard Civil Rights-Civil Liberties Law Review* 53 (2018): 337–79.

Antonovich, Jacqueline D. "Medical Frontiers: Women Physicians and the Politics and Practice of Medicine in the American West, 1870–1930." PhD diss., University of Michigan, 2018. https://deepblue.lib.umich.edu/handle/2027.42/145867.

Archambault, David, II. "Second Declaration." Standing Rock Sioux Tribe v. US Army Corps of Engineers, No. 20-5197 (D.C. Cir., 2021). https://www.govinfo.gov/app/details/USCOURTS-dcd-1_16-cv-01534.

Baldwin, James. *The Fire Next Time*. London: Michael Joseph, 1963.

Banner, Stuart. *How the Indians Lost Their Land: Law and Power on the Frontier*. Cambridge MA: Belknap Press of Harvard University, 2005.

Barber, Katrine. "'We Are at Our Journey's End': Settler Sovereignty Formation in Oregon." *Oregon Historical Quarterly: White Supremacy and Resistance* 120, no. 4 (Winter 2019): 382–413. https://doi.org/10.5403/oregonhistq.120.4.0382.

Barker, Joanne. "Confluence: Water as an Analytic of Indigenous Feminisms." *American Indian Culture and Research Journal* 43, no. 3 (2019): 1–40. doi:10.17953/aicrj.43.3.barker.

———. "For Whom Sovereignty Matters." In *Sovereignty Matters: Locations of Contestation and Possibility in Indigenous Struggles for Self-Determination*, 1–31. Lincoln: University of Nebraska Press, 2005.

Barreyre, Nicholas. "The Politics of Economic Crises: The Panic of 1873, the End of Reconstruction, and the Realignment of American Politics." *Journal of the Gilded Age and Progressive Era* 10, no. 4 (2011): 403–23. doi: 10.1017/s1537781411000260.

Beavers, Olivia, and Melanie Zanona. "MTG's Eye-Popping Fundraiser Haul." *Politico*, April 7, 2021. www.politico.com/newsletters/huddle/2021/04/07/mtgs-eye-popping-fundraising-haul-492390.

Beda, Steven. "Landscapes of Solidarity: Timber Workers and the Making of Place in the Pacific Northwest, 1900–1964." PhD diss., University of Washington, 2014. http://search.ebscohost.com/login.aspx?direct=true&db=ddu&AN=AB5C80EB6C46B830&site=ehost-live.

Benjamin, Ruha. "Black AfterLives Matter: Cultivating Kinfulness and Reproductive Justice." In *Making Kin Not Population*, edited by Donna Haraway and Adele E. Clarke, 43–46. Chicago: Prickly Paradigm, 2018.

Benjamin, Walter. "On the Concept of History." Translated by Dennis Redmond. Marxists.org. https://www.marxists.org/reference/archive/benjamin/1940/history.htm.

———. *Selected Writings*. Vol. 4, *1938–1940*. Edited by Howard Eiland and Michael Jennings. Cambridge MA: Belknap Press of Harvard University Press, 2003.

———. "Theses on the Philosophy of History." In *Illuminations: Essays and Reflections*, translated by Harry Zohn, edited by Hannah Arendt, 253–64. New York: Schocken, 1969.

Bergland, Renée L. *The National Uncanny: Indian Ghosts and American Subjects*. Hanover NH: University Press of New England, 2000.

Berkman, Joyce. "The Question of Margaret Sanger." *History Compass*, June 2, 2011. https://doi.org/10.1111/j.1478-0542.2011.00769.x.

Berman, Terri. "For the Taking: The Garrison Dam and the Tribal Taking Area." *Cultural Survival Quarterly Magazine* 12, no. 2 (June 1988). https://www.culturalsurvival.org/publications/cultural-survival-quarterly/taking-garrison-dam-and-tribal-taking-area.

Bessire, Lucas. *Running Out: In Search of Water on the High Plains*. Princeton NJ: Princeton University Press, 2021.

"Bethenia Owens-Adair." *History of American Women* (blog), accessed August 2021. https://www.womenhistoryblog.com/2014/07/bethenia-owens-adair.html.

Bitsui, Sherwin. *Flood Song*. Port Townsend WA: Copper Canyon, 2009.

Black, Edwin. *War against the Weak: Eugenics and America's Campaign to Create a Master Race*. New York: Dialog, 2012.

Bogue, Allan G. "The Land Mortgage Company in the Early Plains States." *Agricultural History* 25, no. 1 (January 1951): 20–33. https://www.jstor.org/stable/3740295.

Bogue, Margaret Beattie. "Swampland Act and Wet Land Utilization in Illinois, 1850–1890." *Agricultural History* 25, no. 4 (1951): 169–80. https://nationalaglawcenter.org/publication/bogue-the-swamp-land-act-and-wet-land-utilization-in-illinois-1850-1890-25-agricultural-history-169-180-1951/.

Boime, Eric. "'Beating Plowshares into Swords': The Colorado River Delta, the Yellow Peril, and the Movement for Federal Reclamation, 1901–1928." *Pacific Historical Review* 78, no. 1 (2009): 27–53.

Bonderson, Aaron. "Old Hospital in Walthill Being Restored." Nebraska Public Media, August 2, 2021. https://nebraskapublicmedia.org/en/news/news-articles/old-hospital-in-walthill-being-restored.

Bowes, John P. "American Indian Removal beyond the Removal Act." *Native American and Indigenous Studies* 1, no. 1 (Spring 2014): 65–87. https://www.jstor.org/stable/10.5749/natiindistudj.1.1.0065.

Boyd, David. *A History: Greeley and the Union Colony of Colorado*. Greeley CO: Greeley Tribune Press, 1890.

Braude, Ann. *Radical Spirits: Spiritualism and Women's Rights in Nineteenth Century America*. 2nd ed. Bloomington: Indiana University Press, 1989, 2001.

Brown, Alleen. "Five Spills, Six Months in Operation: Dakota Access Track Record Highlights Unavoidable Reality—Pipelines Leak." *Intercept*, January 9, 2018. https://theintercept.com/2018/01/09/dakota-access-pipeline-leak-energy-transfer-partners.

Brown, Alleen, Will Parish, and Alice Speri. "Counterterrorism Tactics at Standing Rock." In *Standing with Standing Rock: Voices from the #NoDAPL Movement*, edited by Nick Estes and Jaskiran Dhillon, 198–208. Minneapolis: University of Minnesota Press, 2019.

Brown, Kate. "The Pandemic Is Not a Natural Disaster." *New Yorker*, April 13, 2020.

Brown, Marty. "Armistice Day in Centralia—100 Years Later." Oregon State University Press (blog), November 7, 2019. https://osupress.oregonstate.edu/blog/armistice-day-in-centralia%E2%80%94100-years-later.

Buchanan, Rex, et al. "The High Plains Aquifer." Kansas Geological Survey, Public Information Circular (PIC) 18, accessed September 2021. http://www.kgs.ku.edu/Publications/pic18/.

Bulla, William D. *Biography of Thomas P. Bulla*. South Bend IN: South Bend Center for History, January 1890.

Burbank, Garin. *When Farmers Voted Red: The Gospel of Socialism in the Oklahoma Countryside, 1910–1924*. Westport CT: Greenwood, 1976.

Burch, Katrina. "Bibliomania: Causes, Cases, and Prevention: Final paper for Preservation 259." May 16, 2011 (page discontinued). https://cportkbb.weebly.com/uploads/ . . . /burch_katrina_preservation_259_paper.docx.

Butler, Judith. *The Force of Nonviolence: An Ethico-Political Bind*. New York: Verso, 2020.

———. *Precarious Life: The Power of Mourning and Violence*. New York: Verso, 2004.

Byerly, Carol R. "War Losses (USA)." *International Encyclopedia of the First World War*, updated October 8, 2014. https://encyclopedia.1914-1918-online.net/article/war_losses_usa.

Byrd, Jodi. *Transit of Empire: Indigenous Critiques of Colonialism*. Minneapolis: University of Minnesota Press, 2011.

Caldwallader, Mary. *Mary S. Vanderbilt: A Twentieth Century Seer*. Chicago: Progressive Thinker, 1921.

Campbell, Stanley W. *Slave Catchers: Enforcement of the Fugitive Slave Law, 1850–1860*. Chapel Hill: University of North Carolina Press, 1970.

Campion, Thomas J. "Indian Removal and the Transformation of Northern Indiana." *Indiana Magazine of History* 107, no. 1 (2011): 32–62. https://www.jstor.org/stable/10.5378/indimagahist.107.1.0032.

Canovan, Margaret. *Populism*. New York: Houghton Mifflin, 1981.

Carey, Jane. "The Racial Imperatives of Sex: Birth Control and Eugenics in Britain, the United States and Australia in the Interwar Years." *Women's History Review* 21, no. 5 (2012): 733–52.

Carlson, Anthony. "Drain the Swamps for Health and Home: Wetlands, Drainage, Land Conservation, and National Water Policy, 1850–1917." PhD diss., University of Oklahoma, 2010.

Carr, Cynthia. *Our Town: A Heartland Lynching, a Haunted Town and the Hidden History of White America*. New York: Broadway Books, 2007.

Cashman, Sean Dennis. *America in the Gilded Age: From the Death of Lincoln to the Rise of Theodore Roosevelt.* 3rd ed. New York: New York University Press, 1993.

Catte, Elizabeth. "Finding the Future in Radical Rural America." *Boston Review*, Winter 2019. http://bostonreview.net/forum/elizabeth-catte-finding-future-radical-rural-america.

Celan, Paul. "The Meridian." In *Collected Prose*, 37–56. Translated by Rosemarie Waldrop. New York: Routledge, 2003.

Census of Agriculture. "Montrose County, Colorado." 2017. https://www.nass.usda.gov/Publications/AgCensus/2017/Online_Resources/County_Profiles/Colorado/cp08085.pdf.

Center for Sustainable Systems. "Carbon Footprint Factsheet." University of Michigan, accessed September 2021. https://css.umich.edu/factsheets/carbon-footprint-factsheet.

Center on Budget Policy and Priorities. "Fact Sheets: States with Biggest K–12 Funding Cuts." December 18, 2015. https://www.cbpp.org/research/state-budget-and-tax/fact-sheets-states-with-biggest-k-12-funding-cuts.

Centers for Disease Control. "Department of Commerce and Labor Bureau of the Census, Bulletin 109: Mortality Statistics 1910." Accessed September 2021. https://www.cdc.gov/nchs/data/vsushistorical/mortstatbl_1910.pdf.

———. "Infant Mortality." Accessed September 2021. https://www.cdc.gov/reproductivehealth/maternalinfanthealth/infantmortality.htm.

———. "Zoonic Disease." Accessed September 2021. https://www.cdc.gov/onehealth/basics/zoonotic-diseases.html.

Cep, Casey. "Kindred Spirits: Why Did So Many Victorians Try to Talk to the Dead?" *New Yorker*, May 31, 2021.

Chafe, William H. "The Negro and Populism: A Kansas Case Study." *Journal of Southern History* 34, no. 3 (1968): 402–19. www.jstor.org/stable/2205135.

Chapman, Berlin Basil. *The Otoes and Missourias: A Study of Indian Removal and the Legal Aftermath.* Oklahoma City OK: Times Journal Publishing, 1965.

Child, Brenda J. *Boarding School Season: American Indian Families 1900–1940.* Lincoln: University of Nebraska Press, 1998.

Christensen, Chris. Interview with Steve Oatley. *Wake Up, America!* (podcast), October 18, 2020. https://www.youtube.com/watch?v=wzRfm2x_HGI.

Christophi, Helen. "Standing Rock Sioux Claim Major Victory against Dakota Access." *Sierra: The Magazine of the Sierra Club*, March 28, 2020. https://www.sierraclub.org/sierra/standing-rock-sioux-claim-major-victory-against-dakota-access.

Cillizza, Chris. "How the Ugly, Racist, White 'Replacement Theory' Came to Congress." CNN *Politics*, April 15, 2021. https://www.cnn.com/2021/04/15/politics/scott-perry-white-replacement-theory-tucker-carlson-fox news/index.html.

Cole, Peter. *Ben Fletcher: The Life and Times of a Black Wobbly*. Chico CA: AK Press, 2006.

Colorado Encyclopedia Staff. "Nathan Meeker." *Colorado Encyclopedia*, accessed September 2021. https://coloradoencyclopedia.org/article/nathan-meeker.

Congressional Research Service. "The Federal Role in Groundwater Supply: Overview and Legislation in the 115th Congress." July 18, 2018. https://fas.org/sgp/crs/misc/r45259.pdf.

———. "U.S. Income Distribution." January 13, 2021. https://fas.org/sgp/crs/misc/r44705.pdf.

Conklin, Julia S. "The Underground Railroad in Indiana." *Indiana Quarterly Magazine of History* 6, no. 2 (June 1910): 63–74. http://www.jstor.org/stable/27785269.

Connolly, Noreen R. "Attorney Lutie A. Lytle: Options and Obstacles of a Legal Pioneer." *Nebraska Lawyer*, January 1999, 10.

Coolidge, Calvin. "Whose Country Is This?" *Good Housekeeping* 72, no. 2 (February 1921): 13–14, 109.

Cottage Grove Historical Society. *Golden Was the Past: 1850–1970*. Cottage Grove OR, 1970, 1972.

Courtwright, Julie. "A Slave to Yellow Peril: The 1886 Chinese Ouster Attempt in Wichita, Kansas." *Great Plains Quarterly* 22 (Winter 2002): 23–33. https://digitalcommons.unl.edu/greatplainsquarterly/2351.

Cowger, Thomas W. "Dr. Thomas A. Bland, Critic of Forced Assimilation." *American Indian Culture and Research* 16, no. 4 (1992): 77–97. https://meridian.allenpress.com/aicrj/article/16/4/77/211580/Dr-Thomas-A-Bland-Critic-of-Forced-Assimilation.

Cozzens, Peter. *The Earth Is Weeping: The Epic Story of the Indian Wars for the American West*. New York: Knopf, 2016.

Crenshaw, Kimberlé. "Looking Back to Move Forward: The Insurgent Origins of Critical Race Theory." *Intersectionality Matters!* (podcast), September 2, 2021. https://soundcloud.com/intersectionality-matters.

Cunfer, Geoff, and Bill Waiser, eds. *Bison and People on the North American Great Plains: A Deep Environmental History*. College Station: Texas A&M University Press, 2004.

Custer County, Nebraska. "County History." Accessed August 2021. https://co.custer.ne.us/webpages/about/history.html.

Dahl, Thomas E., and Gregory J. Allord. "History of Wetlands in the Conterminous United States." *US Geological Survey: National Water Summary on Wetland Resources*, March 7, 1997. https://water.usgs.gov/nwsum/WSP2425/history.html.

Davies, Kevin. *Editing Humanity: The Crispr Revolution and the New Era of Genome Editing*. New York: Pegasus, 2020.

Davis, Angela. *Woman, Race, and Class*. New York: Knopf Doubleday, 1983.

Davis, Wynne. "The Remains of 215 Indigenous Children Have Been Found at a Former School in Canada." NPR, May 29, 2021.

Dayan, Colin. *The Law Is a White Dog: How Legal Rituals Make and Unmake Persons*. Princeton NJ: Princeton University Press, 2011, 2013.

Debs, Eugene. "Freedom Is the Goal." *Birth Control Review* 2, no. 4 (May 1918): 7.

Decker, Peter R. *The Utes Must Go! American Expansion and the Removal of a People*. Golden CO: Fulcrum, 2004.

Deer, Sarah. *The Beginning and End of Rape: Confronting Sexual Violence in Native America*. Minneapolis: University of Minnesota Press, 2015.

Deloria, Philip J. *Playing Indian*. New Haven CT: Yale University Press, 1998.

Denison, Brandi. *Ute Land Religion in the American West, 1879–2009*. Lincoln: University of Nebraska Press, 2017.

Denver Homeless Outloud. "Myths and Reality of Homelessness." Accessed August 2021. https://denverhomelessoutloud.org/myths-and-reality-of-homelessness/.

———. "Press Release, November 5, 2018." https://denverhomelessoutloud.org/2018/11/05/denver-homeless-out-loud-encouraging-city-of-denver-to-give-back-shelter-after-taking-it-in-cold-weather-front/.

Derrell, Anna. "The Women of Reform: Kansas Eugenics." Master's thesis, University of Missouri-Kansas, 2014. http://hdl.handle.net/10355/43560.

Deverell, William. "Fighting Words: The Significance of the American West in the History of the United States." In *A New Significance: Re-envisioning the History of the American West*, edited by Clyde A. Milner, 29–55. Oxford: Oxford University Press, 1996.

Dickens, Charles. *American Notes for General Circulation*. London: Chapman and Hall, 1842. Reissued, New York: Penguin Classics, 2001.

Diouf, Sylviane A. *Slavery's Exiles: The Story of the American Maroons*. New York: New York University Press, 2014.

Dix, Robert H. "Populism: Authoritarian and Democratic." *Latin American Research Review* 20, no. 2 (1985): 29–52.

Dorey, Annette Vance. *Better Baby Contests: The Scientific Quest for Perfect Childhood Health in the Early Twentieth Century*. Jefferson NC: McFarland, 1999.

Dray, Phillip. *At the Hands of Persons Unknown: The Lynching of Black America*. New York: Modern Library, 2003.

Dubofsky, Melvyn. *We Shall Be All: A History of the Industrial Workers of the World*. Abridged ed. Chicago: University of Chicago Press, 2000.

Du Bois, W. E. B. "The African Roots of War." *Atlantic*, May 1915. https://www.theatlantic.com/magazine/archive/1915/05/the-african-roots-of-war/528897/.

———. *Black Reconstruction in America: 1860–1880*. Philadelphia: Albert Saifer, 1935. Reissued, New York: Free Press, 1998.

———. "Close Ranks." *Crisis* 16, no. 3 (July 1918): 1. https://modjourn.org/journal/crisis/.

———. "Opinion." *Crisis* 24, no. 6 (October 1922): 247–53. https://modjourn.org/journal/crisis/.

———. *The Souls of Black Folk*. Oxford: Oxford University Press, 2007.

———. "A Word from Dr. Du Bois." *Birth Control Review* 3, no. 9 (September 1919): 15. https://lifedynamics.com/app/uploads/2015/09/1919-09-September.pdf.

Dunbar-Ortiz, Roxanne. *An Indigenous Peoples' History of the United States*. Boston: Beacon Press, 2014.

Early, Frances H. *A World without War: How U.S. Feminists and Pacifists Resisted World War I*. Syracuse NY: Syracuse University Press, 1997.

Eastman, John. "Born in the USA? Reconsidering the Fourteenth Amendment's Citizenship Clause." Lecture sponsored by the Benson Center, University of Colorado, Boulder, November 18, 2019. https://www.youtube.com/watch?v=5maYvdlkMrM.

Edwards, Richard, Jacob K. Friefeld, and Rebecca S. Wingo. *Homesteading the Plains: Toward a New History*. Lincoln: University of Nebraska Press, 2017.

Ellis, Havelock. *The Problem of Race Regeneration*. London: Cassell, 1911.

Ellis, Mark. "J. Edgar Hoover and the 'Red Summer' of 1919." *Journal of American Studies* 28, no. 1 (April 1994): 39–59. https://www.jstor.org/stable/27555783.

Emery, Sarah E. V. "Demonetization of Silver." In *A Populist Reader: Selections from the Works of American Populist Leaders*, edited by George B. Tindall, 52–59. New York: Harper Torch, 1966.

Emmitt, Robert. *The Last War Trail: The Utes and the Settlement of Colorado*. Boulder: University of Colorado Press, 2000.

Engelman, Peter C. *A History of the Birth Control Movement in America*. Santa Barbara CA: Praeger, 2011.

Erdrich, Louise. *The Sentence*. New York: Harper, 2021.

Estes, Nick. *Our History Is the Future: Standing Rock versus the Dakota Access Pipeline, and the Long Tradition of Indigenous Resistance*. New York: Verso, 2019.

Estes, Nick, and Jaskiran Dhillon, eds. *Standing with Standing Rock: Voices from the #NoDAPL Movement*. Minneapolis: University of Minnesota Press, 2019.

Ethnicity, Race, and Migration. "Remembering the Sand Creek Massacre." Yale University, December 3, 2014. https://erm.yale.edu/news/remember-sand-creek-massacre.

Fanon, Frantz. *Black Skin, White Masks*. New York: Grove, 2008.

Fantina, Robert. *Desertion and the American Soldier: 1779–2006*. New York: Algora, 2006.

Farrow, Anne, Joel Lang, and Jennifer Frank. *Complicity: How the North Promoted, Prolonged and Profited from Slavery*. New York: Ballantine, 2006.

Fehrenbacher, Donald E. *The Slaveholding Republic: An Account of the United States Government's Relations to Slavery*. Oxford: Oxford University Press, 2001.

Ferkiss, Victor C. "Populist Influences on American Fascism." *Western Political Quarterly* 10, no. 2 (June 1957): 350–73. https://www.jstor.org/stable/443694.

Finkelman, Paul. "Sorting Out *Prigg v. Pennsylvania*." *Rutgers Law Journal* 24, no. 3 (Spring 1993): 605–65. https://msa.maryland.gov/megafile/msa/speccol/sc5400/sc5496/051200/051268/images/finkelman_rutgers.pdf.

Fletcher, Calvin. *The Diaries of Calvin Fletcher*. Edited by Galye Thornbrough, Dorothy L. Riker, and Paula Corpuz. Indianapolis: Indiana Historical Society, 1975.

Floyd, M. Ryan. *Abandoning American Neutrality: Woodrow Wilson and the Beginning of the Great War, August 1914–December 1915*. New York: Palgrave MacMillan, 2013.

Fluence. "Wildfires Linked to Groundwater Depletion." September 20, 2018. https://www.fluencecorp.com/wildfires-linked-to-groundwater-depletion/.

Foner, Philip S. *The Industrial Workers of the World, 1905–1917*. Vol. 4 of *History of the Labor Movement in the United States*. New York: International Publishers, 1965.

Food and Agriculture Organization of the United Nations. "Key Facts and Findings." Accessed September 2021. http://www.fao.org/news/story/en/item/197623/icode/.

Foucault, Michel. "Right of Death and Power over Life." In *The Foucault Reader*, edited by Paul Rabinow, 258–72. New York: Pantheon, 1984.

———. *Society Must Be Defended*. Translated by David Macey. New York: Picador, 2003.

Frankel, Jeremy. "Crisis on the High Plains: The Loss of America's Largest Aquifer—the Ogallala." *University of Denver Water Law Review*, May 17, 2018. http://duwaterlawreview.com/crisis-on-the-high-plains-the-loss-of-americas-largest-aquifer-the-ogallala/.

Fraser, Caroline. *Prairie Fires: The American Dream of Laura Ingalls Wilder*. New York: Picador, 2017.

Friedheim, Robert L. *The Seattle General Strike*. Centennial ed. Seattle: University of Washington Press, 1964, 2018.

Friedler, Delilah, and Danny Wilcox Frazier. "Get the Hell Off: The Indigenous Fight to Stop a Uranium Mine in the Black Hills." *Mother Jones*, March/April 2020. https://www.motherjones.com/politics/2020/05/the-black-hills-are-not-for-sale/.

Frymer, Paul. *Building an American Empire*. Princeton NJ: Princeton University Press, 2017.

Gago, Veronica. *Feminist International: How to Change Everything*. Translated by Liz Mason-Deese. New York: Verso, 2021.

Gandesha, Samir. "Understanding Right and Left Populism." In *Critical Theory and Authoritarian Populism*, edited by Jeremiah Morelock, 49–70. London: University of Westminster Press, 2018.

Garza, Cristina Rivera. *Lilianna's Invincible Summer: A Sister's Search for Justice.* New York: Hogarth, 2023.

Gates, Henry Louis, Jr. "Who Were the Harlem Hellfighters?" PBS, accessed September 2021. https://www.pbs.org/wnet/african-americans-many-rivers-to-cross/history/who-were-the-harlem-hellfighters/.

Genealogy Trails History Group. "Wayne County, Indiana: Omer Madison Kem." Accessed September 2021. http://genealogytrails.com/ind/wayne/bios.html.

Genetin-Pilawa, C. Joseph. *Crooked Paths to Allotment: The Fight over Federal Indian Policy after the Civil War.* Chapel Hill: University of North Carolina Press, 2012.

Gerbaudo, Paolo. *The Great Recoil: Politics after Populism and Pandemic.* New York: Verso, 2021.

Gerteis, Joseph. *Class and the Color Line: Interracial Class Coalition in the Knights of Labor and the Populist Movement.* Durham NC: Duke University Press, 2007.

Gerteis, Joseph, and Alyssa Goolsby. "Nationalism in America: The Case of the Populist Movement." *Theory and Society* 34, no. 2 (2005): 215–17. www.jstor.org/stable/4501721.

Giddings, Paula. *When and Where I Enter: The Impact of Black Women on Race and Sex in America.* New York: William Morrow, 1984.

Gilmore, Glenda. *Defying Dixie: The Radical Roots of Civil Rights.* New York: W. W. Norton, 2008.

Giscombe, C. S. *Prairie Style.* Dallas TX: Dalkey Archive, 2008.

Glad, John. *Future Human Evolution: Eugenics in the Twenty-First Century.* Tenafly NJ: Hermitage, 2006.

Goldberg, David J. "Unmasking the Ku Klux Klan: The Northern Movement against the KKK, 1920–1925." *Journal of American Ethnic History* 15, no. 4 (Summer 1996): 32–48. https://www.jstor.org/stable/27502105.

Goldman, Emma. *Anarchism and Other Essays.* New York: Mother Earth, 1910.

Goldsby, Jacqueline. *A Spectacular Secret: Lynching in American Life and Literature.* Chicago: University of Chicago Press, 2006.

Goodwyn, Lawrence. *The Populist Moment: A Short History of the Agrarian Revolt in America.* Oxford: Oxford University Press, 1978.

Gordon, Avery. *Ghostly Matters: Haunting and the Sociological Imagination.* Minneapolis: University of Minnesota Press, 2008.

———. *The Hawthorn Archive: Letters from the Utopian Margins.* New York: Fordham University Press, 2017.

Gordon, Linda. *Woman's Body, Woman's Right.* New York: Viking, 1976.
Gossett, Thomas F. *Race: The History of an Idea in America.* Oxford: Oxford University Press, 1997.
Gould, Stephen Jay. "William Jennings Bryan's Last Campaign." In *Bully for Brontosaurus*, 416–31. New York: W. W. Norton, 1991.
Govinfo.gov. "Indian Issues: Damages and Compensation for Tribes at Seven Reservations Affected by Dams on the Missouri River." Accessed August 2021. https://www.govinfo.gov/content/pkg/GAOREPORTS-GAO-08-249T/html/GAOREPORTS-GAO-08-249T.htm.
Graeber, David. *Debt: The First 5,000 Years.* New York: Melville House, 2012.
Grandin, Greg. *The End of the Myth: From the Frontier to the Border Wall in the Mind of America.* New York: Metropolitan, 2019.
———. Interview with Daniel Denvir. *Dig* (podcast), March 20, 1919.
Grann, David. *Killers of the Flower Moon: The Osage Murders and the Birth of the FBI.* New York: Doubleday, 2017.
Grant, Madison. *The Passing of the Great Race, Or the Racial Basis of European History.* New York: Scribner, 1916.
Grant, Richard. "Deep in the Swamps, Archaeologists Are Finding How Fugitive Slaves Kept Their Freedom." *Smithsonian Magazine*, September 2016.
Gregory, James N. "Introduction to the Centennial Edition." In *The Seattle General Strike*, by Robert L. Friedheim, centennial ed., vii–xxix. Seattle: University of Washington Press, 1964, 2018.
Grossman, Zoltan. *Unlikely Alliances: Native Nations and White Communities Join to Defend Rural Lands.* Seattle: University of Washington Press, 2017.
Guth, Delloyd John. "Omer Madison Kem: The People's Congressman." Master's thesis, Creighton University, 1962.
Gyory, Andrew. *Closing the Gate: Race, Politics, and the Chinese Exclusion Act.* Chapel Hill: University of North Carolina Press, 2000.
Hale, William Harlan. "When Karl Marx Worked for Horace Greeley." American Heritage, accessed August 2021. https://www.americanheritage.com/when-karl-marx-worked-horace-greeley.
Hamalainen, Pekka. "The First Phase of Destruction Killing the Southern Plains Buffalo, 1790–1840." *Great Plains Quarterly* 21, no. 2 (Spring 2001): 101–14. https://digitalcommons.unl.edu/greatplainsquarterly/2227.
Hambly, Thomas C. *Argument of Mr. Hambly of York, (Pa.) in the Case of Edward Prigg vs. the Commonwealth of Pennsylvania in the Supreme Court of the United States.* Baltimore MD: Lucas and Deaver, 1842. https://msa

.maryland.gov/megafile/msa/speccol/sc5400/sc5496/051200/051268/images/hambly_prigg_v_pennsylvania_ocr.pdf.

Hanand, Nikhil. "Public Water and the Intimacy of Hydraulics." *e-flux Architecture*, November 27, 2019. https://www.e-flux.com/architecture/liquid-utility/259641/public-water-and-the-intimacy-of-hydraulics/.

Hannigan, Robert. *The Great War and American Foreign Policy, 1914–1924*. Philadelphia: University of Pennsylvania Press, 2016.

Haraway, Donna. *Staying with Trouble: Making Kin in the Chthulucene*. Durham NC: Duke University Press, 2016.

Haraway, Donna, and Adele E. Clarke, eds. *Making Kin Not Population*. Chicago: Prickly Paradigm, 2018.

Harris, Cheryl. "Whiteness as Property." In *Critical Race Theory: The Key Writings That Formed the Movement*, edited by Kimberlé Crenshaw, Neil Gotanda, Gary Peller, and Kendall Thomas, 276–91. New York: New Press, 1995.

Hartman, Saidiya. *Scenes of Subjection: Terror, Slavery, and Self-Making in Nineteenth-Century America*. Oxford: Oxford University Press, 1997.

———. "Venus in Two Acts." *small axe* 26 (June 2008): 1–14.

Henslow, Professor G. *The Proofs of the Truths of Spiritualism*. New York: Dodd, Mead, 1919.

Hershberger, Mary. "Mobilizing Women, Anticipating Abolition: The Struggle against Indian Removal in the 1830s." *Journal of American History* 86, no. 1 (June 1999): 15–40. https://www.jstor.org/stable/2567405.

Hicks, John D. *Populist Revolt: A History of the Farmer's Alliance and the People's Party*. Minneapolis: University of Minnesota Press, 1931, 1961.

Higgins, Elizabeth. *Out of the West, a Novel*. New York: Harper and Brothers, 1902.

Hild, Matthew. *Arkansas' Gilded Age: The Rise, Decline, and Legacy of Populism and Working-Class Protest*. Columbia: University of Missouri Press, 2018.

History of Wayne County Indiana. Vol. 2. Chicago: Interstate Publishing, 1884.

Hoff, Aliya R. "The Passing of the Great Race." *The Embryo Project Encyclopedia*, July 12, 2021. https://embryo.asu.edu/pages/passing-great-race-or-racial-basis-european-history-1916-madison-grant.

Hofstadter, Richard. *The Age of Reform*. New York: Vintage, 1955.

Holleran, Michael. *Historic Context for Irrigation and Water Supply: Ditches and Canals in Colorado*. Colorado Center for Preservation Research, University of Colorado at Denver and Health Sciences Center, June

2005. https://www.fcgov.com/historicpreservation/pdf/holleran.pdf ?1508793205.

Horn, Martin. "A Private Bank at War: J. P. Morgan & Co. and France, 1914–1918." *Business History Review* 74, no. 1 (2000): 85–112. www.jstor.org/stable/3116353.

Howe, Craig, and Tyler Young. "Minisose." In *Standing with Standing Rock: Voices from the #NoDAPL Movement*, edited by Nick Estes and Jaskiran Dhillon, 56–69. Minneapolis: University of Minnesota Press, 2019.

Huebner, Timothy S. "Roger B. Taney and the Slavery Issue: Looking beyond—and before—*Dred Scott*." *Journal of American History* 97, no. 1 (June 2010): 17–38. https://www.jstor.org/stable/40662816.

Hughes, Hugh J. "The Abuse of the Homestead Law." *Watson's Magazine*, reprinted in *American Lawyer* 14 (1906): 350–53. https://heinonline.org.

Hughes, Langston. *The Collected Poems of Langston Hughes*. New York: Knopf, 1994.

Huhndorf, Shari. *Going Native: Indians and the American Cultural Imagination*. Ithaca NY: Cornell University Press, 2001.

Hunter, Lea. "The U.S. Is Still Forcibly Sterilizing Prisoners." Talk Poverty, August 23, 2017. https://talkpoverty.org/2017/08/23/u-s-still-forcibly -sterilizing-prisoners.

Indiana Constitutional Convention. "Report of the Debates and Proceedings of the Convention for the Revision of the Constitution of the State of Indiana, 1850." Ann Arbor: University of Michigan Library, 2005. http://name.umdl.umich.edu/AEW7738.0001.001.

Indigenous Environmental Network. "Just Transition." Accessed September 2021. https://www.ienearth.org/justtransition/.

Industrial Workers of the World. "Preamble, Constitution, and General Bylaws." https://iww.org/assets/iww-constitution.pdf.

Johnson, Benjamin. "Red Populism? T. A. Bland, Agrarian Radicalism, and the Debate over the Dawes Act." In *The Countryside in the Age of the Modern State*, edited by Catherine McNicol Stock and Robert D. Johnston, 15–37. Ithaca NY: Cornell University Press, 2001.

Johnston, Robert D. *The Radical Middle Class: Populist Democracy and the Question of Capitalism in Progressive Era Portland, Oregon*. Princeton NJ: Princeton University Press, 2006.

Jones, Sondra G. *Being and Becoming Ute: The Story of an American Indian People*. Salt Lake City: University of Utah Press, 2019.

Joron, Andrew. *Fathom*. New York: Black Square, 2003.

Journeyman Pictures. *Sterilized behind Bars*. Produced by the Center for Investigative Journalism, 2021. http://www.journeyman.tv/film/6001.

Kaelber, Lutz. "Eugenics: Compulsory Sterilization in 50 American States." University of Vermont. https://www.uvm.edu/~lkaelber/eugenics/.

Kammer, Sean M. "Land and Law in the Age of Enterprise: A Legal History of Railroad Land Grants in the Pacific Northwest, 1864–1916." PhD diss., University of Nebraska, 2015. http://digitalcommons.unl.edu/historydiss/84.

Kammeyer, Cora. "Corporate Water Stewardship in the Colorado River Basin." Pacific Institute, April 6, 2020. https://pacinst.org/water-sustainability-colorado-river-basin-businesses/.

Kantrowitz, Stephen. "Ben Tillman and Hendrix McLane, Agrarian Rebels: White Manhood, 'The Farmers,' and the Limits of Southern Populism." *Journal of Southern History* 66, no. 3 (August 2000): 497–524. https://www.jstor.org/stable/2587866.

Kardec, Allan. *Spiritism in Its Most Simple Expression: A Short Exposition of Spirits' Doctrine and Their Manifestations*. Translated form the French. Leipzig: Franz Wagner, 1865.

Karuka, Manu. *Empire's Tracks: Indigenous Nations, Chinese Workers, and the Transcontinental Railroad*. Oakland: University of California Press, 2019.

Kautzer, Chad. "The Occupy Movement and the Reappearance of the Polis." In *Routledge Handbook of Philosophy of the City*, edited by Sharon M. Meagher, Samantha Noll, and Joseph S. Biehl, 238–50. New York: Routledge, 2019.

———. "Self-Defensive Subjectivity: The Diagnosis of a Social Pathology." *Philosophy and Social Criticism* 40, no. 8 (2014): 743–56.

Kazanjian, David. *The Colonization Trick: National Culture and Imperial Citizenship in Early America*. Minneapolis: University of Minnesota Press, 2003.

Kazin, Michael. *American Dreamers: How the Left Changed a Nation*. New York: Vintage, 2011.

———. "The Rise of the Security State: from the Great War to Snowden." *Dissent*, Fall 2017. https://www.dissentmagazine.org/article/world-war-i-aftermath-security-state-nsa.

———. *War against War: The American Fight for Peace 1914–1918*. New York: Simon & Schuster, 2017.

Keith, LeeAnna. *The Colfax Massacre: The Untold Story of Black Power, White Terror, and the Death of Reconstruction*. Oxford: Oxford University Press, 2008.

Kelley, Robin D. G. *Freedom Dreams*: Boston: Beacon Press, 2002.

———. *Hammer and Hoe: Alabama Communists during the Great Depression*. Chapel Hill: University of North Carolina Press, 1990.

Kem, Omer M. "Certain Lands of the Confederated Otoe and Missouria Tribes of Indians in Nebraska and Kansas." Committed to the Committee of the Whole House on the State of the Union and ordered to be printed, July 7, 1892. United States congressional serial set. 3048 (1891/92), 757. https://hdl.handle.net/2027/hvd.hj1gz5.

———. "Home Rule for America." Speech to the House of Representatives, August 23, 1893. Fraser, accessed August 2021. https://fraser.stlouisfed.org/title/money-question-53rd-congress-289/home-rule-america-6055.

———. *Report to Accompany H.R. 67*. Report No. 1205, 52nd Congress, 1st Session, April 26, 1892.

Kennedy, David M. *Over Here: The First World War and American Society*. Oxford: Oxford University Press, 1980, 2004.

Kennedy, Ross A. "Review of *Abandoning American Neutrality: Woodrow Wilson and the Beginning of the Great War*, by M. Ryan Floyd." *Journal of American History* 101, no. 3 (2014): 962–63. http://www.jstor.org/stable/44286399.

———. *The Will to Believe: Woodrow Wilson, World War I, and America's Strategy for Peace and Security*. Kent OH: Kent State University Press, 2009.

Kevles, Daniel. *In the Name of Eugenics: Genetics and the Uses of Human Heredity*. Cambridge MA: Harvard University Press, 1985, 1995.

Kimmelman, Barbara A. "The American Breeders' Association: Genetics and Eugenics in an Agricultural Context, 1903–13." *Social Studies of Science* 13, no. 2 (May 1983): 163–204. https://www.jstor.org/stable/284589.

King, Martin Luther, Jr. *Where Do We Go from Here? Chaos or Community*. Boston: Beacon Press, 1968.

Klein, Ezra. "Noam Chomsky on Anachronism, Human Nature, and Joe Biden." *Ezra Klein Show* (podcast), April 23, 2021. www.nytimes.com/2021/04/23/opinion/ezra-klein-podcast-noam-chomsky.html.

Kline, Wendy. *Building a Better Race: Gender, Sexuality, and Eugenics from the Turn of the Century to the Baby Boom*. Berkeley: University of California Press, 2005.

Kühl, Stefan. *The Nazi Connection: Eugenics, American Racism, and German National Socialism*. Oxford: Oxford University Press, 2002.

Largent, Mark A. *Breeding Contempt: The History of Coerced Sterilization in the United States*. New Brunswick NJ: Rutgers University Press, 2011.

———. "'The Greatest Curse of the Race': Eugenic Sterilization in Oregon, 1909–1983." *Oregon Historical Quarterly* 103, no. 2 (Summer, 2002): 188–209. https://www.jstor.org/stable/20615229.

LaRoche, Cheryl Janifer. *The Geography of Resistance: Free Black Communities and the Underground Railroad.* Champaign: University of Illinois Press, 2014.

Laughlin, Harry. *Eugenical Sterilization in the United States.* Chicago: Psychopathic Laboratory of the Municipal Court of Chicago, 1922.

Lause, Mark. *Free Spirits: Spiritualism, Republicanism and Radicalism in the Civil War Era.* Champaign: University of Illinois Press, 2016.

Lawrence, Edward. *Spiritualism among the Savage and Civilized Races: A Study in Anthropology.* London: A. & C. Black, 1921.

Lawson, Michael L. *Dammed Indians Revisited: The Continuing History of the Pick-Sloan Plan and the Missouri River Sioux.* Pierre: South Dakota State Historical Society Press, 2009.

———. "'We Lost Our Way of Living': The Inundation of the White Swan Community." *South Dakota History* 36, no. 2 (Summer 2006): 135–71.

Lay, Shawn, ed. *The Invisible Empire in the West: Toward a New Historical Appraisal of the Ku Klux Klan in the 1920s.* Champaign: University of Illinois Press, 2003.

Lazzarato, Maurizio. *The Making of the Indebted Man: An Essay on the Neoliberal Condition.* Translated by Joshua David Jordan. Boston: Semiotext(e), 2012.

Lentz-Smith, Adriane. *Freedom Struggles: African Americans and World War I.* Cambridge MA: Harvard University Press, 2009.

Leonard, Devin. "The Life and Times of a True American Moral Hysteric." *Literary Hub*, March 2, 2016. https://lithub.com/the-life-and-times-of-a-true-american-moral-hysteric/.

———. *Neither Snow nor Rain: A History of the United States Postal Service.* New York: Grove, 2017.

Leonard, Thomas C. *Illiberal Reformers: Race, Eugenics, and American Economics in the Progressive Era.* Princeton NJ: Princeton University Press, 2016.

Lepore, Jill. *These Truths: A History of The United States.* New York: W. W. Norton, 2018.

Limerick, Patricia. *The Legacy of Conquest: The Unbroken Past of the American West.* New York: W. W. Norton, 1987.

———. "The New Significance of the American West." In *A New Significance: Re-envisioning the History of the American West*, edited by Clyde A. Milner, 61–65. Oxford: Oxford University Press, 1996.

Long Soldier, Layli. *Whereas.* Minneapolis MN: Graywolf, 2017.

Lovett, Laura. *Conceiving the Future: Pronatalism, Reproduction, and the Family in the United States, 1890–1930*. Chapel Hill: University of North Carolina Press, 2007.

Mackay, James. "Review of *Specter of the Indian*, by Kathryn Troy." *Transmotion* 4, no. 1 (2018): 168–70. https://doi.org/10.22024/UniKent/03/tm.517.

Mahmud, Tayyab. "Debt and Discipline." *American Quarterly* 64, no. 3 (September 2012): 469–94. https://doi.org/10.1353/aq.2012.0027.

Manela, Erez. *The Wilsonian Moment: Self-Determination and the International Origins of Anticolonial Nationalism*. Oxford: Oxford University Press, 2009.

Martin & McCoy and Culp & Kelly, LLP. *Ten Strategies for Climate Resistance in the Colorado River Basin*. https://eab9d4f3-11ef-48fa-b86f-bcc50a6b2318.filesusr.com/ugd/a4c8f1_17ecc9178a9d430e94e4c43e0d5eab91.pdf?index=true.

Martinez, Monica Muñoz. *The Injustice Never Leaves You: Anti-Mexican Violence in Texas*. Cambridge MA: Harvard University Press, 2018.

Mathes, Valerie Sherer, and Richard Lowitt. *The Standing Bear Controversy: Prelude to Indian Reform*. Champaign: University of Illinois Press, 2003.

Mayer, Heather. *Beyond the Rebel Girl: Women and the Industrial Workers of the World in the Pacific Northwest 1905–1924*. Corvallis: Oregon State University Press, 2018.

McAdams, Mallory, and Judith Wang. "Gunnison Tunnel: Engineering History of an Early American Reclamation Project." *Journal of Performance of Constructed Facilities* 27, no. 6 (December 2013): 826–35. https://ascelibrary.org/doi/10.1061/%28ASCE%29CF.1943-5509.0000375.

McCann, Carole. *Birth Control Politics in the United States, 1916–1945*. Ithaca NY: Cornell University Press, 1999.

———. "Introduction." In *What Perspectives Did African American Advocates Bring to the Birth Control Movement and How Did Those Perspectives Shape the History of the Harlem Branch Birth Control Clinic?* Binghamton NY: State University of New York at Binghamton, 2006. https://documents.alexanderstreet.com/d/1000671764.

McClanahan, Annie. *Dead Pledges: Debt, Crisis, and Twenty-First-Century Culture*. Stanford CA: Stanford University Press, 2016.

McCool, Daniel. *Command of the Waters: Iron Triangles, Federal Water Development, and Indian Water*. Berkeley: University of California Press, 1987.

McCorvie, Mary R., and Christopher L. Lant. "Drainage District Formation and the Loss of Midwestern Wetlands, 1850–1930." *Agricultural History* 67, no. 4 (Autumn 1993): 22.

McDonald, Earl E. "The Negro in Indiana before 1881." *Indiana Magazine of History* 27, no. 4 (1931): 291–306. https://scholarworks.iu.edu/journals/index.php/imh/article/view/6622/6965.

McGarry, Molly. *Ghosts of Futures Past: Spiritualism and the Cultural Politics of Nineteenth Century America.* Oakland: University of California Press, 2012.

McKittrick, Katherine. "Mathematics Black Life." *Black Scholar* 44, no. 2 (Summer 2014): 16–28. doi:10.1080/00064246.2014.11413684.

McWhirter, Cameron. *Red Summer: The Summer of 1919 and the Awakening of Black America.* New York: Henry Holt, 2011.

Medak-Saltzman, Danika. "Empire's Haunted Logics: Comparative Colonialisms and the Challenges of Incorporating Indigeneity." *Critical Ethnic Studies* 1, no. 2 (Fall 2015): 11–32. https://www.jstor.org/stable/10.5749/jcritethnstud.1.2.0011.

Media Matters for America. "Tucker Carlson Gives Passionate Defense of 'White Replacement Theory.'" April 8, 2021. www.mediamatters.org/fox-news/tucker-carlson-gives-passionate-defense-white-replacement-theory.

Meeker, Josephine. *The Ute Massacre: Brave Miss Meeker's Captivity, Her Own Account of It.* Philadelphia: Old Franklin, 1879.

Meyer, Carter Jones, and Diana Royer, eds. *Selling the Indian: Commercializing & Appropriating American Indian Cultures.* Tucson: University of Arizona Press, 2001.

Minnesota Board of Water and Soil Resources. "Carbon Sequestration in Wetlands." Accessed August 2021. http://bwsr.state.mn.us/carbon-sequestration-wetlands.

Montrose County Historical Society and Museum. *Montrose.* Mount Pleasant SC: Arcadia, 2017.

Moore, Jason W. *Capitalism in the Web of Life: Ecology and the Accumulation of Capital.* New York: Verso, 2015.

Moorehead, Caroline, ed. *Selected Letters of Martha Gellhorn.* New York: Owl, 2007.

Moreton-Robinson, Aileen. *The White Possessive: Property, Power, and Indigenous Sovereignty.* Minneapolis: University of Minnesota Press, 2015.

Morgan, Philip. *Italian Fascism 1915–1945.* New York: Palgrave, 2004.

Morrison, Toni. "Nobel Lecture." Nobel Prize, December 7, 1993. https://www.nobelprize.org/prizes/literature/1993/morrison/lecture/.

Mosier, Ron. "The Settling of the Grand Marsh of the Kankakee River." Interview by Laverne Terpstra, March 15, 1996. Transcribed by Flo Riley.

Sponsored by DeMotte-Kankakee Valley Rotary Club Oral History Project. Accessed September 2021. http://www.myjcpl.org/sites/default/files/documents/pdf/4260/mosier.pdf.

Moten, Fred. *In the Break: The Aesthetics of the Black Radical Tradition.* Minneapolis: University of Minnesota Press, 2003.

———. *Stolen Life: Social Essays.* Durham NC: Duke University Press, 2018.

Moten, Fred, and Stefano Harney. *The Undercommons: Fugitive Planning and Black Study.* Wivenhoe NY: Minor Compositions, 2013. https://www.minorcompositions.info/wp-content/uploads/2013/04/undercommons-web.pdf.

Mouffe, Chantal. *For a Left Populism.* New York: Verso, 2018.

Murphy, Angela F. *The Jerry Rescue: The Fugitive Slave Law, Northern Rights, and the American Sectional Crisis.* Oxford: Oxford University Press, 2014.

Mussolini, Benito. "Strength in Numbers." *Gerarchia*, September 9, 1928. https://bibliotecafascista.blogspot.com/2012/03/strength-in-numbers.html.

National Archives, Educator Resources. "Margaret Sanger: The Woman Rebel." https://www.archives.gov/education/lessons/sanger.html.

National Bureau of Economic Research. "The Economics of World War I." *Digest* 1 (January 1, 2005). https://www.nber.org/digest/jan05/economics-world-war-i.

National Institute of Health. "Changing the Face of Medicine: Dr. Susan La Flesche Picotte." Accessed September 2021. https://cfmedicine.nlm.nih.gov/physicians/biography_253.html.

National Park Service. "African American Homesteaders on the Great Plains." Accessed September 2021. https://www.nps.gov/articles/african-american-homesteaders-in-the-great-plains.htm.

———. "A Complex Prairie Eco-System." Accessed October 2017 (page discontinued). https://www.nps.gov/tapr/learn/nature/a-complex-prairie-ecosystem.htm.

"National People's Party Platform (1892)." History Matters: The US Survey Course on the Web, accessed August 2021. http://historymatters.gmu.edu/d/5361/.

Nebraska Legislature. *Nebraska Blue Book.* https://nebraskalegislature.gov/about/blue-book.php.

Nebraska Studies. "Standing Bear Arrested." Accessed August 2021. http://nebraskastudies.org/1875-1899/the-trial-of-standing-bear/standing-bear-arrested/.

Neiberg, Michael S. *The Path to War: How the First World War Created Modern America.* Oxford: Oxford University Press, 2016.

———. "Why the U.S. Entered the First World War and Why It Matters." Lecture sponsored by U.S. Army War College, June 14, 2018. https://www.youtube.com/watch?v=-F7OAIRLKN0.

Nelson, Jennifer. *More Than Medicine: A History of the Feminist Women's Health Movement.* New York: New York University Press, 2015.

Newlands, F. G. "A Western View of the Race Question." ANNALS *of the American Academy of Political and Social Science* 34, no. 2 (1909): 49–51. https://www.jstor.org/stable/i242600.

Ngai, Mae. *Impossible Subjects: Illegal Aliens and the Making of Modern America.* Princeton NJ: Princeton University Press, 2004.

Novak, Nicole, Natalie Lira, Kate O'Connor, Sioban Harlow, Sharon Kardia, and Alexandra Minna Stern. "Disproportionate Sterilization of Latinos Under California's Eugenic Sterilization Program, 1920–1945." *American Journal of Public Health,* May 2018. https://ajph.aphapublications.org/doi/10.2105/AJPH.2018.304369.

NPR. "Fact Check: Donald Trump's Republican Convention Speech, Annotated." July 21, 2016. https://www.npr.org/2016/07/21/486883610/fact-check-donald-trumps-republican-convention-speech-annotated.

Nugent, Walter. *The Tolerant Populists: Kansas Populism and Nativism.* Chicago: University of Chicago Press, 1963, 2013.

O'Brien, Sean. "The Stationmaster." *Notre Dame Magazine,* Summer 2017. https://magazine.nd.edu/news/the-stationmaster/.

Ohio History Central. "Ku Klux Klan." Accessed September 2021. https://ohiohistorycentral.org/w/Ku_Klux_Klan.

Oklahoma Historical Society. "Land Run of 1889." Accessed September 2021. https://www.okhistory.org/publications/enc/entry.php?entry=LA014.

Okrent, Daniel. *The Guarded Gate: Bigotry, Eugenics and the Law That Kept Two Generations of Jews, Italians, and Other European Immigrants out of America.* New York: Scribner, 2019.

Oliver, Mariana. *Migratory Birds.* Translated by Julia Sanchez. Oakland CA: Transit, 2021.

Olson, James C. *History of Nebraska.* Lincoln: University of Nebraska Press, 1955.

Ordover, Nancy. *American Eugenics: Race, Queer Anatomy, and the Science of Nationalism.* Minneapolis: University of Minnesota Press, 2003.

Ost, Suzanne. "Doctors and Nurses of Death: A Case Study of Eugenically Motivated Killing under the Nazi 'Euthanasia' Programme." *Liverpool Law Review* 27 (2006): 5–30. doi:10.1007/s10991-005-5345-2.

Otoe-Missouria Tribe. "Who We Are." https://www.omtribe.org/who-we-are/history/.

Owen, Chandler. "Women and Children of the South." *Birth Control Review* 3, no. 9. (September 1919): 9. https://lifedynamics.com/app/uploads/2015/09/1919-09-September.pdf.

Owens-Adair, Bethenia. *Human Sterilization: It's [sic] Social and Legislative Aspects*. Portland OR: Metropolitan, 1922.

Parziale, Amy. "'As Little as Possible': Trauma Aesthetics and the Case of Chinatown." CEA *Critic* 80, no. 1 (March 2018): 53–71. doi:10.1353/cea.2018.0005.

Paul, Diane B. *The Politics of Heredity: Essays on Eugenics, Biomedicine, and the Nature-Nurture Debate*. Albany: State University of New York Press, 1998.

Pierce, Jason E. *Making the White Man's West: Whiteness and the Creation of the American West*. Boulder: University Press of Colorado, 2016.

Pinsker, Matthew. "After 1850: Reassessing the Impact of the Fugitive Slave Law." In *Fugitive Slaves and Spaces of Freedom in North America*, edited by Damien Alan Pargas, 93–115. Gainesville: University Press of Florida, 2018.

Pisani, Donald J. "Beyond the Hundredth Meridian: Nationalizing the History of Water in the United States." *Environmental History* 5, no. 4 (October 2000): 466–82. https://doi.org/10.2307/3985582.

———. *To Reclaim a Divided West: Water Law and Public Policy 1848–1902*. Albuquerque: University of New Mexico Press, 1992.

Popenoe, Paul. *Applied Eugenics*. New York: MacMillan, 1918.

Porterfield, Sara. "Creating an American Nile: The International Origins of Colorado River Development." Paper for European Society for Environmental History Conference, July 1, 2017.

Postel, Charles. *The Populist Vision*. Oxford: Oxford University Press, 2007.

Pouty, Andrew Mason. *More Deadly Than War: Pacific Coast Logging 1827–1981*. New York: Garland, 1985.

Powalski, Caitlin. "Radical Transmissions: Isaac and Amy Post, Spiritualism and Progressive Reform in Nineteenth Century Rochester." *Rochester History* 71, no. 2 (Fall 2009): 1–29. https://www.libraryweb.org/~rochhist/v71_2009/v71i2.pdf.

Preston, William, Jr. *Aliens and Dissenters: Federal Suppression of Radicals 1903–1933.* Cambridge MA: Harvard University Press, 1963.

Prince, Hugh. "A Marshland Chronicle, 1830–1960: From Artificial Drainage to Outdoor Recreation in Central Wisconsin." *Journal of Historical Geography* 21, no. 1 (January 1995): 3–23. https://ur.booksc.eu/book/16389714/d922c7.

———. *Wetlands of the American Midwest: A Historical Geography of Changing Attitudes.* Chicago: University of Chicago Press, 2014.

Ptacin, Mira. *The In-Betweens: The Spiritualists, Mediums, and Legends of Camp Etna.* New York: Liveright, 2019.

Public Broadcasting Service. "Suffragist Alice Paul Clashed with Woodrow Wilson." Accessed September 2021. https://www.pbs.org/wgbh/americanexperience/features/suffragist-alice-paul-clashed-woodrow-wilson/.

Quashie, Kevin. *Black Aliveness, or, a Poetics of Being.* Durham NC: Duke University Press, 2021.

Raheja, Michelle. "Reading Nanook's Smile: Visual Sovereignty, Indigenous Revisions of Ethnography, and Atanarjuat (The Fast Runner)." *American Quarterly* 59, no. 4 (December 2007): 1159–85. https://doi.org/10.1353/aq.2007.0083.

Rainn. "Victims of Sexual Violence." Accessed August 2021. https://www.rainn.org/statistics/victims-sexual-violence.

Randall, A. Philip, and Chandler Owen. "Who Shall Pay for the War." *Messenger* 1, no. 11 (November 1917): 7–8. https://babel.hathitrust.org/cgi/pt?id=uc1.c2904887&view=page&seq=7&skin=2021.

Regan-Dinius, Jeannie. "With Bodily Force and Violence, the Escape of Peter." *Black History News & Notes*, no. 100 (May 2005). Reprinted by the Indiana Historical Bureau. Accessed September 2021. https://www.in.gov/history/3128.htm.

Reisner, Marc. *Cadillac Desert: The American West and Its Disappearing Water.* New York: Penguin, 1986.

Rivas, Jorge. "California Prisons Caught Sterilizing Female Inmates without Approval." ABC *News*, July 8, 2013.

Roberts, Dorothy. *Killing the Black Body: Race, Reproduction, and the Meaning of Liberty.* New York: Vintage, 1997.

Rodrique, Jessie. "The Afro-American Community and the Birth Control Movement, 1918–1942." PhD diss., University of Massachusetts, Amherst,

1991. https://www.proquest.com/docview/303970725?pq-origsite=gscholar&fromopenview=true.

———. "The Black Community and the Birth Control Movement." *NWSA Journal* 1, no. 4 (Summer 1989): 755–56. https://www.jstor.org/stable/4315980.

Roediger, David R. *The Wages of Whiteness: Race and the Making of the American Working Class*. New York: Verso, 1991.

Ross, Loretta J. "African American Women and Abortion." In *Abortion Wars: A Half Century of Struggle 1950–2000*, edited by Rickie Solinger, 161–207. Berkeley: University of California Press, 1998.

Ross, Loretta, et al. "The 'SisterSong Collective': Women of Color, Reproductive Health, and Human Rights." *American Journal of Health Studies* 17, no. 2 (2001): 79–88.

Rudwick, Elliott M. *Race Riot at East St. Louis*. Champaign: University of Illinois Press, 1982.

Sachs, Jeffrey. "Steep Rise in Gag Orders: Many Sloppily Drafted." Penn.org, January 24, 2022. https://pen.org/steep-rise-gag-orders-many-sloppily-drafted/.

Samet, Elizabeth D. *Looking for the Good War: American Amnesia and the Violent Pursuit of Happiness*. New York: Farrar, Straus and Giroux, 2021.

Sanger, Margaret. *Family Limitations*. Rev. 6th ed., 1917. https://archive.lib.msu.edu/DMC/AmRad/familylimitations.pdf.

———. *The Pivot of Civilization*. New York: Brentano's, 1922. https://www.gutenberg.org/files/1689/1689-h/1689-h.htm.

———. *The Selected Papers*. Vols. 1 and 2. Champaign: University of Illinois Press, 2007.

Saxton, Alexander. *The Rise and Fall of the White Republic: Class Politics and Mass Culture in Nineteenth-Century America*. New York: Verso, 1990.

Sayers, Daniel O. *A Desolate Place for a Defiant People: The Archeology of Maroons, Indigenous Americans, and Enslaved Laborers in the Great Dismal Swamp*. Gainesville: University Press of Florida, 2014.

———. "Marronage Perspective for Historical Archaeology in the United States." *Historical Archaeology* 46, no. 4 (2012): 135–61. www.jstor.org/stable/43491350.

Schaeffer, Katherine. "6 Facts about Economic Inequality in the U.S." Pew Research Center, February 7, 2020. https://www.pewresearch.org/fact-tank/2020/02/07/6-facts-about-economic-inequality-in-the-u-s/.

Schoen, Joanna. *Coercion and Control: Birth Control, Sterilization, and Abortion in Public Health and Welfare.* Chapel Hill: University of North Carolina Press, 2005.

Schuller, Kyla. *The Biopolitics of Feeling: Race Sex and Science in the Nineteenth Century.* Durham NC: Duke University Press, 2017.

Schwartz, Carley, Anette Kocbach Bølling, and Christopher Carlsten. "Controlled Human Exposures to Wood Smoke: A Synthesis of the Evidence." *Part Fibre Toxicol* 17, no. 49 (2020). https://doi.org/10.1186/s12989-020-00375-x.

Seager, Richard, and Celine Herweijer. "Causes and Consequences of Nineteenth Century Droughts in North America." Lamont-Doherty Earth Observatory, Earth Institute at Columbia University, accessed August 2021. http://ocp.ldeo.columbia.edu/res/div/ocp/drought/nineteenth.shtml.

Sedgwick, Eve. *Touching Feeling: Affect, Pedagogy, Performativity.* Durham NC: Duke University Press, 2003.

Shannon, Fred Albert. *The Farmer's Last Frontier: Agriculture, 1860–1897.* New York: Routledge, 1977.

Shaw, Jhelene R. "'Yours for Colorado': Applicants to the 1870 Union Colony at Greeley." Undergraduate honor's thesis, University of Colorado, 2016. https://scholar.colorado.edu/concern/file_sets/1n79h4762.

Silbernagel, Robert. *Troubled Trails: The Meeker Affair and the Expulsion of the Utes from Colorado.* Salt Lake City: University of Utah Press, 2011.

Silliman, Jael, Loretta Ross, Elena Gutierrez, and Marlene Gerber Fried, eds. *Undivided Rights: Women of Color Organize for Reproductive Justice.* Cambridge MA: South End, 2004.

Smith, Andrea. "Beyond Pro-choice versus Pro-life: Women of Color and Reproductive Justice." *NWSA Journal* 17, no. 1 (2005): 119–40. http://www.jstor.org/stable/4317105.

Smythe, William E. *The Conquest of Arid America.* New York: Harper and Brothers, 1900.

Solinger, Rickie. *Pregnancy and Power: A History of Reproductive Politics in America.* Rev. ed. New York: New York University Press, 2019.

Soloway, Richard A. "The 'Perfect Contraceptive': Eugenics and Birth Control Research in Britain and America in the Interwar Years." *Journal of Contemporary History* 30, no. 4 (October 1995): 637–64. https://www.jstor.org/stable/261086.

Southern Ute Indian Tribe. "Early History." Accessed August 2021. https://www.southernute-nsn.gov/history/.

Spitz, Lila. "'More Tons, Less Huns': World War I Shipbuilding in Alexandria." *Boundary Stones*, December 23, 2016. https://boundarystones.weta.org/2016/12/23/more-tons-less-huns-world-war-i-shipbuilding-alexandria.

Sprague, Marshall. *Massacre: The Tragedy at White River.* Lincoln: University of Nebraska Press, 1957.

Stanford Report Staff. "New Report Reveals the Environmental and Social Impact of the 'Livestock Revolution.'" *Stanford Report*, March 16, 2010. https://news.stanford.edu/news/2010/march/livestock-revolution-environment-031610.html.

Starita, Joe. *"I Am a Man": Chief Standing Bear's Journey for Justice.* New York: St. Martin's, 2008.

Stein, Samuel. *Capital City: Gentrification and the Real Estate State.* New York: Verso, 2019.

Stern, Alexandra Minna. *Eugenic Nation: Faults and Frontiers of Better Breeding in Modern America.* Berkeley: University of California Press, 2005.

———. "Making Better Babies: Public Health and Race Betterment in Indiana, 1920–1935." *American Journal of Public Health* 92, no. 5 (2002): 742–52. https://doi.org/10.2105/AJPH.92.5.742.

———. *Proud Boys and the White Ethnostate: How the Alt-Right Is Warping the American Imagination.* Boston: Beacon Press, 2019.

Stock, James H. "Real Estate Mortgages, Foreclosures, and Midwestern Agrarian Unrest, 1865–1920." *Journal of Economic History* 44, no. 1 (March 1984): 89–105. https://doi.org/10.1017/S0022050700031387.

Strathern, Marilyn, et al., eds. "Forum on *Making Kin Not Population: Reconceiving Generations.*" *Feminist Studies* 45, no. 1 (2019): 159–72. https://www.jstor.org/stable/10.15767/feministstudies.45.1.0159.

Strausberg, Stephen F. "Indiana and the Swamp Lands Act: A Study in State Administration." *Indiana Magazine of History* 73 (September 1977): 191–203. https://www.jstor.org/stable/i27790213.

Stubbendieck, James, Stephan L. Hatch, and Cheryl D. Dunn. *Grasses of the Great Plains.* College Station: Texas A&M AgriLife Research and Extension Service Series, 2017.

Sullivan, Shannon. "Inheriting Racist Disparities in Health: Epigenetics and the Transgenerational Effects of White Racism." *Critical Philosophy of Race* 1, no. 2 (2013): 190–218. https://doi.org/10.5325/critphilrace.1.2.0190.

Supreme Court of the United States. *U.S. Reports: Plessy v. Ferguson, 163 U.S. 537*. 1895. Periodical. https://www.loc.gov/item/usrep163537/.

Sy, Stephanie. "Texas Homeless Suffer due to Lack of Public Housing." *PBS Newshour*, August 25, 2021. https://www.pbs.org/newshour/show/texas-homeless-suffer-due-to-lack-of-public-housing-as-public-camping-is-criminalized.

"Tales from Pauling's Boyhood." *Pauling Blog*, May 26, 2009. https://paulingblog.wordpress.com/2009/05/26/tales-from-paulings-boyhood-the-1917-shipbuilders-strike/.

TallBear, Kim. "Making Love and Relations beyond Settler Sex and Family." In *Making Kin Not Population*, edited by Donna Haraway and Adele E. Clarke, 145–57. Chicago: Prickly Paradigm, 2018.

———. "Making Love and Relations beyond Settler Sexualities." Talk at Social Justice Institute Noted Scholars Lecture Series and the Ecologies of Social Difference Research Network at the University of British Columbia, February 24, 2016. https://www.youtube.com/watch?v=zfdo2ujRUv8.

Taney, Roger Brooke, and Supreme Court of the United States. *U.S. Reports: Prigg v. The Commonwealth of Pennsylvania, 41 U.S. 16 Pet. 539*. 1842. Periodical. https://www.loc.gov/item/usrep041539/.

Taylor, Catherine. *You, Me, and the Violence*. Columbus: Ohio State University Press, 2017.

Taylor, Jared. "The Racial Revolution: Race and Racial Consciousness in American History." *American Renaissance*, August 3, 2019. https://www.amren.com/news/2019/08/race-and-racism-in-american-history/.

Taylor, Stephen J. "Fletcher's Swamp and Bacon's Swamp." *Hoosier State Chronicles*, March 31, 2015. http://blog.newspapers.library.in.gov/fletchers-swamp-and-bacons-swamp/.

Ten Tribes Partnership. "Keepers of the River." Accessed August 2021. https://tentribespartnership.org.

———. "Water Study." Accessed August 2021. https://tentribespartnership.org/wp-content/uploads/2019/12/WaterStudy.pdf.

Terrell, Mary Church. "Lynching from a Negro's Point of View." *North American Review* 178, no. 571 (June 1904): 853–68. https://www.jstor.org/stable/25150991.

Thompson, KT. *Blanket*. New York: Bloomsbury, 2018.

———. "Stock Histories." *Social Text* 138, no. 1 (March 2019): 107–15.

Thorson, John E. *River of Promise, River of Peril: The Politics of Managing the Missouri River.* Lawrence: University Press of Kansas, 1994.

Tibbles, Thomas. *Buckskin and Blanket Days: Memoirs of a Friend of the Indians.* Lincoln NE: Bison, 1969.

———. *The Ponca Chiefs: An Account of the Trial of Standing Bear.* Edited by Kay Graber. Lincoln: University of Nebraska Press, 1972.

"Timeline Tuesday: Drought and Depression in 1890s Nebraska." *History of Nebraska* (blog), accessed August 2021. https://history.nebraska.gov/blog/timeline-tuesday-drought-and-depression-1890s-nebraska.

Tindall, George B., ed. *A Populist Reader: Selections from the Works of American Populist Leaders.* New York: Harper Torch, 1966.

Tom, Gloria, Carolynn Begay, and Raylene Yazzie. "Climate Adaptation Plan for the Navajo Nation." Navajo Nation Department of Fish and Wildlife, 2018. https://www.nndfw.org/docs/Climate%20Change%20Adaptation%20Plan.pdf.

Tooze, Adam. "American Power in the Long 20th Century." Lecture sponsored by *London Review of Books*, March 27, 2019. https://www.youtube.com/watch?v=09s-T778ciA.

———. *Deluge: The Great War, America, and the Remaking of the Global Order 1916–1931.* New York: Penguin, 2015.

Treuer, David. *The Heartbeat of Wounded Knee: Native America from 1890 to the Present.* New York: Riverhead, 2019.

Troy, Kathryn. *The Specter of the Indian: Race, Gender, and Ghosts in American Seances, 1848–1890.* Albany: State University of New York Press, 2017.

Trump, Donald. "Remarks by President Trump during Visit to the Border Wall, San Diego, CA." Trump White House Archives, September 18, 2019. https://trumpwhitehouse.archives.gov/briefings-statements/remarks-president-trump-visit-border-wall-san-diego-ca/.

U.S. Bureau of Reclamation. "Lower Colorado Water Supply Report." August 19, 2021. https://www.usbr.gov/lc/region/g4000/weekly.pdf.

———. "Uncompahgre Project." 1994. https://www.usbr.gov/projects/pdf.php?id=203.

U.S. Department of the Interior. "Drought in the Colorado River Basin." Accessed August 2021. https://www.doi.gov/water/owdi.cr.drought/en/.

US ex Rel. Standing Bear v. Crook, 25 F. Cas. 695 (D. Neb. 1879). https://casetext.com/case/us-ex-rel-standing-bear-v-crook.

U.S. Holocaust Memorial Museum. "Nazi Racial Science." Accessed August 2021. https://www.ushmm.org/collections/bibliography/nazi-racial-science.

U.S. Meat Export Federation. "Strong Momentum Continues for U.S. Beef and Pork Exports." Accessed August 2021. https://www.usmef.org/news-statistics/press-releases/strong-momentum-continues-for-u-s-beef-and-pork-exports/.

Vasudevan, Pavithra. "Brown Scholar, Black Studies: On Suffering, Witness, and Materialist Relationality." In *Feminist Geography Unbound: Discomfort, Bodies, and Prefigured Futures*, edited by Banu Gökariksel, Michael Hawkins, Christopher Neubert, and Sara Smith, 27–47. Morgantown: West Virginia University Press, 2021.

Vials, Christopher. *Haunted by Hitler: Liberals, the Left, and the Fight against Fascism in the United States.* Boston: University of Massachusetts Press, 2014.

Walzer, Michael. *Political Action: A Practical Guide to Movement Politics.* New York: NYRB Classics, 1971.

Wang, Jackie. *Carceral Capitalism.* Boston: Semiotex(t), 2018.

Waring, George E. *Draining for Profit, Draining for Health.* New York: Orange Judd, 1967.

Warren, Louis. *God's Red Son: The Ghost Dance Religion and the Making of Modern America.* New York: Basic Books, 2017.

Watson, Tom. "The Negro Question in the South." In *A Populist Reader: Selections from the Works of American Populist Leaders*, edited by George B. Tindall, 18–28. New York: Harper Torch, 1966.

Webb, Patterson. "Seattle Shipyard Workers on the Eve of the General Strike." Seattle General Strike Project, University of Washington, Winter 2011. https://depts.washington.edu/labhist/strike/shipyards_webb.shtml.

Webb, Walter Prescott. *The Great Plains: A Study in Institutions and Environment.* Lincoln: University of Nebraska Press, 1931, 1959, 1981.

Weheliye, Alexander. *Habeas Viscus: Racializing Assemblages, Biopolitics, and Black Feminist Theories of the Human.* Durham NC: Duke University Press, 2014.

Welch, Steven R. "Military Justice." *International Encyclopedia of the First World War*, accessed August 2021. https://encyclopedia.1914-1918-online.net/article/military_justice.

Wells-Barnett, Ida B. *Southern Horrors: Lynch Law in All Its Phases.* Pamphlet. New York, 1892, 1893, 1894. https://archive.org/stream/southernhorrors14975gut/14975.txt.

White, Richard. *It's Your Misfortune and None of My Own: A New History of the American West.* Norman: University of Oklahoma Press, 1991.

———. *The Republic for Which It Stands: The United States during Reconstruction and the Gilded Age, 1865–1896.* Oxford: Oxford University Press, 2017.

Whitman, James Q. *Hitler's American Model: The United States and the Making of Nazi Race Law.* Princeton NJ: Princeton University Press, 2017.

Wilderson, Frank B., III. *Red, White and Black: Cinema and Structure of US Antagonisms.* Durham NC: Duke University Press, 2010.

Wilkinson, Isabel. *Caste: The Origins of Our Discontent.* New York: Random House, 2020.

Williams, A. Park, Edward R. Cook, Jason E. Smerdon, Benjamin I. Cook, John T. Abatzoglou, Kasey Bolles, Seung H. Baek, Andrew M. Badger, and Ben Livneh. "Large Contribution from Anthropogenic Warming to an Emerging North American Megadrought." *Science* 386, no. 6448 (April 17, 2020): 314–18.

Williams, William J. "Accommodating American Shipyard Workers, 1917–1918: The Pacific Coast and the Federal Government's First Public Housing and Transit Programs." *Pacific Northwest Quarterly* 84, no. 2 (1993): 51–59. https://www.jstor.org/stable/40491344.

Williamson, Joel. "Wounds Not Scars: Lynching, the National Conscience, and the American Historian." *Journal of American History* 83, no. 4 (March 1997): 1221–53. https://www.jstor.org/stable/2952899.

Wilson, Dorothy Clarke. *Bright Eyes: The Story of Susette La Flesche, an Omaha Indian.* New York: McGraw Hill, 1974.

Wishart, David. *Great Plains Indians.* Lincoln NE: Bison, 2016.

———. *An Unspeakable Sadness: The Dispossession of the Nebraska Indians.* Lincoln: University of Nebraska Press, 1994.

Wolcott, Victoria W. "Suffragists Used Hunger Strike as Powerful Tool of Resistance." *UBNow*, University of Buffalo, August 21, 2020. http://www.buffalo.edu/ubnow/stories/2020/08/wolcott-conversation-suffragists.html.

Wolfe, M. Melissa. "'Proving Up' on a Claim in Custer County, Nebraska: Identity, Power, and History in the Solomon D. Butcher Photographic Archive: 1886–1892." PhD diss., Ohio State University, 2005.

Wolfe, Patrick. "Race and the Trace of History: For Henry Reynolds." In *Studies in Settler Colonialism*, edited by Fiona Bateman and Lionel Pilkington, 272–96. London: Palgrave Macmillan, 2011.

———. "Settler Colonialism and the Elimination of the Native." *Journal of Genocide Research* 8, no. 4 (2006): 387–409. doi:10.1080/14623520601056240.

Women's Earth Alliance and Native Youth Sexual Health Network. *Violence on the Land Violence on Our Bodies*. Accessed August 2021. http://landbodydefense.org/uploads/files/VLVBReportToolkit2016.pdf.

Woodward, C. Vann. *Tom Watson: Agrarian Rebel*. New York: Rinehart, 1938.

World War I Casualties. Vol. 1. Accessed September 2021. http://www.digifind-it.com/hoboken/data/scrapbooks/1918-1919%20Part_0001.pdf.

Worster, Donald. *Rivers of Empire: Water, Aridity, and The Growth of the American West*. New York: Pantheon, 1985.

Wortman, Roy. "Denver's Anti-Chinese Riot, 1880." *Colorado Magazine* 42 (Fall 1965): 275–91. https://www.historycolorado.org/sites/default/files/media/document/2018/ColoradoMagazine_v42n4_Fall1965.pdf.

Wright, George C. *Racial Violence in Kentucky: Lynchings, Mob Rule, and "Legal Lynchings."* Baton Rouge: Louisiana State University Press, 1990.

Wright, Richard. *Black Boy*. 75th anniversary ed. New York: Harper Perennial, 2020.

Yazzie, Melanie K., and Andrew Curley. "Decolonizing Development, Challenging Patriarchy: Colonialism, Capitalism, and Gender in Diné Bikeyah." *Environment and Society* 9 (2018): 25–39. https://www.jstor.org/stable/26879576.

Yazzie, Melanie K., and Cutcha R. Baldy. "Introduction: Indigenous Peoples and the Politics of Water." *Decolonization: Indigeneity, Education & Society* 7, no. 1 (2018): 1–18.

Youngkin, Stephen D. "Prelude to Wounded Knee: The Military Point of View." *South Dakota History* 4, no. 3 (Summer 1974): 333–51. https://www.sdhspress.com/journal/south-dakota-history-4-3/prelude-to-wounded-knee-the-military-point-of-view/vol-04-no-3-prelude-to-wounded-knee.pdf.

Zimmer, Kenyon. *Immigrants against the State: Yiddish and Italian Anarchism in America*. Champaign: University of Illinois Press, 2015.

Index

Page numbers in italics refer to illustrations.

abolitionists and abolitionism, 30, 78, 259n7
abortion, 145, 257n59
Adams, Charles, 113
Addams, Jane, 201
AFL (American Federation of Labor), 237n109, 242n15, 277n69
African Blood Brotherhood, 277n74
agents. *See* Indian agents; slave catchers
agriculture, 120–22, 224n30, 231n40, 249n93, 250nn99–100
air quality, 252n109
alcoholism, 131, 179
Ali, Omar, 53–54
Allies, 194, 271n21
Allotment Act (1887), 247n76
allotments, land, 46, 71, 226n49, 236n97, 247n76
America. *See* United States
America First Caucus, 173–74, 266n59, 267n72
American Birth Control Conference (New York, 1920), 149

American Federation of Labor. *See* AFL (American Federation of Labor)
Americanism, 4, 197, 262n25
Americanness, 170–71, 262n25
American Union against Militarism, 200
Amy (enslaved person), 14
Anarchist Exclusion Act (1918), 197
anarchy and anarchists, 102, 144, 145, 150–51, 202–3, 242n13
Anderson, Mr. (settler), 98–99
Anderson, Steve, 104, 121–22
Anglo-Saxon bias, 103, 168, 173–74, 242n16
Anthony, Susan B., 78
antisemitism, 59–61, 182–83, 233n50
anti-war sentiment, 145, 197, 200–201, 203–4, *205*, 273n39, 276n60
archeological studies, 25–26, *26*, 219n36
archives and archival study, 4–5, 10–11, 51, 164
Army, U.S., 68, 112, 199

313

Army Corps of Engineers, 248n84
Article 13 (Indiana Constitution), 30–31, 221n54
Ashmore, John, 21
Ashmore, Margaret, 21
assimilation of Indians, 44, 47, 66, 81, 87, 167, 169, 226n53, 236n98
Assiniboine Indians, 115
Atlantic, 276n66

Baldwin, James, 129
Baldwin, Simeon E., 262n32
Banner of Light, 89, 222n8
barbed wire, 41, 224n24
Barker, Joanne, 116, 117
Barnes, Djuna, 272n33
Barrett, William, 52
Bear Shield (Ponca boy), 39
Beda, Steven, 269n5
Bell, John, 104
Bellamy, Edward: *Looking Backward*, 64
Bemis, Mr. (slave hunter), 21
Benga, Ota, 128
Benjamin, Walter, 189; *Selected Writings*, 269n2
Benson Center, 172–73
Bergland, Renée, 87
Berkman, Alexander, 201, 203, 253n22
Berkman, Joyce, 257n48
Bet (enslaved person), 14
Biden, Joe, 229n12
Big Blue River Reservation, 227n62
Big Snake (Ponca man), 39, 226n49
birth control: availability of, 133, 146; for Blacks, 147–48, 255n32; effectiveness of, 253n13; and

eugenics, 148–51, 153–54, 171, 256n39, 257n48; knowledge about, 142–43, 154–55; laws affecting, 143, 144, 254n27, 254n31; and power, 142; support for, 141–42, 144–48
Birth Control Review, 147–48, 149, 255n33
birthday party for white children, 8–10, 126, 128, 159–60, 163–64, 258n2
The Birth of a Nation (film), 197
Bitsui, Sherwin: *Flood Song*, 117
Black Canyon, 139
blackface minstrelsy, 80, 238n17
Black Hills Agreement (1877), 222n8
Black Hills region, 222n8
Black Lives Matter movement, 188, 259n8
Blackness, 55, 161, 230n24, 259n6
Black Populists and Populism, 53–54, 74, 210, 230n16, 237n105
Black Reconstruction (Du Bois), 74
Blacks: and birth control, 147–48, 255n32; in Congress, 228n3; and eugenics, 261n18; as homesteaders, 98–99, 223n22; infant mortality rate of, 148, 255n36; and labor issues, 259n4; laws affecting, 30–31, 270n6; and mixed-race issues, 9, 126, 128; perceptions about, 102, 161, 230n24; and Populism, 53–54, 73–75, 210, 230n16, 237n105; in professional jobs, 230n17; and racialized debt, 234n63; resistance by, 203, 277n74; and spiritualism, 238n17; spurning of,

by president, 272n31, 277n75; in Underground Railroad, 217n2; violence against, 52–53, 54–55, 143–44, 159–60, 197, 228n6, 229n10, 262nn30–31; and voting rights, 74, 197; in World War I, 202, 203, 272n28, 276nn65–66
Bland, Cora, 81
Bland, Thomas, 81
Bland family, 81–82, 84–85, 239nn18–20
blood: and air, 185–86, 269n101; in habeas corpus, 45; and immigration policy, 170; and nationalism, 172, 173–74; and Populism, 180; in racial purity, 9–10, 160–61, 164, 167–68, 171, 179, 259n6; and slavery, 21; symbolism of, in film, 117–18
Blumberg, Stephen "Book Bandit," 2–3, 5, 12
boarding schools, 44, 65–69, 71, 235n76, 235n81
Boasberg, James, 248n84
book theft, 2–3, 5–6, 12
border wall, 153, 269n1
Boston Indian Citizenship Committee, 45–46
boundaries, non-physical, 11–12, 51, 72, 95–96, 171, 179, 212
Braude, Anne, 77–78, 238nn7–8; *Radical Spirits*, 77
Bread and Roses Strike (1912), 253n22
breath and breathing, 185–86, 189, 213, 269n2
Bright Eyes (Omaha woman). *See* La Flesche, Susette "Bright Eyes"

Bright Eyes (spirit control), 89–91, 240n35
Brosius, Marriott, 66–67, 226n53
Brown sawmill, 191, *191*
Brunot Agreement (1873), 110, 245n48
Bryan, William Jennings, 73–74, 200, 237n111, 275n57
Buchanan, Joseph, 168
Buck, Carrie, 260n15
Buck v. Bell, 163, 260n15
Buffon, Comte de: *Histoire naturell*, 220n44
Bulla, Martha, 13
Bulla, Thomas (grandson of Thomas Jr.), 13–14
Bulla, Thomas, Jr., 14, 217n5
Bulla, Uriah, 13
Bulla, William, 13–14
Bulla family, 13, 15
Burch, Guy Irving, 149
Bureau of Reclamation, 122
burials, 39–40, 49, 225n42
Burrill, Mary, 147–48
Butcher, Solomon D., 34
Butler, Judith, 199, 206, 275n49
Butler, Pierce, 260n15
Byrne, Ethel, 254n31

California, 120, 121
Calloway, Bertha, 261n19
A Call to Action (Weaver), 64
Cambridge Neighborhood Committee on Vietnam, 277n79
Cameron Peak fire, 252n109
Campbell, Verne, 128–29
Camp Etna, 88–89
Campion, Thomas, 15

canals, 16, 18, 99, 100, 110–11, 218n11
Canella (Ute man), 112
capitalism: consequences of, 247n75; and immigration, 145; and irrigation, 101; and Populism, 176, 177, 209, 211, 234n62; and race issues, 7–8, 31, 74–75; resistance to, 202–3; and settler legacy, 11; and war, 198; and wetlands drainage, 27, 29; and women's rights, 145–46
Carey Act (1894), 242n10
Carlisle Indian Industrial School, 65–67
Carlson, Anthony, 27, 29, 220n44
Carlson, Tucker, 173
Carr, Carolyn (later Grace), 182–83, 204, 205, 277n79
Carr, Julie: activism of, 116–17, 173; dreams of, 47–48, 76, 97–98, 155, 213; interviews by, 88, 104, 121–22, 190; Jewish heritage of, 60–61, 182–83; legacy inherited by, 7, 11, 123, 184–86; memories of, 97, 133–34, 154–55, 204; as researcher, 51, 69, 72–73, 125, 126, 128–31, 135–37, 139–40, 164; and spiritualism, 187–88
Carr, Lynch, Hack and Sandell (architectural firm), 216n16, 249n87
Carr, Stephen: advantages of, 258n63; in dreams, 97–98; and family history, 8, 209, 212, 278n87; during pandemic, 157; values of, 11; views of, 7; work of, 216n16; in youth, 108, 137

Cashman, Sean, 64
Cassdall, H. D., 210
cattle industry, 42, 223n21, 228n64, 236n98
Census Bureau, 153
censuses, 23, 263n34
Central Labor Council, 277n69
Central Valley CA, 105, 244n28
Chafe, William, 74, 230n16
Chapman, Brett, 44
Cheatham, Henry P., 228n3
Cherokee Indians, 15, 70
Chicago Bee, 276n60
Chicago Tribune, 114
Chinatown (film), 108–9, 117–20, *118*, *119*, 245n46
Chinese Exclusion Act, 168–69, 263n35, 264n39. *See also* Geary Act
Chinese residents, 168–70, 264nn40–41
Chipeta (Ute woman), 152
Choctaw Indians, 70
Chomsky, Noam, 234n62
Christensen, Chris, 75, 125, 128, 129–30, 131–32, 252n5, 270n6
Christensen, Valerie, 128
Christianity, 29, 65, 78, 81–82, 164–65, 175, 225n42
Christy, George, and Christy Minstrels, 238n17
City of Montrose (boat), 103
Civil War, 23, 234n63
class differences: and birth control, 143, 256n39; and capitalism, 145–46, 190–91, 201–2; and eugenics, 260n16, 261n22; in national politics, 7–8; and pro-

316 Index

natalism, 171; and racism, 163–64, 210, 267n82; in war, 202
Clay, Henry, 22
clay fragments, archeological, 26
Colfax, Schuyler, 31, 253n18
Colfax Massacre (1873), 143–44, 253n17
colonialism, 247n75
colonization, 15, 30, 197–98, 224n24, 235n83, 236n84, 259n7, 273n38
Colorado, 93, 107
Colorado River, 104–5, 121–22, 244n28
Colorado River Basin Tribal Coalition, 251n104
communism, 61–62, 216n8
commutation clause (1891), 59, 232n47
Compromise of 1877, 222n8
Comstock, Anthony, 143–44, 253n14, 253n18
Comstock Act (1873), 143–44
Congress: on birth control, 144; Blacks in, 228n3; on eugenics, 263nn34–35, 265n45; on immigration, 169–71, 263nn34–35, 265n45; and Indian policy, 37–38, 65–68, 71, 114, 217n8, 236n92, 236n98, 246n73; and land ownership, 237n100; Populists in, 6, 56, 165, 167, 265n45; on race issues, 54–55, 229n12, 229n14; self-absorption of, 50–51; and slavery laws, 20, 22; on state's rights, 52–53; war legislation of, 195; on water issues, 102, 104

Conklin, Julia, 19
conscription, mandatory, 202. *See also* draft, military
Constitution, U.S., on slavery, 20, 21–22
Constitutional Convention (Indiana, 1850), 30
Corey, Anita, 140
Corey, Elaine, 140
Corey, Gardner Brooks, 137, 140
Corey family, 151–52
Corn Belt, 23, 221n60
corporations, 101–2, 211, 249n93
Corvallis Gazette Times, 181
Cottage Grove Electric and Light, 191–92, *191*
Cottage Grove OR, 252n109
Council Fire and Arbiter, 81, 239n18
Counterpath, 116, 140, 249n87
Courtright, Julie, 264n40
COVID-19. *See* pandemic (COVID-19)
Crawford, Dave, 2–3, 4–5, 8
creditor-debtor dynamic, 61–62, 232n48, 233n56
creditors, nations as, 194–95, 271n19
Creighton University, 2, 5, 215n4
criminality, eugenic concept of, 174, 177–78
criminals, 166, 181, 196
Crisis, 148
Crook, George, 40, 45, 224n33
crops, 32, 42, 57, 58, 64, 105, 231n37, 232n46
Cruce, Micaela, 229n7
Crusius, Patrick, 251n106
Cruz, Ted, 4

Index 317

crying, 225n43
Custer County NE, 228n64
cyclone, 140
Czolgosz, Leon, 102, 144, 242n13

Dakota Access Pipeline (DAPL), 115, 248n84
daughters and daughterhood, 138
Davenport, Charles, 150, 268n93
Davidson, George, 243n18
Davis, Maggie, 81–83
Dawes, Henry L., 46
Dawes Act (1887), 46–47, 71, 81, 224n33, 227n62, 239n18
death, 51, 66, 81, 135–37, 157–58, 189
Debs, Eugene, 150, 203, 255n33
debt: humiliation of, 61–64; labor working off, 233n61; and land issues, 57–59, 141, 237n100; migration caused by, 231n32; moral, 234n63; in political theater, 235n75; of settlers, 233n53; social aspects of, 232n48, 233n54, 233n56; in war, 194, 200
Declaration on the Rights of Indigenous Peoples (United Nations), 226n54
Deer, Sarah, 113, 247n75
Deloria, Philip J., 85
Democrats, 7, 73–74
Denison, Brandi, 113–14, 245n47
Dennett, Mary Ware, 256n39
Denver CO, 48, 227n58
Denver Tribune, 111
desertion, military, 200, 275n52
development compared to wetlands drainage, 220n46

Dhillon, Jaskiran, 115, 117
Diane (spiritualist), 88–90
Diouf, Sylviane A., 220n37; *Slavery's Exiles*, 24–25
Dix Dam, 160, 259n4
Dixon, Thomas, 197
Dobbs v. Jackson Women's Health Organization, 257n59
Donnelly, Ignatius, 210, 278n89
Douglass, Frederick, 44, 54, 78, 238n9
Doyle, Henry, 237n105
draft, military, 195, 202, 234n62, 271n25, 274n45
Draining for Profit, Draining for Health (Waring), 27
dreams, 47–48, 76–77, 97–98, 100, 155, 213
drought, 58, 121, 231nn31–32, 231n39, 232n46, 251n104
Dubofsky, Melvyn, 203
Du Bois, W. E. B., 143, 147–48, 210, 229n9, 255n34, 261n18, 274n41, 276n66; *Black Reconstruction*, 74
Dundy, Judge, 45, 225n44
Dyer Bill (1922), 203, 229n12, 277n74
dysentery, 16, 18

East Colfax Neighborhood Association, 249n87
Eastman, Crystal, 201
Eastman, John, 172–73, 266n56
Eastman, Max, 203
education, cost of, 5–6, 216n7
education, laws affecting, 216n8
Education Week, 216n8
Ellis, Havelock, 149, 256n40

Emery, Sarah E. V., 59–60
Emmett Till Antilynching Act, 229n12
The End of the Myth (Grandin), 153–54
Energy Transfer Partners, 248n84
enlistment papers, *195*
environmentalism, 122, 241n7, 248n84, 251n104, 257n52
epigenetics, 264n37, 269n99
Erdrich, Louise: *The Sentence*, 241n46
Espionage Act (1917), 197, 203
Estes, Nick, 63, 115, 117, 224n24, 224n33
eugenics: acceptance of, 267n77, 268n95; and antisemitism, 182–83; and birth control, 256n39; ethics of, 149–50; ideology of, 148–49; and immigration policy, 167–70, 263nn34–35; influence of, 234n66; as other-focused, 268n97; paranoia causing, 179; and Populism, 165–67, 176, 178–79, 262n27, 278n87; press on, 261n23; and pro-natalism, 171; racism of, 126, 161, 163–64, 167–71, 257n56, 258n1, 267n82; as religion substitute, 261n21; and reproductive rights, 183–84, 257n48; roots of, 260n16; and sterilization, 259n12, 261n18; support for, 268n93; targets of, 161–63, 180–81, 196, 256n46, 260n15; women encouraging, 152–53
Europe, 33, 150, 193, 231n19, 231n21, 273n40, 274n41

euthanasia, 181, 268n87
Evelyn Mulwray (fictional character), 108–9, 118
expansionism, 63, 153

Family Limitation (Sanger), 146–47, 254n31
Fanon, Frantz, 230n24, 236n84
farmers: as activists, 64, 73; and capitalism, 31; comparisons to, 234n62; and eugenics, 262n25; film treatment of, 108; financial difficulties of, 58–59, 232n46; in Germany, 223n22; home meaningful to, 227n55; inexperience of, 231n40; and Jews, 265n46; and land ownership, 41, 85, 179, 209; and Populism, 215n3, 240n25; and railroad, 235n72; supporters of, 235n68; and swampland, 219n30; and water supply, 98, 101, 103–4, 120, 121–22. *See also* homesteading; settlers
Farmers Alliance, 64, 215n3, 233n61, 235n68
farms, 16, *43*, 59, 98–99, 137, 140, 231n41
fascism, 7, 208–9, 210, 271n19
fathers, 11, 98
February Revolution, 271n21
Fellows, Abraham, 103, 243n19
Felton, Mr. (senator), 169
feminists and feminism, 77–78, 145, 201, 238nn7–8, 247n75, 256n39, 259n12
Ferrer Center, 253n22
Finkelman, Paul, 218nn19–20

fires, 124, *124*. See also wildfires
Fleet Wind (Indian spirit), 7, 37, 85–87, 93–94, 129, 240n25, 240n42
Fletcher, Ben, 276n60
Fletcher, Calvin, 26, 30–31, 220n41
Fletcher Swamp, 25–26, 33
flooding, 23, 115, 248n82
Flood Song (Bitsui), 117
Floyd, M. Ryan, 270n14
Flynn, Elizabeth Gurley, 150, 201, 253n22
food sources, community, 116, 140, 249n87
forest fires, 111, 213, 246n57, 252n109. See also wildfires
Fort Berthold Reservation, 115, 248n82
Fort Laramie Treaty, 38
Fort Peck Dam, 115
Fort Randall Dam, 115
Forwood, Mr. (slave hunter), 21
Foster, Benjamin F., 53
Foucault, Michel, 254n25
Fourier, Charles, and Fourierism, 105, 244n31, 244n38
Fourteenth Amendment, 172–73
fragmentation (grassland farming), 41, 42, 46–47
free range, 41
free speech, 144, 197
Free-State militias, 42
fruit trees, 98–99
Fugitive Slave Act (1793), 20, 22, 218n20
Fugitive Slave Act (1850), 20, 22–23, 52–53
Fuller, Edna, and family, 174

Gamble, John R., 50–51
gardening, 116, 249n87
Garrison, William Lloyd, 78
Garrison Dam, 115
Garvey, Marcus, 54, 148. See also UNIA (Universal Negro Improvement Association)
Geary Act, 169–71. See also Chinese Exclusion Act
gender issues, 161, 216n8, 227n55, 242n16
genealogy, 184
Genealogy (Kem), 217n5
genetics, 161, 164n37, 167–68, 183, 269n99
Genetin-Pilawa, C. Joseph, 239n18
genocide: and abolitionists, 15; basis of, 243n17; birth control as, 148; and eugenics, 181; in Europe, 183, 208; of Indians, 37, 110, 236n88; justification for, 153, 252n2; and Populists, 69, 177
Germany, 150, 194, 223n22, 271n20
Gerteis, Joseph, 171, 262n25, 265n46
ghosts, 76–77, 78–80, 81, 89, 93–94, 96, 187–88, 241n46
Gidden, J. F., 224n24
Gilded Age, 4, 53
Giscombe, C. S.: *Prairie Style*, 10
Giuliani, Rudy, 4, 266n56
Goldman, Emma, 145, 150, 201, 203, 242n13, 253n22, 254n25
gold mining, 110, 222n8
Goldsby, Jacqueline, 53
Goolsby, Alyssa, 171, 262n25, 265n46

Gordon, Avery, 26, 80, 84, 96
Graber, Kay, 40
Graeber, David, 61–62, 233n54
Grandin, Greg, 234n64, 276n65;
  The End of the Myth, 153–54
Grann, David: *Killers of the Flower
  Moon*, 236n88
Grant, Madison: *The Passing of the
  Great Race*, 149, 183, 265n48
Gray, Alexander, 14, 217n5
Great Britain, 193, 194, 270n14,
  271n24
Great Compromise (1850), 22–23, 24
Great Depression (1873), 143
Great Depression (1930s), 138,
  140, 141
Great Plains, 37, 222n8
Great Plains Black History
  Museum, 164, 261n19
Great Sioux Reservation, 38, 222n8
Greeley, Horace, 105–7, 244n31
Greeley CO, 106, 107
Greeley daughters, 107
Greeley Tribune, 111
Greene, Marjorie Taylor, 173–74,
  266n59, 267n72
greenhouse gases, 120, 250n94
Grimke, Sarah, 78
Guggenheim, Samuel, 252n2
Gunnison River, 100, 103–4
Gunnison Tunnel, 103–5, 137, 241n2
Guth, Delloyd, 57, 75, 215n4,
  231n31
Guthrie, Woody, 132
Gyory, Andrew, 263n35, 264n41,
  265n45

Haaland, Deb, 251n104

habeas corpus, 43–44, 45, 169,
  265n45
Hagerstown IN, 13, 16, *17*
Hambly, Thomas, 21
Hannigan, Robert, 273n37
Harlem Hellfighters, 202
Harris, Cheryl, 216n10
Harris, Chris, 227n61
Harris, Kamala, 172
Harris, Mr. (medium), 78–79
Harrison, Benjamin, 54
Hartman, Saidiya, 234n63
The Haunted Camera (film), 125–26
hauntings, 84, 187–88
Hayes, Rutherford, 39–40, 90
Haywood, Bill, 150, 201, 253n22
heartbeat bills, 257n59
Hector Rosado y Su Orquesta
  Hache, *185*
Henslow, G., 238n14
Hereditary Homestead Law,
  223n22
Hershberger, Mary, 217n8
Herweijer, Celine, 231n39
Hicks, John, 42, 58, 231n32
Histoire naturell (Buffon), 220n44
History of American Women (blog),
  259n12
A History of the American People
  (Wilson), 272n32
History of Wayne County Indiana,
  217n5
Hitler, Adolf, 183, 265n48
Hofstadter, Richard, 233n50
Hollis Mulwray (fictional character), 109
Holmes, K. J., 269n101
Holmes, Oliver Wendell, 260n15

Holt, Sam, 262n31
home, symbolism of, 227n55
homelessness, 48–49, 179, 227n58, 227nn60–61
home ownership, 123, 251n105
Homestead Act (1862), 6, 32, 58–59, 223n22
homesteading, 6, 32, 58–59, 63, 114, 223n22, 228n64, 232n47
Homestead Strike (1892), 56
homosexuality, 179, 267n78
Hooker, Charles E., 170, 265n45
Hoover, Andrew, 13
Hoover, J. Edgar, 203
house, Kem family, *124*
House of Morgan, 194. *See also* Morgan, J. P., Jr.
Howe, Craig, 115–16
Hughes, Langston, 208–9
Huhndorf, Shari, 93, 240n42
humanity, makeup of, 45, 161, 259nn8–9
Human Sterilization (Owens-Adair), 181, 267n86
humor, 154
hunger strikes, 197, 254n31, 272n33
Huxley, Thomas Henry, 126

Ignacio, Chief, 70–71, 236n97
"illegal alien" concept, 168, 264n39
immigrants and immigration: and eugenics, 167–71, 263nn34–35, 265n49, 267n72; in national politics, 4, 123, 189, 269n1; and puppet analogy, 131–32; and racism, 102–3; and violence, 251n106; and women's rights, 146, 254n31
incest, 108–9, 245n46
Independent, 91
Independent Party, 64. *See also* Populists and Populism
India, 243n18
Indiana, 17, 23, *28*, 29–31, 218n11, 218nn25–26, 220n39, 221n49
Indian agents, 107–8, 110–13, 114, 222n10, 226n49
Indianapolis Journal, 25–26, 31
Indian Appropriations Act (1851), 37–38
Indian Removal Act (1830), 15
Indian reservations. *See* reservations
Indians: activism by, 248n84, 251n104; agricultural knowledge of, 231n40; attitudes toward, 29, 111–12; fear of, 228n64; free range concept of, 41; irrigation affecting, 110–11; and land issues, 14–15, 63, 70–71, 85, 151–52, 224n24, 226n49, 241n46, 270n6; laws affecting, 37–38, 40, 46–47, 222n8, 222n10; numbers of, 221n5; as slaves, 220n39; sovereignty for, 226n54; and spiritualism, 85–88, 89–92, 240n42; support for rights of, 81, 239nn18–19; violence against, 226n49, 235n83, 247n75; and water use, 122; in White River incident, 112–14; white values placed on, 65–69, 224n24, 225n42, 225n44, 226n53. *See also specific tribes*

Indigenous Environmental Network, 122
Industrial Workers of the World. *See* IWW (Industrial Workers of the World)
infanticide, 180–82, 267n86
International Conference of Eugenics, 149, 268n93
International Workers' Defense League, 202
ironing and electrical use, 270n7
irrigation, 98, 100–101, 102–3, 104–8, 110–11, 112, 114, 120–24, 242nn10–11, 243n18
IWW (Industrial Workers of the World): and birth control, 254n31; on economic issues, 145, 202; influence of, 180; as interracial organization, 74, 237n109; and labor issues, 253n22, 277n69; misstatements of, 234n62; rights of, violated, 144, 203, 276n60

Jackson, Andrew, 15
Jacobs, Harriet, 78, 238n9
Jake Gittes (fictional character), 108, 117–18
Jazz on the Green, *185*
Jews, 59–61, 118, 182–83, 257n47, 265n46
Jim Crow laws, 167, 258n1
John C. Bell (boat), 103
Johnson, James Weldon, 272n31, 277n74
Johnson-Reed Act. *See* National Origins Act (1924)
Johnson v. M'Intosh, 14–15, 45, 217n6
Jones, Sondra G., 71, 114, 246n73

Just Transition, 122, 251n104

Kansas, 58–59, 121, 166
Kansas-Nebraska Act, 38
Kantrowitz, Stephen, 74
Katherine (fictional character), 108–9, 118
Kazin, Michael, 201, 272n28
Keeler, P. O. L., 238n17
Keith, LeeAnna, 253n18
Kem, Alice (Lockhart), *192*; accident of, 134; correspondence with, 8, 215n4; and family business, 269n4; family life of, 36–37, 49, 57, 65, 135, 164–65; problems of, 140–41; and spiritualism, 77, 86
Kem, Charley, 131, 190
Kem, Claude, 35–36, 140–41, 215n4
Kem, Earl, 35
Kem, Edwin, 143
Kem, Ellen (later Ross), 18, 82–83
Kem, Ely, 125
Kem, Happie, 9, 128, 160, 258n2
Kem, Huxley, 8–9, 57, 87, 125–26, 128, 160–61, 216n12, 258n2
Kem, Iris (later Corey), *139*; and birth control, 141–42, 151; in childhood and youth, 137; and eugenics, 9–10, 150–51, 153–54; family life of, 140–41; and Indian relocation, 151–52; in memory, 140; and spiritualism, 86; values of, 137–39, 156–58; wedding of, 135
Kem, Kathleen (later Carr), 1, 76–77, 86, 99, 108, *130*, 133–34, 141, 213, 215n4

Kem, Linda, 34–35, 86, 99–100, 134–37, 178–79, 207
Kem, Madison, 14, 15–18
Kem, Malinda (Bulla), 13–14, 15, 17–18, 79
Kem, Mary (Huxley's daughter), 8–9, *12*, 125–29, *127*, 132, 159, 216n12
Kem, Mary Esther, 16, 18
Kem, Maude (later Shinn), 1, 34–36, 135, 191, 269n4
Kem, Myrtle, 179
Kem, Nan (Benson), 19–20, 31–32, 35, 143
Kem, Norma-Marie "Marie," 86, 99, *100*, 134, 139, 207
Kem, Omer, *192*, *208*; about, 1–2, 6–7; affiliations of, 64, 168; ancestry of, 266n61; awareness lacking in, 178–80; on birth control, 141–42, 150–51; as businessman, 190–92; in childhood and youth, 13, 15–16, 18–19; community activities of, 135, 252n2; as congressman, 56, 64–65, 68–72, 73, 167, 215n4, 236n92, 239n19; and debt, 57–59, 62, 237n100; and eugenics, 8–10, 150–51, 164–66, 180–82, 261n22, 266n60, 269n100; family life of, 19–20, 25–27, 35–37, 57, 99–100, 134, 136–37, 138–39, 143, 156–58, 195–96, 270n8; friendships of, 175–78; *Genealogy*, 217n5; health of, 140–41; and Indian relocation, 49, 85, 88, 116; as inspiration, 75, 131–32; and irrigation, 101–4; and Jews, 60, 182; as landowner, 40, 41–42, 63–64, 98–99, 114–15, 231n40; legacy of, 123–24, 187–88, 208, 278n87; limitations of, 204–5; and Margaret Sanger, 155; in memory, 55–56, 212–13; poems of, 196; as racist, 174–75; on slavery, 217n5; and spiritualism, 76–77, 78–80, 81–87, 93–95, 156–57, 238n17, 239n20, 240n42; *Spiritualist Notes*, 79, 93, 94; values of, changing, 160–61, 209–10; and war economy, 198–202, 274n48; work life of, 31–32, 36, 42, 143
Kem, Omer Albert (Omer's son), 37, 57, 82–83
Kem, Randy, 125, 130–31, 190
Kem, Sophronia (later Mellett), 16, 191–92, *192*
Kem, Thelma, 133, 140–41, 164, *192*
Kem, Victor, *195*, *207*; about, 1–2; conduct of, 130–31, 141, 179; in military, 195–96, 278n83; as parent, 190; in youth, 76–77, 207
Kemble, E. C., 39
Kem family, 2, 13, 15, 16–18, *35*, 79–80, 86–87, 134–35, 140–41, 151–52, 213
Kennedy, David, 272n28
Kennedy, Ross, 197, 273n36
Kevles, Daniel, 260n16, 261nn21–22
Killers of the Flower Moon (Grann), 236n88
Klein, Ezra, 234n62
Kline, Wendy, 257n56

Knights of Labor, 64, 168
Kocher, Ruth Ellen, 159
Ku Klux Klan, 197, 229n9, 258n1
Ku Klux Klan Act (1876), 52

Lacombe, Beatriz, 164, 184–86
La Flesche, Francis, 45–46
La Flesche, Joseph, 223n18
La Flesche, Susette "Bright Eyes," 45–46, 89–92, 92, 223n18
La Flesche family, 225n45
La Follette, Robert, 201
Lakota Indians, 38, 50–51, 115–16
land speculators, 29–30, 46, 59, 221n53, 221n57, 232nn47–48, 265n46
Lansing, Robert, 197, 271n21, 273n38
Largent, Mark, 166, 262n28
Laughlin, Harry, 162
Laughlin, S. B., 180–81
Laurent, L. D., 210
Lause, Mark, 77
Lauzon, Francoise "Frank," 100
Law for the New Formation of the German Farmerstock, 223n22
Lawson, Michael, 248n82
League for Democracy, 277n74
Leedy, John, 166
Leise (puppeteer), 125, 128, 129, 131
L. E. Myers (construction company), 259n4
lenders and loan agents, 58–60, 232n43
Lentz-Smith, Adriane, 203
Lepore, Jill, 231n41
Lewelling, Lorenzo, 166
Lewis, Mr. (congressman), 67

Lewis, Mr. (slave hunter), 21
Limerick, Patricia, 51, 72
Lincecum, Gideon, 262n28
Lincoln, Abraham, 6, 160–61
livestock industry, 120, 122–23, 249n93, 250n94
Loblolly Marsh, 26–27
Lodge Bill (1890), 230n16
Loehmann, Timothy, 188–89
Looking Backward (Bellamy), 64
love, 11–12, 129, 133, 155–56, 158, 183, 211–12
Lovett, Laura, 103
Lowitt, Richard, 46
Lynch, Kevin, 216n16
Lynch, Mr. (congressman), 66
lynching, 52–55, 73–74, 166, 203, 228n6, 229n7, 229n9, 229n12, 229n14, 262n32
Lytle, Lutie A., 54, 230n17

Macdonald, John, 235n81
Mackay, James, 77
Magnes, Judah L., 201
maleness and masculinity, 56, 123
Mansur, Mr. (congressman), 67–68
maroons and *marronage*, 24–27, 216n1, 219n36, 220n37, 221n47. *See also* Blacks; slaves and slavery
marriages, 71, 135, 139, 174–75
Marshall, John, 14–15
Martin, Mr. (Oregon governor), 181
Martinez, Monica Muñoz, 224n24
Marx, Karl, 244n31
Marxists, 267n77
Mary (Indian woman), 67–68
masturbation, 143, 162, 253n14
Mathes, Valerie Sherer, 46

McCann, Carole, 254n31
McClanahan, Annie, 233n56
McDowell, Calvin, 52, 54–55, 228n6
McInnes, Gavin, 234n66
McKinley, William, 74, 102, 144, 237n111
McNary, Charles, 199, 274n48
McWhirter, Cameron, 203
Meacham, Alfred, 81, 239n18
mediums, 78–79, 81–82, 88–90, 238n17
Meeker, Arvilla, 112, 246n73
Meeker, Josephine, 112–14, 269n1; *The Ute Massacre*, 113, *119*
Meeker, Nathan, 105–8, 110–13, 245n51
Meeker, Ralph, 111, 114
Mejia, Eswin, 189
Mellett, Lottie, 191–92, *192*, 270n8
Mellett, Louise, 191–92, *192*, 270n8
Menominee Indians, 65–66
menstruation, 171
mental illness, 34, 99–100, 178–79
mercury chloride, 16
Messenger, 148, 201, 276n60
Mexicans, 133–34, 261n18
Mexico, 153, 194
Michigan, *28*
migration, reverse, 231n32
militarism, 199–201
militias, 42, 112, 144
Miller, Mr. (senator), 168
minstrels, 80, 238n17
Missouri River, 115, 248n82
mongrel (term), 266n61
Montrose CO, 100, *124*, 140
Mooney, Tom, 202

Morgan, Jerry, 21, 22
Morgan, J. P., 198
Morgan, J. P., Jr., 198, 200, 273n39
Morgan, Margaret, 21, 22
Mormons, 236n98
morphology, false, 128, 252n2
Morrison, Toni, 209
mortality rate, infant, 148, 255n36
mortgage companies, 59, 232n43, 232n45
mortgages, 57–58, 59, 62, 65, 98, 231n41
Mos Def, 272n33
Moss, Thomas, 52, 54–55, 228n6
mothers: as activists, 204, 277n79; and childbearing, 145; and daughters, 138; in dreams, 47–48; and eugenics, 257n56; film treatment of, 118; and spiritualism, 78–79, 82, 84; and stepmothers, 34–35; and superiority, 155; and water, 97–98, 123
Mott, Lucretia, 78
Mourning (enslaved person), 14
mud, 32–33
Muenter, Erich, 273n39

NAACP, 203, 229n12, 272n31
National Birth Control League, 256n39
National Indian Defense Association. *See* NIDA (National Indian Defense Association)
nationalism, 130, 170–71, 173–74, 234n66, 262n25, 274n41
National Origins Act (1924), 167, 170, 263n34
Navajo Indians, 251n103

Nazism, 150, 163, 172, 181, 182–83, 223n22, 257n47
Nebraska, 43, 58–59, 64–65, 121, 228n64, 232n46
Nebraska Blue Book, 221n5
The Negro (Shufeldt), 268n89
New Freedom (reform program), 197, 272n31
Newlands, Francis, 102
Newlands Reclamation Act (1902). *See* Reclamation Act (1902)
newspapers, 53, 64, 171, 246n73
Newsweek, 172
New York Herald, 111
New York Times, 44, 91
New York Tribune, 105, 244n38
Ngai, Mae, 263n34, 264n39
Nicaagat ("Captain Jack," Ute man), 112, 245n51
Nicholson, Jack, 108, 117, *118*
NIDA (National Indian Defense Association), 81, 239n18
Nieberg, Michael, 193
Ni Una Menos, 267n83
Noah Cross (fictional character), 108–9, 118
NO GODS NO MASTERS (slogan), 145
noise and silence, 55–56
Non-Conscription League, 201
Nordic Aryan League of America, 174
North, the, 23, 144
Norton, Charles, 169

Oatley, Steve, 252n5
Obama, Barack, 248n84
Oberly, John, 224n24

Occupy Wall Street movement, 232n48, 235n75
Ogallala Aquifer, 120
oil industry, 70, 128, 236n88, 248n82, 248n84
Oklahoma, 70
Okrent, Daniel, 261n23
Olathe CO, 140, 253n8
Olathe Women's Club, 151
"The Old Bachelor" (song), 18, 83
Omaha Congress and Platform, 210–12
Omaha Herald, 42–43
Omaha Indians, 223n18
Ordover, Nancy, 263n35
Oregon, 130, 132
Oregon Donation Land Act (1850), 270n6
Oregonian, 174, 181, 199
Osborn, Fairfield, 149
Ost, Suzanne, 268n87
Otoe-Missouria Indians, 227n62
Otoe-Missouria Reservation, 49, 237n100
Ouray (Ute chief), 112–13, 245n51
Owen, Chandler, 148, 150, 201, 276n60
Owens-Adair, Bethenia, 162–63, 259n12, 268n89; *Human Sterilization*, 181, 267n86
ownership: of humans, 20–22, 52–53, 225n38; and Indian relocation, 14–15, 32–33, 63, 70, 72, 237n100; of land, 41, 46, 226n49; power of, 44; private, 224n24; of property, 10, 234n64; rejection of, 5

pacifism. *See* anti-war sentiment

Index 327

Palmer, A. Mitchell, 203
Palmer, Belinda, *119*
pandemic (COVID-19), 135–36, 157–58, 213, 258n63
parenting as human experience, 155, 183–84
Parziale, Amy, 245n46
The Passing of the Great Race (Grant), 149, 183, 265n48
Paul, Alice, 201, 272n33
Paul, Julius, 262n27
Paul, Rand, 229n12
Pelton Expedition, 103
PEN America, 216n8
Pennsylvania, 20–22
People's Council of America for Democracy and Peace, 201
People's Grocery, 52
People's Party, 54, 215n3, 230n19. *See also* Populists and Populism
Pepper, George, 91
Perkins, Jo Rae, 252n5
Perry, Scott, 173
personhood, 43–44, 225n38, 225n42
photo as proof of spiritualism, 90, 240n35
Pick-Sloan dam project, 115, 248n82
Picotte, Susan La Flesche, 225n45
Pilcher, F. Hoyt, 166
Pinkerton agents, 52–53, 56
Pisani, Donald, 23–24
Pitkin, Frederick, 111, 112, 245n51
The Pivot of Civilization (Sanger), 149–50
Plessy, Homer, and *Plessy v. Ferguson*, 11, 50, 216n11

Plumb, Preston B., 51
Polanski, Roman, 108, 117–20, *118*, *119*
Political Action (Walzer), 277n79
Politico, 266n59
Polly-Anne (puppet), 129, 131–32
Ponca Indians, 38–40, 42–44, 45–46, 90, 222nn9–10, 223n12, 223n18, 224n32
Popenoe, Paul, 149, 267n82
population growth, 151, 257n52
populism (political movement), 6, 61, 74, 75, 96, 180, 215n3, 262n25
Populists and Populism: about, 85, 210–12, 215n3, 240n25; conflicting views of, 174–78, 180; and eugenics, 164–67, 262n25, 262n27; in government, 167, 265n44; on immigration, 169–70, 265nn45–46; and indebtedness, 62–65; and Jews, 59–60, 233n50; and land ownership, 179–80; and nationalization of utilities, 101–2; portrayals of, 234n62; and race issues, 4, 53–54, 73–75, 170–71, 229n14, 230n16, 237n105; solidarity in, 69–70; and spiritualism, 78, 95; and sterilization, 263n33. *See also* Kem, Omer
Porterfield, Sara, 243n18
Potawatomi Indians, 15, 217n9
poverty, 61, 165, 178, 233n53, 261n22
power company, 190–92, 270n7
prairies, 40–41
Prairie Style (Giscombe), 10

Pratt, Edward, 271n19
Pratt, Richard Henry, 65
Prigg, Edward, and *Prigg v. Pennsylvania*, 20–22
Progressive Era, 165, 243n23
pro-natalism, 171–72
propaganda, 271n24
Proud Boys, 234n66
Pueblo Chieftain, 246n73
puppets, 129, 131–32

Quakers, 13, 217n2
Quashie, Kevin, 259n8
Quinkent ("Douglas," Ute man), 245n51

racism: and blood, 170–72; in capitalism, 31; and class consciousness, 210, 267n82; distractions from, 153; in educational policy, 6; and eugenics, 148–49, 150, 161, 163–64, 181, 268n93; and health risks, 258n63; home as symbol in, 227n55; in homesteading, 223n22; ideology of, 233n57; and immigration, 167–69, 263n34, 264n41, 265n52; and Indian sovereignty, 226n54; and irrigation policy, 102–3; and liberty through ownership, 234n64; in national politics, 7, 188–89, 196–98; and personhood, 225n36, 225n38, 236n84; rejection of, 278n89; in social situations, 8–10, 126, 128, 160; in violence, 268n87; and white insecurity, 129; in women's rights, 156; in World War I, 276n65, 277n78

Radical Spirits (Braude), 77
Raheja, Michelle, 225n40
railroad industry, 62, 102, 235n72, 242n9
Rams Horn project, 121–22
ranchers, 41–42, 98, 122, 228n64
Randolph, A. Philip, 201, 203, 276n60
rape: colonialism as, 120; and film industry, 108–9, 118–20; and racism, 55, 235n83, 247n75; as sterilization justification, 166, 260n15, 262n28, 262nn30–31; in White River incident, 112–14, 246n73
Ream, Annie, 176
Ream, Jim, 36, 95, 175–78, *177*, 180–82, 212, 213, 269n100, 275n53
reclamation, land, 103, 105
Reclamation Act (1902), 102, 104, 231n39, 242n11, 242n15, 243n18, 243n23
Reconstruction, 143–44, 228n3, 272n32
Red Cloud (Lakota man), 38, 81
Red Cloud's War, 38
Red Scare, 150
removal of Indians from land: acceptance of, by whites, 49, 152; and forced marches, 38–39, 217n9; government regulating, 15, 227n62; irrigation encouraging, 110; opponents of, 71, 217n8, 239n18; proponents of, 70–71, 113–14; and spiritualism, 87
Republican, 42
Republican Party, 6, 130, 188, 212, 252n2, 266n59, 278n89

Index 329

reservations: and boarding schools, 65–67; conditions on, 110–11, 115; and Indian relocation, 70–71, 114, 227n62, 237n100; and land ownership, 49; laws affecting, 37–38, 46, 236nn97–98, 247n76, 270n6; natural resources on, 222n8, 248n82
Restoration Act (1937), 247n76
Rice, Tamir, 4, 188–89
Roberts, Tim, 2–3, 88–89, 91, 116, 164
Rockefeller Foundation, 268n93
Rocky Mountain News, 113
Roediger, David, 8
Roger (cousin of Victor Kem), 196
Root, Sarah, 189, 269n1
Ross, Dr. (son-in-law of Madison and Malinda Kem), 18
Ross, Minnie Ha-Ha, 18
Russia, 180, 271n21

Salinas CA, 133
Sanger, Margaret: as activist, 144–48, 253n22, 254n27, 254n31; and Blacks, 255n32; comparisons with, 254n25; and eugenics, 148–50, 256n40; *Family Limitation*, 146–47, 254n31; as inspiration, 154–55; *The Pivot of Civilization*, 149–50; on sterilization, 256n46, 257n47
Sanger, William, 253n22
Save the Colorado, 122
sawmills, 16, 191, *191*
Saxton, Alexander, 264n41
Sayers, Daniel, 24–25, 216n1

Schuller, Kyla, 227n59, 260n16, 263n35, 264n37
Schuman, Mr. (fascist), 174
Schurz, Carl, 39–40, 113–14, 226n49
Seager, Richard, 231n39
sedition, arrests for, 276n60
Sedition Act (1918), 197, 203
Selected Writings (Benjamin), 269n2
The Sentence (Erdrich), 241n46
sentimentalism, 227n59
settlers: agriculture built up by, 228n64; class levels of, 218n11; debt of, 58, 233n53, 237n100; and genocide, 236n88, 243n17; and Indian relocation, 37, 63, 70, 85, 92, 110, 114, 152, 227n62; and land ownership, 44, 46; naming of town by, 253n8; and patriarchy, 11, 243n17; Populists as, 170; and racism, 222n8, 270n6; and ranchers, 41–42; sense of entitlement of, 209–10; and spiritualism, 93, 96, 241n46; as "standard" humans, 44–47; violence by, 247n75; and water supply, 115. *See also* farmers; homesteading
shame, 62, 63–64, 133–34, 210
Sharpell, John L., 5
sheep ranching, 36
Sheldon, George, 13, 217n3
Sherman, John, 265n45
Shinn, Charles, 164, 191–92, 270n7
shipping and shipbuilding industry, 198, 274nn42–43, 274n45
Shufeldt, R. W.: *The Negro*, 268n89

Shylock and "shylocks," 59–60, 182
Silbernagel, Robert, 112, 113
silence as acceptance, 51, 53, 55–56, 188
Silk Strike (1913), 253n22
Simpson, Jerry, 229n14
Sioux Indians, 115, 222n8, 224n33, 248n82
Sixteenth Amendment, 231n29
slave catchers, 13, 20–21, 217n3
slavery as metaphor, 62–63, 233n57, 233n61, 234n62
Slavery's Exiles (Diouf), 24–25
slaves and slavery, 13–14, 20–23, 24, 80, 217nn2–3, 217n5, 218nn19–20, 219nn25–26, 220n39, 252n2
smallpox, 38, 252n2
Smith, Paxton, 257n59
socialism, 105, 176, 201, 216n8, 253n22, 256n40, 267n77
sod and sod houses, 35, 37, 40–41
Solinger, Rickie, 253n19
South, the, 29, 62, 73–74, 143–44, 222n8, 233n61, 276n65
Southern Horrors (Wells-Barnett), 54–55
sovereignty, 15, 47, 81, 226n54
spirit controls, 88, 89, 238n17. *See also* Bright Eyes (spirit control)
spirits, 79, 81–84, 87–88, 89, 93–94. *See also* Fleet Wind (Indian spirit)
spiritualism: about, 77–78; and boundary crossings, 95–96; and healing, 86; and land ownership, 222n8; manifestations of, 78–80, 81–83; and Populism, 6, 78, 93–94, 238n14; and racism, 238n7; skepticism about, 238n9; spirit guides in, 88–92; white, 87–88, 240n42; and women's rights, 238n7
Spiritualist Notes (Kem), 79, 93, 94
Standing Bear (Ponca man), 39–40, 43–47, 225n40, 225n42, 226n49
Standing Rock protest (2016), 115–16, 248n84
Stanton, Elizabeth Cady, 78
State Colony for Epileptics and the Feebleminded, 260n15
state's rights, 21, 52–53, 229n9
steam power, 191, 269n5
Steiner, R. E. Lee, 162
Stellow, Peter. *See* Sheldon, George
sterilization, reproductive: compulsory, 150, 166; and eugenics, 161–63, 259n12, 260nn15–16, 261n22, 262n28, 262n30, 267n86; of feeble-minded, 149, 150, 256n46; of homosexuals, 267n78; and Jews, 257n47; justification for, 178–79; laws on, 165, 183, 196; and lynching, 262n32; opponents of, 263n33; and racism, 208, 261n18, 268n89
Sterilization and Social Justice Lab, 261n18
Stern, Alexandra Minna, 234n66
Stewart, Will, 52, 54–55
Stock, James, 232n48
Stockdale, Mr. (congressman), 67
Story, Joseph, 21–22, 218n20
strikes, hunger, 197, 254n31, 272n33
strikes, labor, 198–99, 202, 253n22, 274n43, 275n50

Supreme Court, 14–15, 20–22, 52–53, 163, 218nn19–20, 231n29, 257n59, 260n15
Sussex pledge (1916), 271n20
Sutcliffe, Robert, 164–65
Swamp Lands Act (1850), 23–24
swamps: drainage of, 23–24, 29–30, 219n29, 219n31, 221n60; loss of, 221n49; as *marronage* sites, 25–27, 221n47; perceptions about, 27, 29, 33, 220n44; value of, 219n30, 221n53, 221n57

Taft, William Howard, 241n2
TallBear, Kim, 243n17
Taney, Roger B., 21, 218n20
taxation, 56, 68–69, 229n9, 231n29
Taylor, Catherine, 129, 194
Taylor, Mr. (senator), 52
Taylor, Stephen, 25
Teller, Mr. (senator), 111
Telluride News, 122
Ten Tribes Partnership, 122
Terrell, Mary Church, 53, 54
Thompson, KT, 77, 222n8
Thornburgh, T. T., 112
Tibbles, Thomas Henry, 42–43, 45–46, 90–91, 225n42
TigerSwan, 248n84
timber industry, 129–30, 191, 269n5
Timber Unity, 129–30
Todd, Samuel, 217n3
tooth rot, 16
Tooze, Adam, 194, 201, 271n19
Torrence, William, 103, 243n19
Trail(s) of Tears, 15, 38–39, 217n9
trauma, ancestral, 184, 269n99

treaties, 38, 109–10, 152
trees, 98–99, 106–7, 140, 191, 213, 219n30
Treuer, David, 44, 66, 224n24
Troy, Kathryn, 87–88
Trumbull Phalanx, 105
Trump, Donald: on campaign, 3–4; and immigration, 4, 123, 189, 251n106; and law, 188–89; and oil industry, 248n84; and racism, 269n1; reaction to election of, 7; supporters of, 75, 130, 172
Tsashin (Ute woman), 112–13
tuberculosis, 34, 135
Tulsa Massacre (1921), 159–60
typhoid fever, 35–36

Uncompahgre River and valley, 99–100, 103–4, 121–22, 135
Uncompahgre Ute Indians, 114–15, 239n18
Uncompahgre Water Users Association, 103–4
Underground Railroad, 13–14, 19, 28, 51, 160, 216n1, 217n2
UNIA (Universal Negro Improvement Association), 54, 148
Uniform Code of Military Justice, 200
Union Colony, 106–7, 244n32, 244n35
United Kingdom. *See* Great Britain
United Nations: *Declaration on the Rights of Indigenous Peoples*, 226n54
United States: educational barriers in, 5; fascism spreading

from, 208–9; nationalism in, 167–71, 173–74; wealth distribution in, 209, 278n86; world power aspirations of, 197–98, 243n18; in World War I, 193–95, 197–98, 271nn19–20, 271n24, 272n28, 273n40, 275n53
United States Geological Survey, 103
United States v. Cruikshank, 52
Unite the Right, 173
Universal Negro Improvement Association. *See* UNIA (Universal Negro Improvement Association)
University of Colorado, 172, 216n7, 266n56
uranium mining, 222n8
Ute Indians: education of children of, 236n94; history of, 245n47; and land allotments, 236n97; land relinquishment by, 245n48, 247n76; misrepresentations of, 246n57; relocation of, 70–71, 110–15, 152, 245n51; reservations of, 236n98; supporters of, 239n18; in White River incident, 112–13, 246n73, 269n1
The Ute Massacre (Meeker), 113, *119*
utopianism, 105–8, 121, 176, 269n100

vaccinations, 252n2
Valdinoci, Carlo, 202–3
Van Amringe, H. H., 244n38
Vanderbilt, Edward, 91, 240n35
Vanderbilt, Mary Scannell Pepper, 89–91, 240n35

Vanderbilt, Minerva, 91
Vickers, William, 111–12
Vietnam War, 204, 277n79
voters and voting, 74, 143–44, 197, 253n17

Wade, Benjamin, 160–61
Wake Up America (podcast), 252n5
Walzer, Michael: *Political Action*, 277n79
war, nature of, 153, 190, 200, 202, 203–4, 206–7
War against War (exhibition), 201
Waring, George: *Draining for Profit, Draining for Health*, 27
Warren, Elizabeth, 75
Warwick, William, 210
water: in agricultural use, 98; and climate change, 250n100; film treatment of, 108–9; for irrigation, 100–101, 103–7, 110, 241n2; in personal use, 97–98, 123–24; privatization of, 241n7; supply of, 120–24, 251n103; understanding of, 115–16; and wetlands drainage, 219n29; in world politics, 243n18
water protectors, 115–16, 248n84
Watkins, Jabez, 59
Watson, Tom, 52, 73–74, 237n105
weather and agriculture, 42, 58, 224n30
Weaver, James: *A Call to Action*, 64
Webb, Walter Prescott, 37
Webster, John Lee, 44, 225n42
Wells-Barnett, Ida B.: *Southern Horrors*, 54–55
West, the, 62, 72, 102–3, 105, 151

Index   333

Westfield IN, 19
wetlands. *See* swamps
wheat, 224n30
White, George Henry, 229n12
White Eagle (Ponca man), 39
Whitehead, Irving, 260n15
whiteness: and Americanism, 262n25; in archival history, 51; and birth rates, 265n52; and Blackness, 55, 236n84; and eugenics, 152–54, 167–68; as exclusive, 216n10; and immigration, 159; and Indians, 44–45, 47, 68, 225n40; and law, 22–23, 32; and masculinity, 11, 56; in national politics, 7–8; and Populism, 170–71, 210; and social expectations, 9–10, 126; as "standard" race, 160–61; and violence, 159–60; and women, 134
white Populists and Populism, 54, 62–63, 73–74, 78, 170, 230n16, 237n105
White River Agency, 107–8, 110
White River incident (1879), 112–14, 246n73
whites: advantages of, 253n19, 258n2; and birth control, 153–55, 256n39, 257n56; birth rate of, 265n52; and Black military, 202–3; and capitalism, 74–75; and "colonization," 259n7; debt of, 57–61, 63; film treatment of, 109; home symbolic to, 227n55; and Indians, 14–15, 37–38, 40, 70–71, 91, 113–14, 152, 220n39, 224n32, 228n64; infant mortality rate of, 148; and labor issues, 259n4; and land ownership, 16, 31, 32–33, 41, 46–47, 222n8; nationalism of, 234n66; poor, 29, 30, 217n5; power of, 189, 270n6; and racism, 225n36; self-acceptance by, 129; and slavery, 220n39, 233n57, 233n61, 234n62; and spiritualism, 80, 85, 86, 87–88; violence by, 52, 53, 144, 159–60, 229nn9–10
white supremacy: and eugenics, 163, 183–84, 257n56, 259n6, 277n78; and immigration, 154, 170; and infrastructure development, 102; in national policy, 197; and Populists, 73–74; and settlers, 222n8; as standard, 56; violence encouraging, 253n17; and water issues, 123
Whitewater Canal, 18
Whitman, James, 183
Widows, Esther (later Bulla), 217n5
Wilder, Laura Ingalls, 233n53
wildfires, 111, 213, 246n57, 252n109
Williams, William J., 274n42
Wilson, Dorothy, 225n40
Wilson, Herbert, 243n18
Wilson, Woodrow: on economic issues, 193, 274n41; *A History of the American People*, 272n32; on labor strikes, 275n50; and national security, 273n36; and race issues, 197–98, 272nn31–32, 273nn37–38, 277n75; and World War I, 194, 196, 198
Wilson-Gorman Tariff Act (1894), 231n29
Wishart, David, 37, 38
Witherspoon, Fannie May, 201

Withycombe, James, 162
Wobblies. *See* IWW (Industrial Workers of the World)
Wockner, Gary, 122
Wolfe, Patrick, 46–47
Woman Rebel, 145–46, *147*
women: abductions of, 111–14, 246n43; as activists, 200–201, 217n8; and birth control, 142–43, 144–45, 146–51, 171, 254n31, 256n39; deaths of, 18; and eugenics, 152–53, 154, 257n56; expectations for, 242n16; freedom as goal of, 255n33; and racism, 155; rights of, 77–78, 238n7, 257n59; slaves compared with, 233n61; and spiritualism, 238n7; sterilization of, 162–63, 166, 259n12, 261n18; and suffrage, 197; support for, 267n83; violence against, 235n83, 247n75; and whiteness, 134
Women's Peace Party, 200
wood waste, 191, 269n5
World Anti-Slavery Convention (London, 1840), 78
World War I: ambivalence toward, 272n28; attitudes toward, 200–201, 276n60, 276n66; deaths from, 194–95, 196, 271n24, 277n78; democracy as justification for, 196; desertion during, 200; draft for, 271n25; economic aspects of, 193–95, 197–98, 201, 270n12, 271nn19–21, 273nn40–41; labor strikes during, 198–99; legacy of, 208, 271n19, 275n57, 277n78; poetry on, 270n16; propaganda of, 271n24; and race issues, 276n65; shipbuilding industry during, 274n43; violence inspired by, 202–4
Worster, Daniel, 106
Wortman, Roy, 264n40
Wounded Knee Massacre (1890), 50–51, 68

Young, Tyler, 115–16
YouTube, 125

Zimmerman, Jean, 267n86
Zimmerman Telegram, 194
Zohn, Harry, 269n2
zoonotic disease, 249n93

www.ingramcontent.com/pod-product-compliance
Lightning Source LLC
Chambersburg PA
CBHW031847220426
43663CB00006B/525